Horse, Bird, and Wildlife Figures of Maureen Love

Hagen-Renaker and Beyond

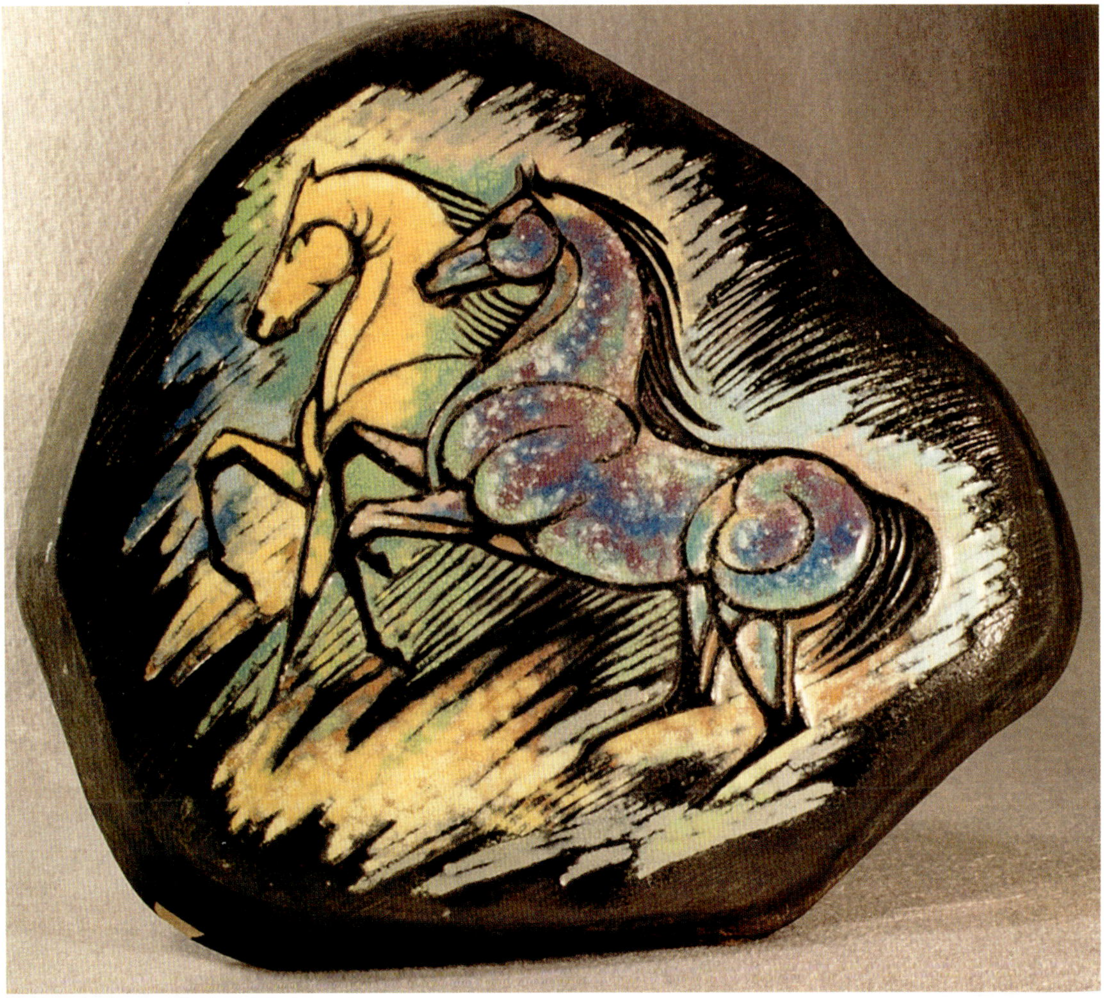

Nancy Kelly

I0808830

Schiffer Publishing Ltd

4880 Lower Valley Road, Atglen, PA 19310 USA

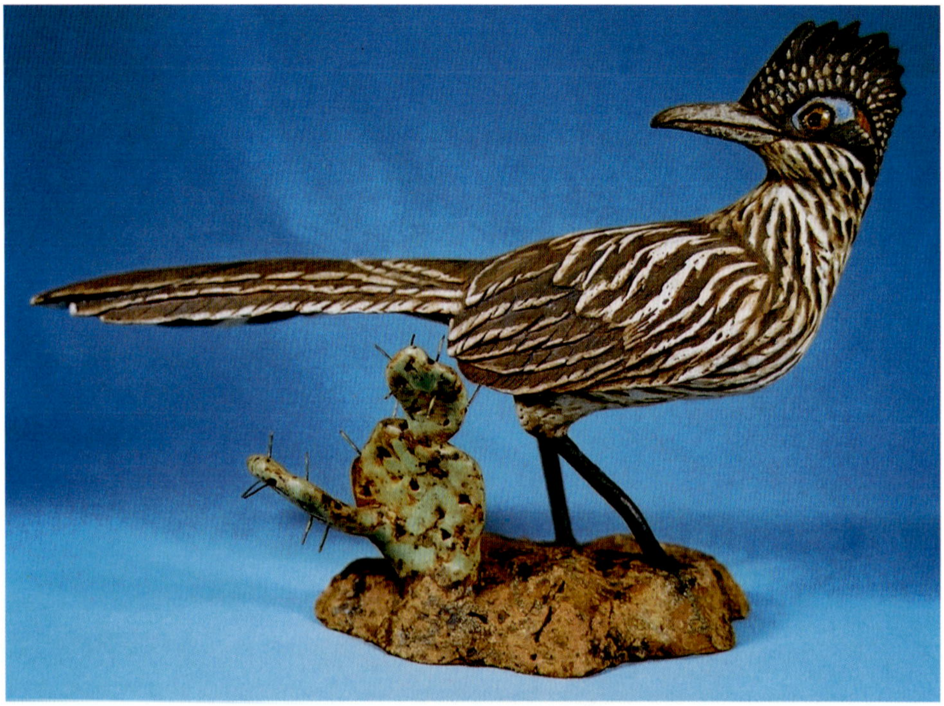

Published by Schiffer Publishing Ltd.
4880 Lower Valley Road
Atglen, PA 19310
Phone: (610) 593-1777; Fax: (610) 593-2002
E-mail: Schifferbk@aol.com
Please visit our web site catalog at **www.schifferbooks.com**
We are always looking for people to write books on new and related subjects. If you have an idea for a book, please contact us at the above address.

This book may be purchased from the publisher.
Include $3.95 for shipping.
Please try your bookstore first.
You may write for a free catalog.

In Europe, Schiffer books are distributed by
Bushwood Books
6 Marksbury Avenue
Kew Gardens
Surrey TW9 4JF England
Phone: 44 (0) 20 8392 8585
Fax: 44 (0) 20 8392 9876
E-mail: Bushwd@aol.com
Free postage in the UK. Europe: air mail at cost.

Library of Congress Control Number: 2002110225

Designed by Joseph M. Riggio Jr.
Type set in ZapfCalligraphy BT/Souvenir Lt BT

ISBN: 0-7643-1705-9
Printed in China
1 2 3 4

Contents

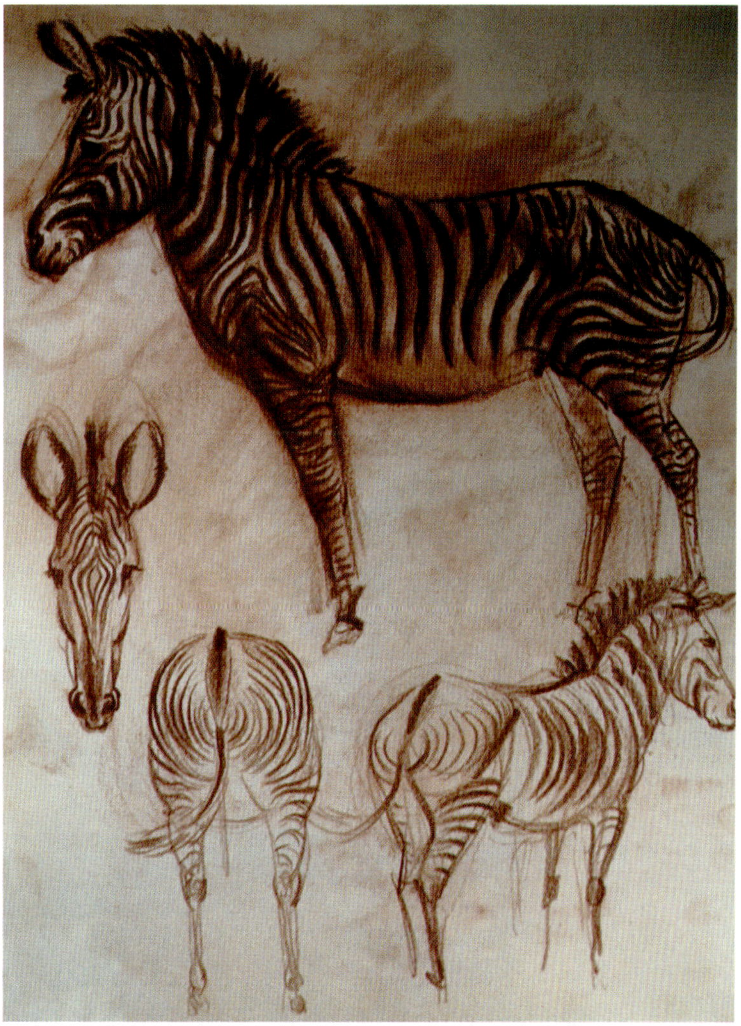

Introduction

Maureen Love is best known to collectors and art aficionados as one of the wildlife designers for the Hagen-Renaker Pottery Company of California. Yet, Maureen's work is so much broader than the limitations imposed by the constraints of mass production. Her realistic style of design is more than just an anatomy lesson in nature—it captures the personality and beauty of the horses, birds, and other creatures she so deeply loves. Her uncompromising spirit and desire to create the perfect model has left a legacy of incredible artwork.

In the following excerpt from a letter to the author, John Renaker, retired president of Hagen-Renaker Pottery, expressed his enthusiasm for Maureen's work:

> "Dear Nancy: I think it's wonderful that you are going to do a book on Maureen and her sculptures. She has spent her life studying, drawing, modeling, caring for, and living with a variety of animals and birds, and not only horses. She deserves commemoration. I have no particular story to tell about her, for she has lived a perfectly consistent life with no vagaries or eccentricities. Her life is her story and what you see is what it is—which, when you come to think of it, is remarkable in itself."

Photo of Maureen Love taken by John Renaker in the early 1970s.

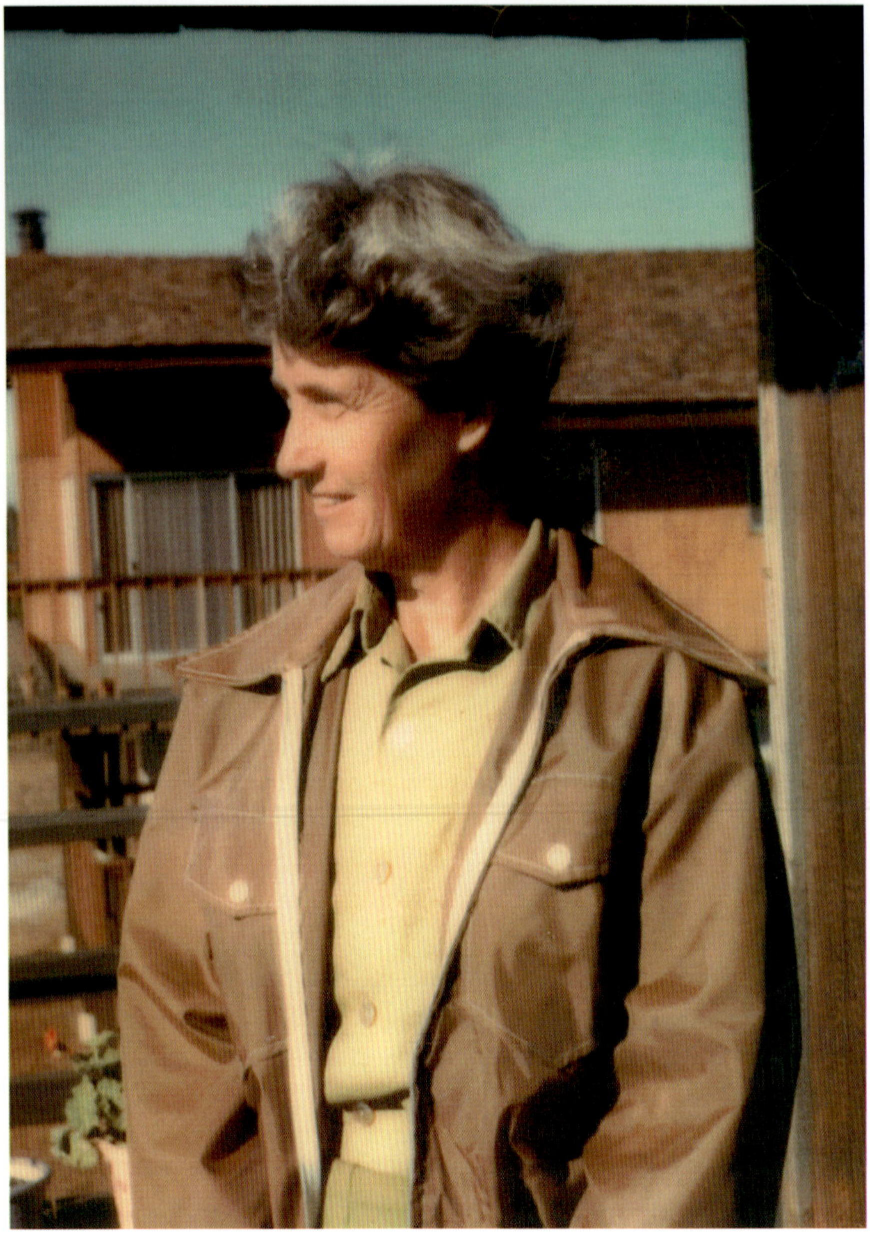

Acknowledgments

This book could not have been created without the assistance of several people. I wish to gratefully acknowledge the contributions of Gayle Roller and Dawn Sinkovich, truly a dynamic duo for getting things done. Others who were very helpful include John Renaker, Nancy Falzone, T. Phillips, Laurilyn Burson, Joan Berkwitz, Margo Potheau, Elizabeth Bouras, Dawn Daugherty Shaw, Elli Heritage-Mench, Tracy Wong Wells, Bonnie Elber, Sharon Carabajal, Maggie Kennedy, Simrat Khalsa, and Patty Albright. I am deeply grateful to Janet DeClark who fussed so carefully over my photos during processing. The handsome covers for this book would not have been possible without the skill and artistry of Richard C. Best...thanks so much! Finally, I wish to thank Maureen Love herself for putting up with this book writing process, and for being a huge help no matter what we asked of her. I know she doesn't like the limelight, but she certainly deserves it.

This book includes price guide information for the majority of the models featured. Although these figures were well researched and represent a fair market value for the items shown, ultimately the value of a piece is determined by the individual buyer and seller in each unique situation.

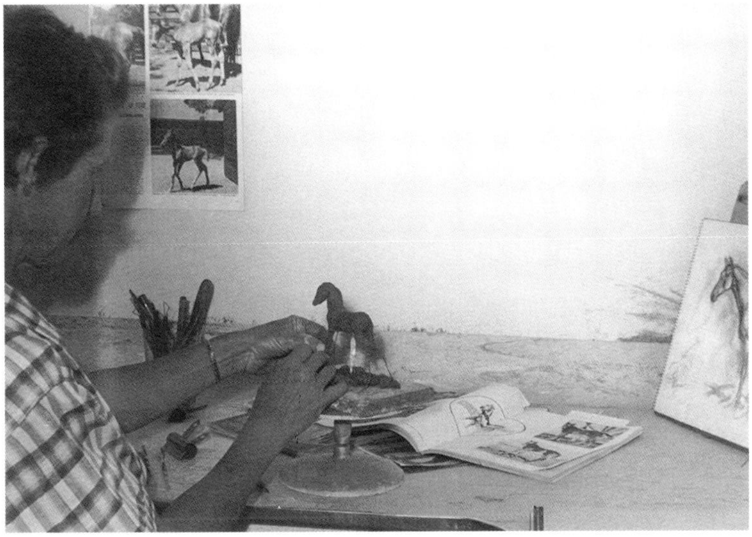

"I do what I like to do." Maureen Love in 1961 modeling a clay horse from reference sketches.

Chapter One

Introducing Maureen Love

Maureen Love would rather talk about any topic but herself. This incredible woman is as modest as she is talented. Her friend and current business partner Laurilyn Burson calls her a "national treasure." Artist Helen Perrin Farnlund says she is "the most genuine person I have ever met." What follows are excerpts from several conversations over the course of two years which are woven together in order to allow Maureen to tell her own story:

I was born in National City, which is kind of near San Diego. When my mother was young, she used to do china painting, so she was artistic. I guess I got that from her. My dad worked as an office man in National City, at the Star and Crescent Ship Company. His name was Tom Love, a Scotch and Irish name. My mother's maiden name was Sarah Aileen Specht, a German name.

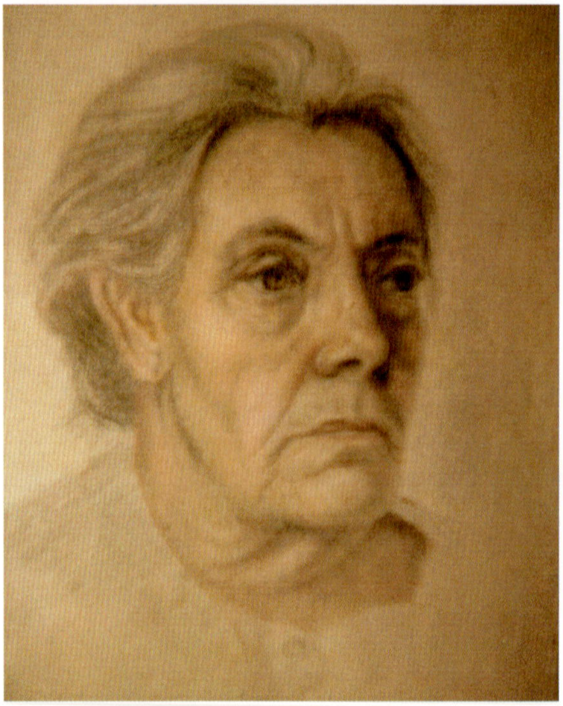

Portrait of Sarah Specht, done by her daughter Maureen Love.

As a girl, I always kind of fooled around and did stuff, like draw for fun. I did that pretty early, from as early as I could scribble probably. One time I made a goat out of clay from the backyard. Of course it never got fired, but it held together for quite a while. I also had art books and stuff that my mom would get me. I was always pretty interested in Western type stuff, so she got me a book on Remington and Russell, and some other books, too. So those kind of influenced me, I'm sure.

In high school I took art classes, whatever they offered. I took anything that was available in that line. I wasn't hunting for mathematics or anything like that. I won several state and national art awards and finally won a scholarship to the California School of Fine Arts in San Francisco. This was the only time in my life that I didn't live in Southern California. I spent two years at the School of Fine Arts. During World War II I helped out by doing welding in the shipyard. I was finished with school by then.

My first art job was drawing portraits of horses. I used to go to the stable and draw them in pastel. I did quite a few of those. I think I got all of about $25 for those. There was also an Arabian magazine that featured my work. Later, I sketched mostly for my own knowledge and experience. The Nelsons, who owned Wagon Wheel, were friends of mine and I sketched their Arabians. They also commissioned me to do one or two models of their horses. I also sketched during the morning workouts at Santa Anita racetrack. In fact, that's where I met my husband, while he was preparing the tip sheets at the track. PG Calvert and I were only married a couple of years, then he died of cancer in the late 1960s.

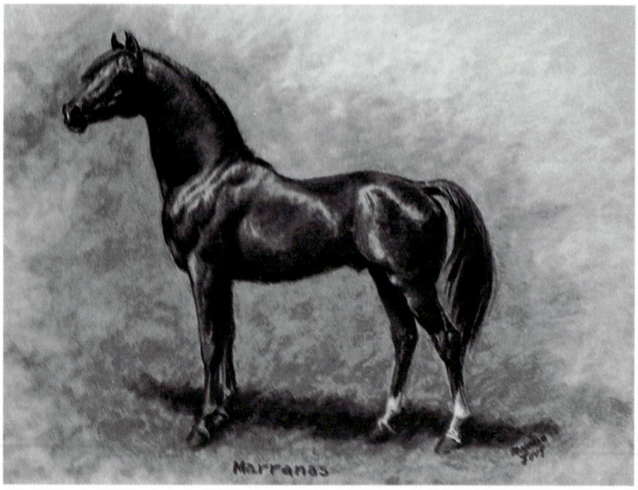

This is a pastel drawing of the Arabian horse "Marranas" done by Maureen in 1963 for the horse's owner.

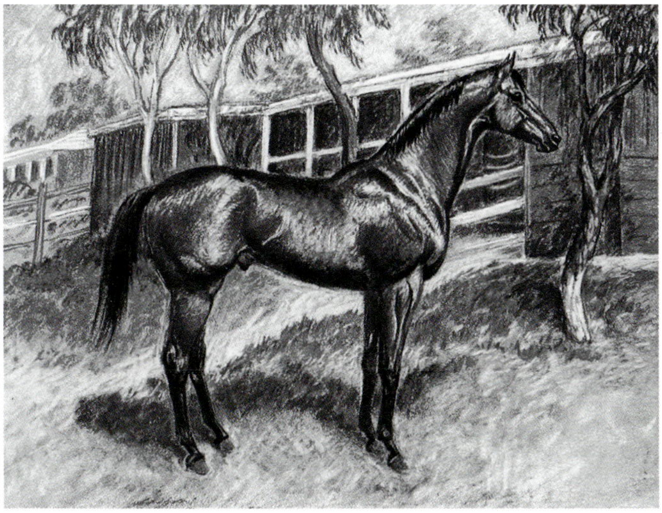

Another pastel sketch done in 1963, on location where this Thoroughbred was kept, for the horse's owner.

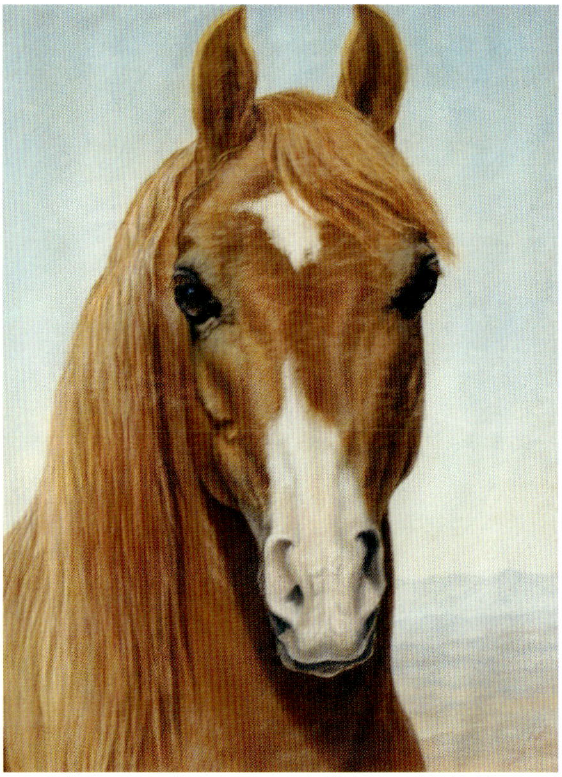

The handsome Arabian "Zillanow" is shown in this pastel portrait.

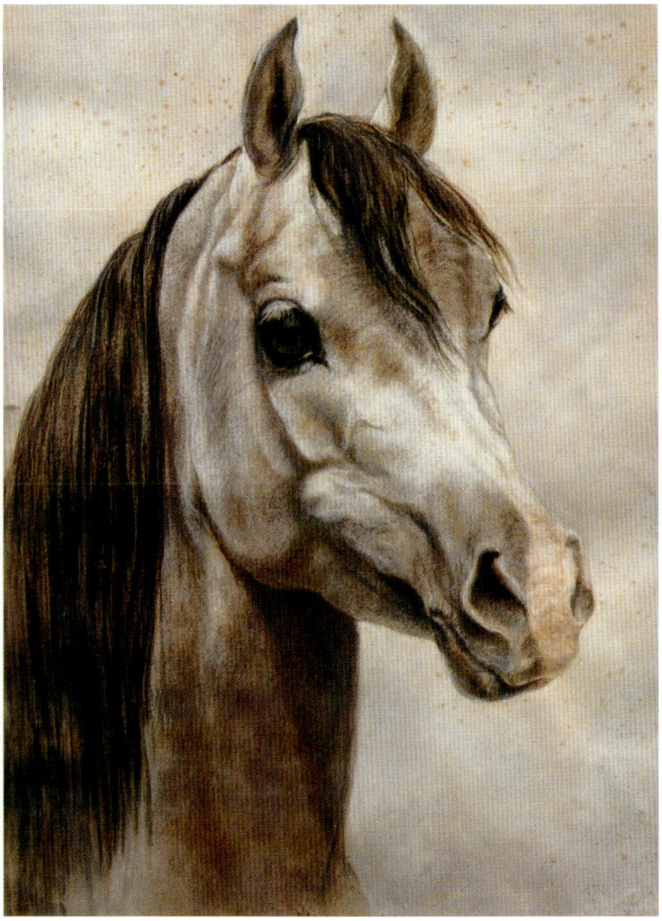

The Arabian "Mahronek" is the subject of this beautifully expressive portrait.

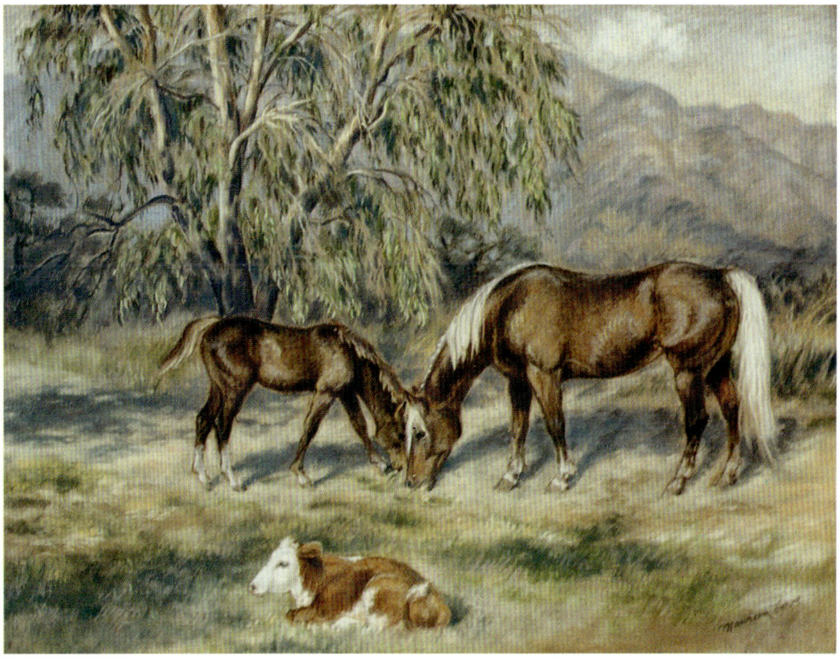

This painting features a Morgan mare and foal, painted in a pasture in Monrovia, California. The man who owned these horses was also the owner of the Morgan stallion Lippett. Hagen-Renaker collectors will recognize the calf in the foreground as the Designers Workshop calf "Candy."

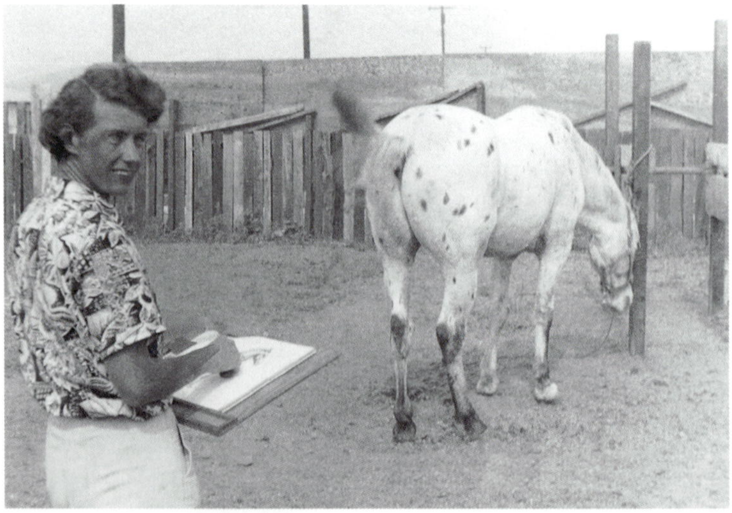

Maureen Love is shown in 1961 sketching the Appaloosa stallion "OK Ya Ta Hey" before producing a model of an Appaloosa horse.

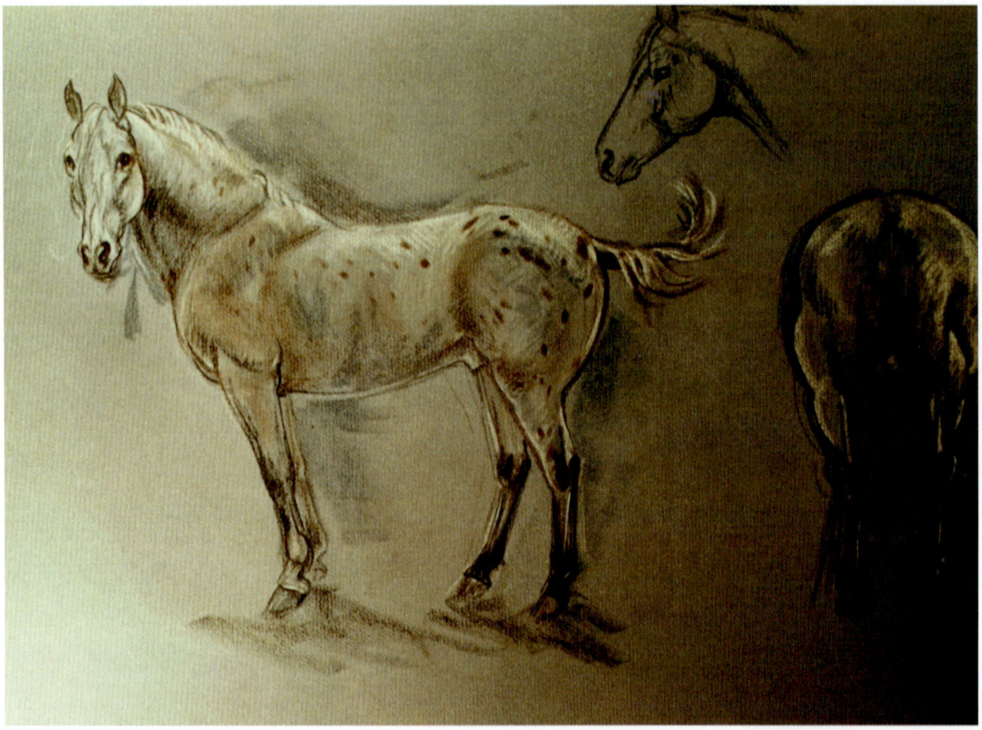

One of the many sketches of "OK Ya Ta Hey."

I never considered any other career. Uh uh. I always wanted to be an artist. I went to work at Hagen-Renaker in 1951, starting out as a decorator. The decorator did just whatever work the piece needed with a brush. I had also done some horses at home. I showed one or two of them to John and he says you can be a designer, you don't have to be a decorator any more. So from then on I designed for them. In the early 1960s when they laid everyone off, I did freelance work for local potteries. I did some work for Twin Wintons, and some others.

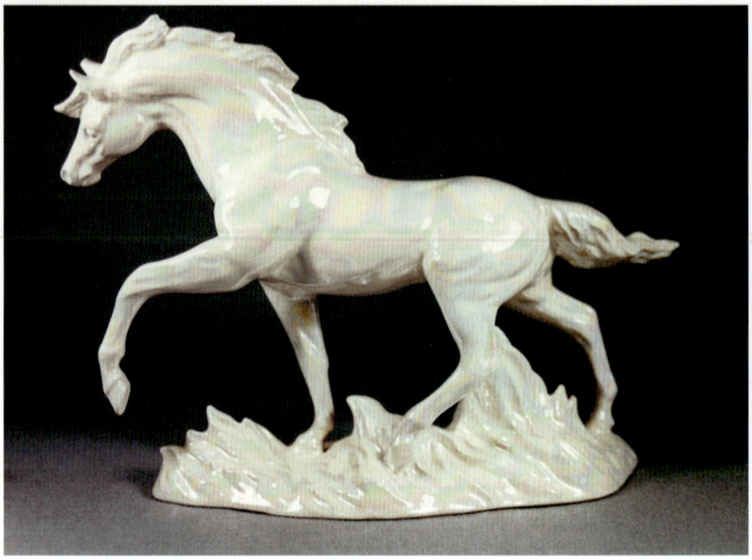

This lively, iridescent charging stallion was designed by Maureen Love during her freelance years. She acknowledges it as her work, but does not recall the company that produced it.

I also had a line of original sculptures, called Maureen Love Originals or MLO. I did a variety of things...not so much horses but birds and other animals...and I used to sell them at a local store here called The Third Bird and through the Hagen-Renaker factory. I did these for a long time. However, working from order sheets can get a little frustrating. If you get orders, then you've got to do them instead of making new stuff. What I really like to do are new things, not repeat orders.

Around 1980 I went back to work with Hagen-Renaker on a contract basis. I also met Laurilyn Burson around that time, when John Renaker bought the Freeman-McFarlin pottery plant where Laurilyn was a mold maker. We've stayed friends over the years, and just recently she has been producing some of my horses. We also started a new pottery line called Made With Love. So far, we've only produced horses, but might go into birds, too. She's real good about decorating them.

I've always loved horses, although I never owned one. As a girl, I had a friend who was a substitute schoolteacher. She had a horse and a pony, and I used to go over there and ride sometimes. There were lots of places to ride then; it was a long time ago. This was the only riding I ever did. I remember when we would go back home, it was a little hard to control the horses, as they were in a big hurry to get home.

I like to draw, and I've done lots of life sketches. I did them primarily for a purpose, because if I was going to make a model of an animal then I would sketch it first. I enjoy that much more than taking photographs, although I also did that. By sketching the animal, you get a better idea of the form and conformation. If you go out and sketch, it takes a whole lot longer than just taking photographs, and you learn a lot more. I don't do so much now, as I've got a big file, plus my old sketchbooks that I've done. Once I was sketching a hippo at the zoo many years ago. You have to sketch from all angles to make a sculpture of something. So, I was working on the back view, and a couple of ladies came up behind me. One of them said "How could anybody draw that ugly thing?" I don't think they wanted me to hear it. The back of a hippo...well, you know, it would be kind of like drawing the back end of a pig. I just ignored it. It's not really a lot of fun to draw at the zoo...you get an audience.

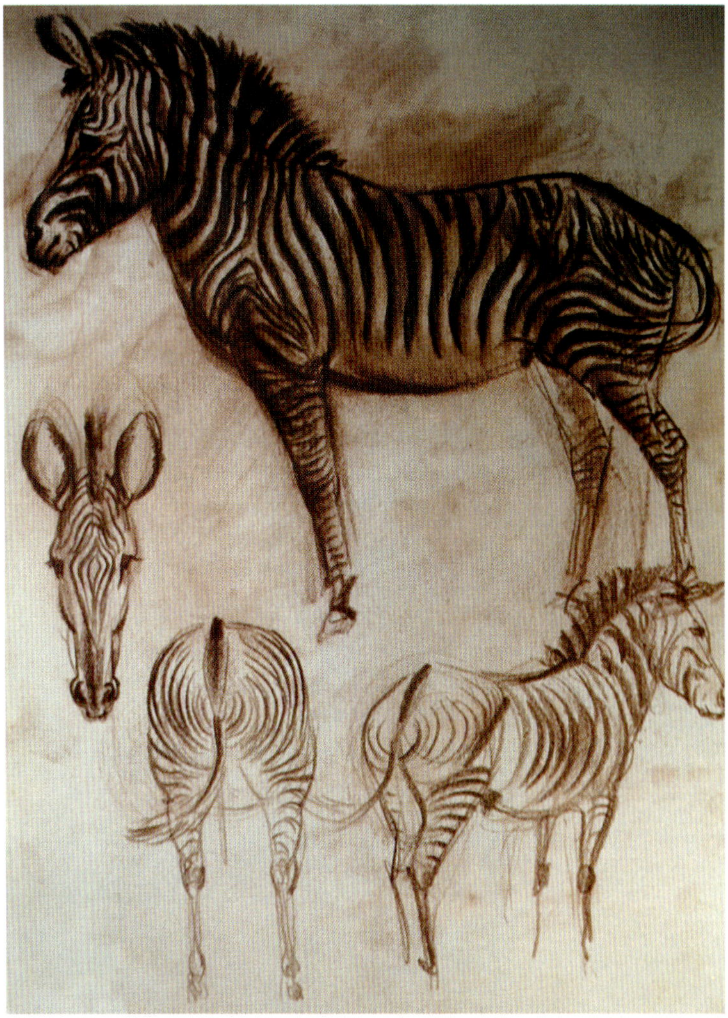

This sketchbook page shows several views of the zebra, as drawn at the zoo. To get good three-dimensional models, Maureen would make several sketches of her subjects.

When I'm sketching, I usually just think about doing it right. You think about the job...if you were doing something technical it would be the same way. You just have to concentrate on it real hard. Your mind doesn't wander very much. At least it shouldn't. When sketching live animals, sometimes I talk to them but it doesn't have much effect. I think it's hard to say what makes a good sculpture. If I think I've succeeded in representing it properly, then I'm fairly happy.

I also like the decorating to be realistic. At first at Hagen-Renaker—this was a long time ago—I used to get kind of perturbed with some of the decorating that they did on some of my horses. For example, horses never really look up. In other words, they would put the white underneath the eye. What it looked like was that somebody hit them over the head with a baseball bat or something. They didn't look right. If you are going to have white in the eye, which you don't really even need at all in a horse unless he's a real wild running horse, it would really be to the front edge of the eye and maybe a little bit to the top. But never underneath it. The tri-color eyes were all right, but it was kind of silly as far as I was concerned. Of course, they thought they were doing something really great. When you look at a horse, you normally see a big, dark eye. It's not like looking at a person's eye where the pupil and iris part are more separate. I remember that, and I used to complain about it. Also, I think the majority of people prefer the shiny glaze. I don't! It reflects all the light so much, you can't see the sculpture nearly as well on a shiny piece. The detail and the muscles. Let's face it...unless it's something that just fell in a pond and climbed out, why, nothing's shiny like that. Not that shiny!

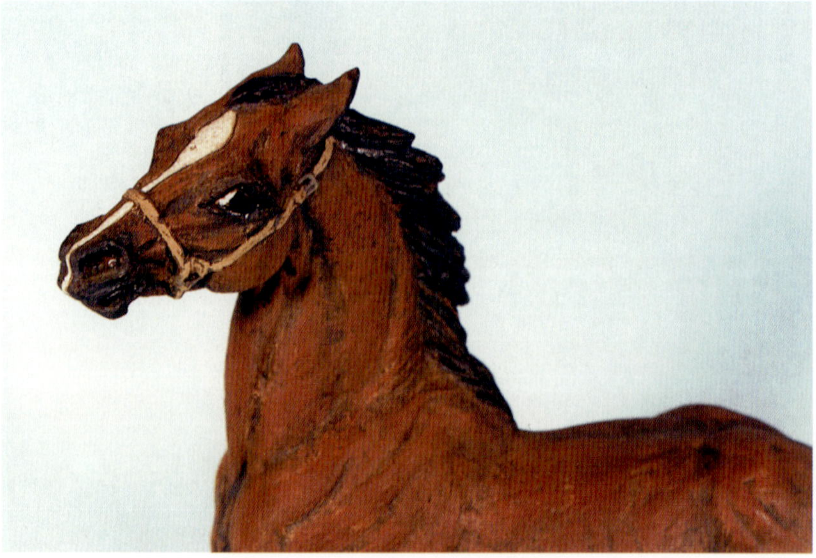

Maureen would consider this a properly done eye-white, as the wildness of this horse is accentuated by just a bit of eye-white to the front.

As far as I'm concerned, I do what I like to do, and what I've always done. You know, I do things just for fun, not necessarily with the idea that I am going to sell them. I do things that I want to do, not necessarily as a job for anybody. For example, take the pelican I did. I see pelicans on the beach and they're kind of a neat looking bird. Sometimes you think of something that you might like to do, or you see a picture of something that might inspire you. I did the egret and heron because I see them at the lagoon and you can get close enough to sketch them there.

I get up around 4:00 am. I do better in the morning, as far as being creative. My best time I like to work is in the morning. I do quite a bit. When the weather's nice, I do quite a bit on my models outside. I have a couple of stands and a chair outside. I like it outside. Besides art, I like to work with plants. I like to grow things from seeds. I don't like to take a large growing plant from a field, but I have done that just before they tore it down to put houses or a shopping center over them. When I think about my life, I have to say that I'm satisfied.

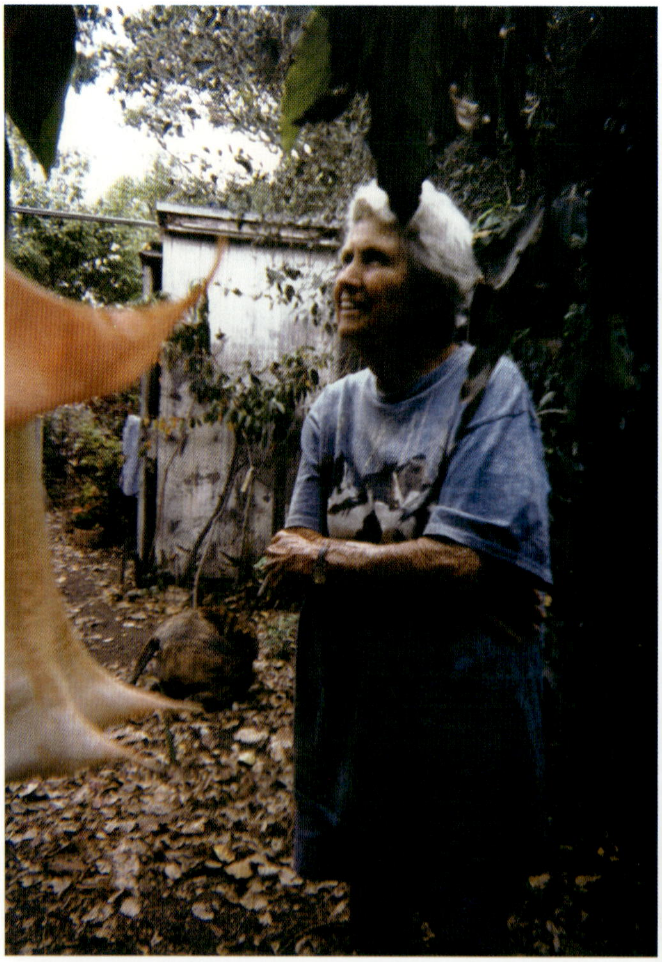

Maureen Love, out in her garden, admiring her tall Angels Trumpet (Datura) tree. She enjoys working outdoors with her plants, and creating her artwork.

The cover of *The Arabian Horse News* magazine dated March, 1951, features portraits in pastel paintings by Maureen Love. The horses shown are Mahronek 3778, Zillanow 2470, and Takris 4766 on the top row and Raas Ali 2749, Roalah 2120, and Gharitez 5078 on the bottom. *This cover was reprinted with permission from the International Arabian Horse Association (IAHA).*

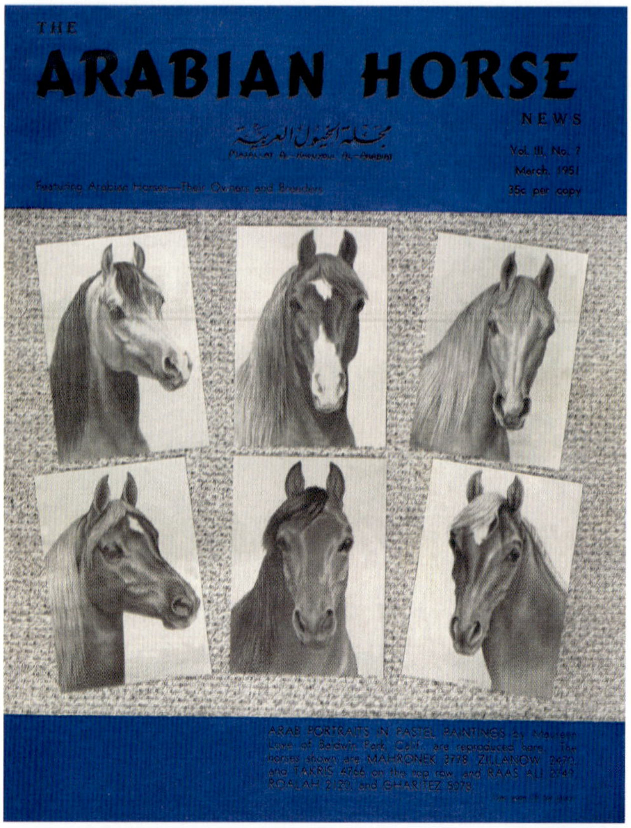

Chapter Two

The Artist's Personal Collection

This chapter features several items Maureen created for her own enjoyment, or for gifts, which were never intended for commercial distribution. She kindly consented to allow photographs to be taken of these so that collectors might enjoy them. They are referred to as the artist's personal collection and are therefore not assigned a value, since they exist as one-of-a-kind artwork and are priceless.

Included on these pages are numerous plaques, which were given to close friends; some experimental pieces; and items made just for the fun of exploration. Many of these items now decorate the inside and outside of Maureen's home.

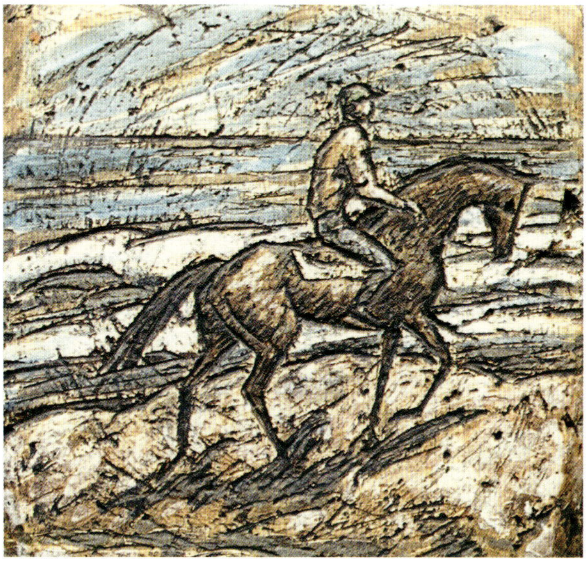

Del Mar racetrack used to bring their horses to the ocean to work out, but it is against the law now. This plaque is 6" tall.

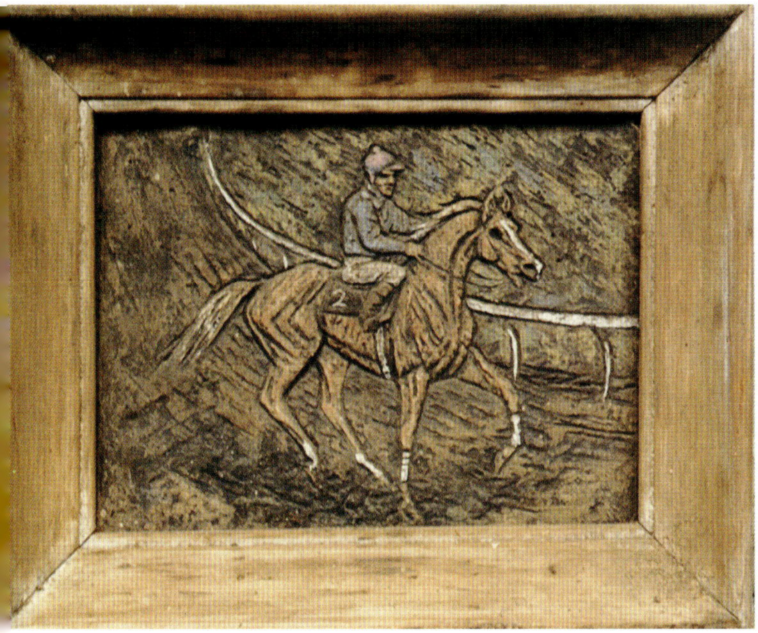

Maureen enjoyed going to the Santa Anita racetrack and sketching the horses during their morning workouts, as this scene shows. This plaque measures 5.25" long without the frame.

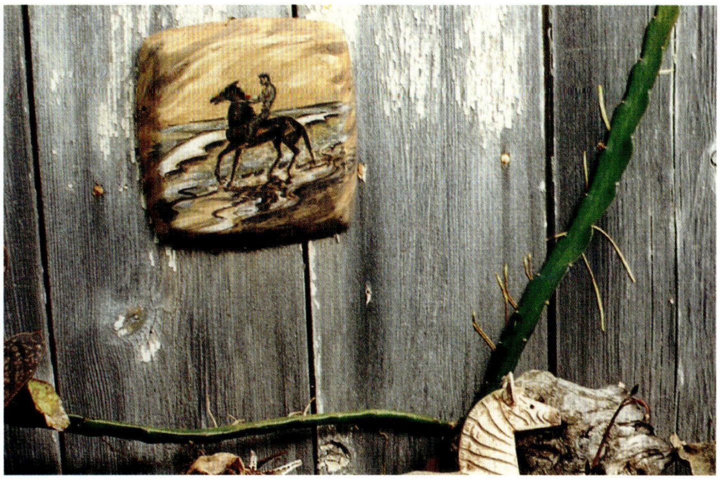

This plaque with the Thoroughbred horse at the ocean casually hangs outside Maureen's house, alongside her numerous repotting projects.

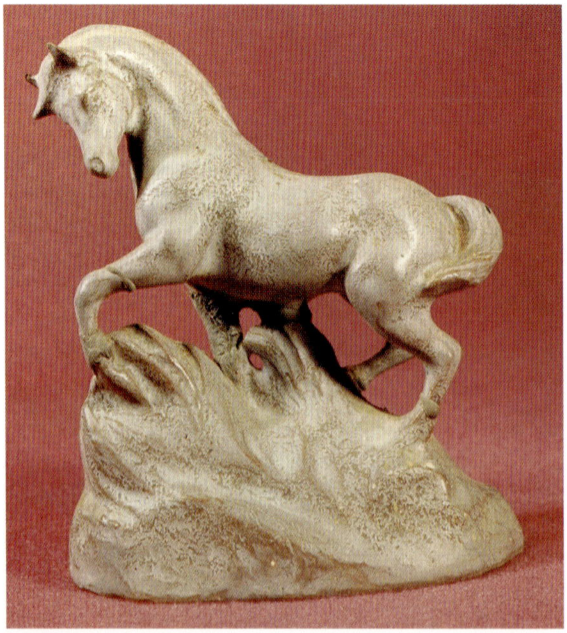

Standing only 3.8" tall on its base, this Morgan stallion was created from Plasti-Carve, a modeling material. Maureen said she did it a long time ago, just for herself.

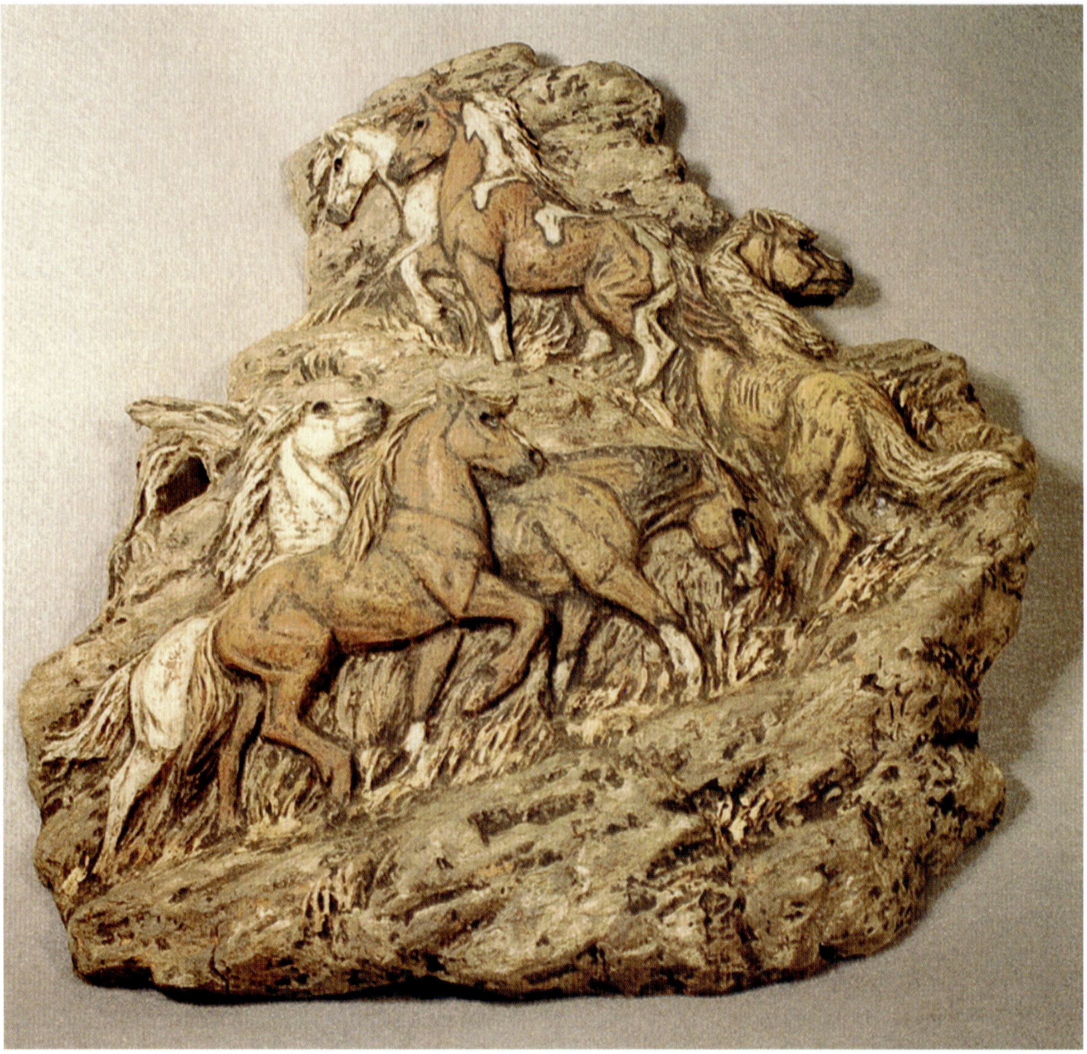

A doctor commissioned this plaque of horses climbing out of a canyon. He bought it, sight unseen, knowing it would be wonderful. It is 12" tall.

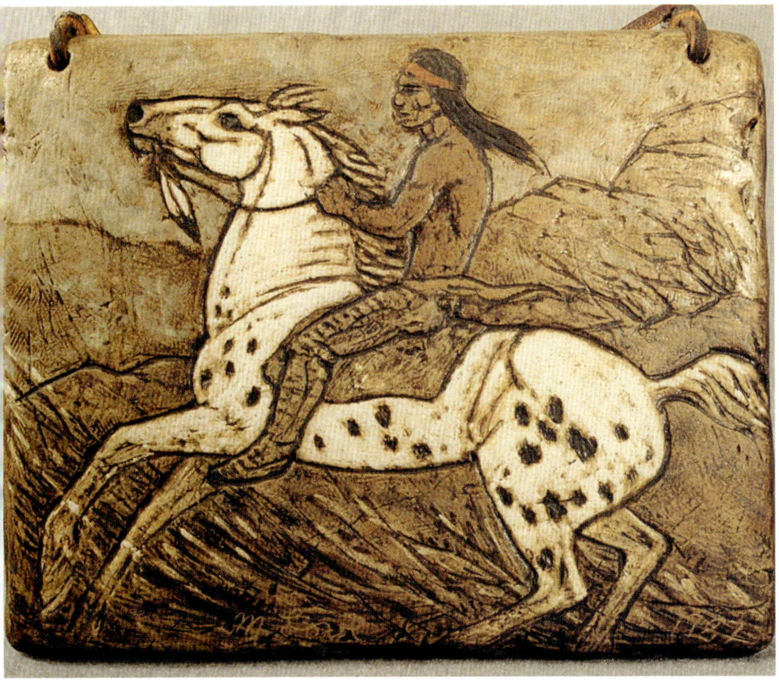

Rugged and handsome, this Indian and horse plaque measures 5" tall and 6" wide. Indians, cowboys, and anything from the old West fascinate Maureen.

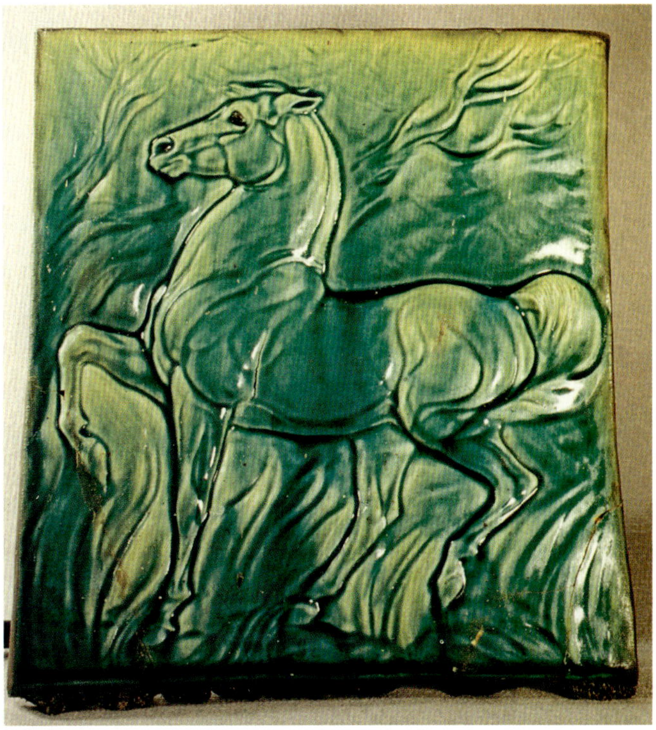

As an experiment, Maureen produced this green horse tile. It measures 10" tall by 9" wide.

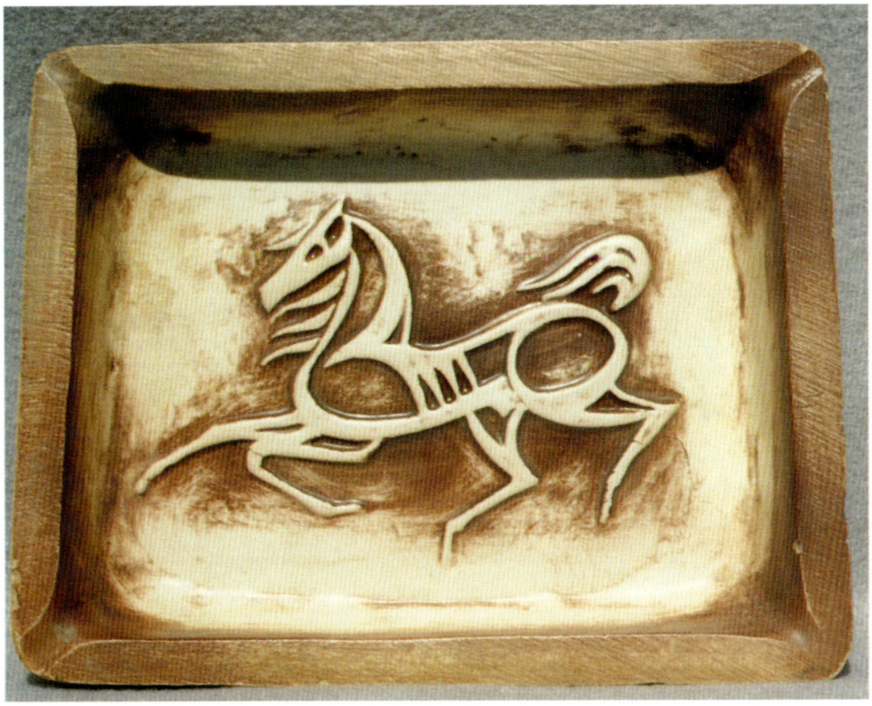

Maureen enjoys working in many different styles. This ashtray represents yet another experimental item. It measures 4.5" by 6".

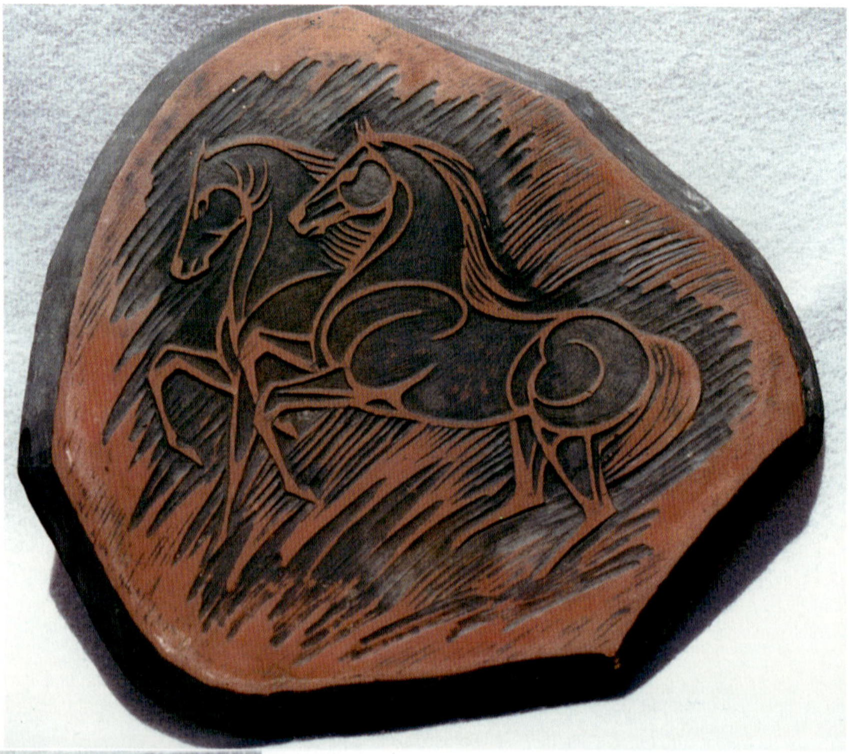

Measuring 8" at the widest point, this unique horse duo plaque is quite the departure from Maureen's usual, realistic style.

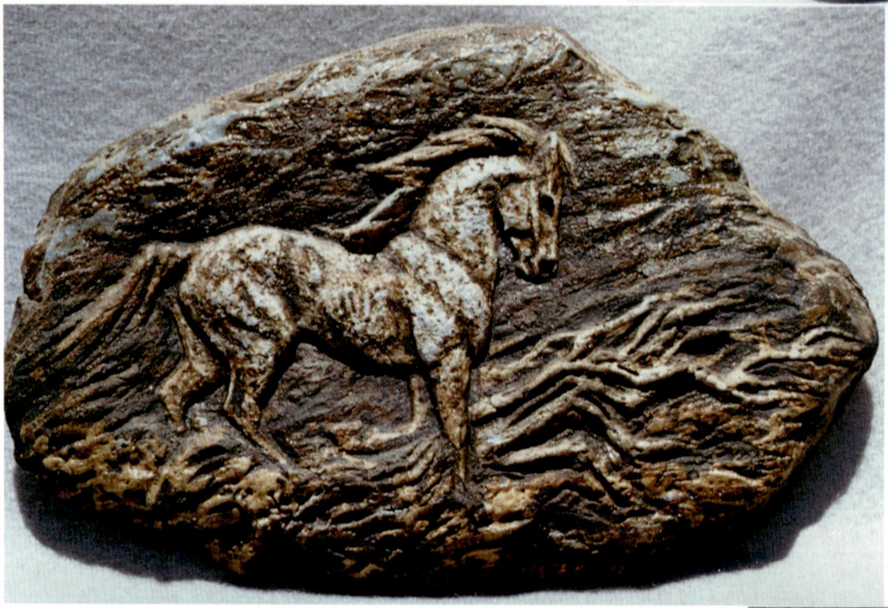

Dated 1976, this wild-looking horse plaque measures 5" by 8".

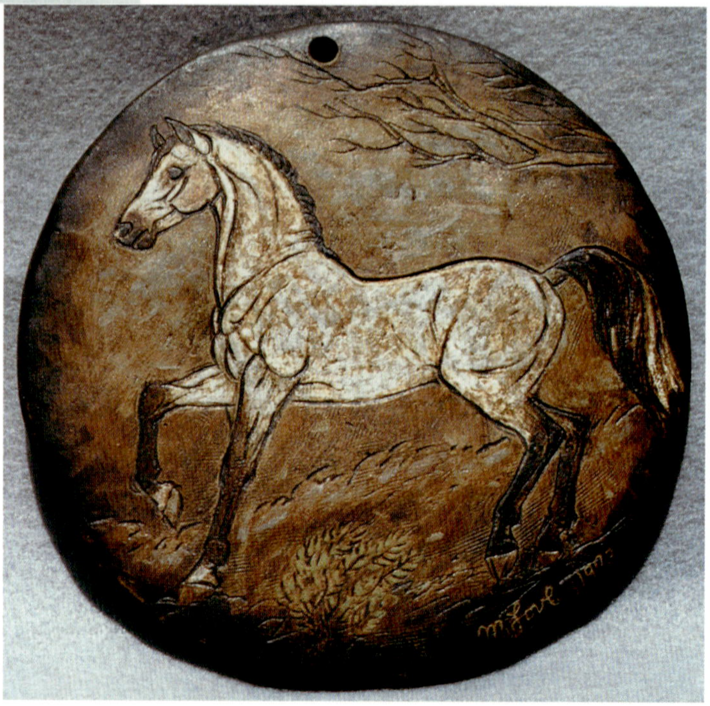

The 1993 seen on the front of this round horse plaque signifies that this was Maureen's Christmas gift that year to her closest friends. It measures 5.75" in diameter.

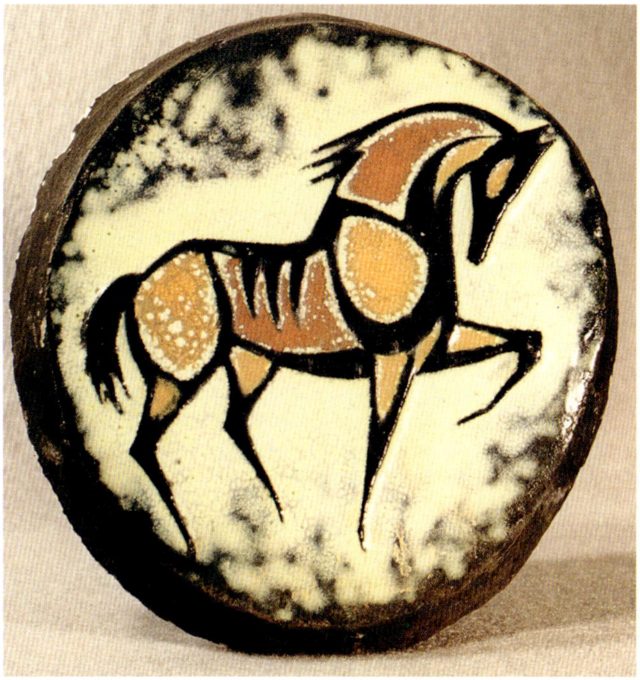

Always experimenting, Maureen created the next two horse plaques using the same enamels that Hagen-Renaker used on their rock plaques in 1959. This single horse piece is 5" in diameter.

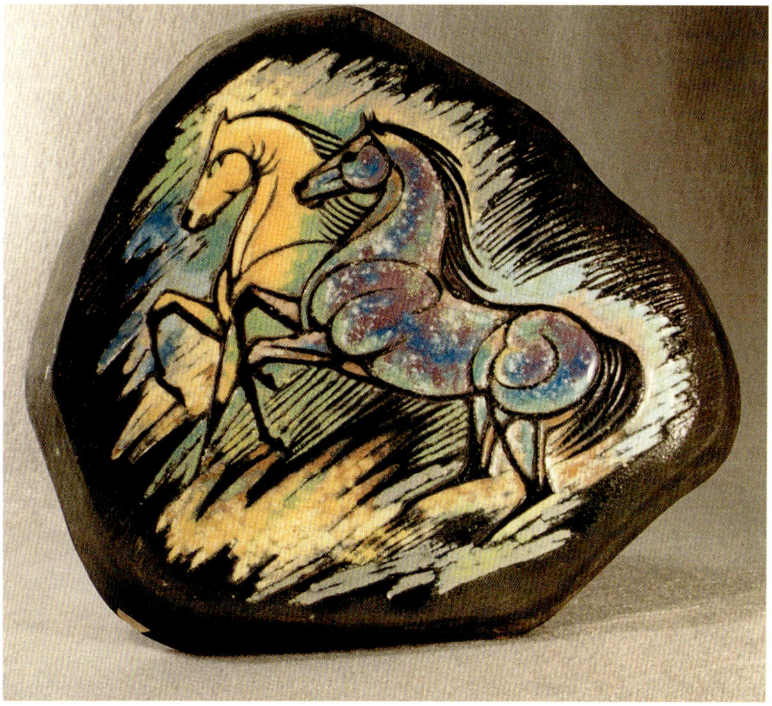

The appealing appearance of these brilliantly colored horses is due to the enamels used experimentally by Maureen. This marvelous plaque measures 8" in diameter. Both Hagen-Renaker and Maureen soon abandoned this expensive process.

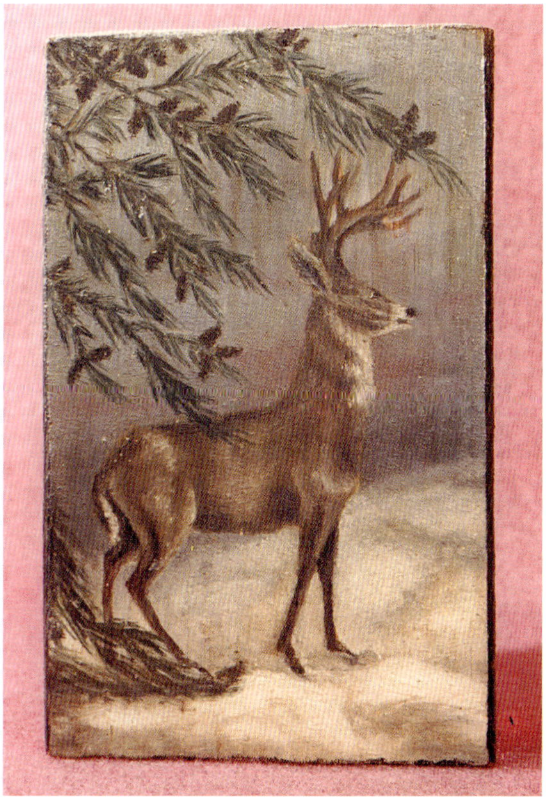

Maureen rarely did any work in oil paint, but this buck plaque, measuring 4.75" by 3", was one of her rare examples. She claims she did it a "jillion" years ago.

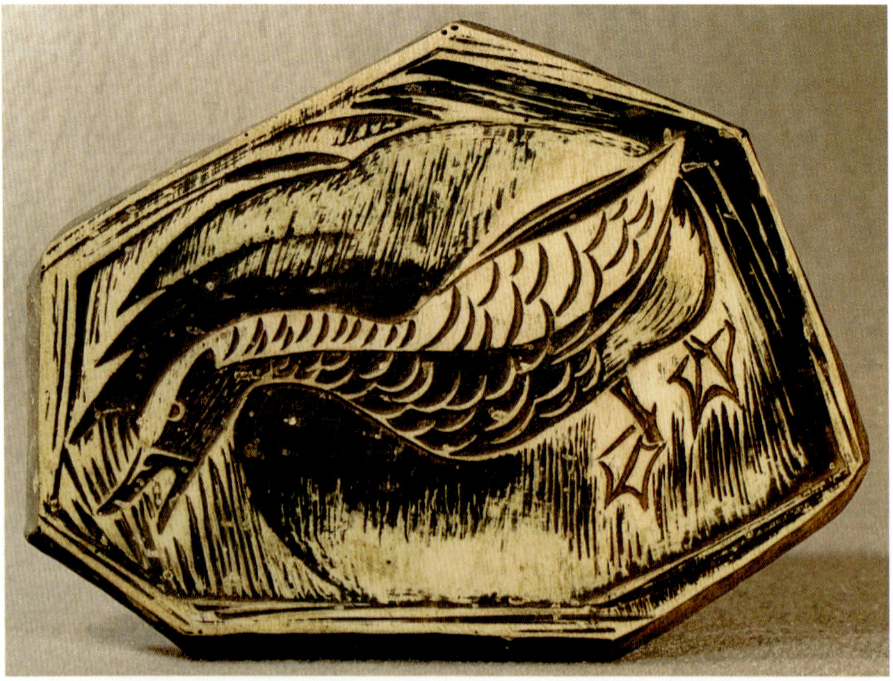

Very stylized, and looking almost like a woodblock, this ceramic goose plaque measures 4.5" by 5.5".

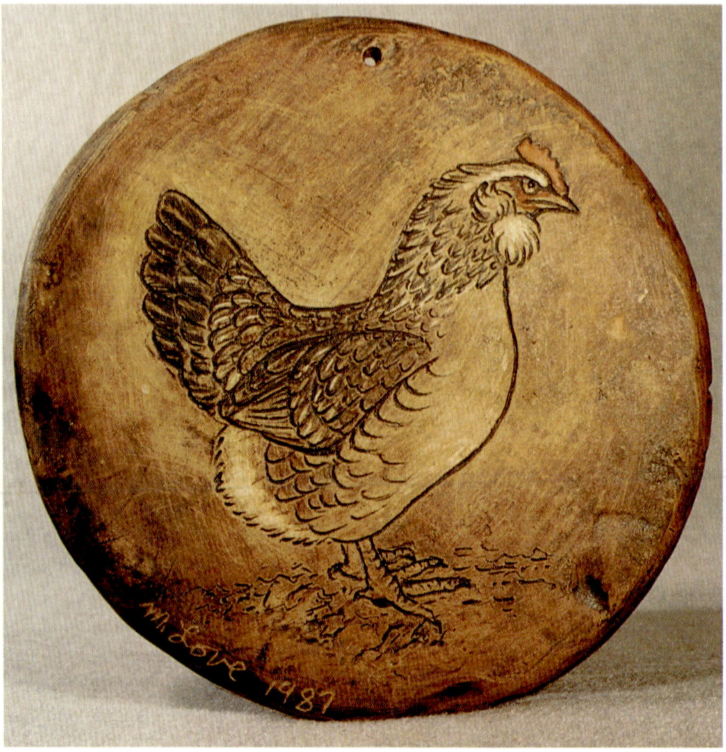

Signed and dated on the front, this chicken plaque was produced in 1987. It is 5" in diameter.

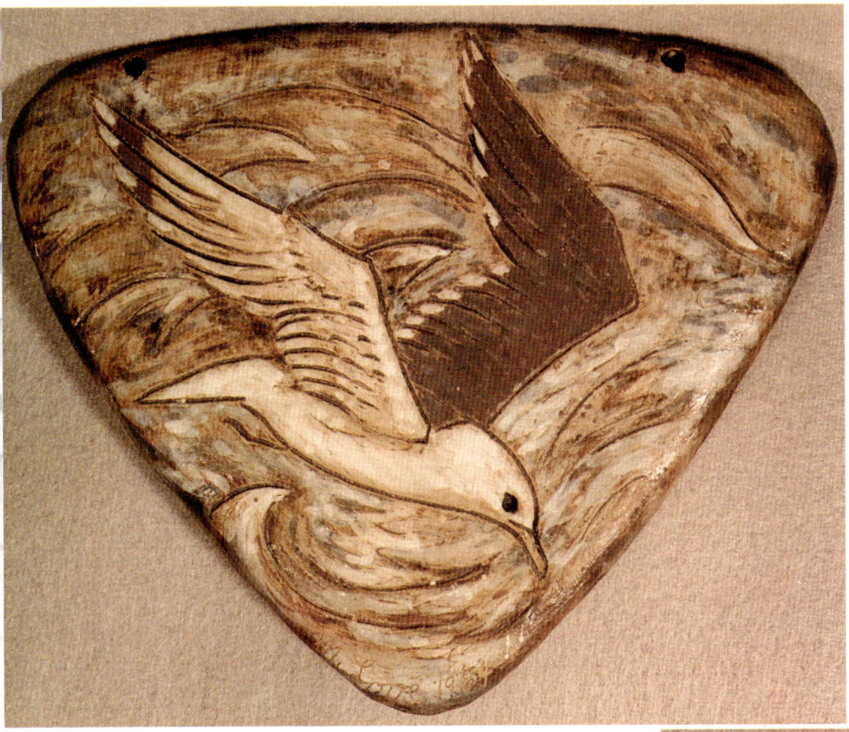

This delightful matched pair of seagull plaques was designed to hang outdoors. They each measure 6" across and have holes in them for rope or leather ties to hang them with.

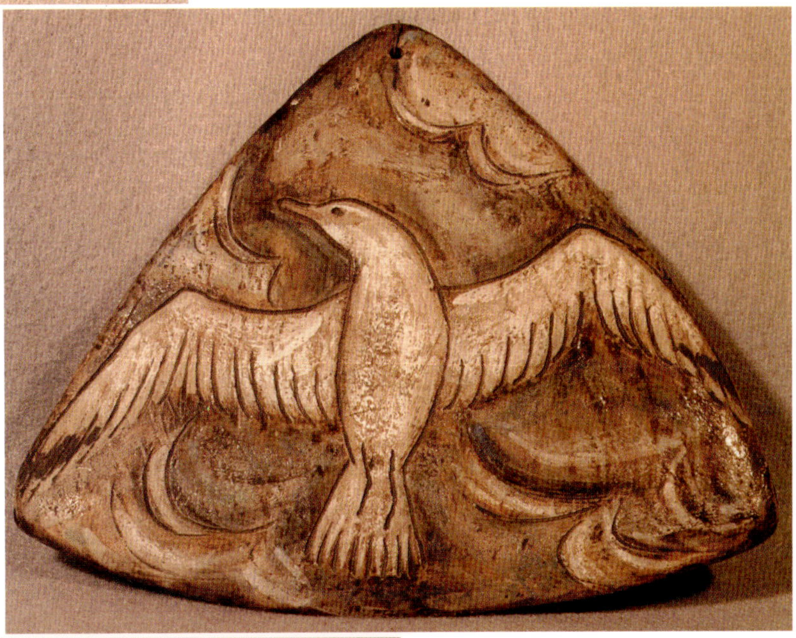

Both seagull plaques show the swirls of the ocean in the background. Their triangular shapes and matching colors make them an attractive set.

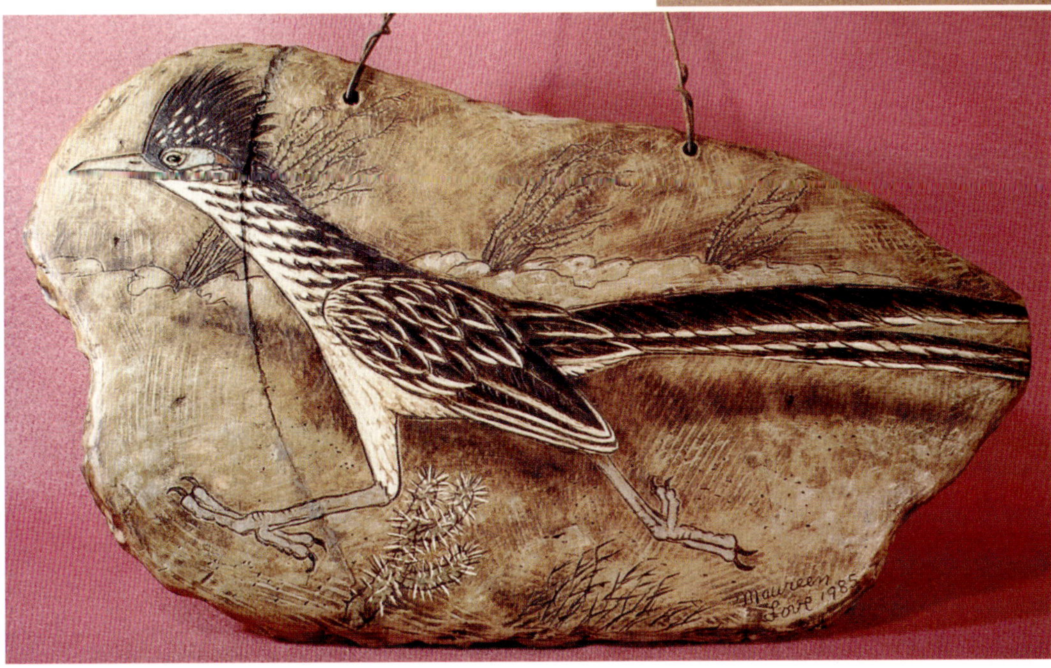

This intensely detailed roadrunner plaque is signed and dated 1985 in the lower right corner. Unfortunately, it suffered a crack over the years. It measures 9" tall and 16" long.

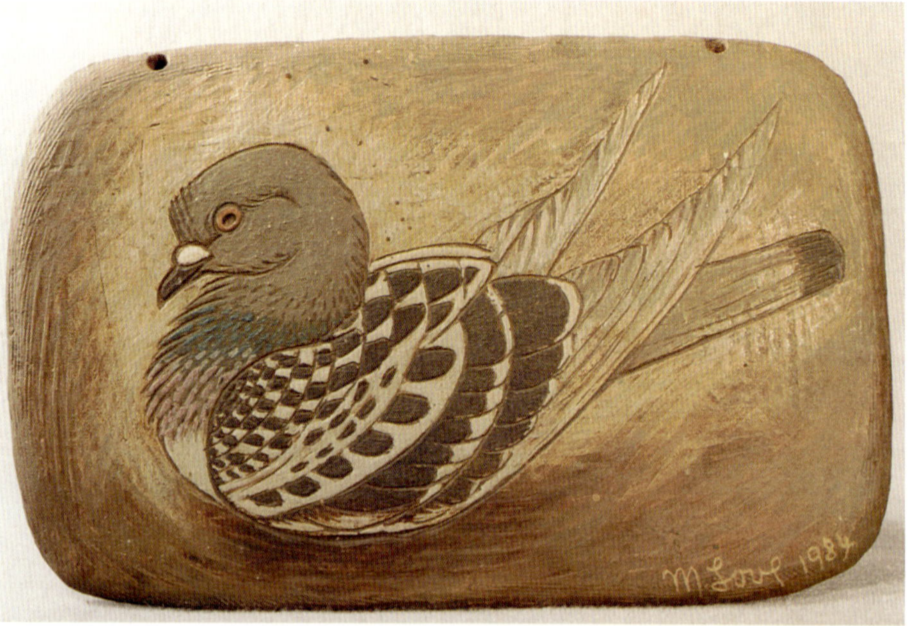

Exhibiting nearly as much detail as her bird sculptures, this pigeon plaque measures 4.75" tall and 7.6" long. It is signed and dated 1984 in the lower right corner.

This tiny Egret plaque has an incredible amount of detail for something only 3.5" in diameter. It is signed "M. Love 89" on the bottom.

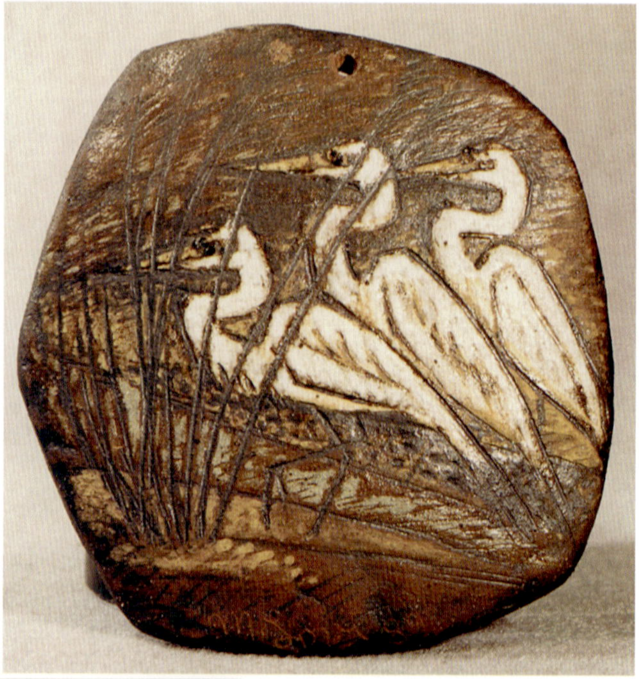

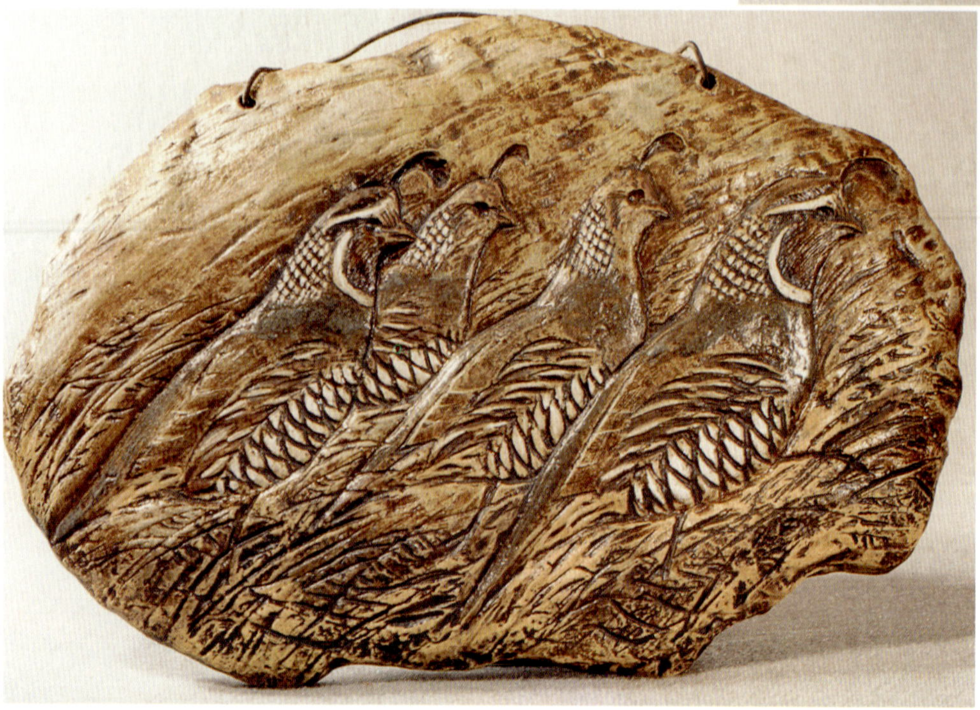

Measuring 5.75" long, this quail plaque has a very appealing texture and appearance.

This adorable little zebra measures 2.5" tall, and looks quite different from most of Maureen's more realistic work.

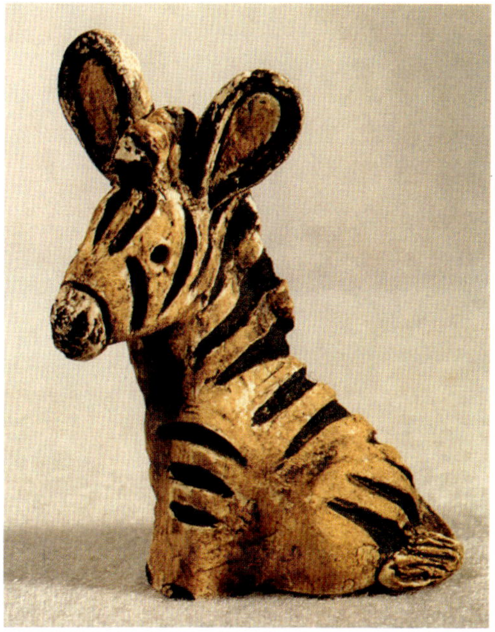

Maureen refers to these pieces as "sketch" pieces, as they are merely quick experiments. Done in the same cute style as the zebra, the giraffe measures 2" tall and the buffalo is 1.5" tall.

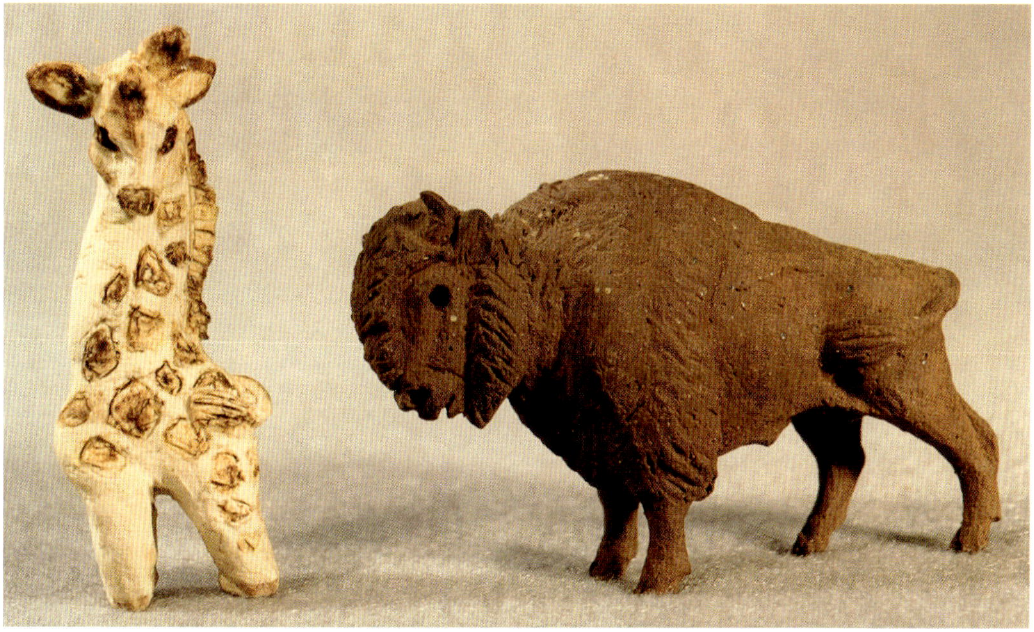

Measuring only 1" tall, this tortoise is intended to look like the little ones that used to be sold to children in dime stores to keep as pets. Maureen comments that it should have had red stripes on its head, to be more realistic.

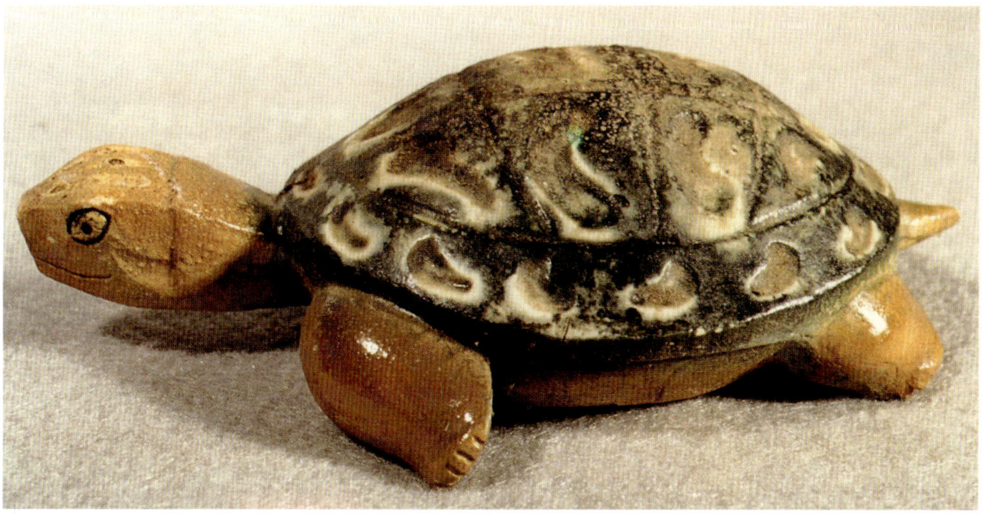

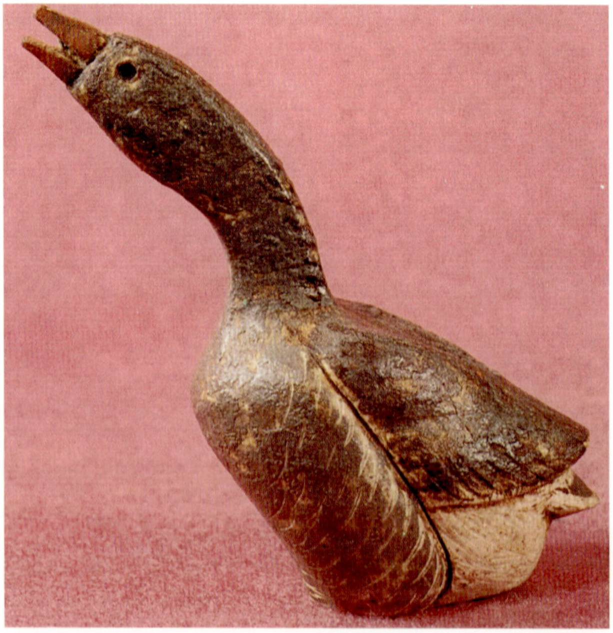

This head-up, honking goose has an almost woodcut appearance to it, but it is made of clay. It stands 3" tall.

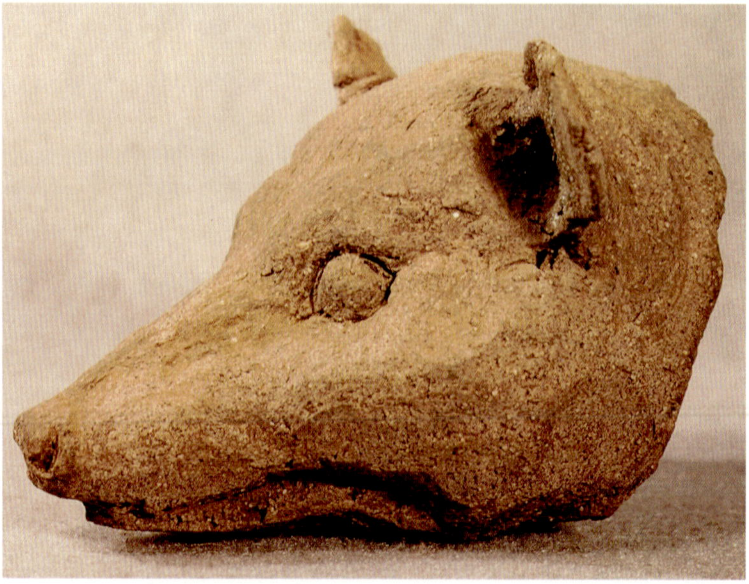

When asked about this opossum head, Maureen comments that she did it a long time ago, inspired by one of the opossums in her yard. It measures 2.5" by 4".

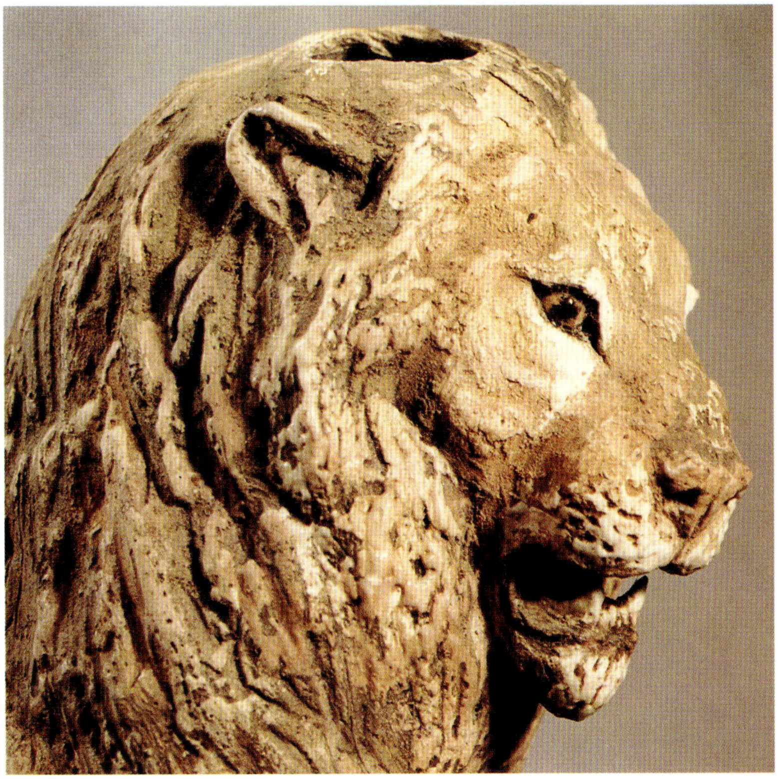

Designed as a sort of planter, as evidenced by the hole in the top of his head, this walking lion has suffered the effects of life outdoors in the elements.

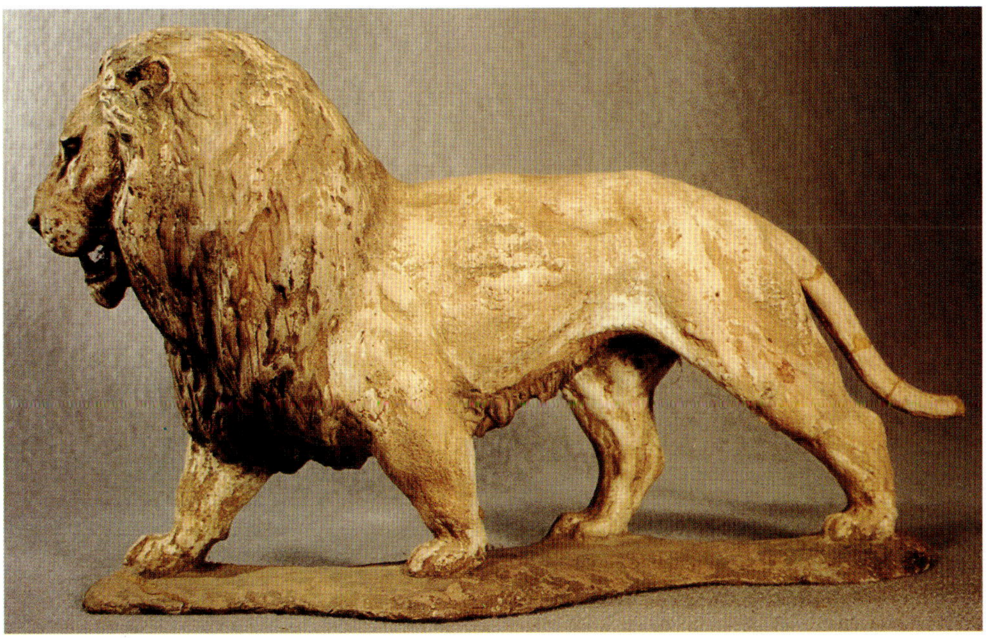

The entire lion measures 5.25" tall, and has lost his tail tip over the years.

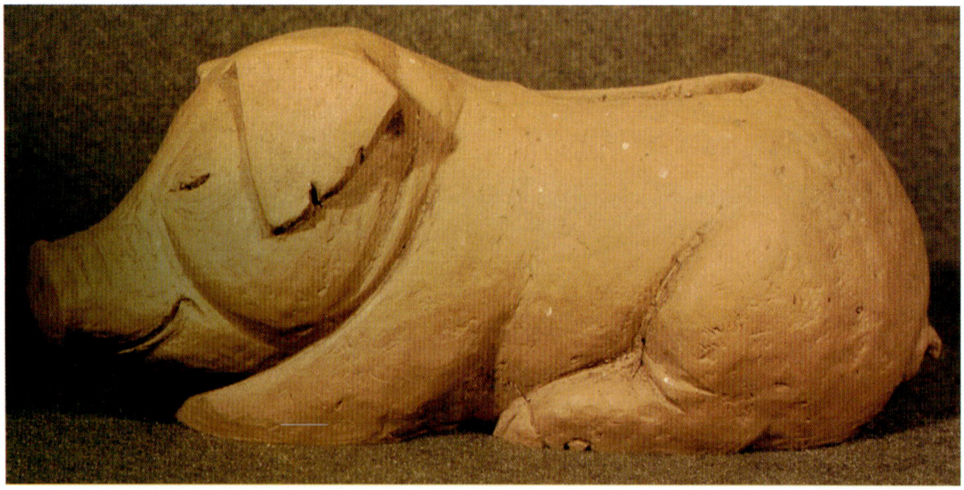

Contently napping, this little pig planter or pot has a large hole in his back for plants. He measures 3" tall by 7.5" long.

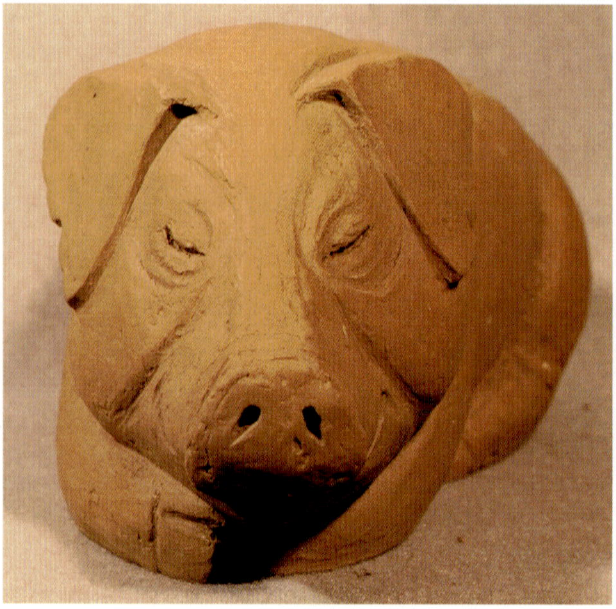

Even in a planter, Maureen has instilled ample detail to make this pig unique and appealing. This front view shows the creases around the eyes and snout.

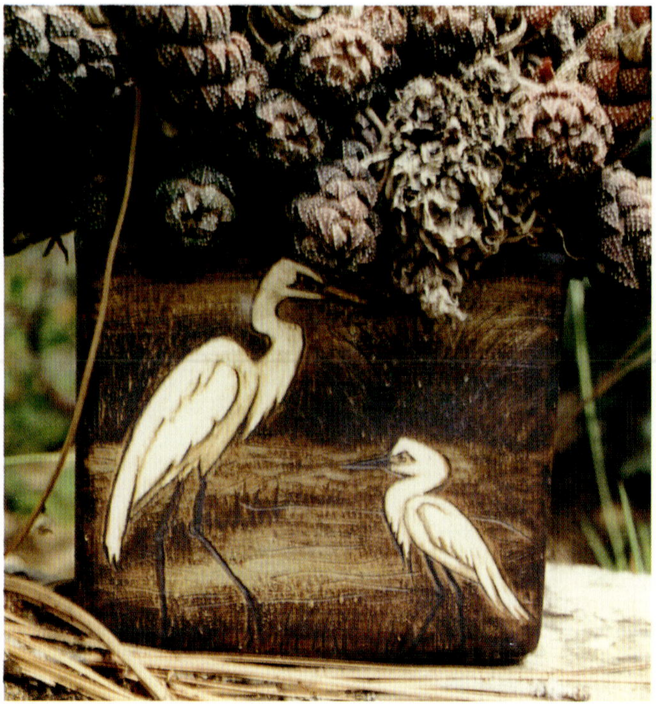

Here is another example of art serving a function. This planter shows a Great Egret and a Snowy (smaller) Egret. It measures 5" tall and 5" wide. Hagen-Renaker produced the pots in their nursery division, and Maureen decorated a few of them.

Maureen created a mold for this quail bell and produced several of them. There is a separately formed clapper inside. It measures 2.25", and can be hung in a tree to function as sort of a wind chime.

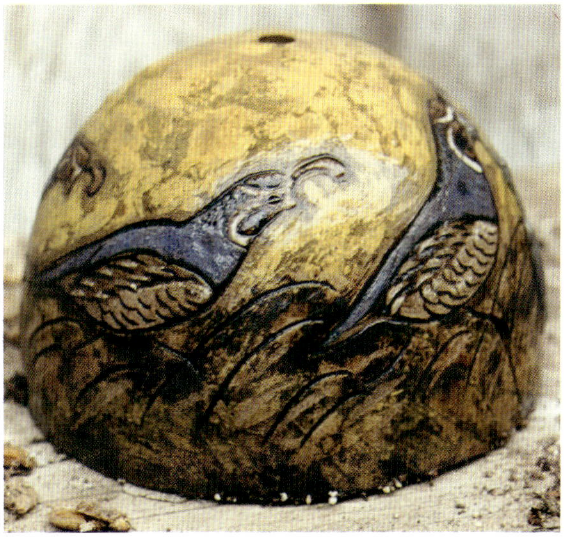

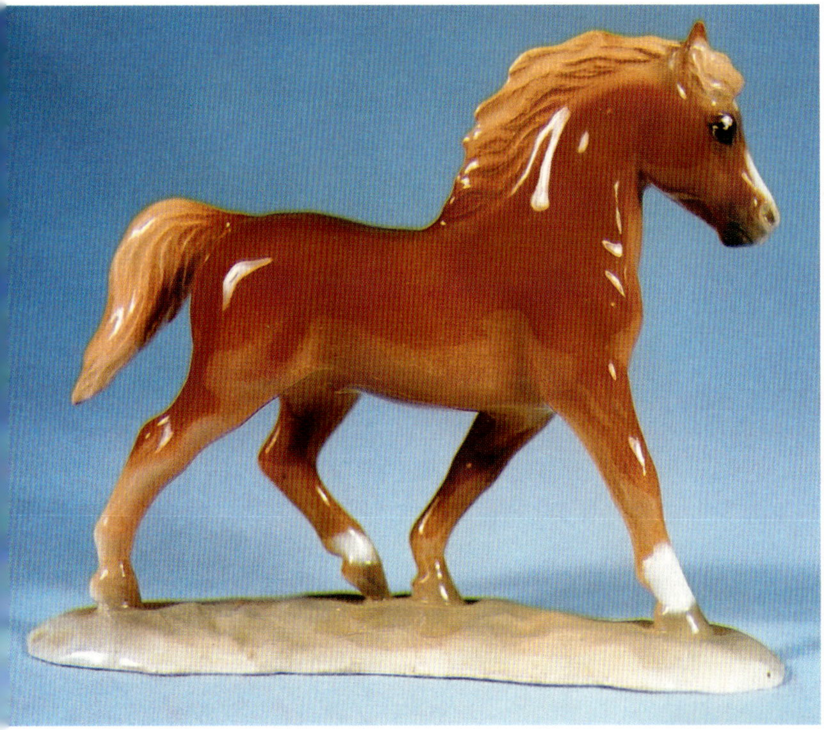

This little horse can be termed the one that started it all, as he was the first horse Maureen produced. When asked what breed it is, she laughs that she was just happy that it looked like a horse, any horse! He measures 3.75" tall at the ear tips.

Maureen would obtain blank planters from the Hagen-Renaker company's nursery division. She would then etch or carve them at home, and finish them with color. This zebra planter (or pencil holder) measures 4.3" tall.

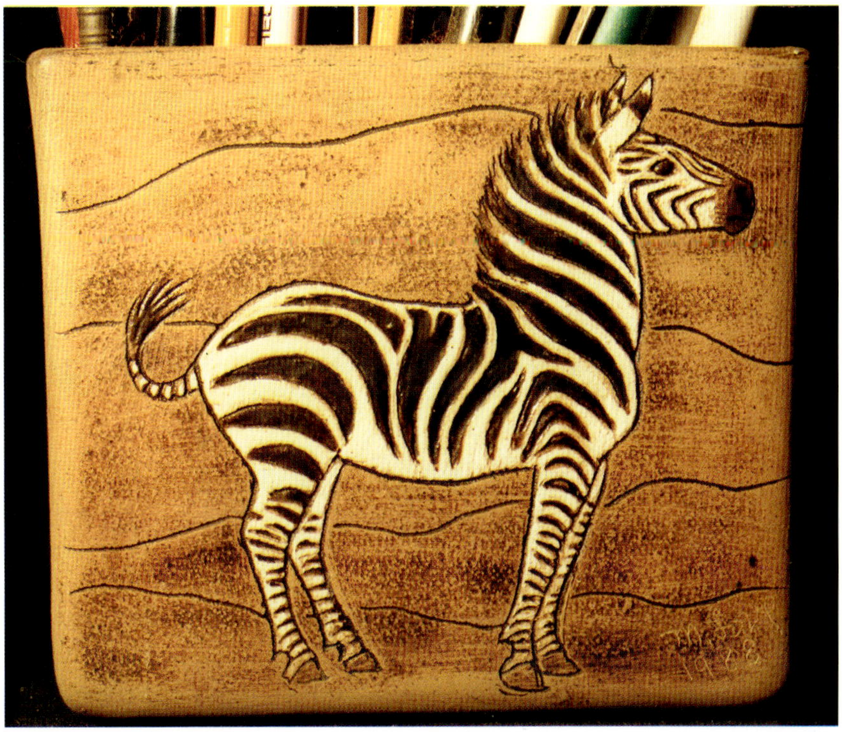

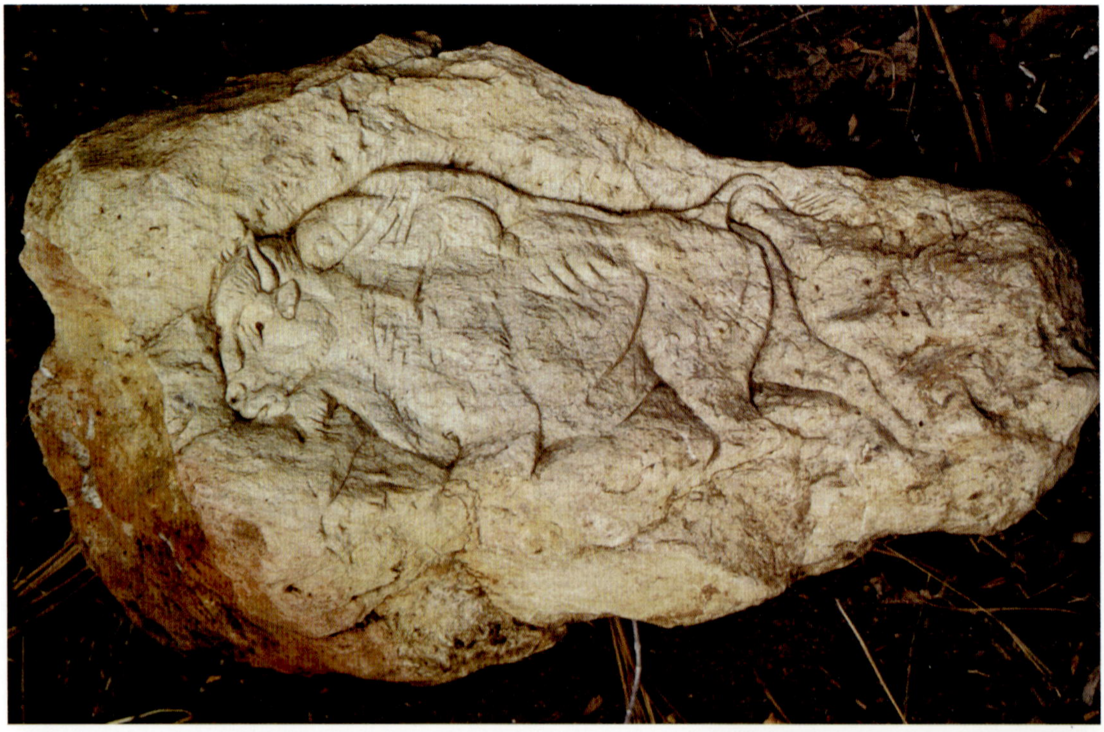

Always looking for new techniques and challenges, Maureen carved this buffalo from a rock. The entire piece measures 16.5" by 10", and the actual carving is 10" long. Hagen-Renaker later made a rock plaque from this in the late 1950s, but very few were produced by the factory due to their size and expense.

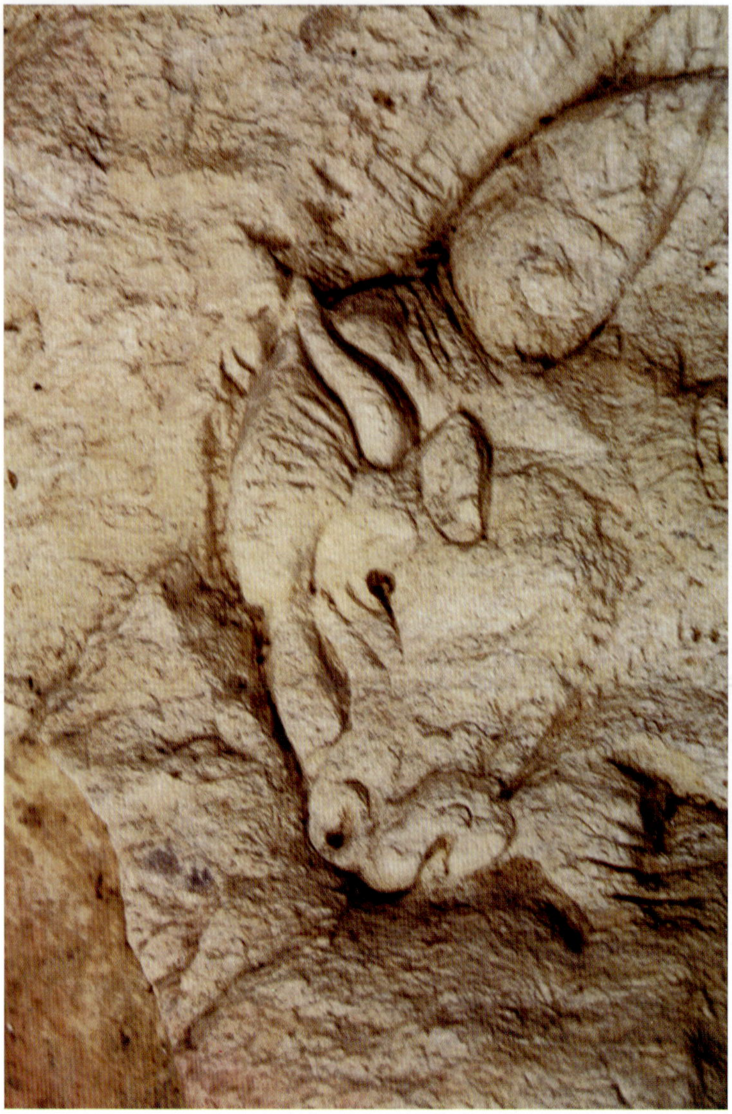

A closer look at the head of the rock buffalo reveals incredible detail and texture for such a difficult medium.

Chapter Three

The Busy 1970s

Maureen Love has created art all of her life, but the 1970s were a particularly busy time for her commercially. Her "Maureen Love Originals" (MLO) were sold through two retail outlets: The Third Bird (a gift shop) and Hagen-Renaker Pottery Company. It was difficult for her to keep up with the demand. The gift shop owner recalls that she would just put a bird out for sale and within minutes it would be headed for its new home.

During this period, time was a real problem for Maureen. She was obligated to fill orders from the adoring public, yet what she really enjoyed most was making new creations. One of the reasons her work was so hard to get was because she would not release a piece until she was convinced that it was ready. "I don't know if I'm ever 100 per cent satisfied, but if it doesn't turn out right, I just won't sell it," Maureen told the local newspaper in 1974.

There was a lot of work involved for this one-person operation. Maureen was making all of her own molds, then casting the bodies using slip (clay). Pretty standard ceramic process up to this point, but then the magic began. Maureen enjoys experimenting and pushing the medium to its limits. She would start with a basic glaze, then alter it so that it could be heated beyond normal standards for interesting results. She also added things to the basic glaze, such as beach sand, clay, and dirt, plus oxides for color variations. This led to bold textures and eye-catching colors. Her favorite subjects were the native birds she saw around her home in ponds, fields, and on the beach, plus the horses that she deeply admires and enjoys. Yet, any creature of nature could show up in her unique, life-like style.

The models in this chapter were all designed and hand-decorated by Maureen Love. Some of what is shown here are creations that fortunate collectors, animal lovers, or art aficionados may have purchased in the 1960s and 1970s under the name Maureen Love Originals. The others are pieces done in the same style but produced in much smaller numbers. All were created with the same attention to detail and realistic feeling. Two Maureen Love Originals sales sheets are included at the end of this chapter.

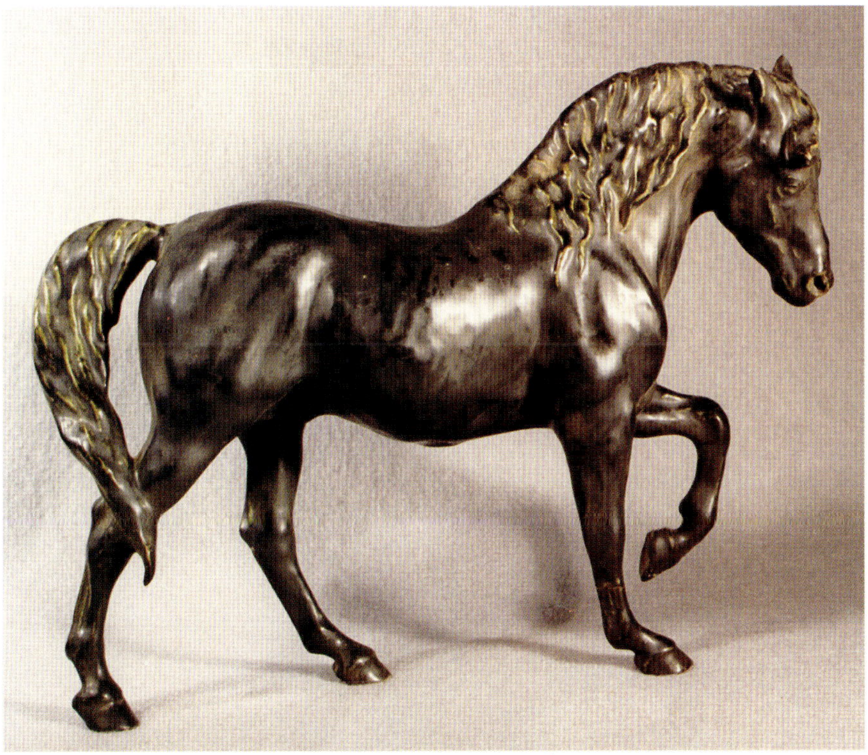

Lippett, a Morgan stallion, served as the model for this figure. He stands 7.75" tall, and has suffered a broken leg over the years. Approximate value $275-300.

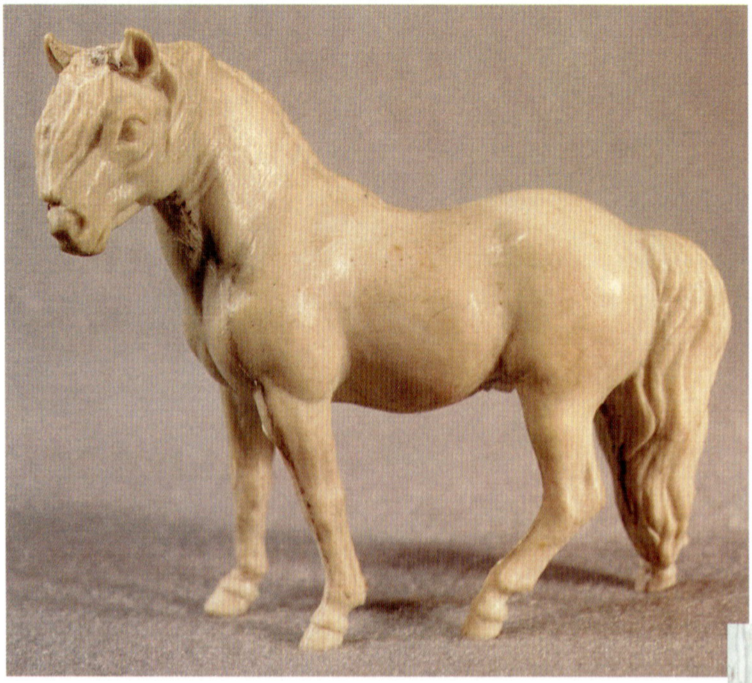

Maureen sculpts using a material called Plasti-Carve. It is sort of a cross between wax and clay, and has the integrity to allow her to put great detail into her pieces. This pony stallion shows a completed sculpture in Plasti-Carve.

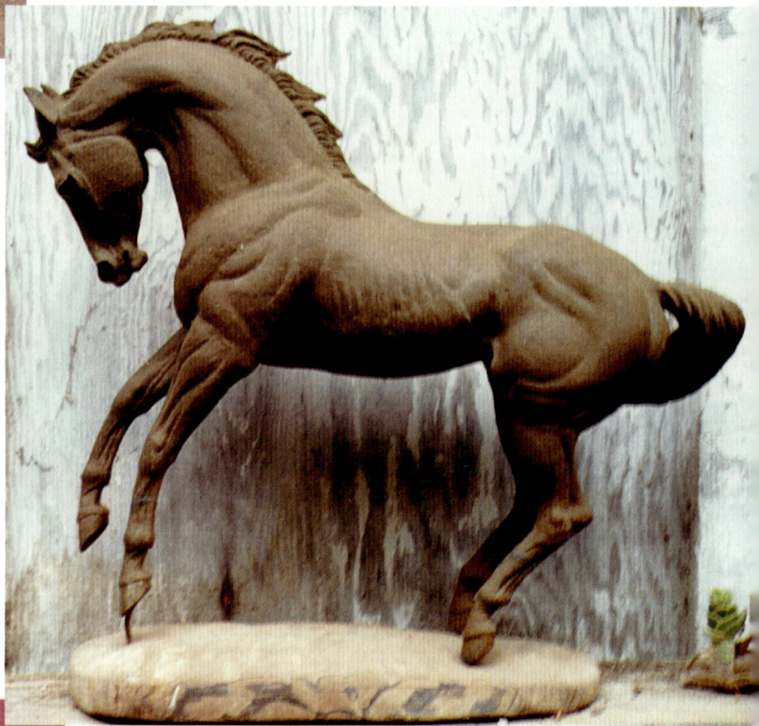

Probably the largest horse Maureen ever produced, this gigantic Thoroughbred measures 17.5" tall, including the wooden base. Laurilyn Burson made a couple of recent horses from this mold, but this is the original. See page 133 for the newer one. Approximate value of this original horse $800-1,000.

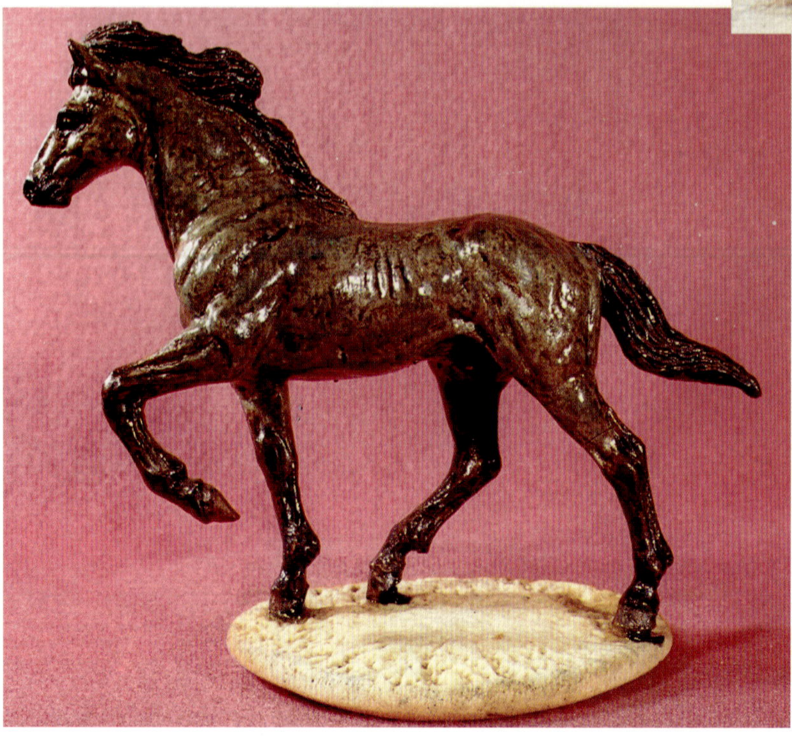

Measuring 5.5" tall, this walking horse has a heavy glaze. Maureen's later pieces feature minimal glaze and a stoneware appearance. Approximate value of this horse is $175-200.

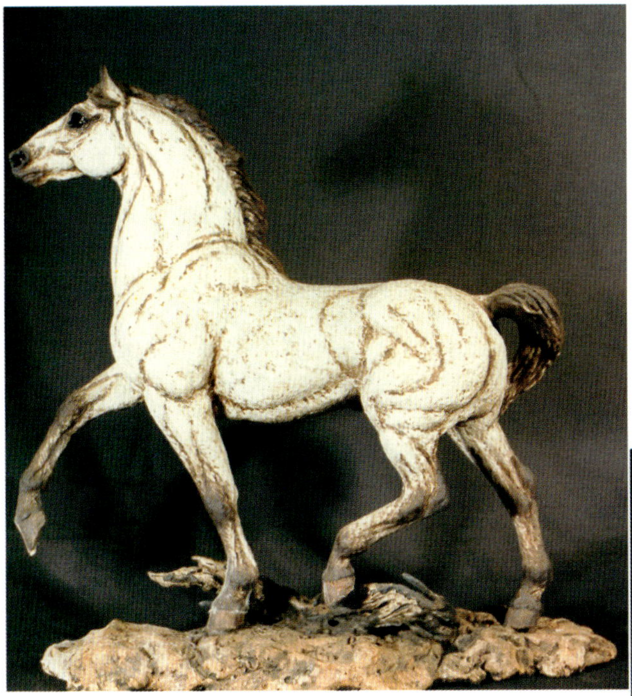

This magnificent stallion was known as the "Wild Horse" and was produced in a variety of colors. He stands 6.5" tall, and has an approximate value of $250-275.

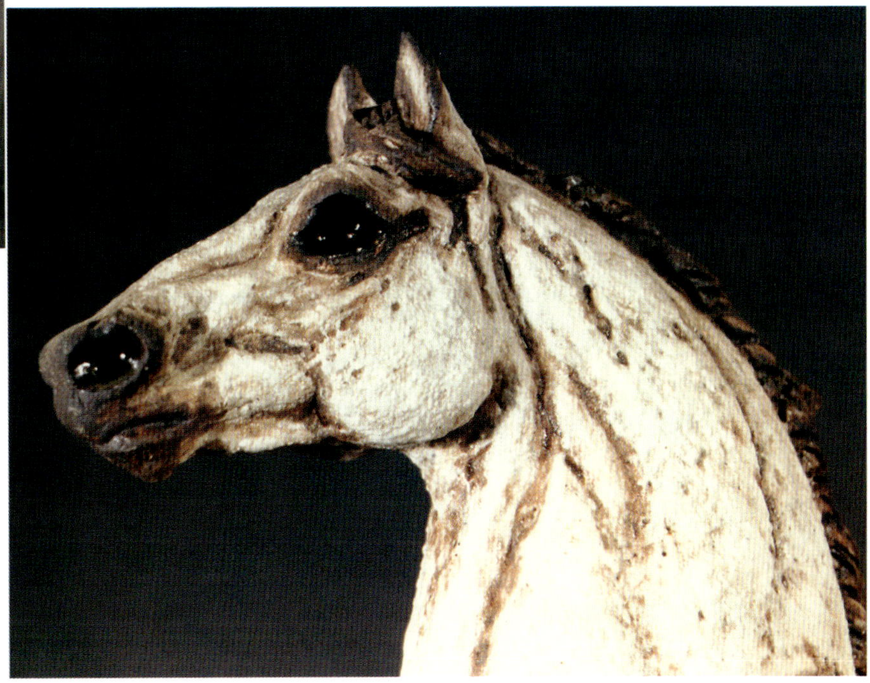

The fiery personality of this stallion comes through well in this head study.

A variation on the "Wild Horse" is this pinto coloring. The "washy" appearance of the brown coloring helps accentuate the muscle and hair detail. This model stands 6.5" tall and has an approximate value of $250-275.

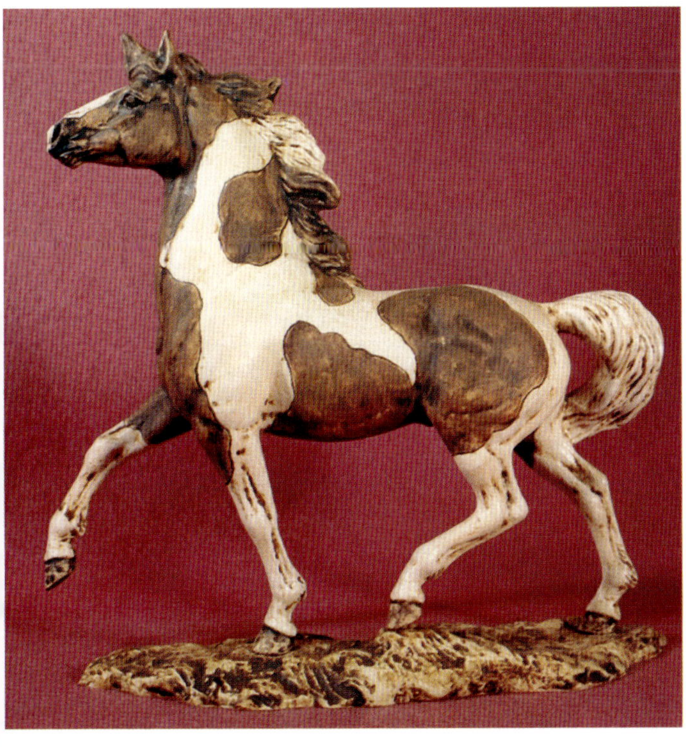

This coloring on the "Wild Horse" gives it a more natural, unfinished appearance. This is probably the most common color for this piece. The model stands 6.5" tall and has an approximate value of $225-250.

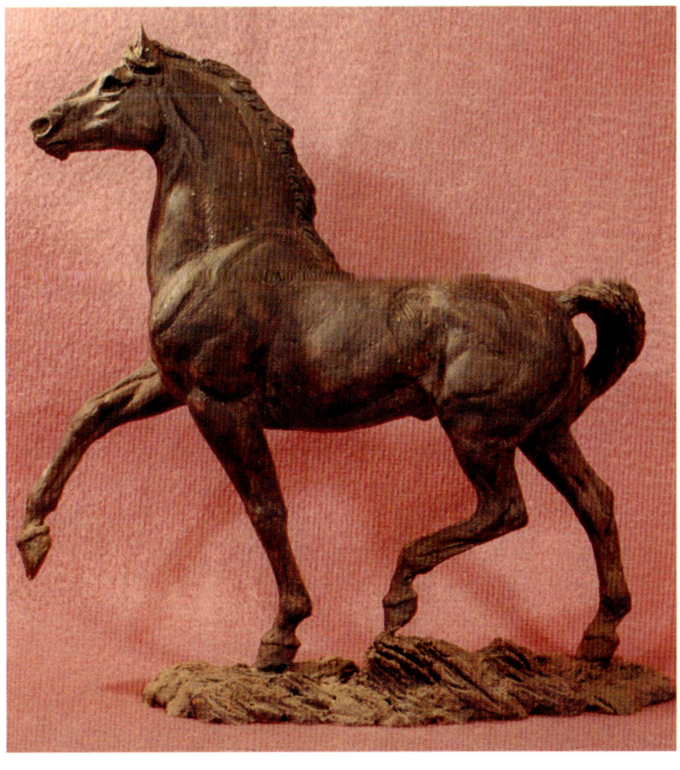

Wild and very artistic-looking, this model was simply referred to as horse/tree. It stands 7" tall and was offered as part of the Maureen Love Originals line. This particular model has Maureen's signature under the base, along with the number 13 and the date 1977. It has an approximate value of $180-210

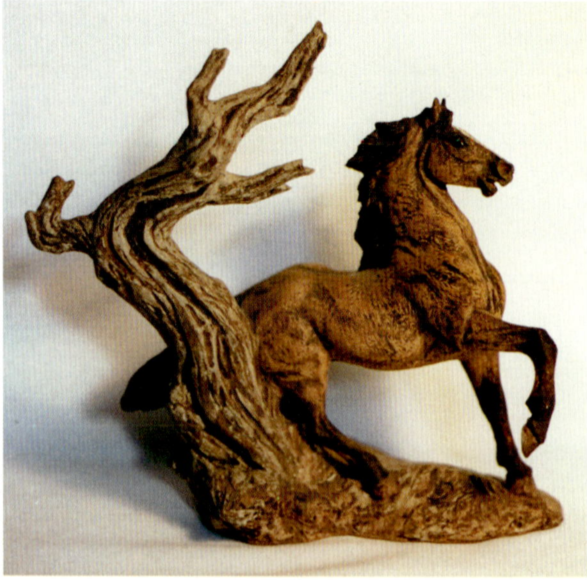

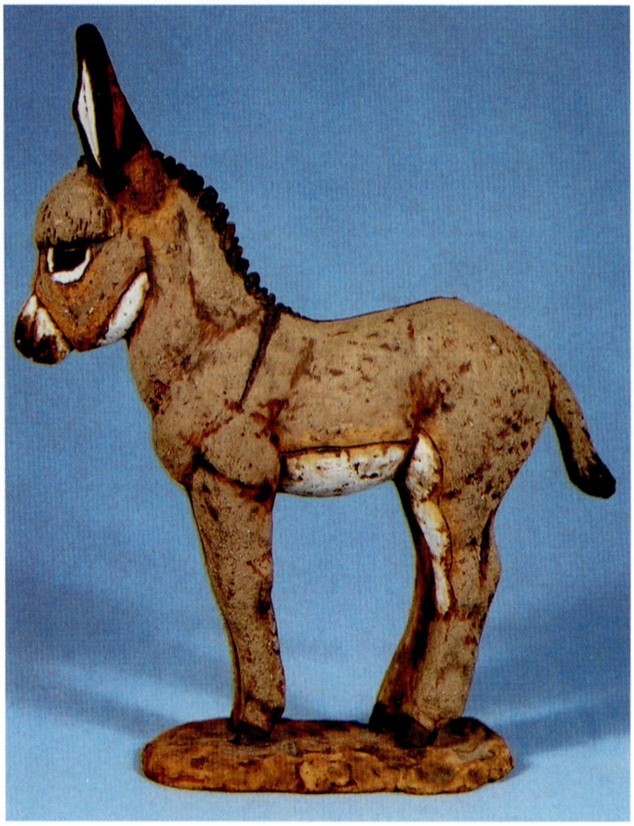

Known as "Baby Burro" on the Maureen Love Originals sales sheets, this little fellow stands 6" tall and has an approximate value of $125-150. The coloring on this model was fairly standard, without much variation during the production run.

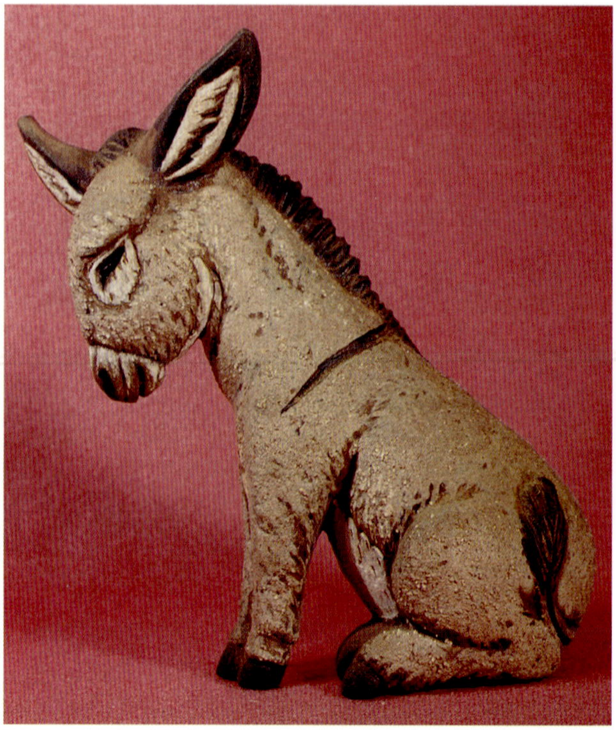

Measuring 5.5" tall, this adult burro was simply called "Burro," and his coloring was similar to that of the baby burro. His approximate value is $100-125.

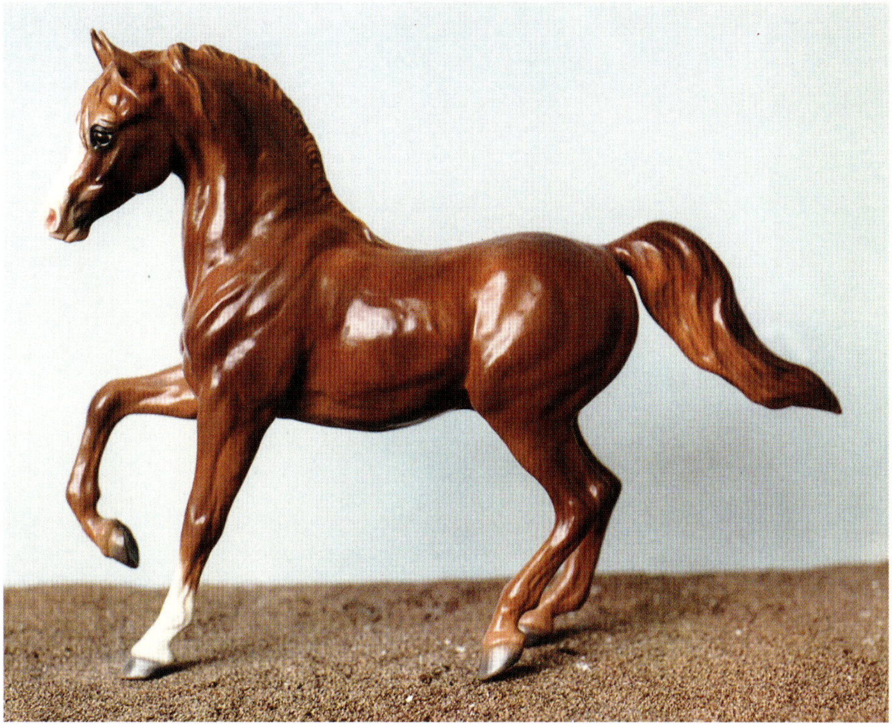

The Arabian stallion "Abu Farwa" served as the model for this handsome chestnut figure. Standing 7.5" tall, he was designed and delicately decorated by Maureen. Very few models of this horse exist, as it was originally submitted to Hagen-Renaker for production in 1954 and rejected. Approximate value $600-700.

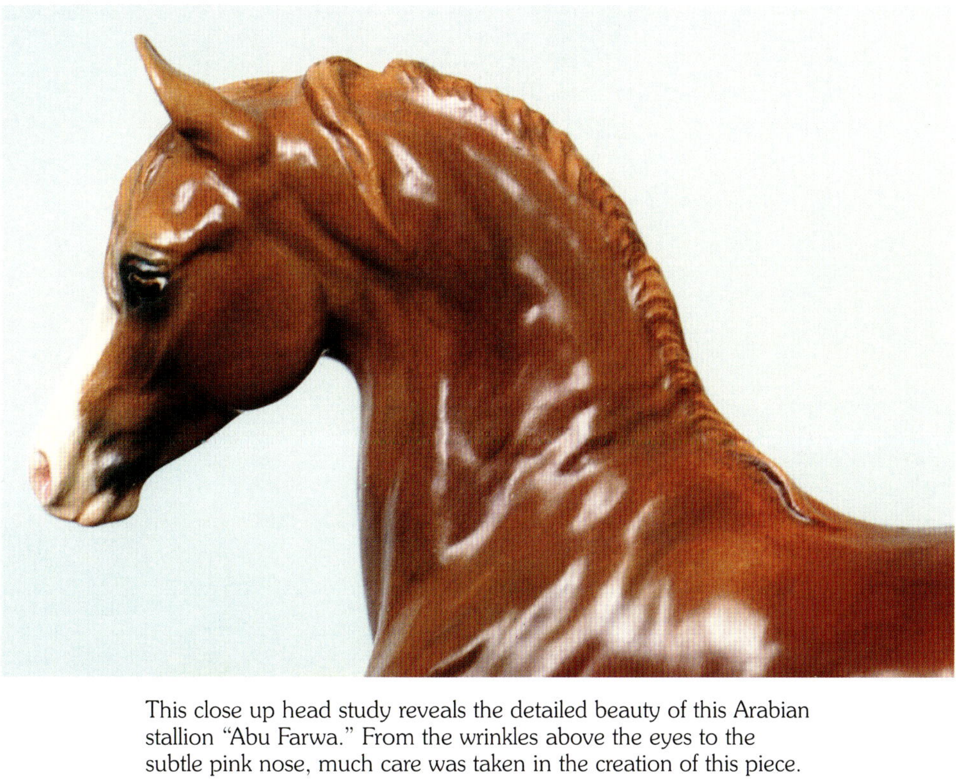

This close up head study reveals the detailed beauty of this Arabian stallion "Abu Farwa." From the wrinkles above the eyes to the subtle pink nose, much care was taken in the creation of this piece.

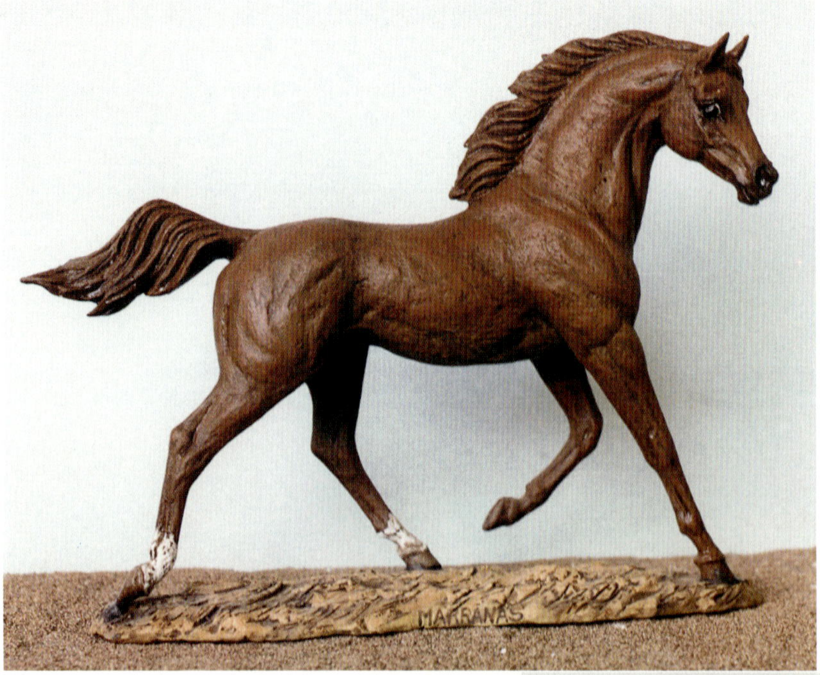

"Marranas," an Arabian stallion owned by Jimmie and Edna Nelson, was the model for this horse. At 9.75" tall, this is one of the tallest horses produced by Maureen Love Originals. This chestnut finish is the most common, but other finishes were also produced. The underside of the base is signed by Maureen and dated 1979. The approximate value of this horse is $500-550.

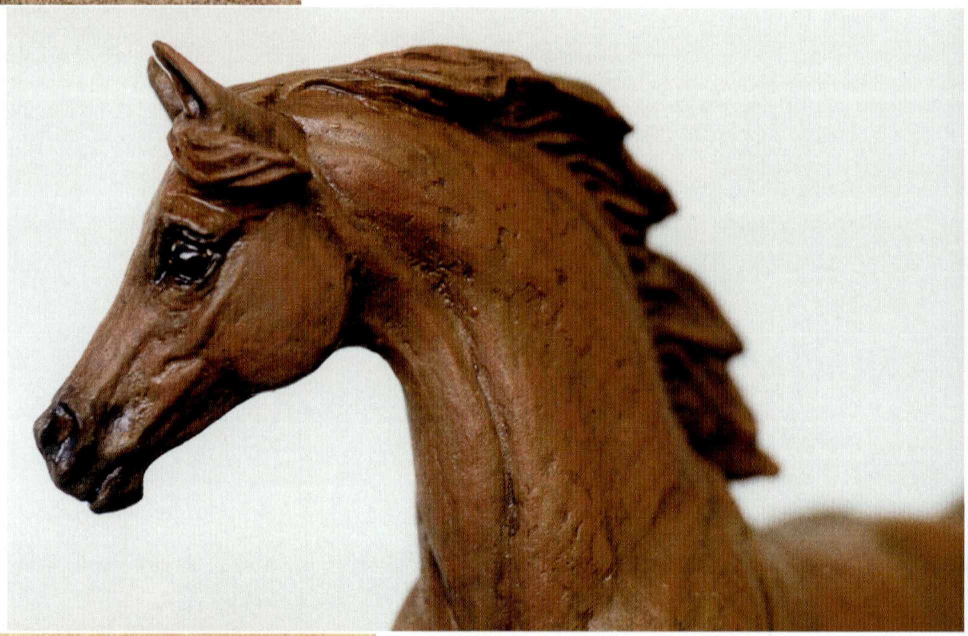

Looking at "Marranas" from the reverse side gives a wonderful view of the spirit and fire of this horse.

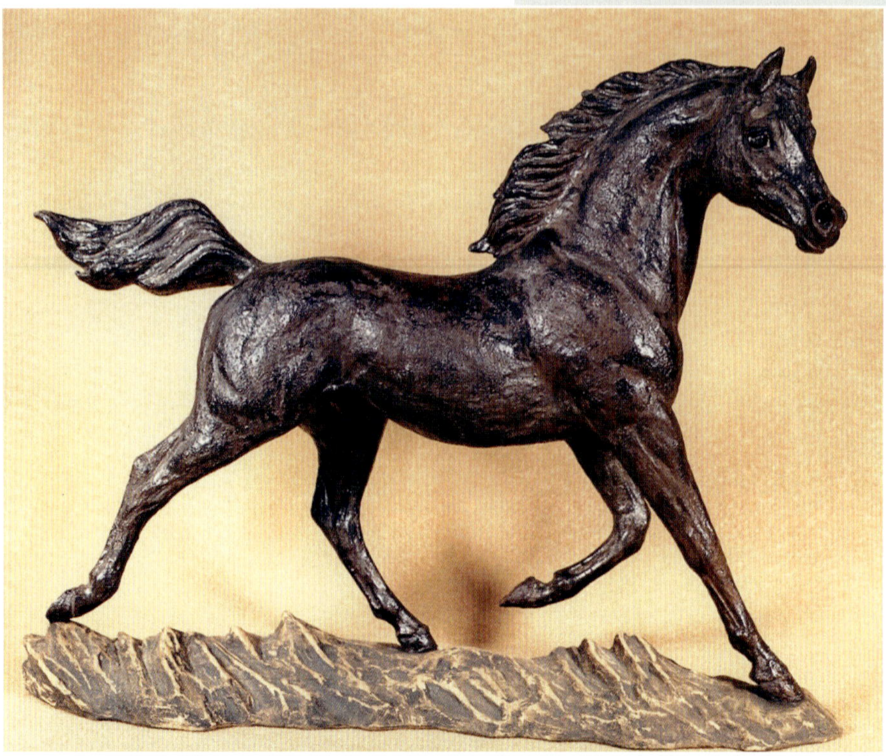

This is a different finish on the same "Marranas" model. Although made of ceramic, it has an almost bronze appearance. Approximate value $500-550.

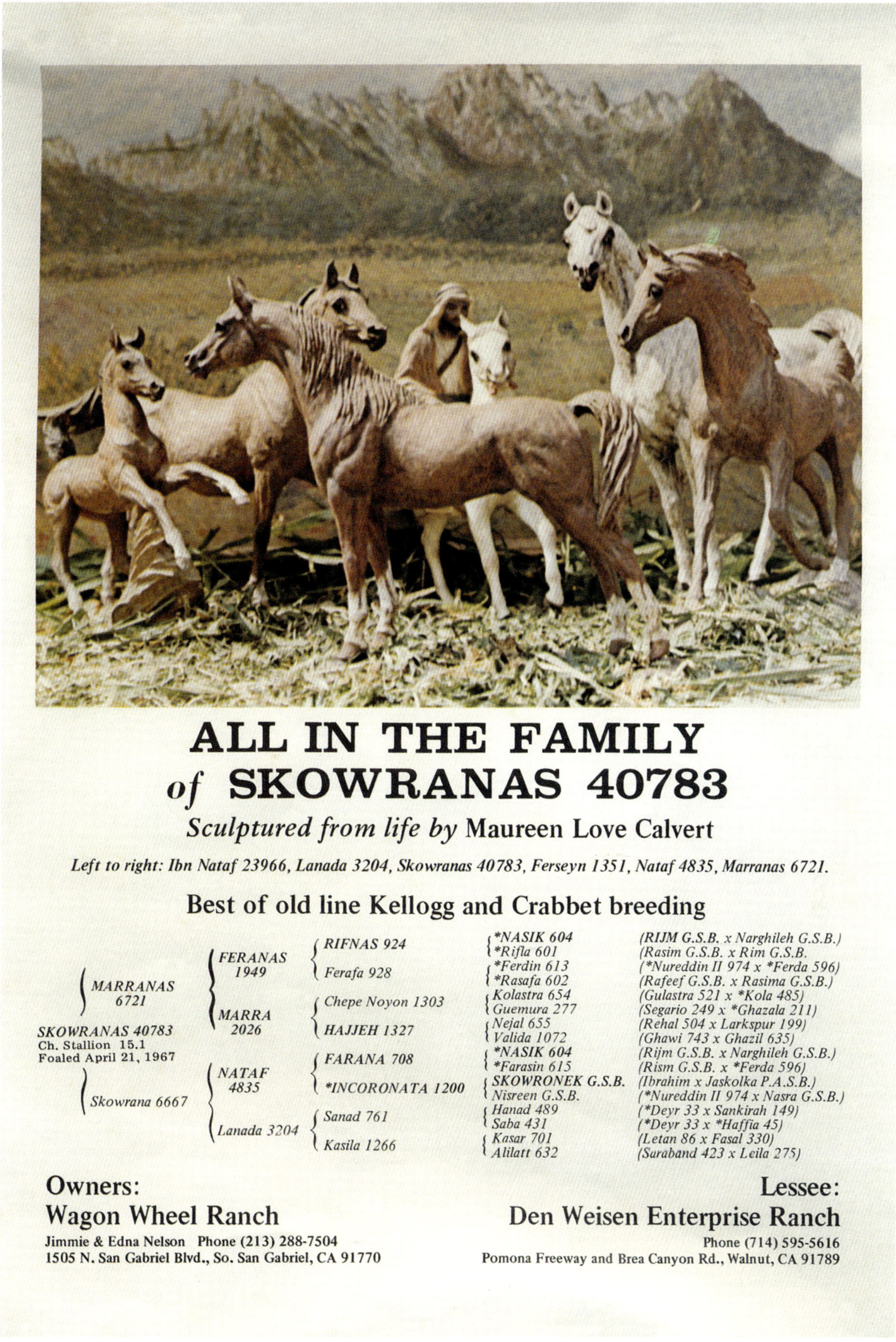

This very detailed promotional poster shows the bloodlines of the Arabian horses at the Wagon Wheel Ranch, owned by Jimmie and Edna Nelson. Maureen Love enjoyed visiting the ranch to sketch their horses, and the photo on the poster shows several of her models that were made for the Nelsons.

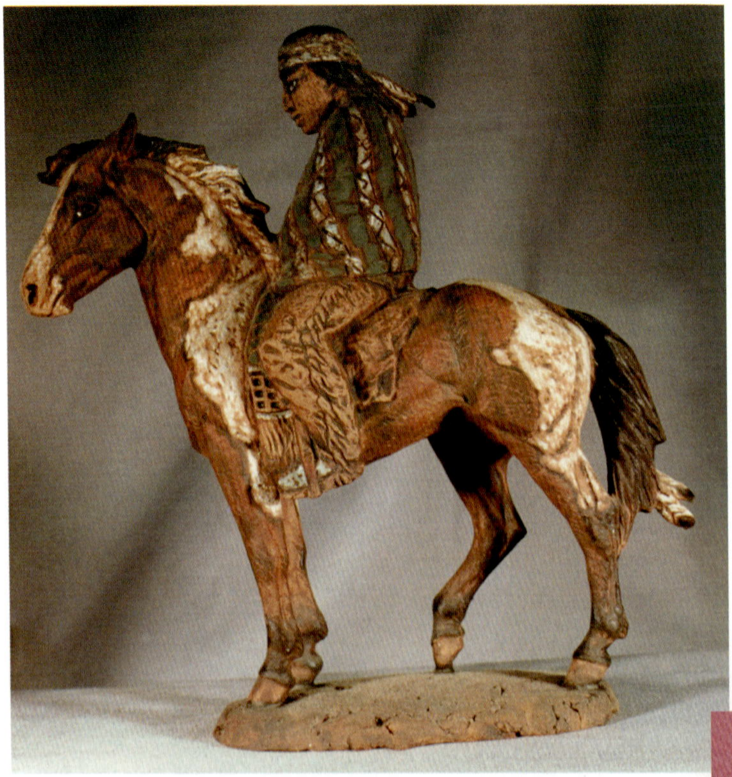

Standing 8" tall on the ceramic base, this Indian pony and rider were produced in a variety of horse and clothing colors. Each version has wonderful hand-painted detail. The approximate value of this horse and rider is $275-325.

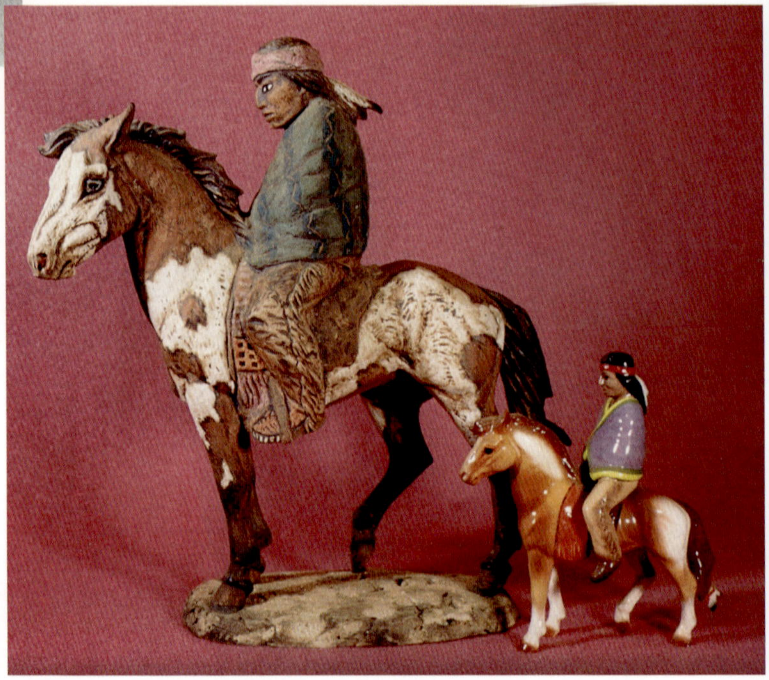

The Maureen Love Originals Indian pony and rider gave rise to a corresponding Hagen-Renaker model several years later. The Hagen-Renaker model stands 3.8" tall and has an approximate value of $20-22. The larger figure is 8" tall, with an approximate value of $275-325.

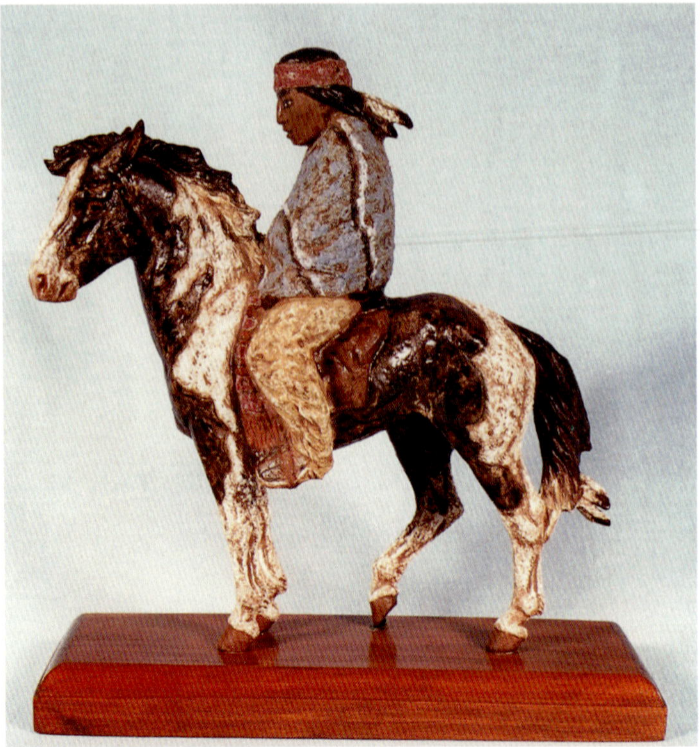

Here is another color version of the pinto Indian pony. This model was mounted on a wooden base for stability, and the wooden base is not original.

The Indian pony was also produced in this solid color version. It gives it a very different appearance from the pinto coloring.

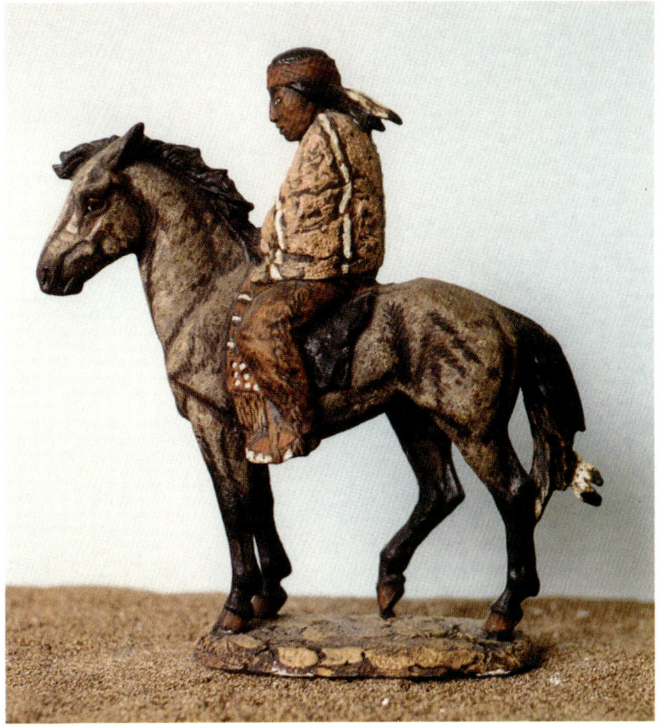

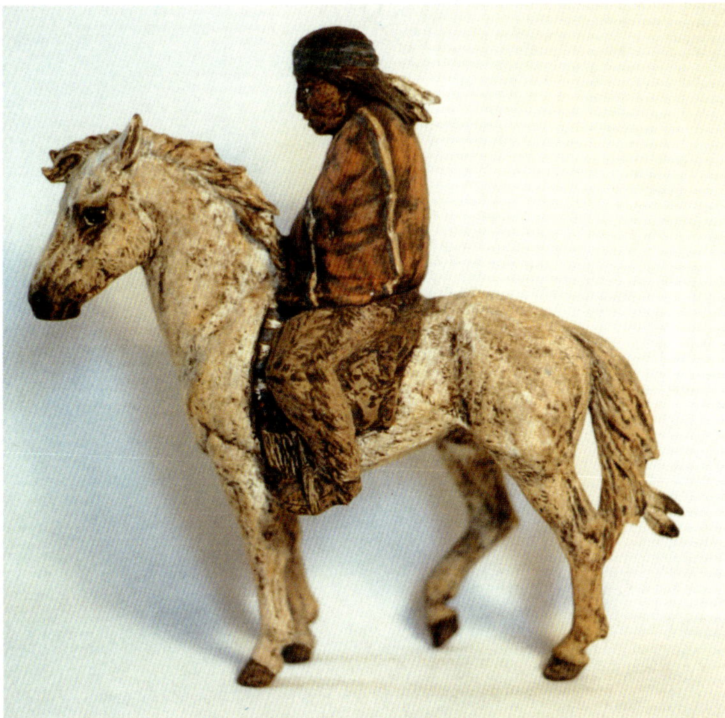

The combination of horse colors, blanket colors, and other details varied quite a bit, giving rise to several unique models. This palomino-colored horse was one of the more unusual versions of this piece.

Incredibly fierce-looking, this Apache with his horse stands 9.5" tall by 8.5" long and has an approximate value of $350-400.

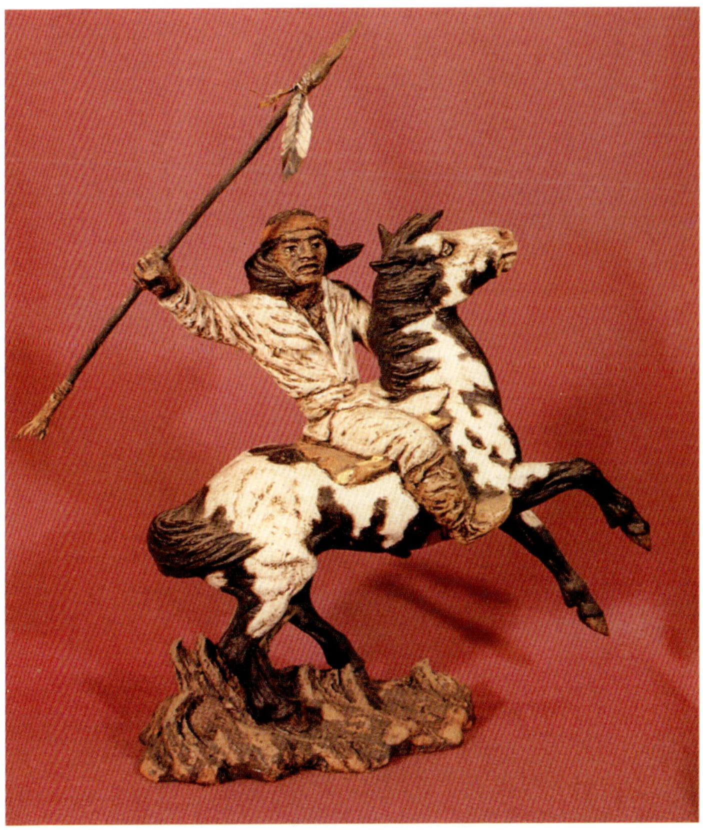

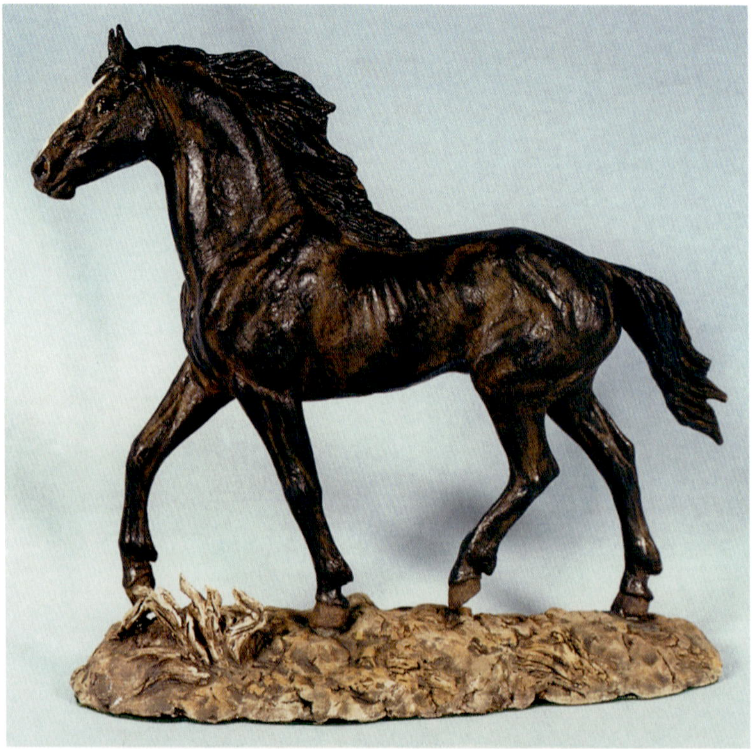

Known as the "Wild Stallion" on the 1970s sales sheet, this horse is considered black, with lighter highlights. He stands 8.75" tall and is dated 1974 underneath the base. His approximate value is $300-350.

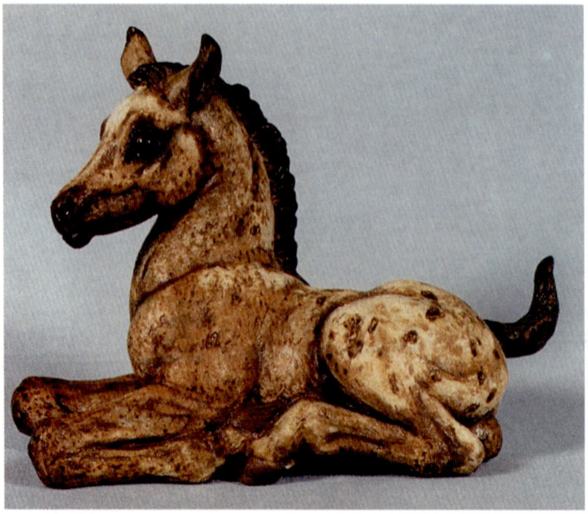

This delightful Appaloosa lying foal is dated 1979 on the underside. He measures 3.5" tall, and has an approximate value of $100-125. Pieces with more elaborate hand decoration are worth more than the simpler pieces.

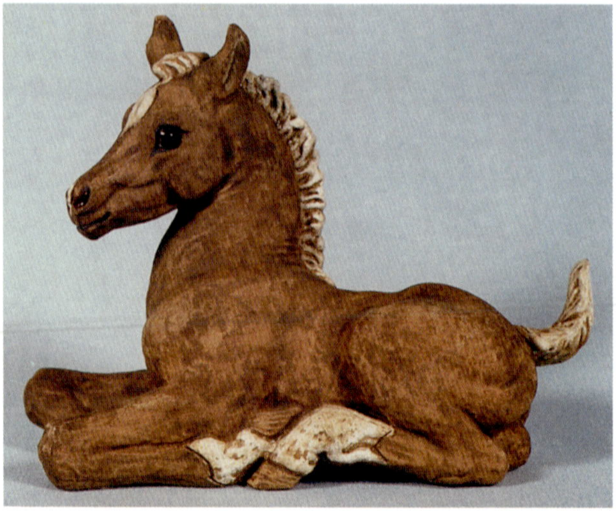

The glossy eye against the matte finish of this chestnut-colored lying foal really gives it a "live" appearance. It measures 3.5" tall, and has an approximate value of $100-125.

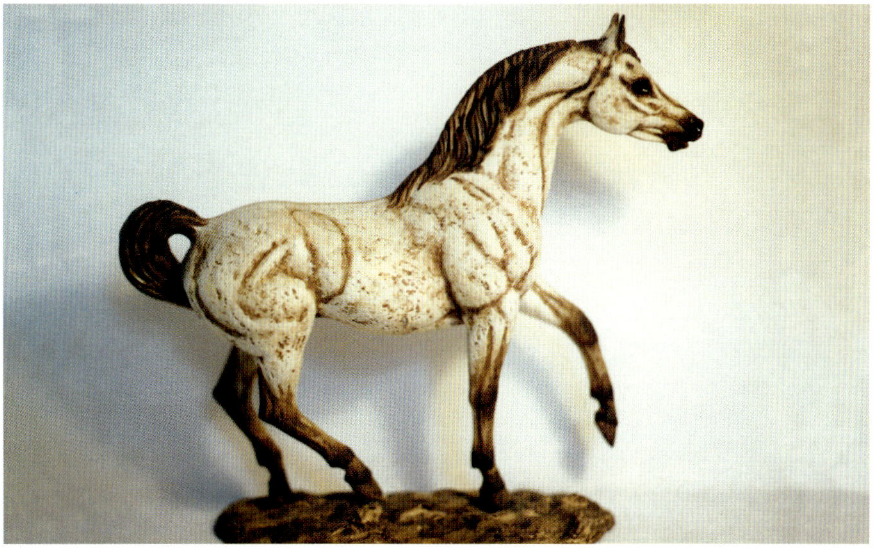

This Arabian stallion was produced in a variety of colors and finishes. This light-colored version is a less common color. He stands 8" tall on his base and has an approximate value of $325-375.

Maureen loves to experiment with glazes. The model underneath this pebbly glaze is smooth. This Arabian stallion stands 8" tall, and has an approximate value of $325-375, with the more unusual finishes being worth more.

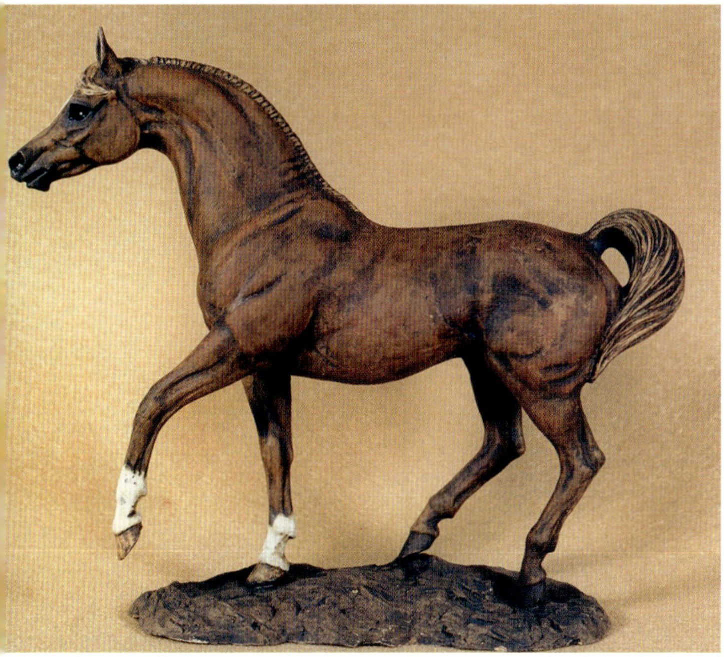

The Arabian stallion is dated 1975, and has the unusual feature of hollow eyes. This color is the more common version for this model.

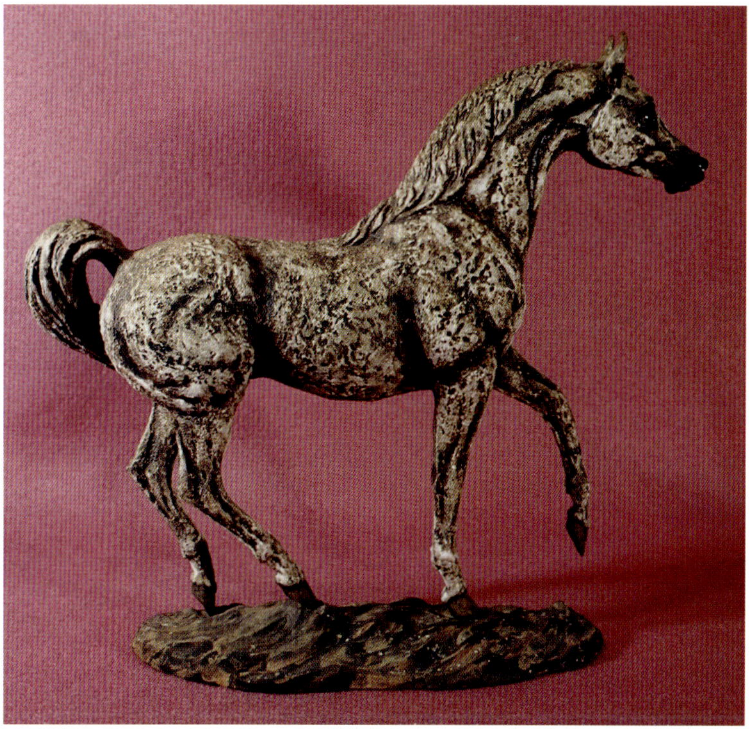

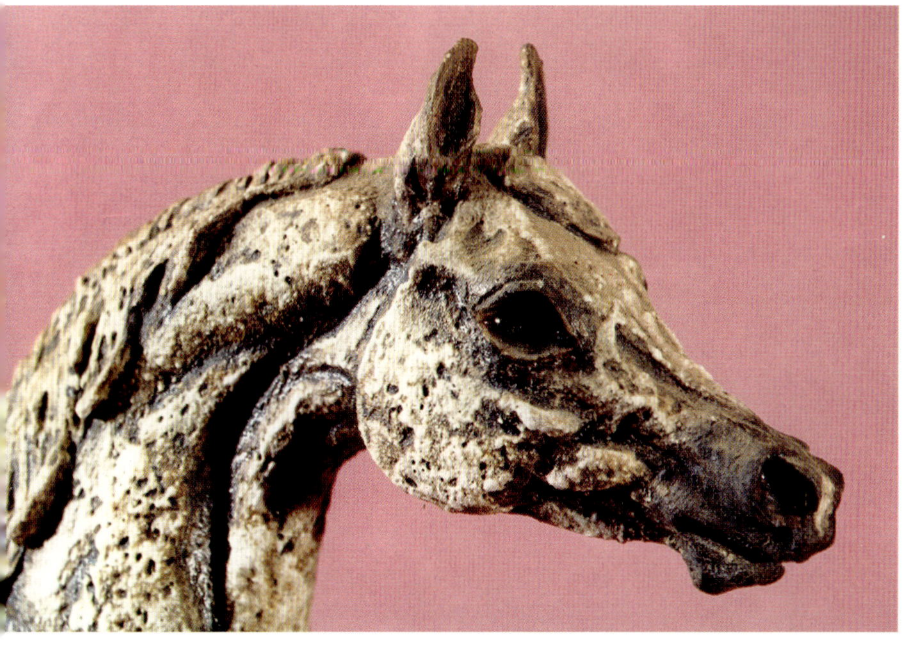

This close-up view of the Arabian stallion's head gives a good view of the bumpy texture of the glaze.

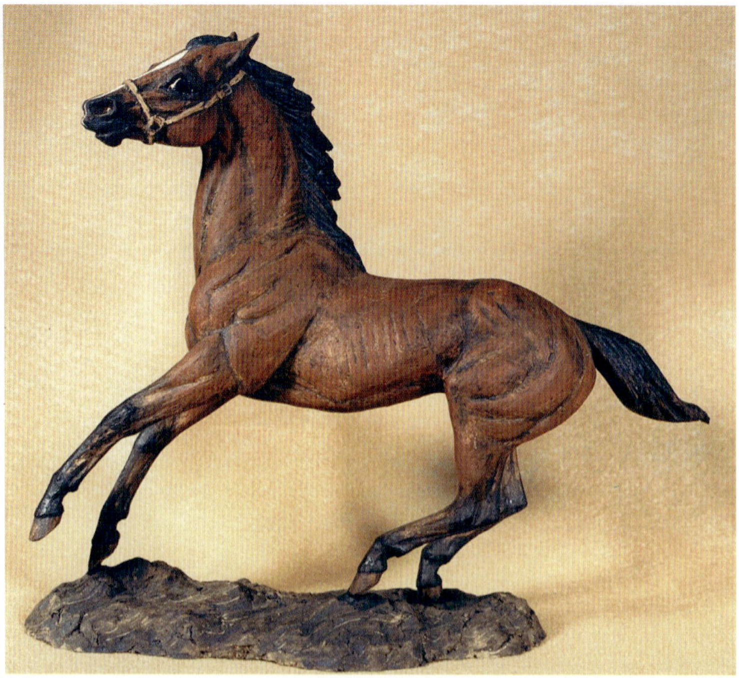

Dated 1974, this Thoroughbred in action is also numbered #7 under the base. It stands 9.5" tall, and is one of the very few pieces Maureen created wearing a halter. The approximate value is $350-400.

The Arabian stallion "Nataf" was the inspiration for this model. At a towering 13" tall, he is one of the tallest pieces created by Maureen during this period. He is dated 1979, and shows a simple version of the bubbly white glaze. His approximate value is $500-550. Note the horse's name appears on the front of the base.

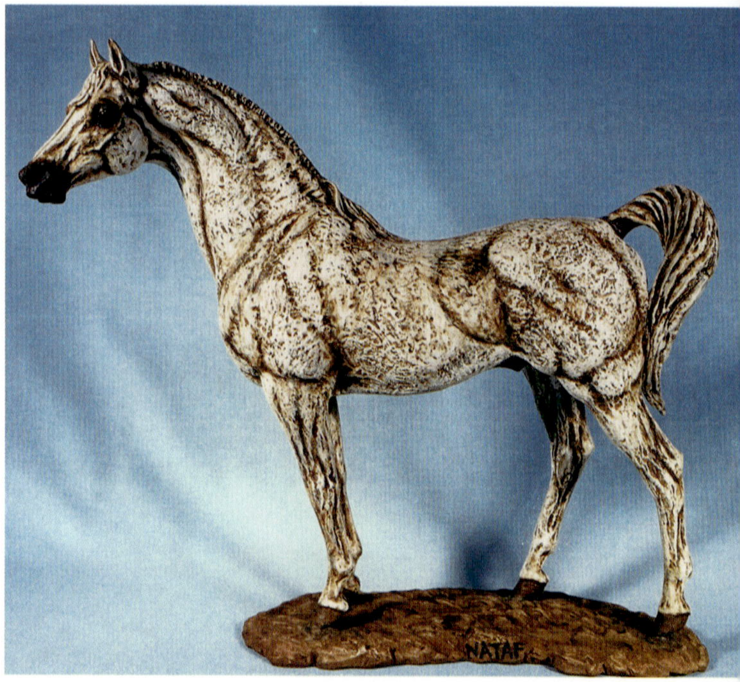

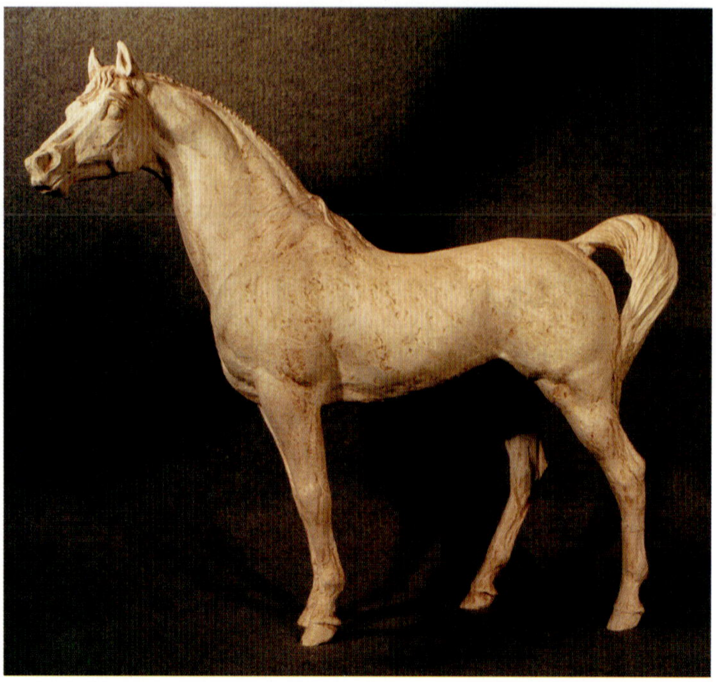

This plain, smooth version of "Nataf" is more common, with a simpler finish. This model looks like the model eventually produced by Hagen-Renaker pottery in the 1980s. This horse stands 12" tall (without a base) and has an approximate value of $500-550.

“Ibn Nataf,” the Arabian foal, is dated 1974 and stands 8.5" tall, making him a much larger scale than the adult horses produced during this time. He was inspired by a foal at the Nelson’s ranch. His approximate value is $325-375.

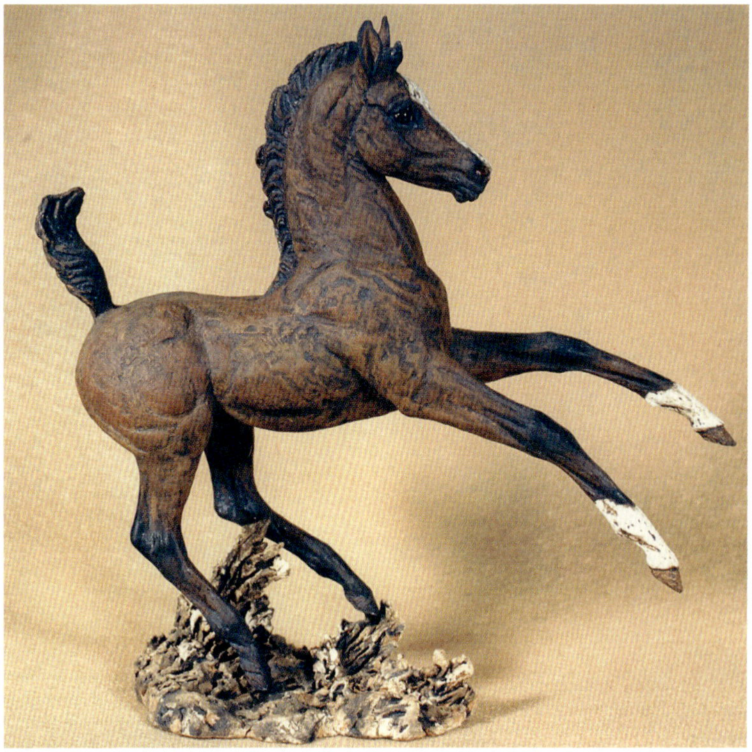

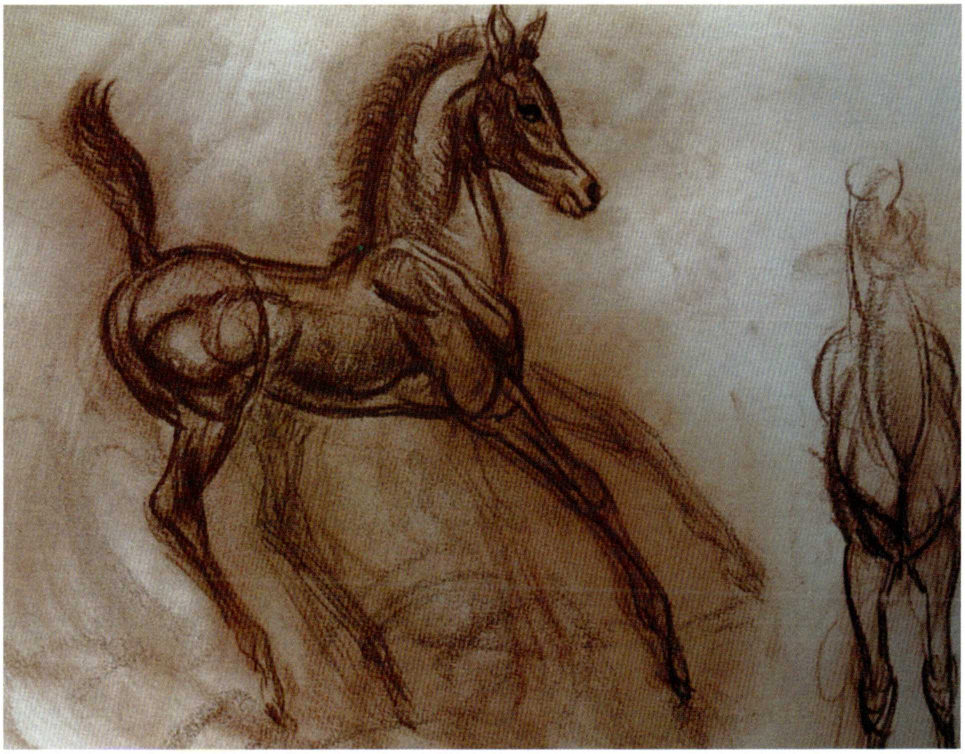

The impish personality of the foal “Ibn Nataf” is captured well in this sketch done by Maureen Love while visiting the Nelson’s ranch. Maureen preferred to sketch her subjects from many angles before attempting to sculpt them.

These two dinosaurs were submitted to the Hagen-Renaker Pottery company for consideration, but were never produced. The Tyrannosaurus Rex stands 3.5" tall and the Corythosaurus is 3" tall. Their approximate value is $40-65 each.

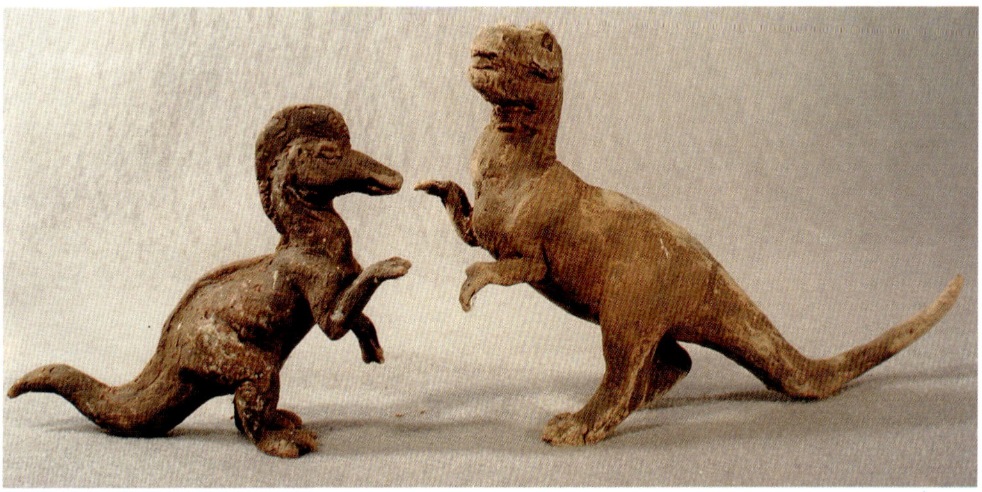

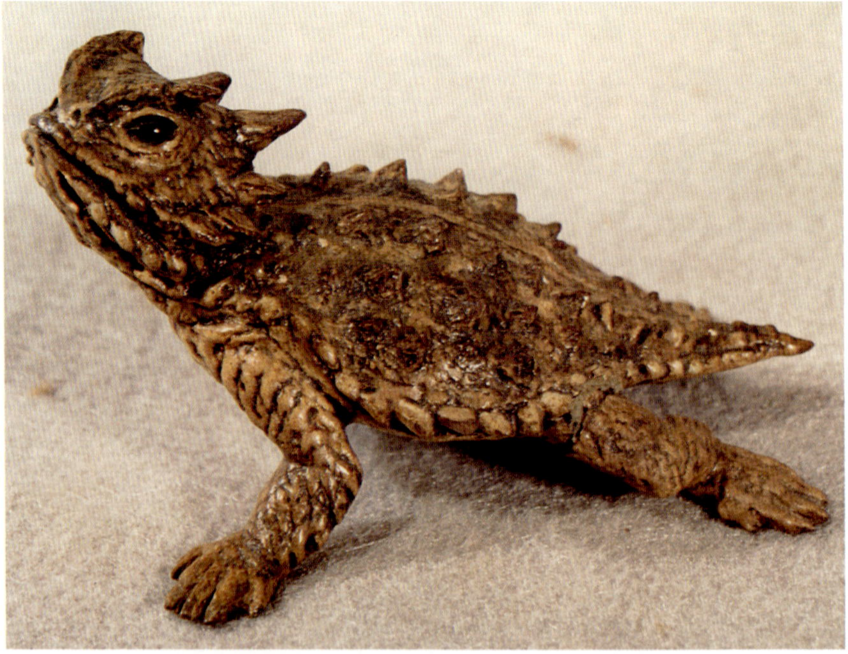

The crusty horned toad has an amazing amount of detail in the bumps of his skin. Measuring 1.5" tall, he is one of the creatures Maureen observed in her garden. His approximate value is $50-75.

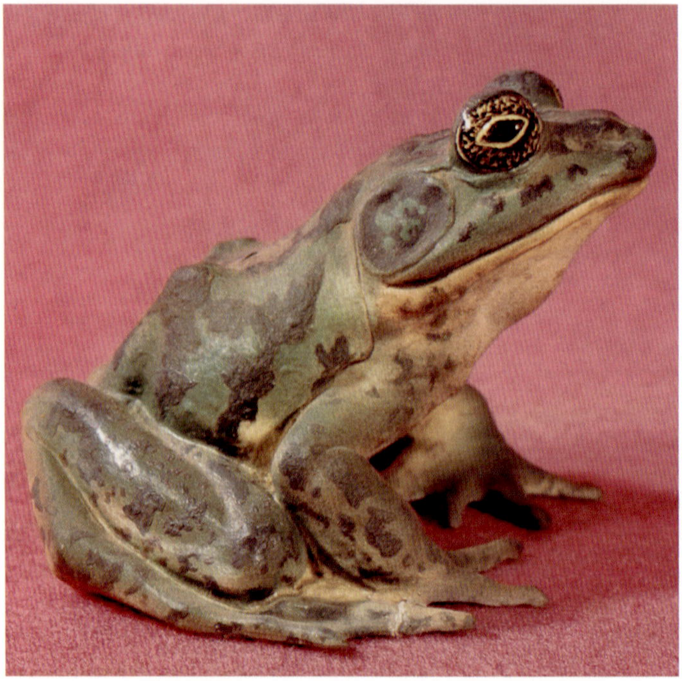

Although this design later went on to become a Hagen-Renaker model, the production pieces could never rival the marvelous hand-painted detail this bullfrog exhibits. It stands 2.75" tall, and has an approximate value of $75-100.

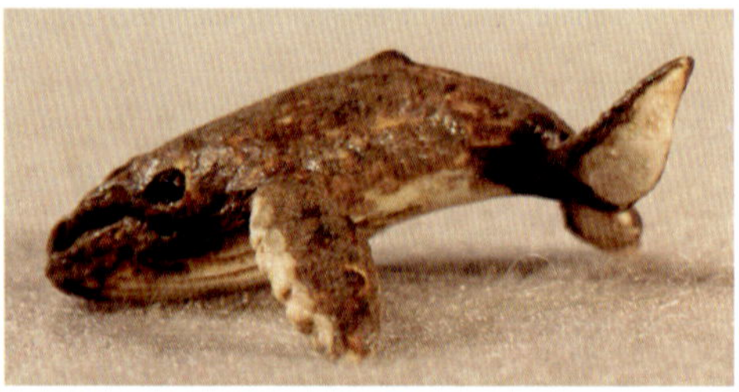

Maureen provided a series of whales to Hagen-Renaker, but this humpback whale baby was never produced. It measures a tiny 0.5" tall, and has an approximate value of $25-40.

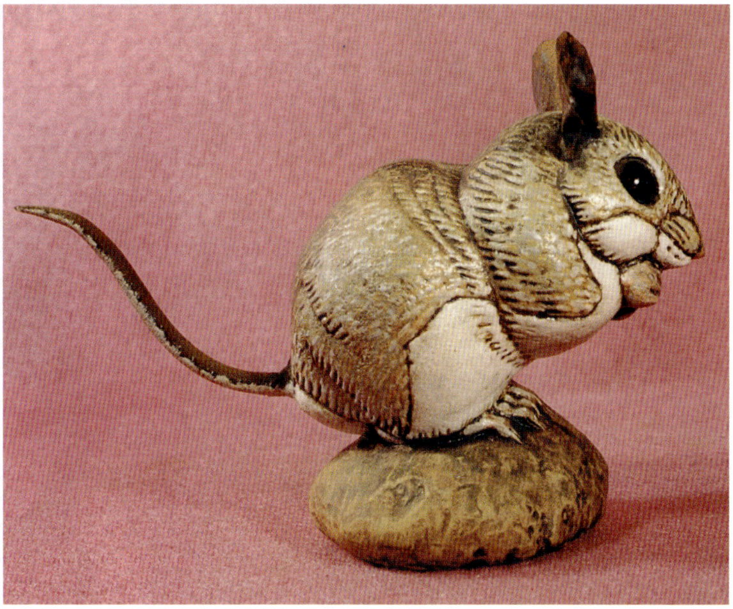

This white-footed mouse sitting on a rock has an unusual feature. Its ears are made of copper, and they are wrinkled to look like the ears of a real mouse. It is 3.25" tall, and has an approximate value of $60-80.

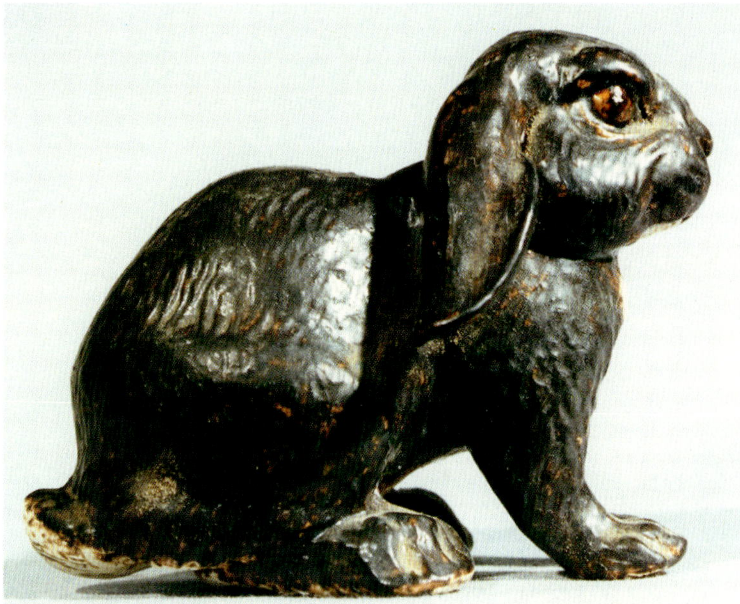

Measuring 3" tall and 6.75" long, this charming lop-eared rabbit has an approximate value of $60-80.

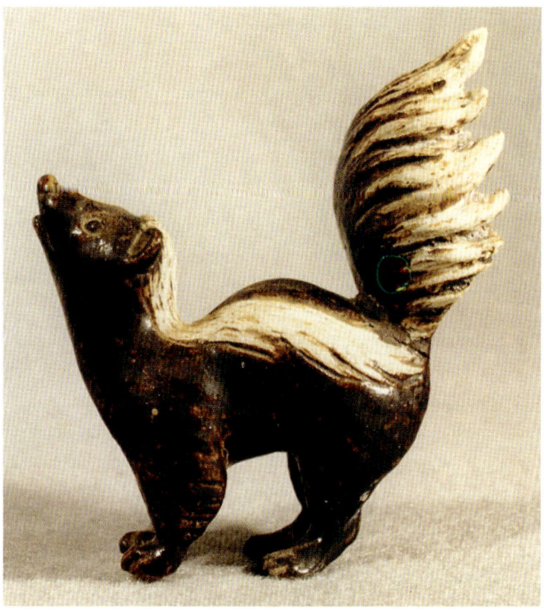

Looking very frightened and alarmed, this skunk measures 2.75" tall and shows a lot of long fur detail over its back and tail. Approximate value for this piece is $40-65.

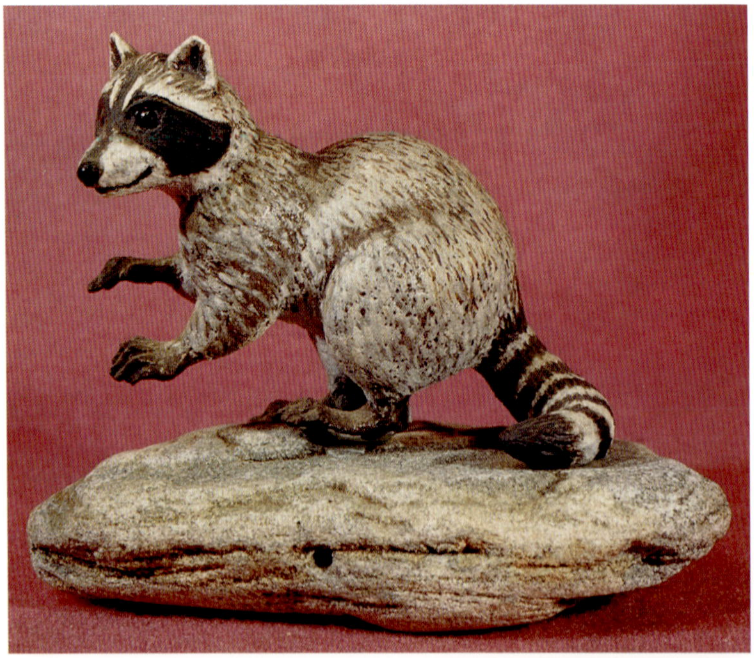

Ready for its next meal, this raccoon model captures the true nature of the animal. Maureen has observed numerous masked visitors in her garden over the years. The raccoon on the rock stands 3" tall, and has an approximate value of $50-75.

The Persian cat shown in the foreground is carved from Plasti-Carve, one of the materials that Maureen uses to create her original models. Behind is the original piece, which she later altered by changing the head position using Plasti-Carve. Both cats stand 3.2" tall.

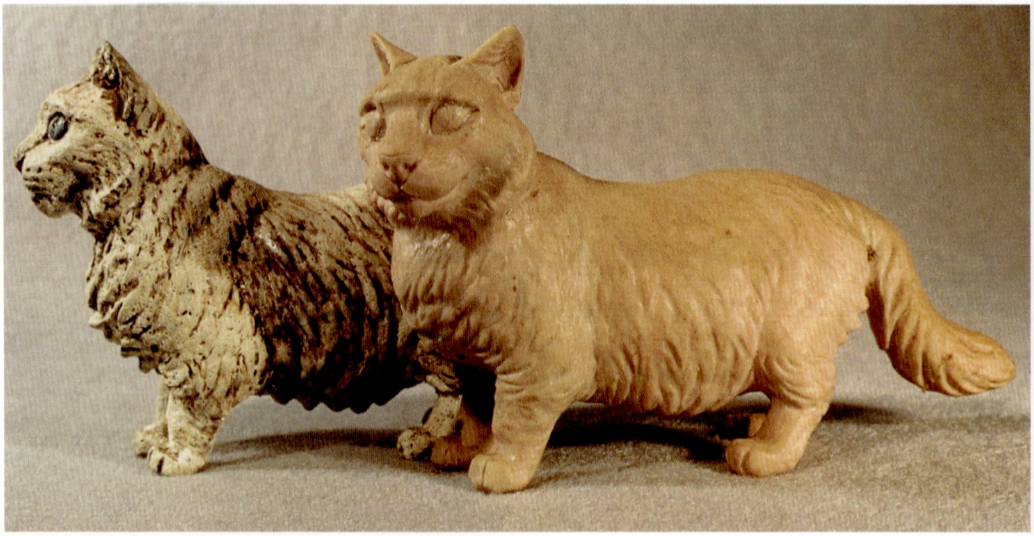

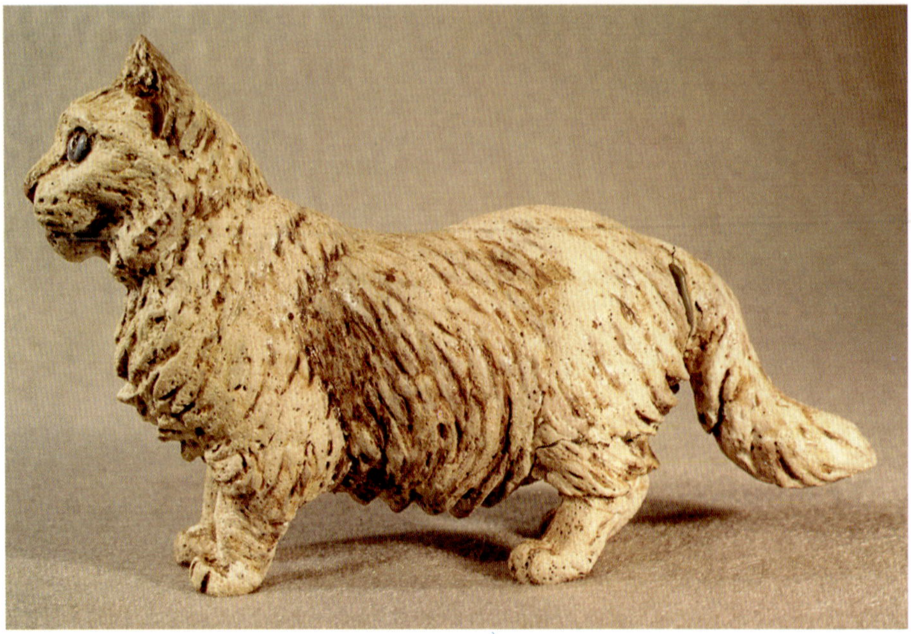

This wonderfully furry Persian cat stands 3.2" tall, and has an approximate value of $60-80.

Measuring a tiny 1.5" tall, this lying cat illustrates Maureen's amazing attention to detail. The cat has an approximate value of $40-60.

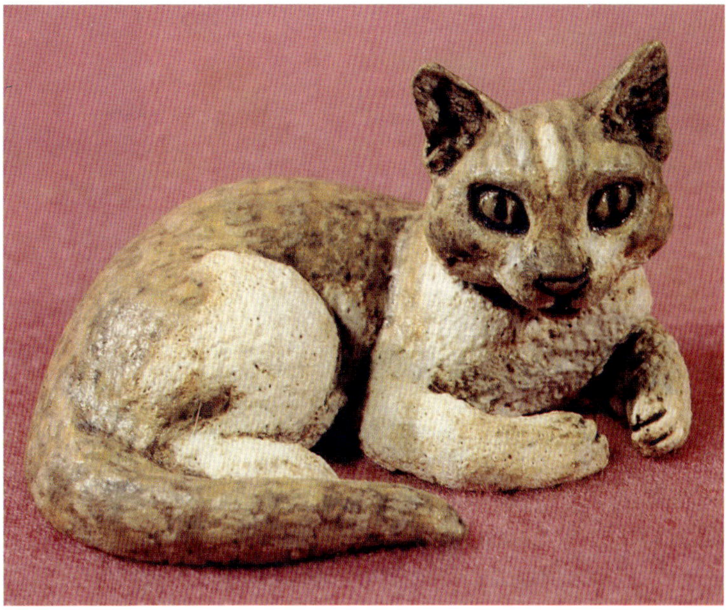

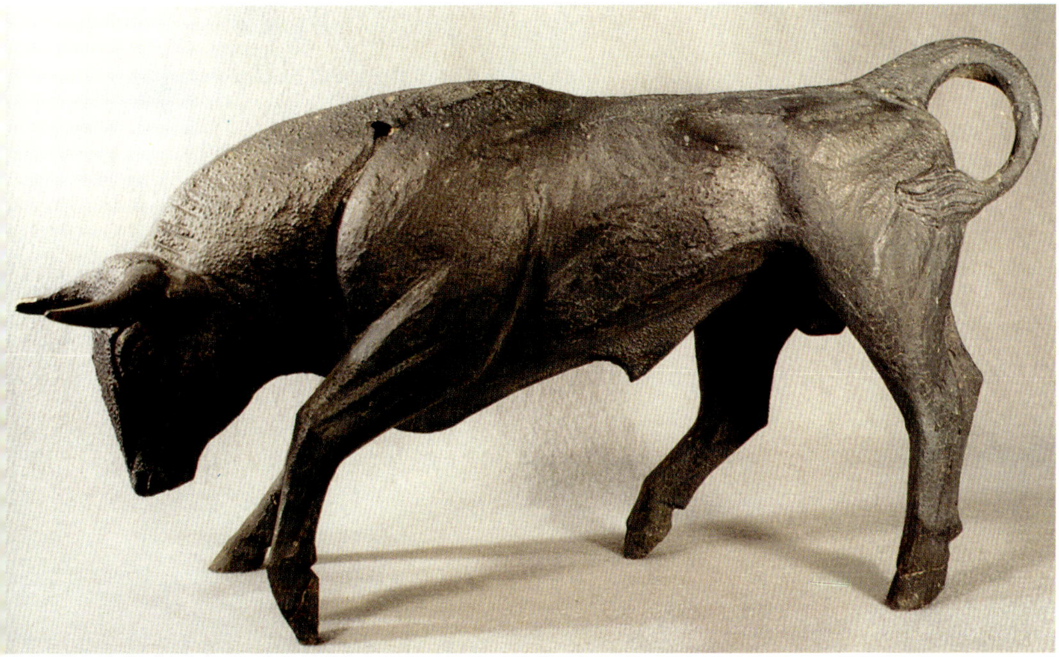

Known as the Spanish Fighting Bull, this stylized model measures 7.5" tall and has an approximate value of $125-150.

The hippopotamus was one of the many animals that Maureen studied at the zoo. See page 9 for the amusing story related to this. Standing 3.75" tall, this hippo has an approximate value of $60-80.

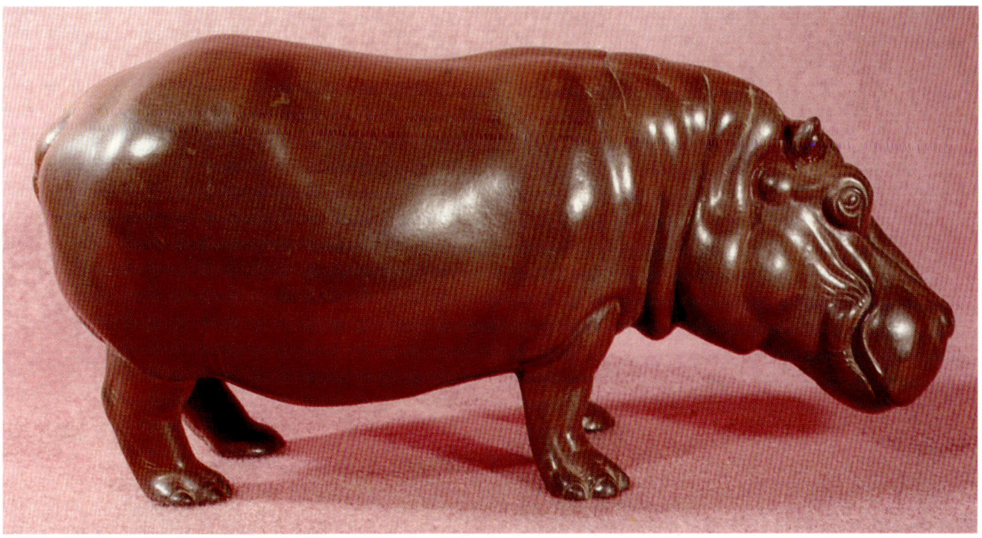

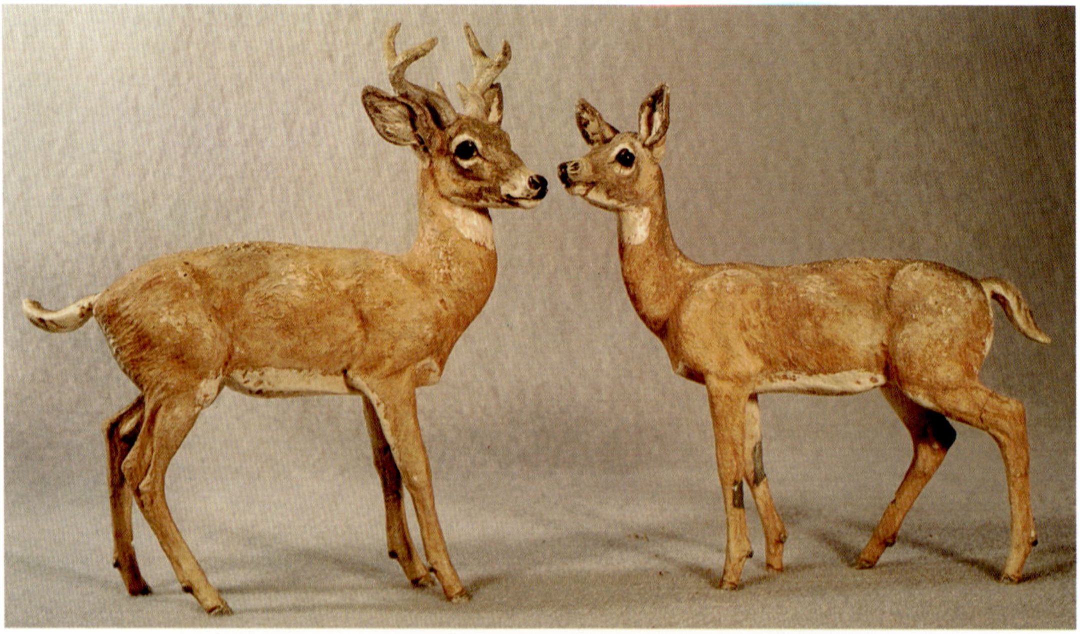

Maureen captured the alert, skittish nature of the White Tailed Deer buck and doe. The buck stands 5" tall and the doe 4.5" tall. This delicate duo has an approximate value of $200-225 for the buck and $175-200 for the doe.

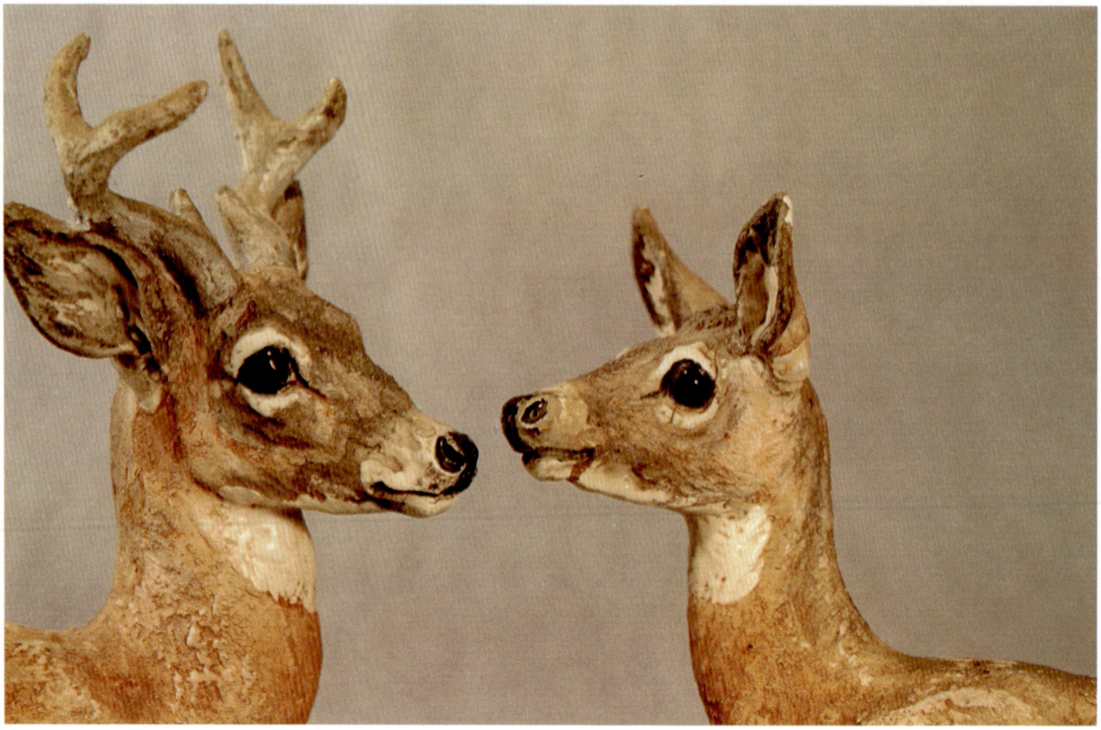

This close up head study shows off the detail and texture of these two deer. Note the glossy eye against the matte body, giving the deer a very life-like appearance.

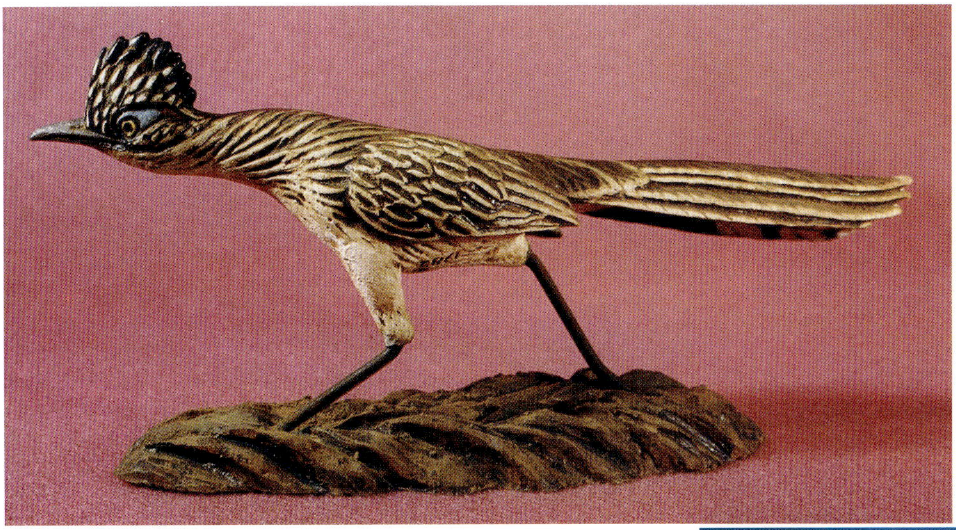

Maureen draws much of her inspiration from the creatures around her. Living in the southwest, the Roadrunner is a common sight. She has done several versions, each with incredible detail. This one stands 3.5" tall and has an approximate value of $45-60.

This larger version of the Roadrunner stands 8" tall. Maureen has added the cactus to the base of this model to give the feel of its natural habitat. The needles on the cactus are actually pieces of metal wire, and the bird's legs are metal rods. His approximate value is $150-175.

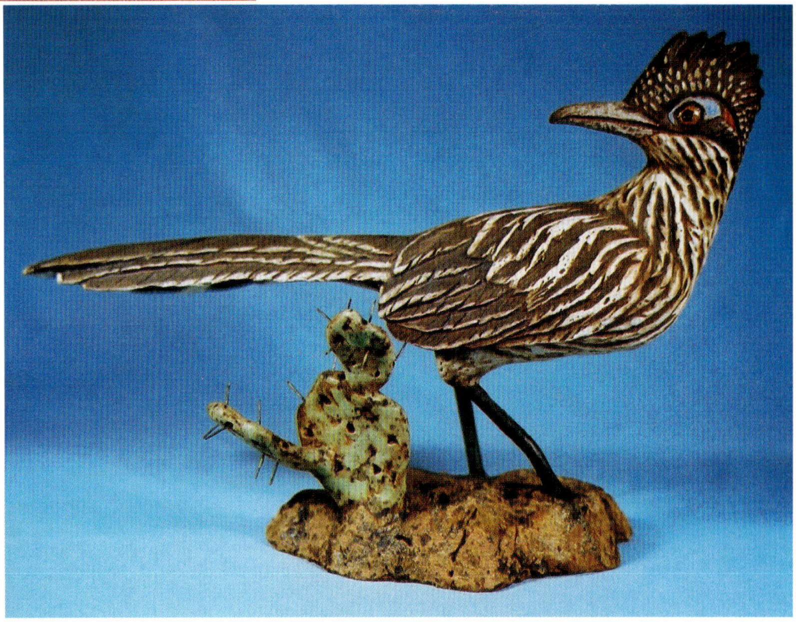

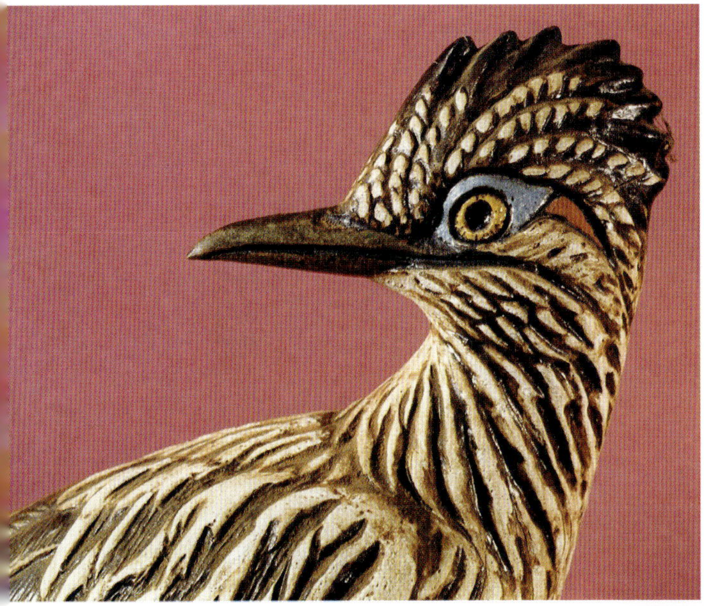

The intricate detail of the feathers and the carved textures in the body are shown well in this close up head study of the roadrunner.

To add interest to the models, Maureen likes to experiment. On the base of this Roadrunner, she added grains of sand to further simulate the desert environment where the Roadrunner lives. This photo also shows the wire cactus needles and the metal legs of the bird.

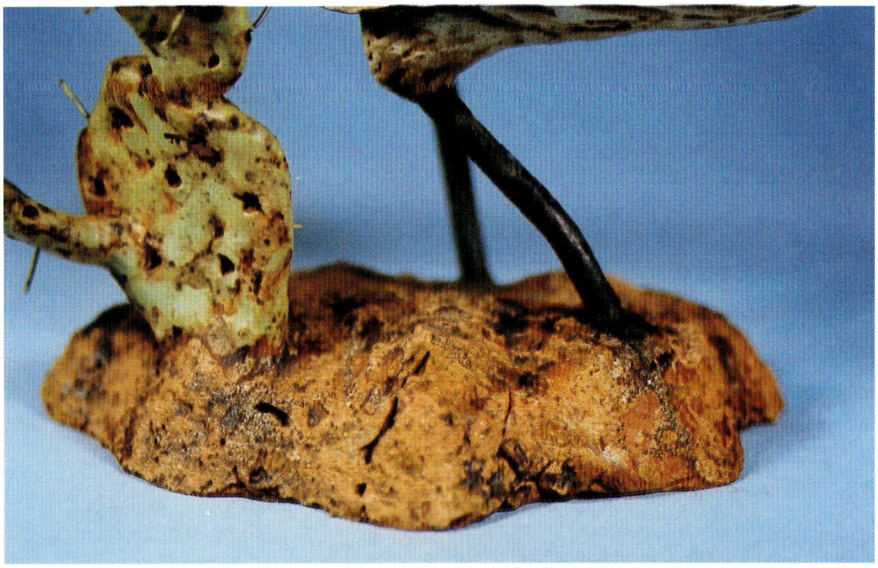

The running Sanderling has the signature of Maureen Love under the base, and the year 1978. It also bears the number 50. Standing 4.5" tall, it has an approximate value of $50-75.

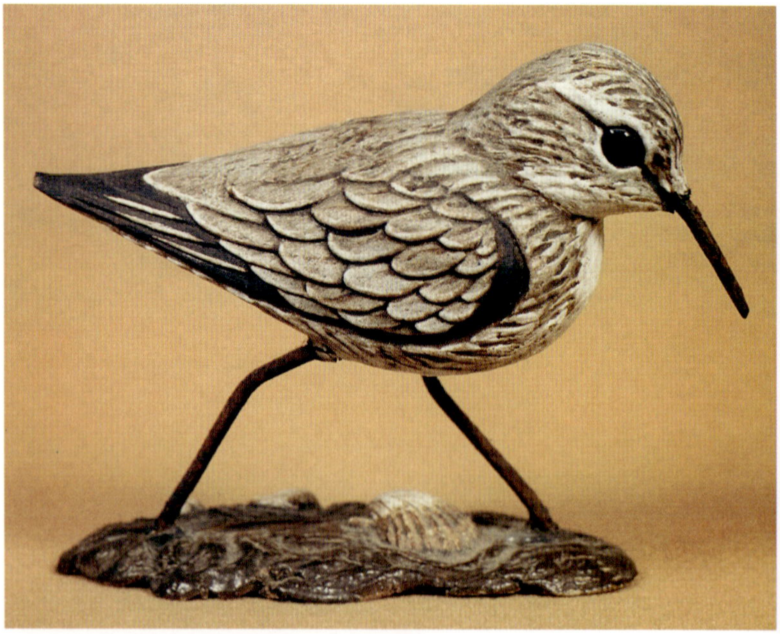

To simulate the shore of the Pacific Ocean, the base of the running Sanderling model shows the swirling patterns of water in the sand, as well as a shell trapped in the sand.

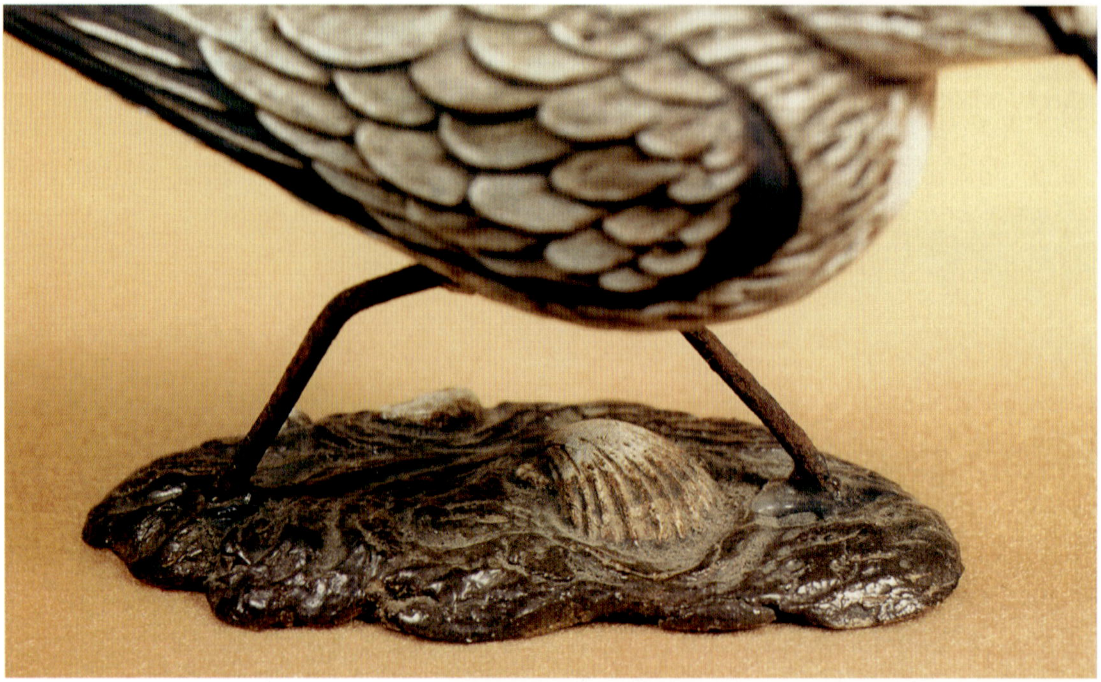

This duo of running Sanderlings represents a variation on the model. Note the added detail in the knee joints, and the different shell and water depictions. They also have a more upright head position, giving them a height of 5". The right bird shows more of the feather detail, and the left bird gives a better view of the chest and face. Their approximate value is $75-100 each.

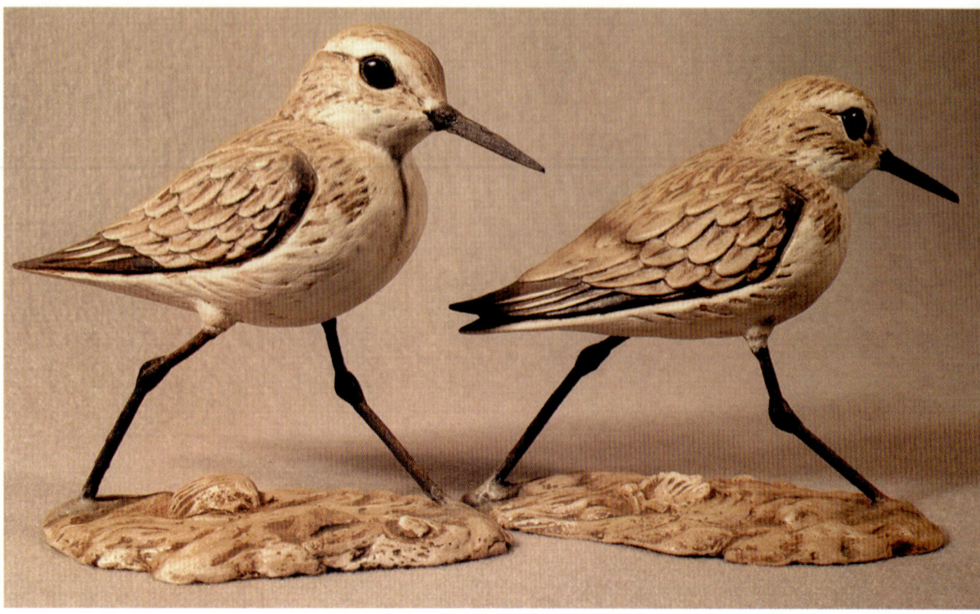

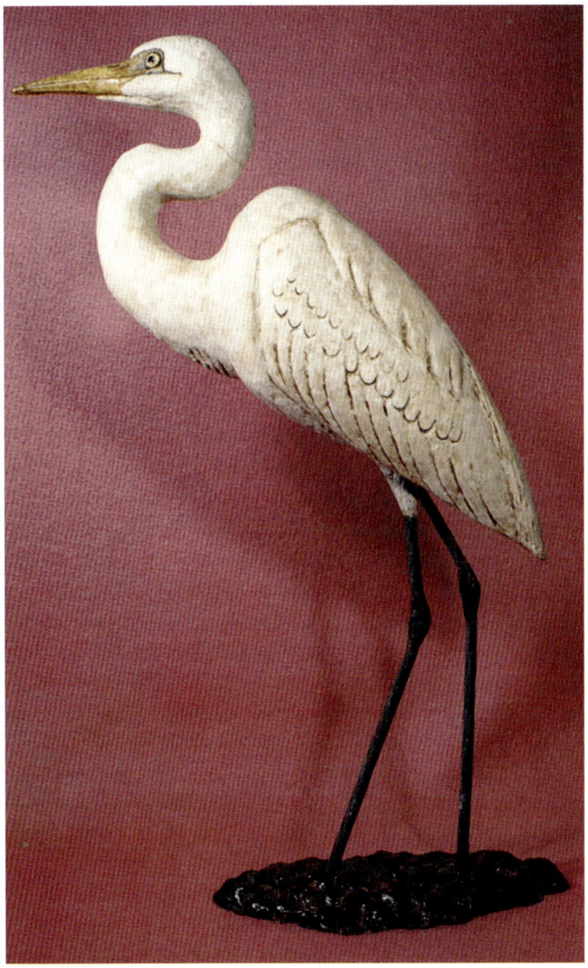

Maureen sees many Egrets around her home, in ponds, ditches, and fields. She has made several variations of this elegant bird. Measuring 19.5" tall, this Great Egret stands huge and very majestic. It has an approximate value of $175-200.

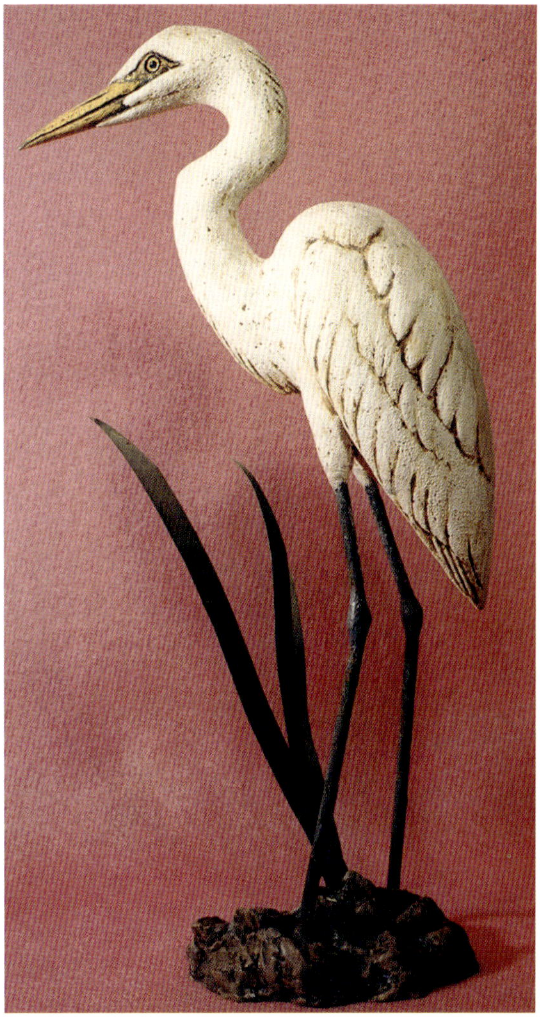

Next in size, this model of the Great Egret stands 11.5" tall. Note the addition of marsh grass to create the feel of the bird's habitat. Approximate value for this model is $150-175.

This 4.5" tall model of the Great Egret is showing more motion than the others. This pose shows off the metal legs, which have developed a bit of rust over the years. Its approximate value is $45-60.

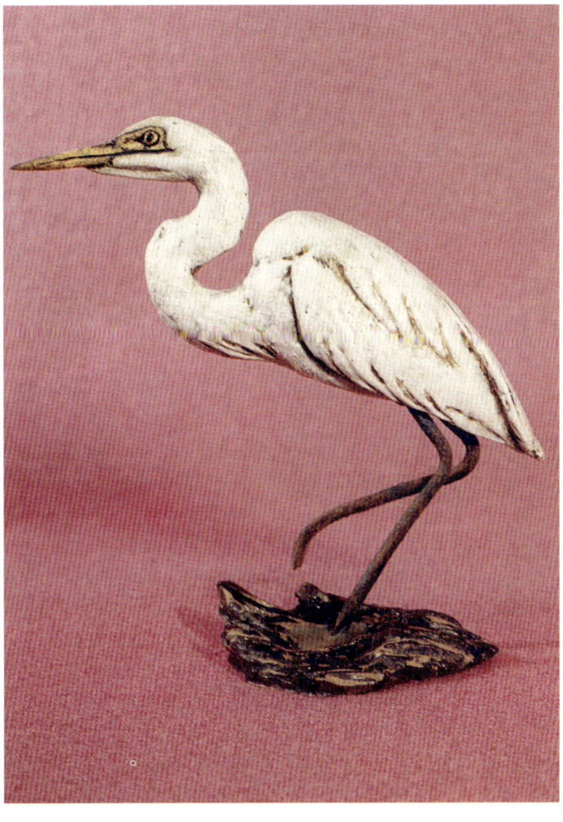

The smallest model of the Great Egret measures a modest 3.5", but shows the same correct form and detail. The waterweeds on the base add an interesting touch to the design. This bird has an approximate value of $45-60.

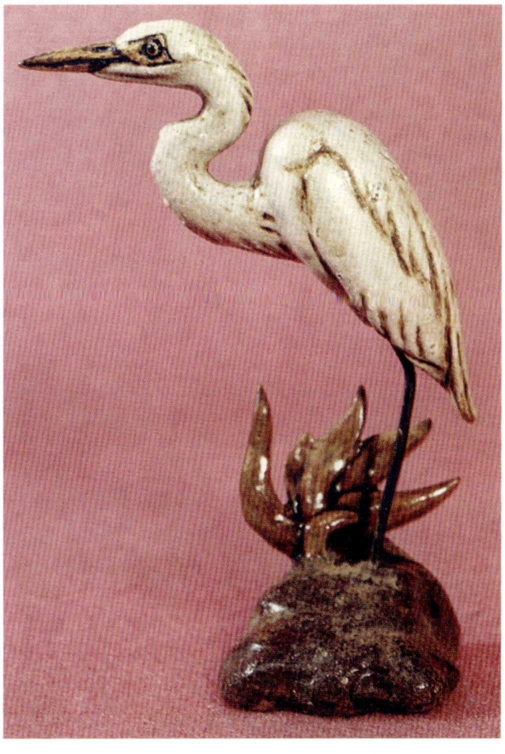

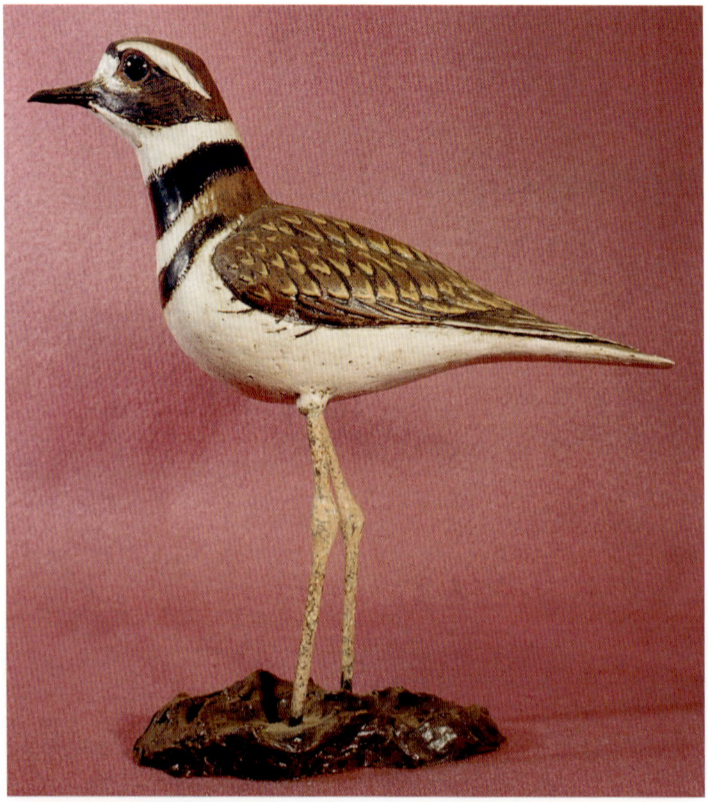

Standing 8" tall, the Killdeer looks ready to run on its spindly legs. It has an approximate value of $90-120.

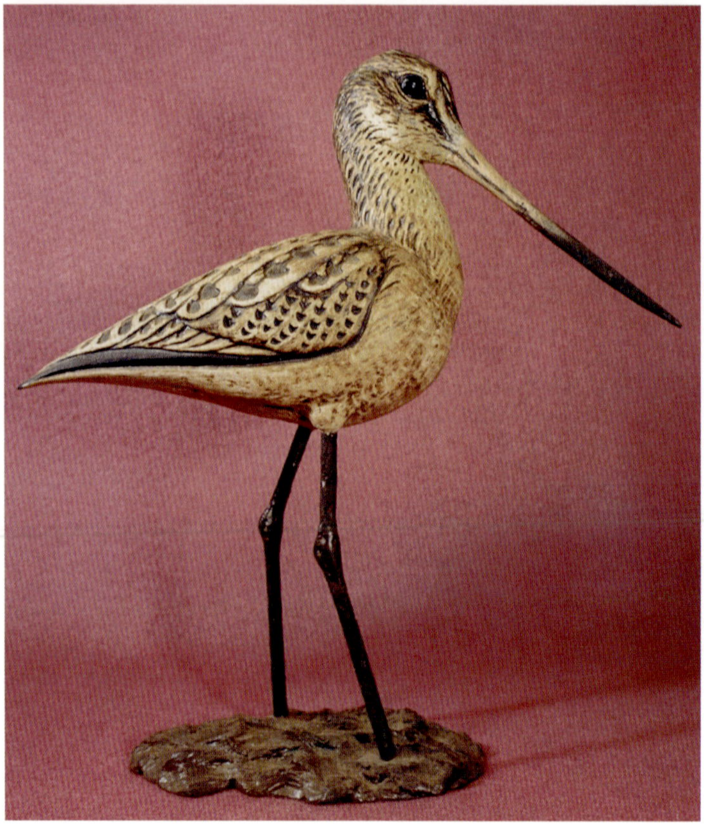

Fine feathery lines around the eyes and head make this model of a Godwit very life-like and appealing. It stands 12" tall, and has an approximate value of $175-200.

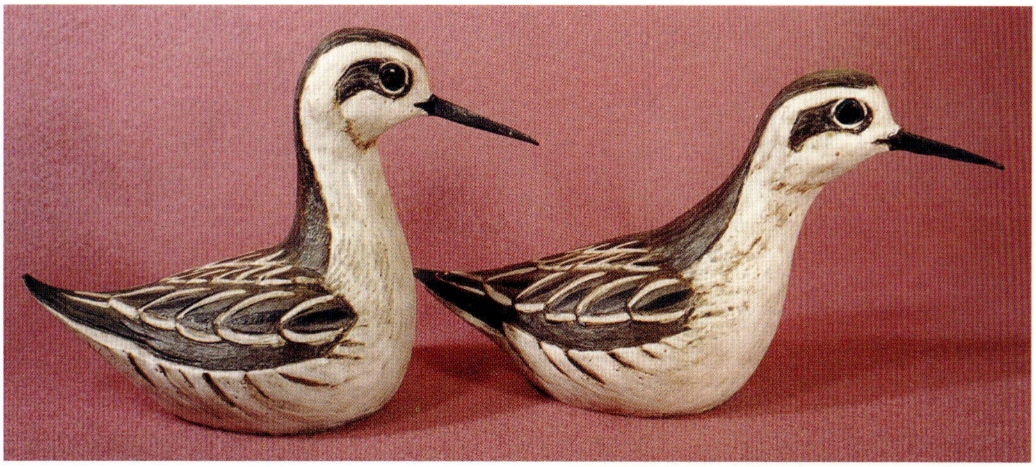

This Phalarope pair measures 3.75" tall. Being water birds, they are designed without legs to simulate swimming. They have an approximate value of $40-55.

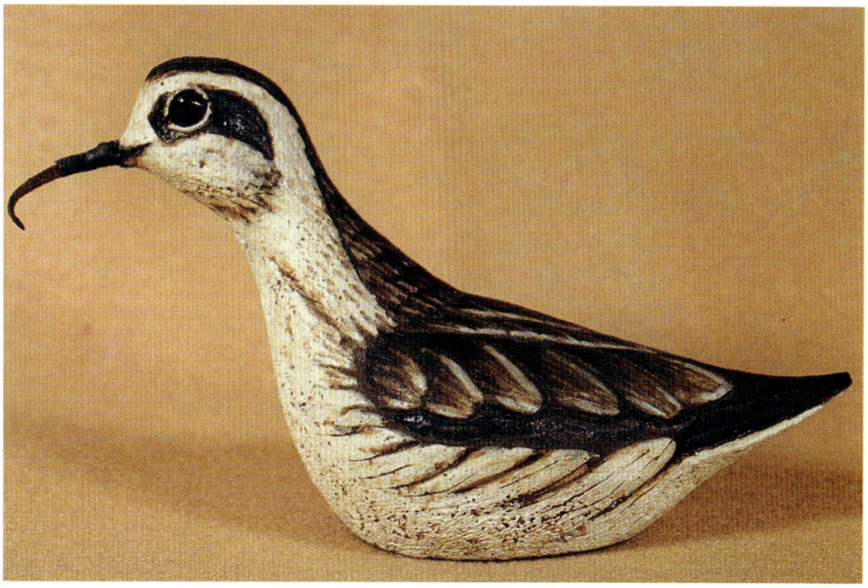

The underside of this bird is marked 1979 and #38. Note the damage to the beak caused by the loss of some of the epoxy that was built up on the framework.

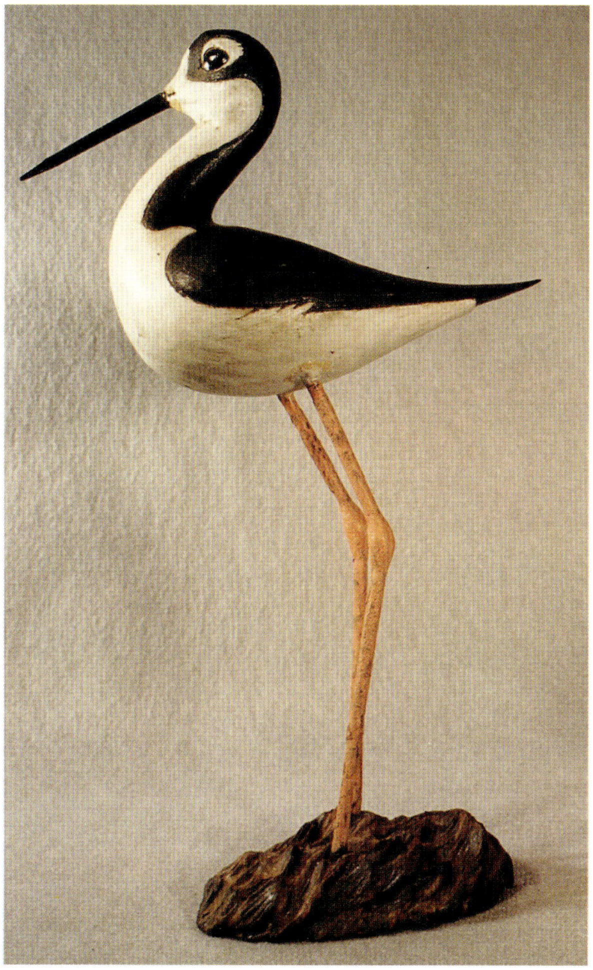

At a towering 10.25" tall, this Black-Necked Stilt has an approximate value of $130-150.

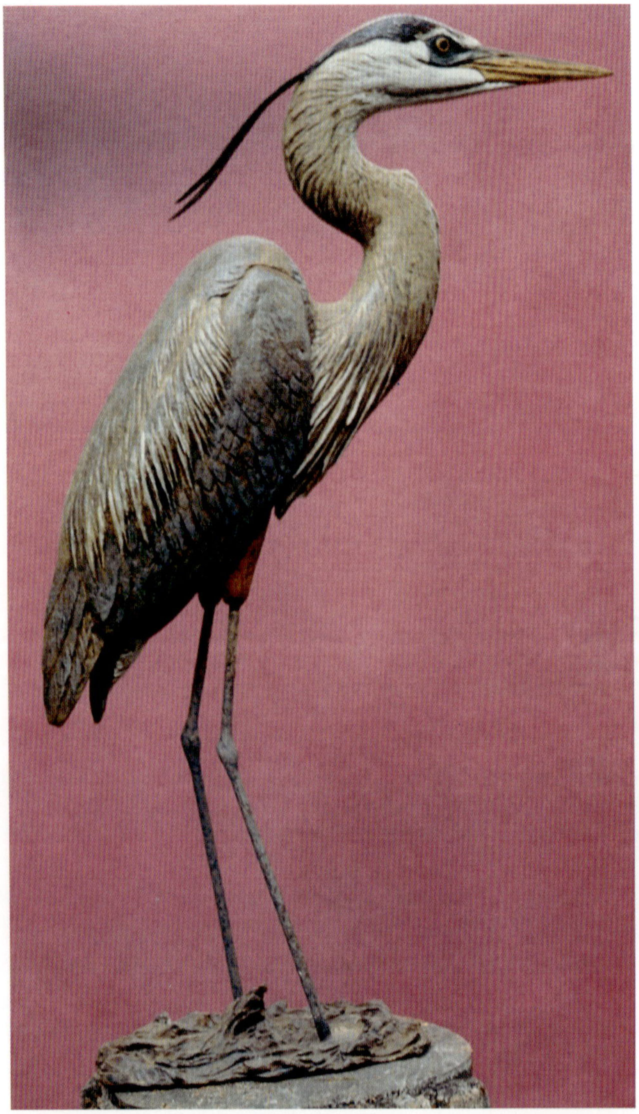

Standing 20" tall, this Great Blue Heron shows incredible detail in the feathers of the body and neck. Its approximate value is $225-250.

Just for fun, here is the Great Blue Heron posed outdoors. The beauty and realism of this model makes it look quite at home in this natural setting.

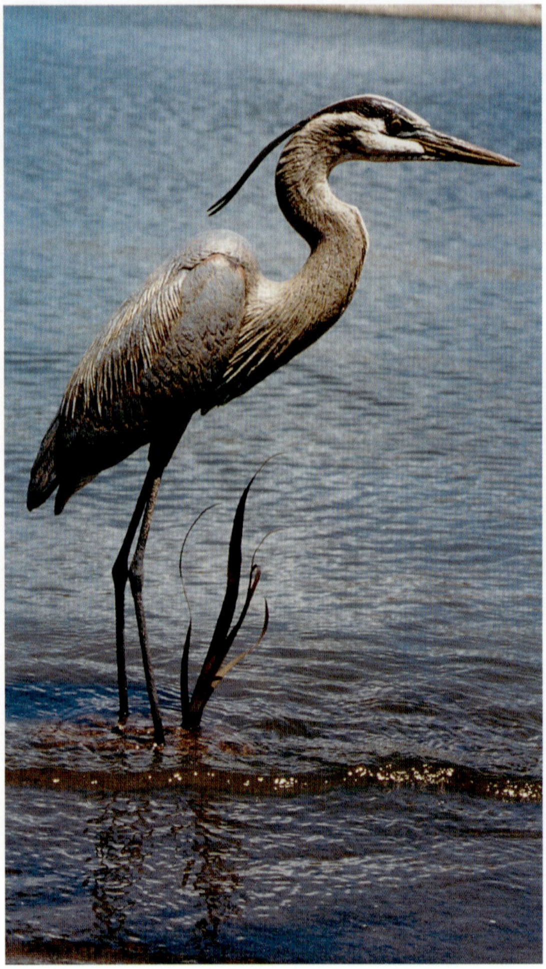

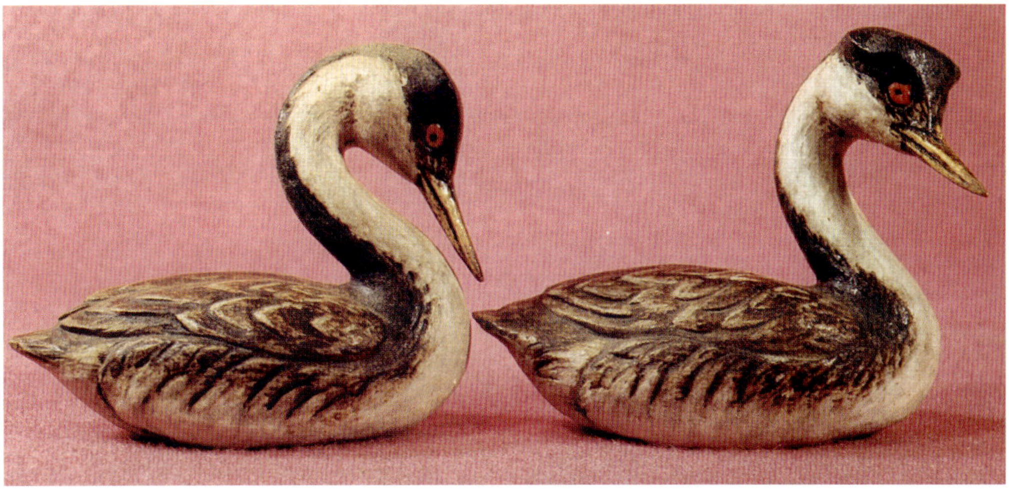

This pair of Western Grebes represents a female and a male. Note the differences in their heads. The left bird is 2.25" tall and the right bird is 2.5" tall. They have an approximate value of $40-55 each.

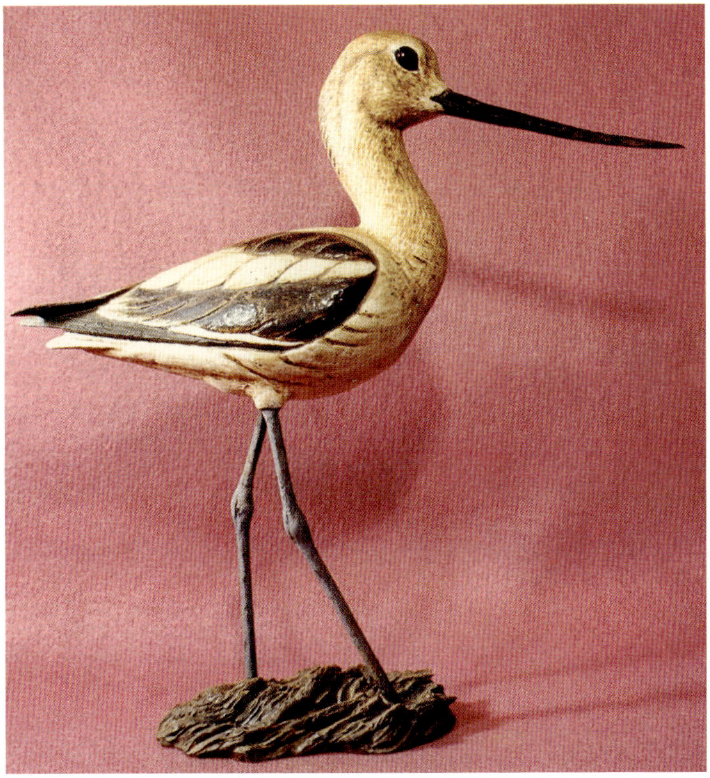

Epoxy was used to form and build up the beak on this American Avocet. It stands 11.75" tall and has an approximate value of $150-175.

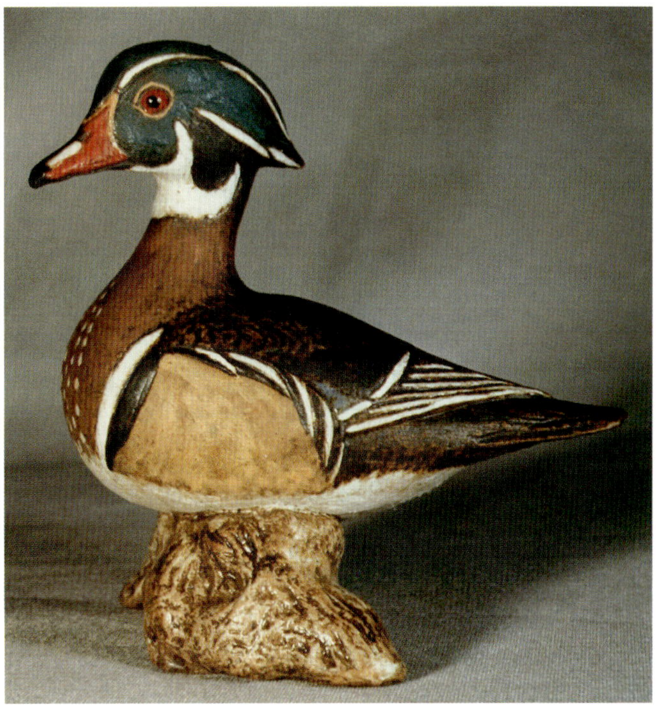

Surrounded by water, Maureen revels in the bounty of water birds around her. This Wood Duck is an example of one of the more colorful local residents. This model is 4.4" tall, and has an approximate value of $90-110.

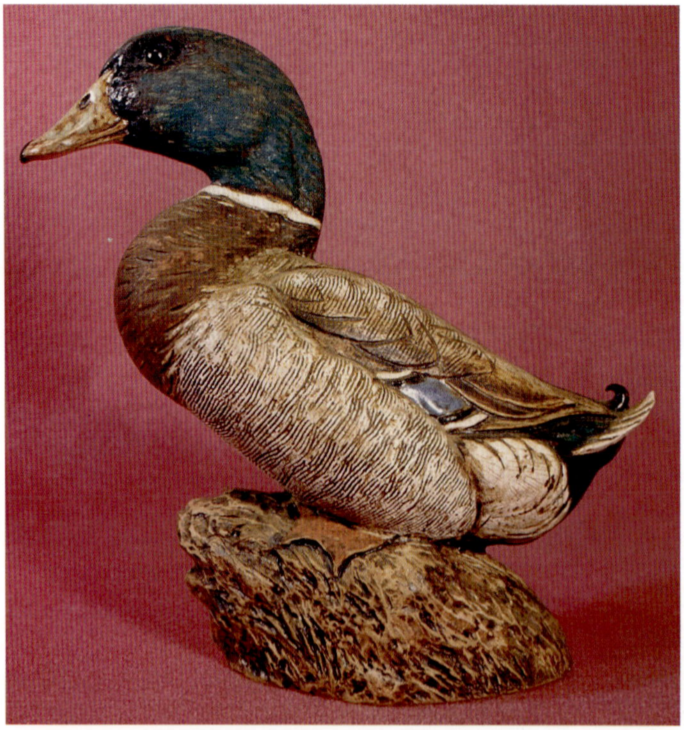

The texture and feather detail on this Mallard duck really brings this model to life. Standing 6" tall, the intricate detail gives it an approximate value of $100-125.

The rough, stoneware-type ceramic that Maureen works with gives her models an interesting, living appearance. This head close-up of the Mallard shows this very well.

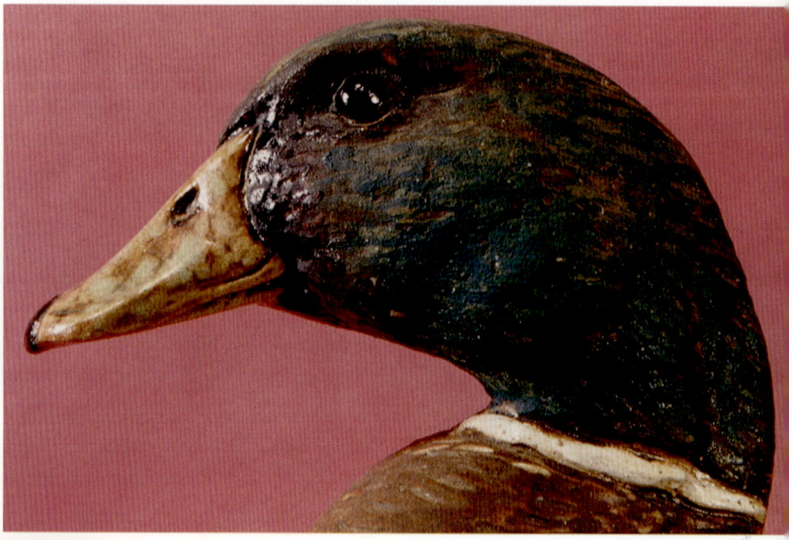

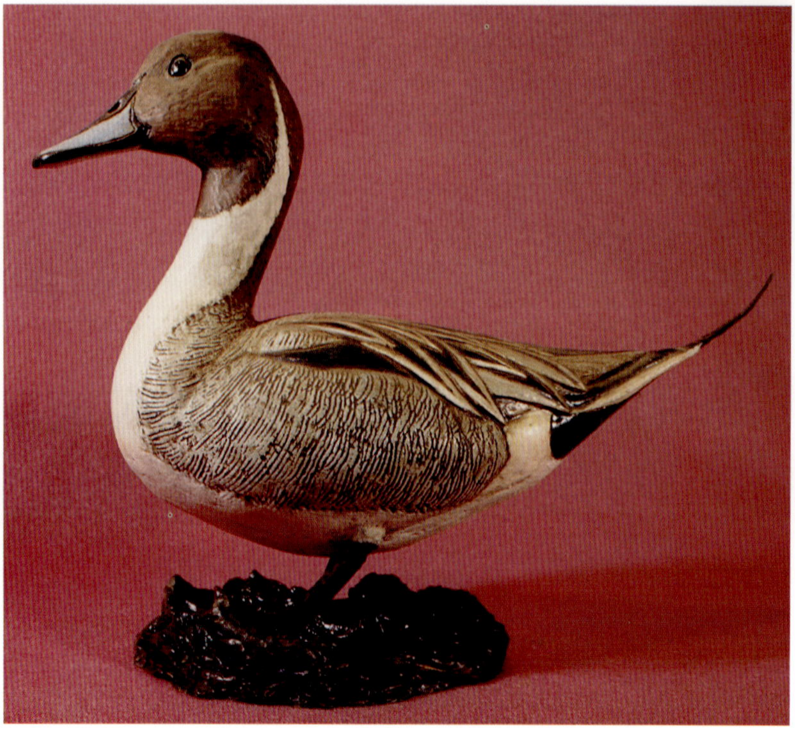

Note the intricate detail of the feathers as they weave together on the back of this Pintail Duck. It stands 7" tall, and has an approximate value of $100-125.

Fascinating patterns in nature make for fascinating models. The Green-Winged Teal has a variety of textures and colors, resulting in this wonderful figure. Standing 5.5" tall, it has an approximate value of $75-100.

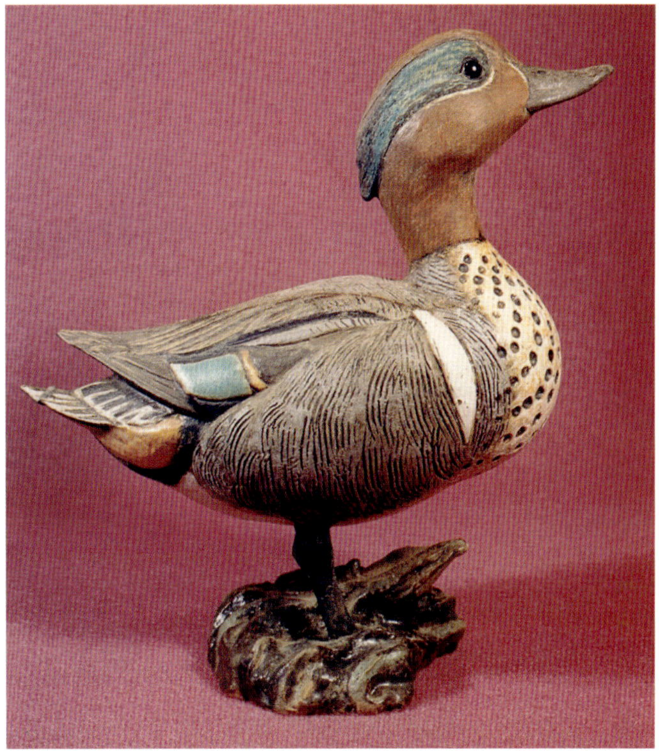

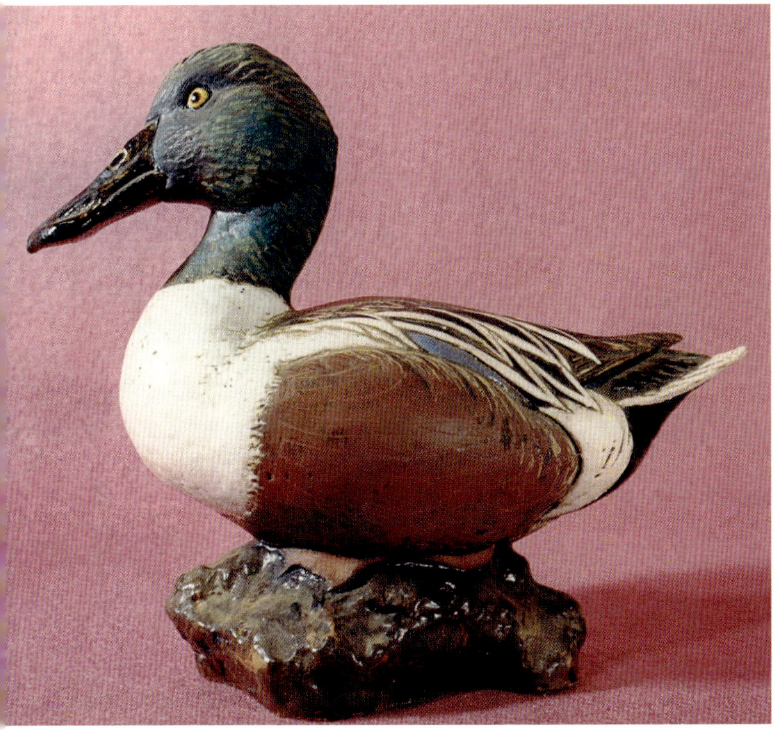

This Shoveler sits 6" tall on his rock perch, and has an approximate value of $75-100.

Maureen has a collection of feathers on her kitchen wall that she has gathered during her morning walks. They serve as valuable references while she is decorating her birds. This Loon measures 3.75" tall, and is posed next to the feather of a real loon. Its approximate value is $45-60.

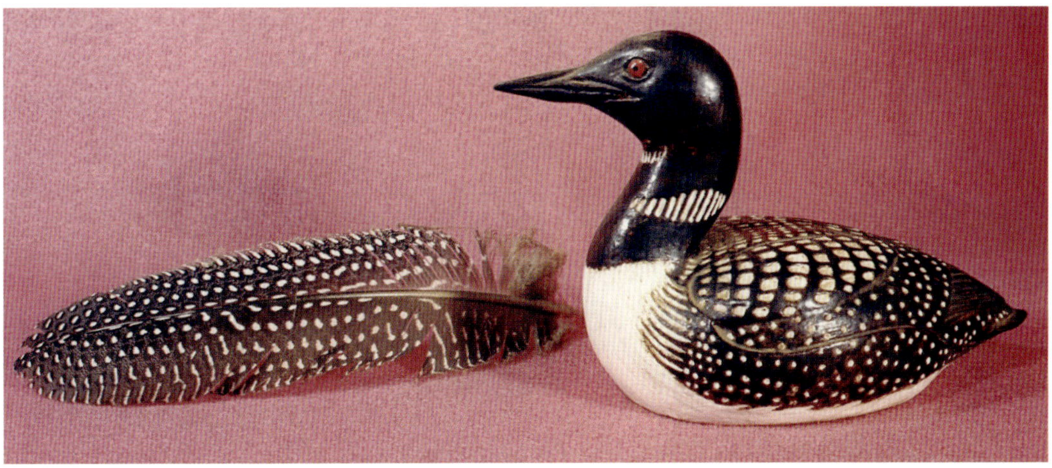

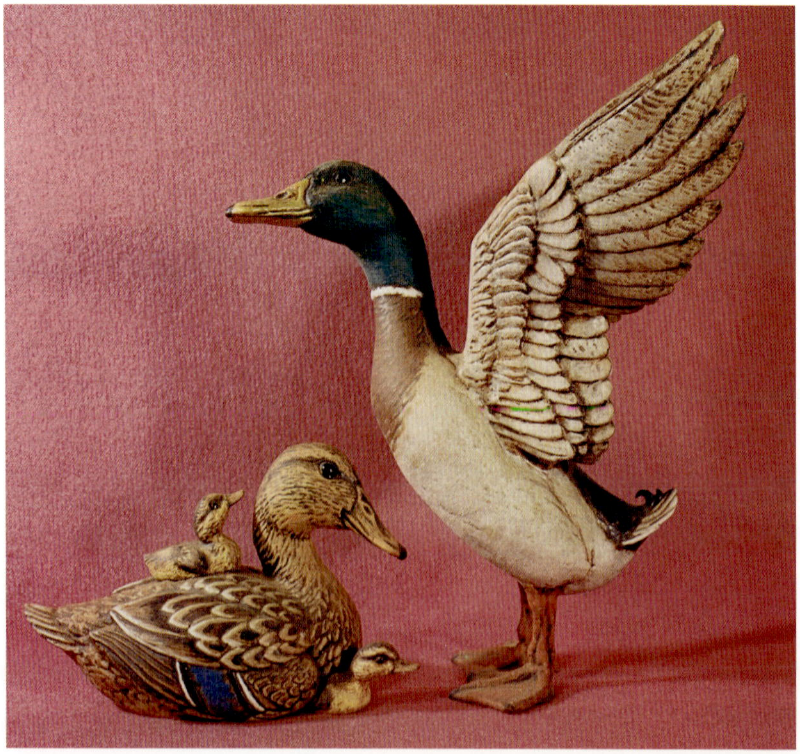

Collectors will recognize this Mallard drake and hen with ducklings as a design that was also produced by Hagen-Renaker. However, the detail, texture, and stoneware-type ceramic leave no doubt that these are original pieces rather than factory-produced items. The hen is 3.25" tall by 5.5" long and the drake is 8" tall. Their approximate value is $90-110 each.

This Mallard Duck pair was made in separate sections from the molds, and then assembled using slip (liquid clay emulsion) to hold them together. Maureen said she made them "a long time ago." The piece stands 8" tall and has an approximate value of $90-110.

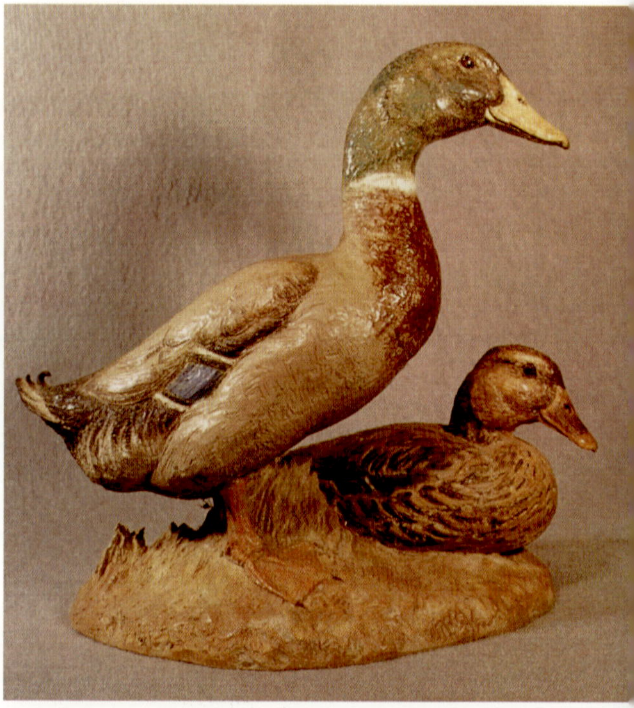

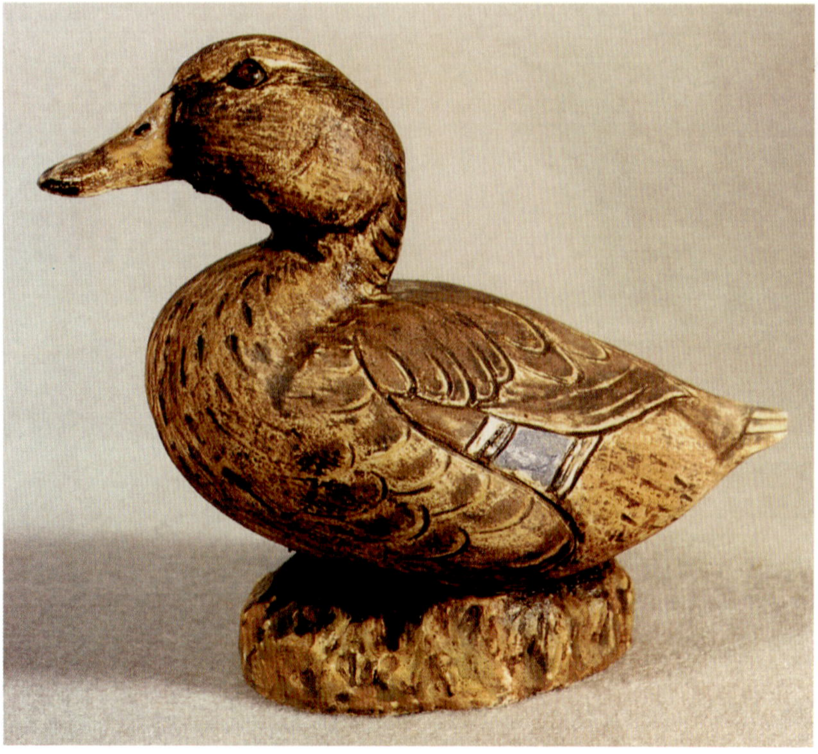

The texture of this Mallard hen makes her look more like a wood carving than a ceramic model. Maureen owned a Mallard pair for several years, giving her readily available subjects to work from. This duck is 3.5" tall and has an approximate value of $40-65.

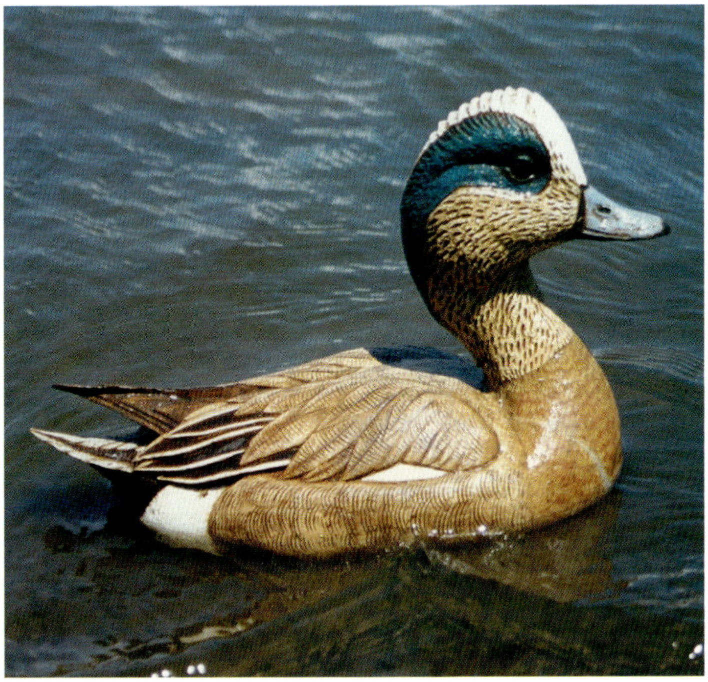

The sunlight on the lake highlights the intricate feather patterns on this American Widgeon. Measuring 8.75" tall, it is nearly life-size. It has an approximate value of $125-150.

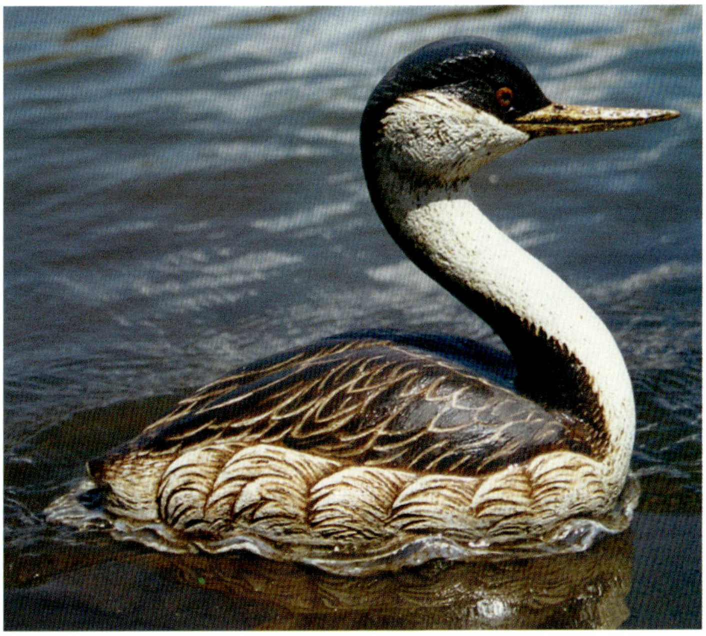

This Western Grebe bears the date 1979 on its underside. Measuring 9.25" tall, it looks quite at home in the waves. Its approximate value is $140-160.

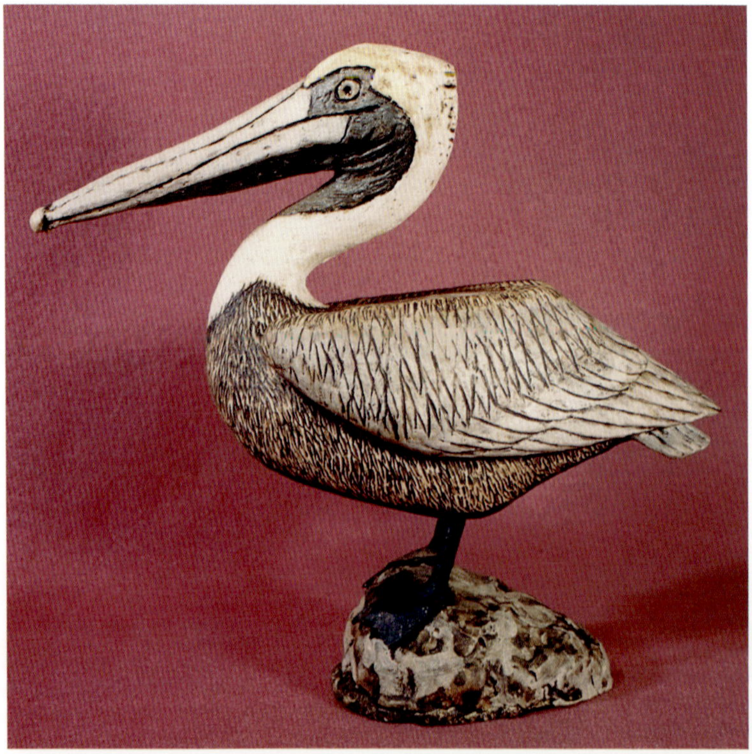

The feet on this standing pelican are made of copper sheet metal. It stands 8" tall on the rock base, and has an approximate value of $100-125.

Captured in flight, this amazing model of a pelican measures 10.2" tall. It has an approximate value of $175-200.

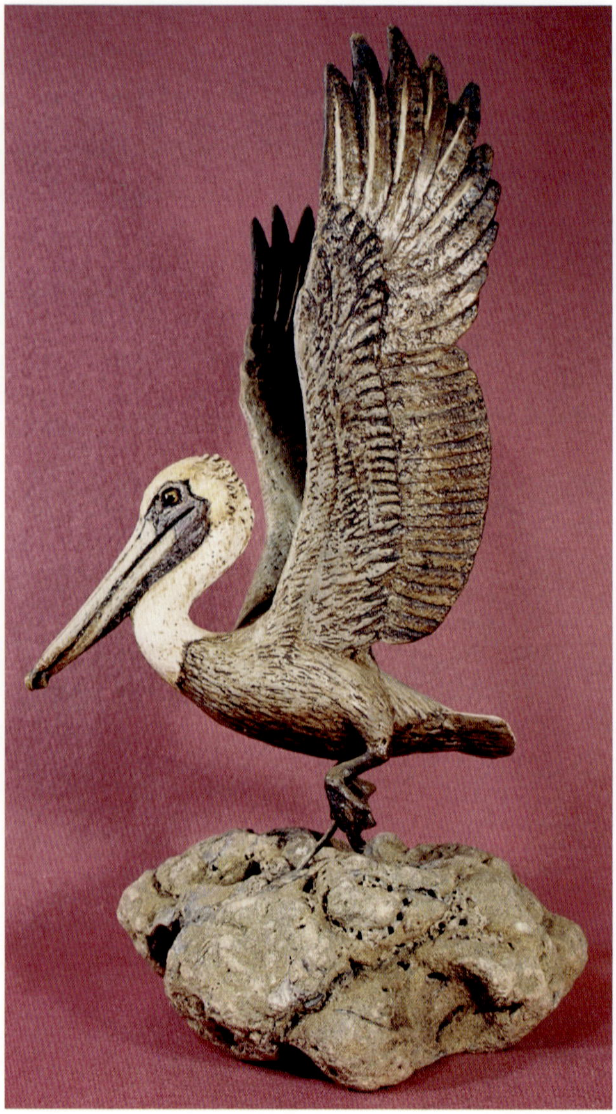

Poised in anticipation, the Black-Bellied Plover stands 5.25" tall, and has an approximate value of $50-65.

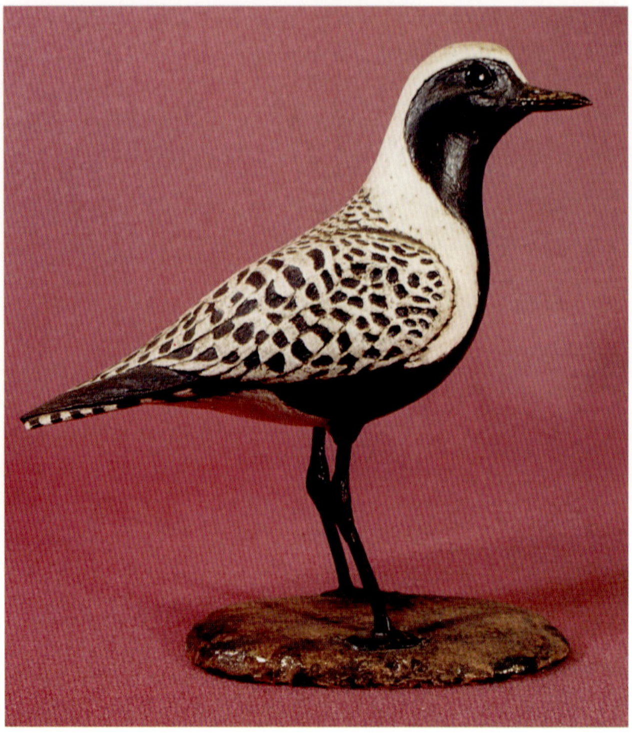

Squabbling over some dispute, this pair of gulls acts out a true-life scene. The flying gull on the base measures 6" tall and the sitting/swimming gull is 2" tall. The gull on the base has an approximate value of $40-65 and the sitting gull has an approximate value of $25-40.

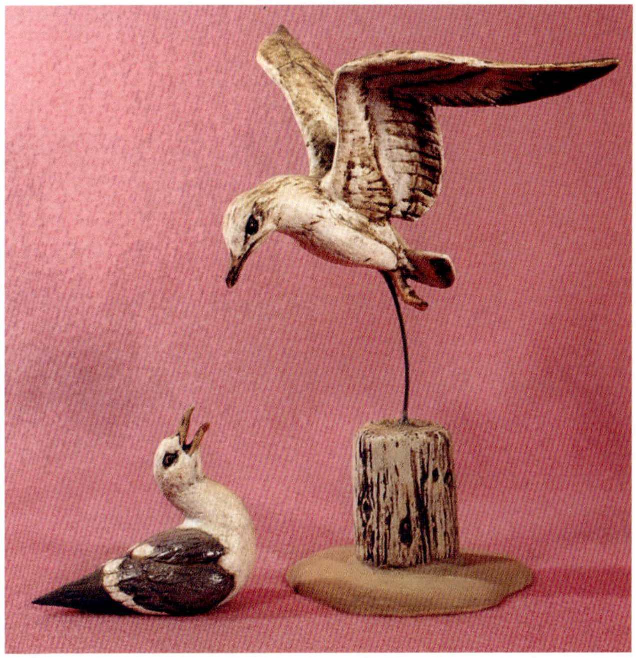

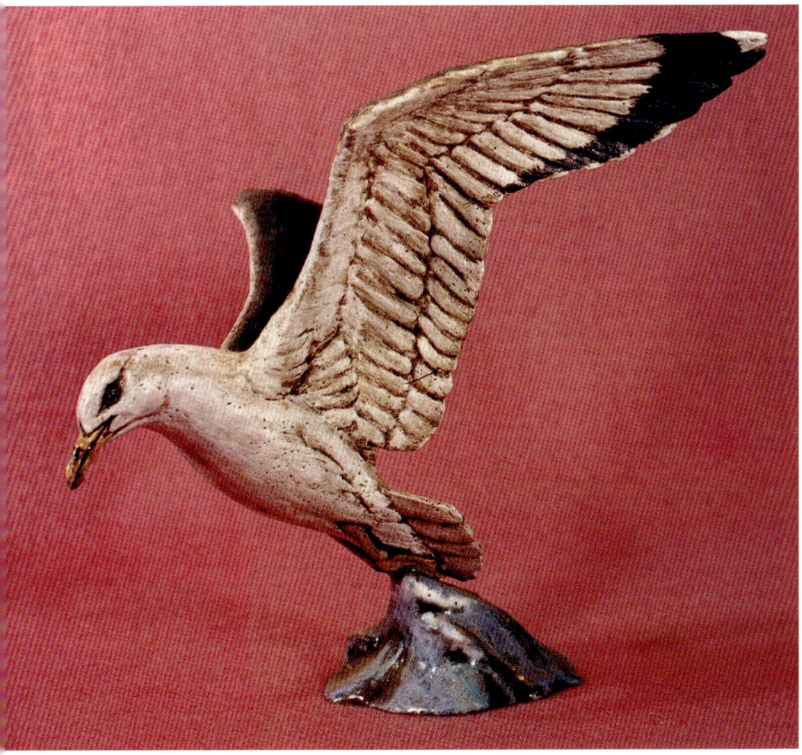

Caught in motion skimming the surface of the water, the base for this Western Gull is a cleverly designed wave crest. Measuring 5" tall, this model has an approximate value of $60-75.

Perched on a rock base, this Seagull has copper sheets of metal for his feet. He stands 9.5" tall and has #31 and 1978 on the underside of his base. His approximate value is $65-80.

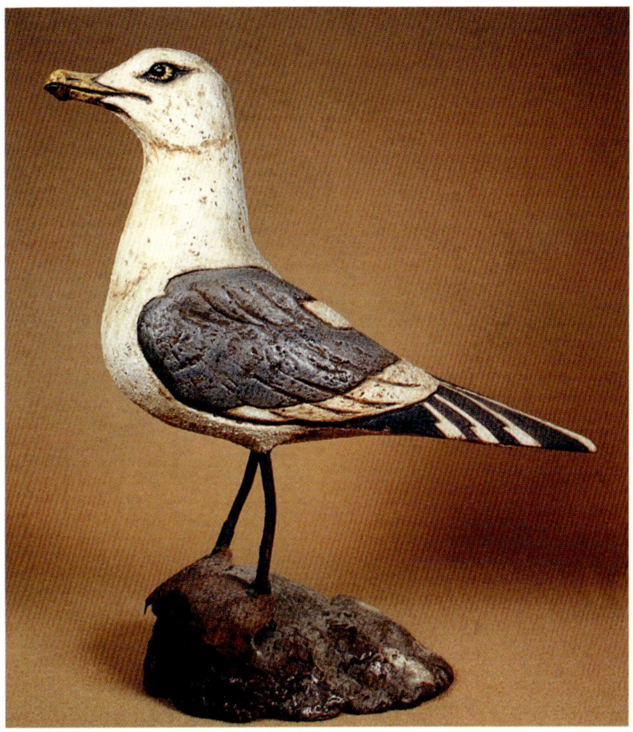

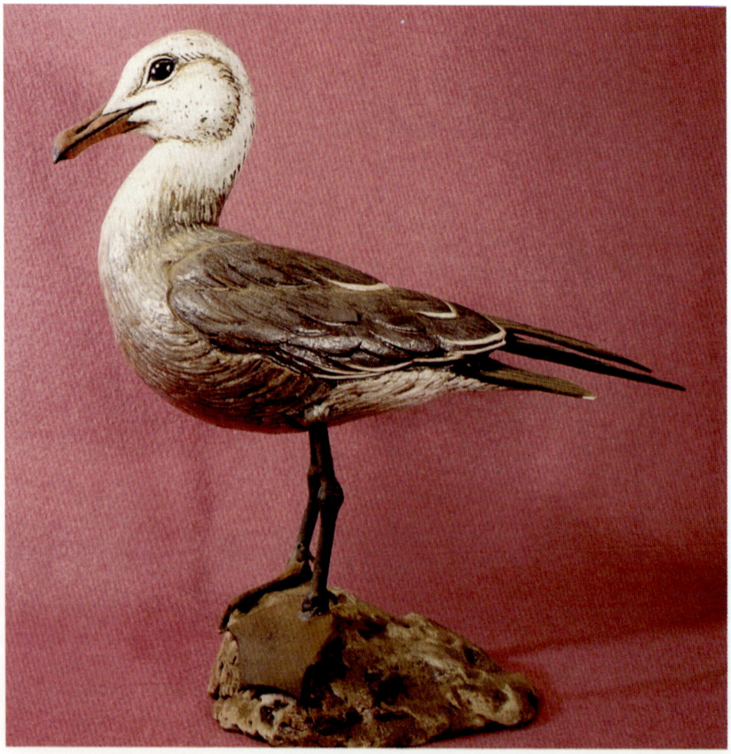

Standing tall on the beach with a starfish at his feet, this Heermann's Seagull measures 10" tall. He has copper metal sheets for his feet, and very detailed feathers and facial features. Approximate value for this model is $100-125.

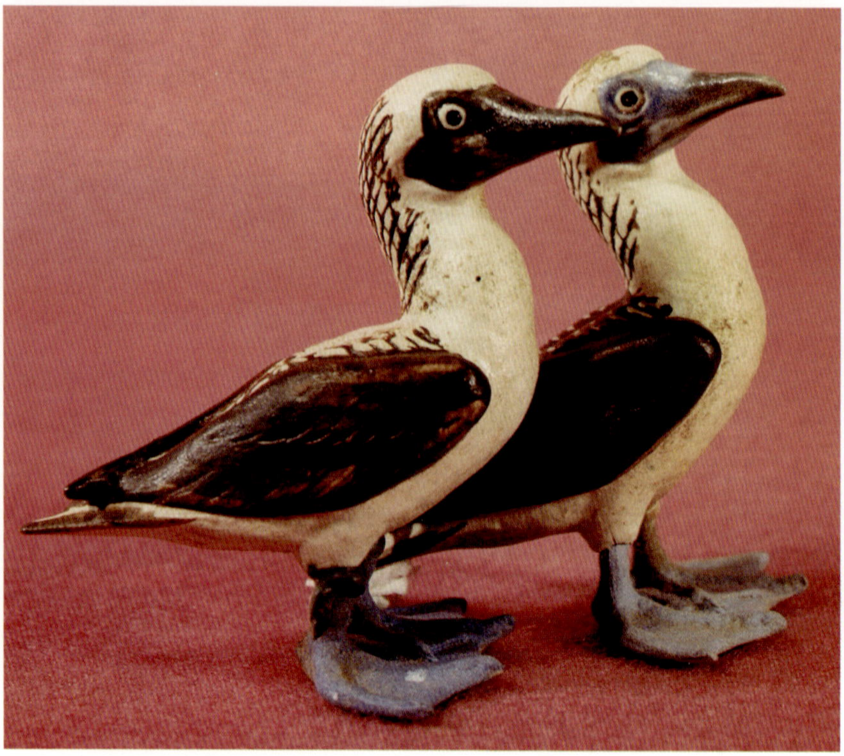

This pair of Blue-Footed Boobies is looking for mischief. Note the variation in the face and beak coloring. They stand 2.2" tall, and have an approximate value of $35-50 each.

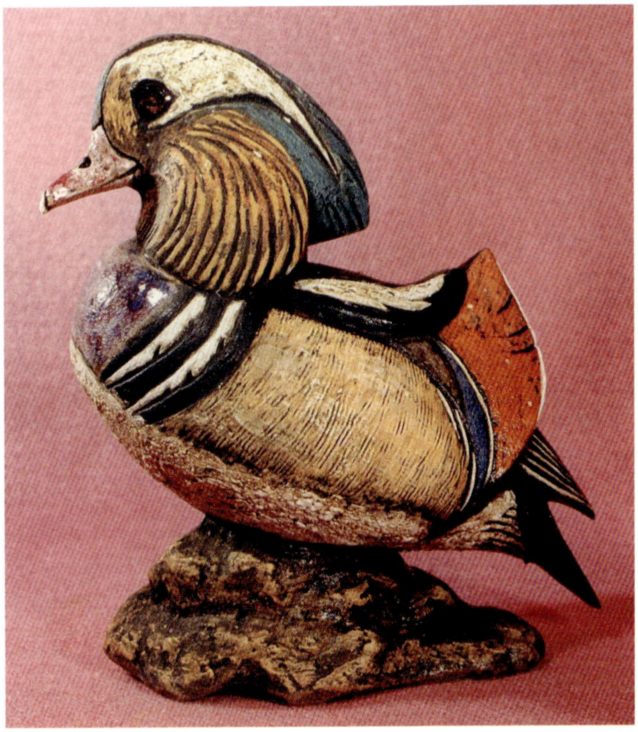

One of the more unusual water dwellers Maureen has created is this exotic Mandarin Duck. He stands 6" tall and has an approximate value of $125-150.

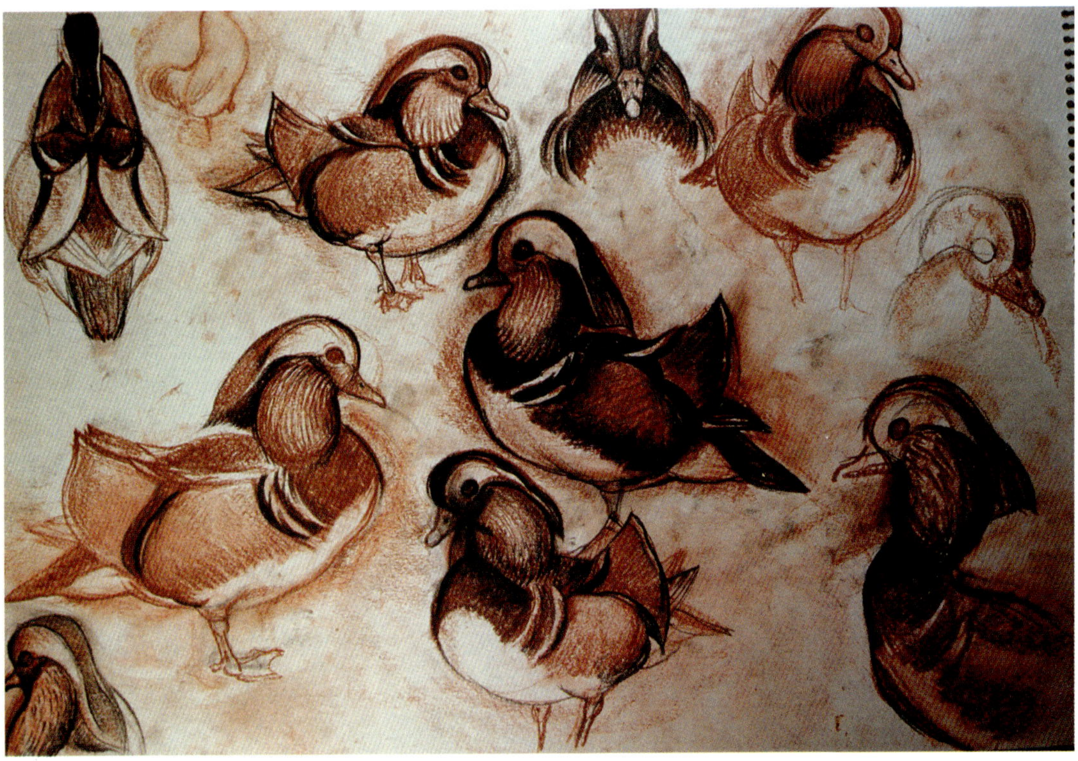

Designing a model as complex as the Mandarin Duck requires a lot of planning. Maureen created several sketches to capture the appearance and personality of this duck before beginning to sculpt it.

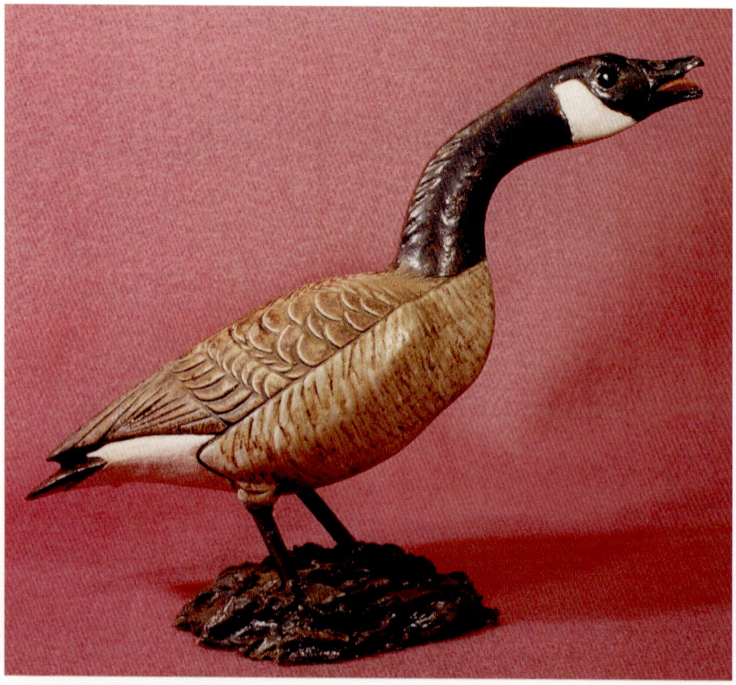

This Canadian Goose is shown in his familiar, honking pose. Standing 5.25" tall, his approximate value is $50-65.

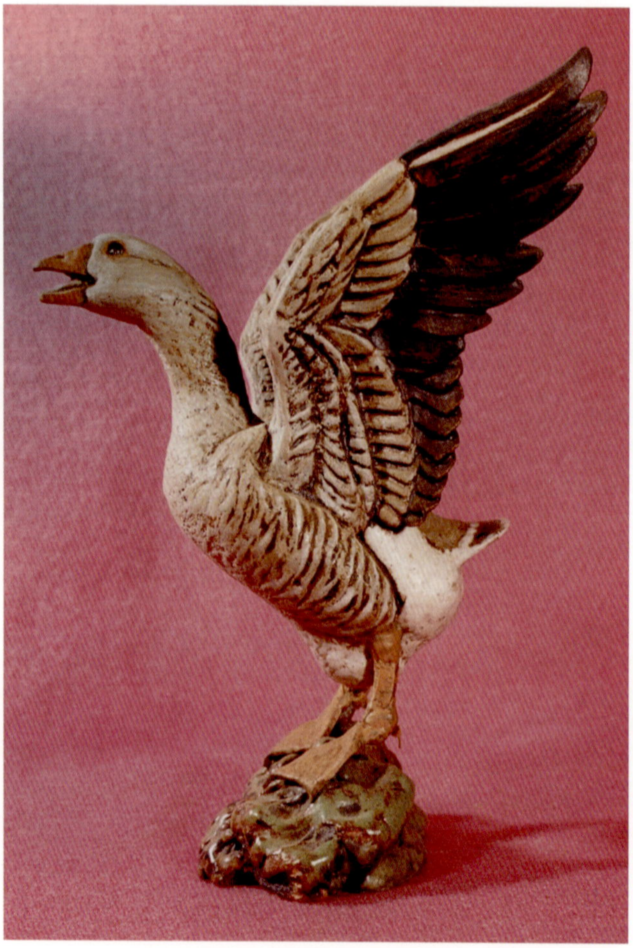

Bearing the unusual name Touloose Goose, this active fellow measures 6.75" tall. His approximate value is $75-100.

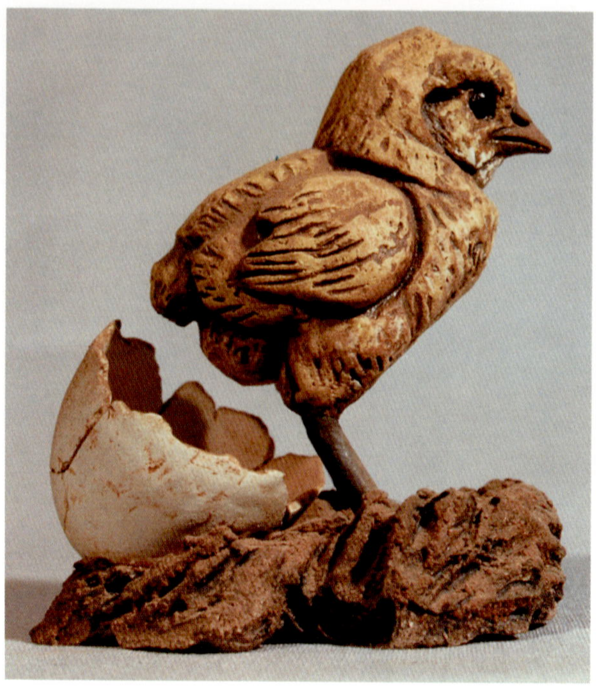

This adorable chick with its eggshell is full of character and spunk. It measures 3" tall and has an approximate value of $45-60.

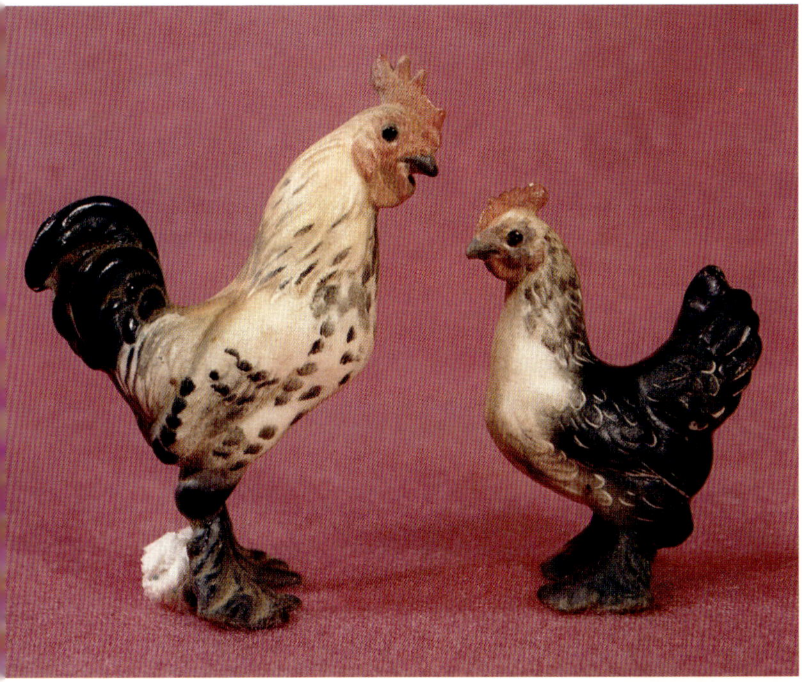

Designed and hand-decorated by Maureen, this Bantam Rooster and Hen later became part of the Hagen-Renaker Miniature line. They measure 2.2" and 1.5" tall, and have an approximate value of $30-45 for the rooster and $25-35 for the hen.

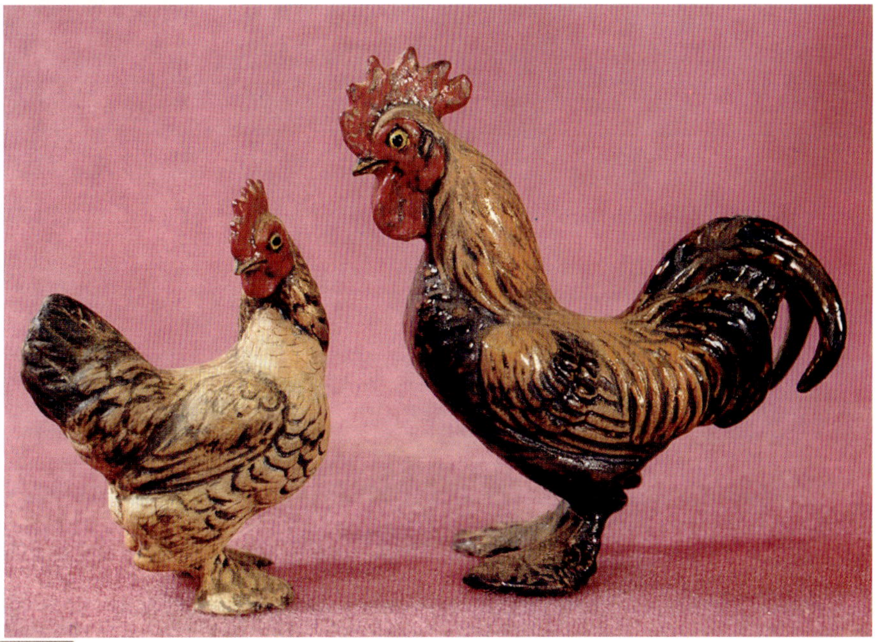

This original Bantam Hen and Rooster set recently was produced in the Hagen-Renaker Specialty line. These pieces, however, are hand-decorated by Maureen, giving them their unique charm. The hen stands 2.2" tall and has an approximate value of $35-50. The rooster stands 2.6" tall and has an approximate value of $45-60.

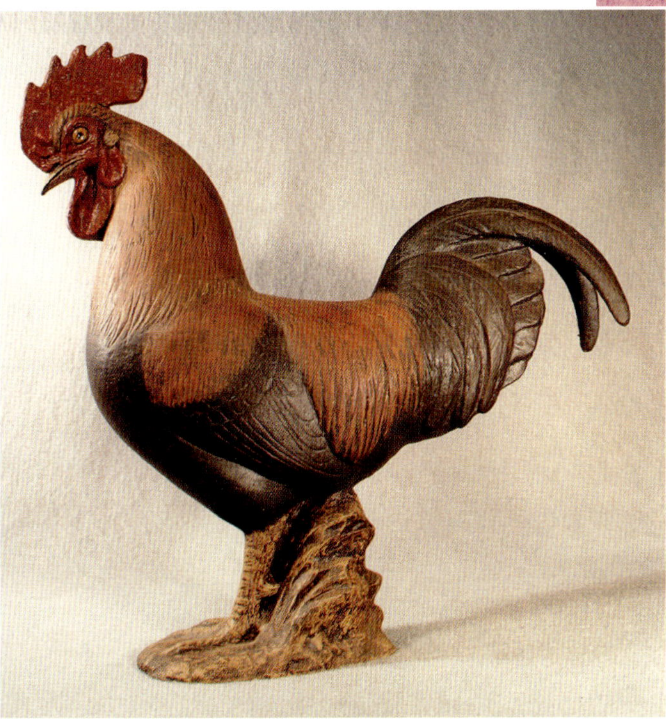

Maureen shares her yard with chickens that have the free-run of the property. Looking like a primitive woodcarving, this ceramic rooster stands 9.75" tall. Somewhat stylized, his approximate value is $90-110.

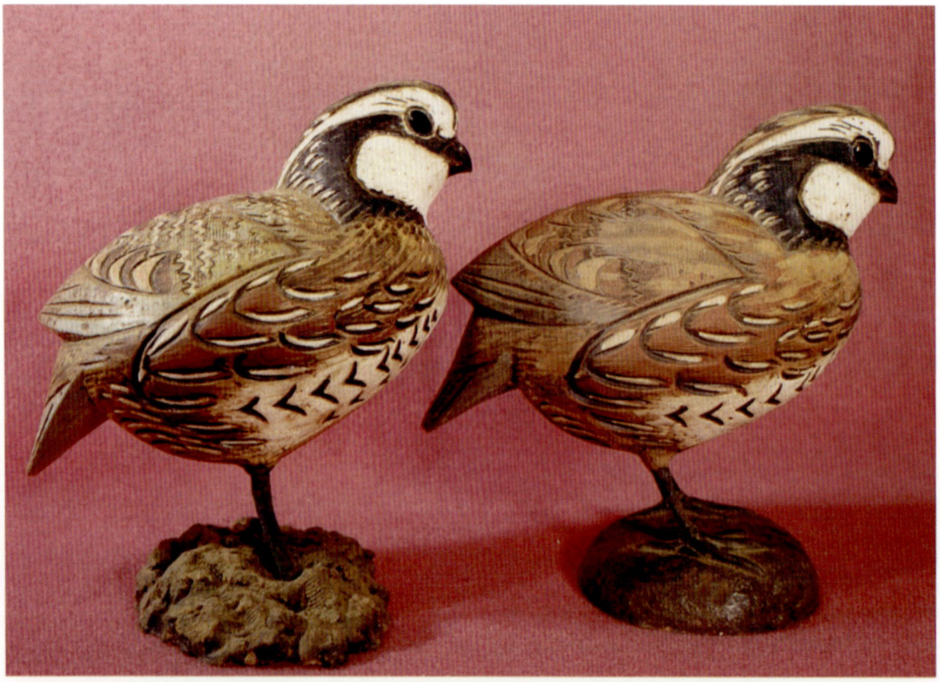

These two Bobwhites were made at different times. The one on the right is the older one, with less detail on the back, but depicted with toes. The newer one on the left has greater detail in the back feathers, but no feet showing. They stand 4.5" tall and have an approximate value of $75-100 each.

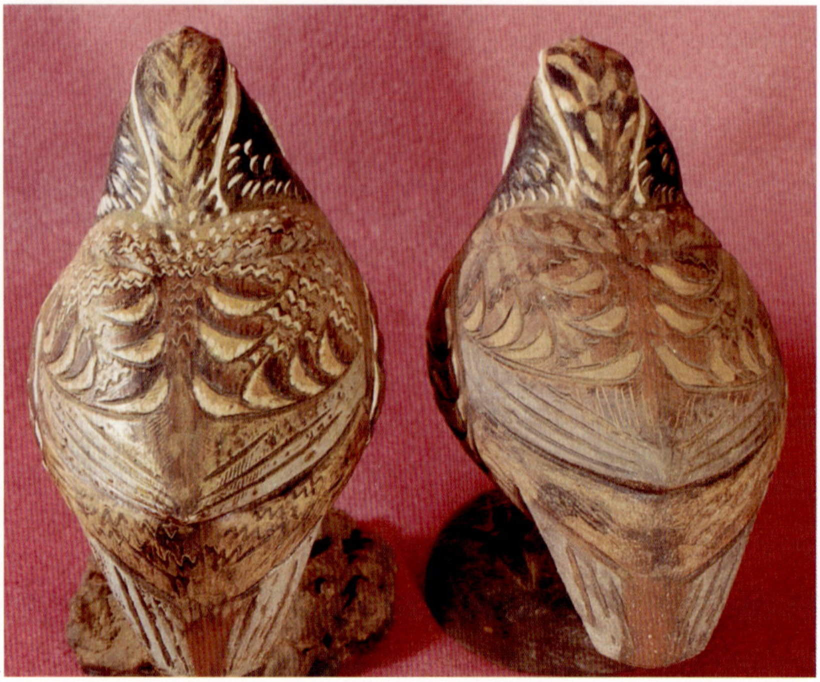

In this back view, it is easy to see the difference in the decoration and detail between the older Bobwhite on the right and the newer one on the left.

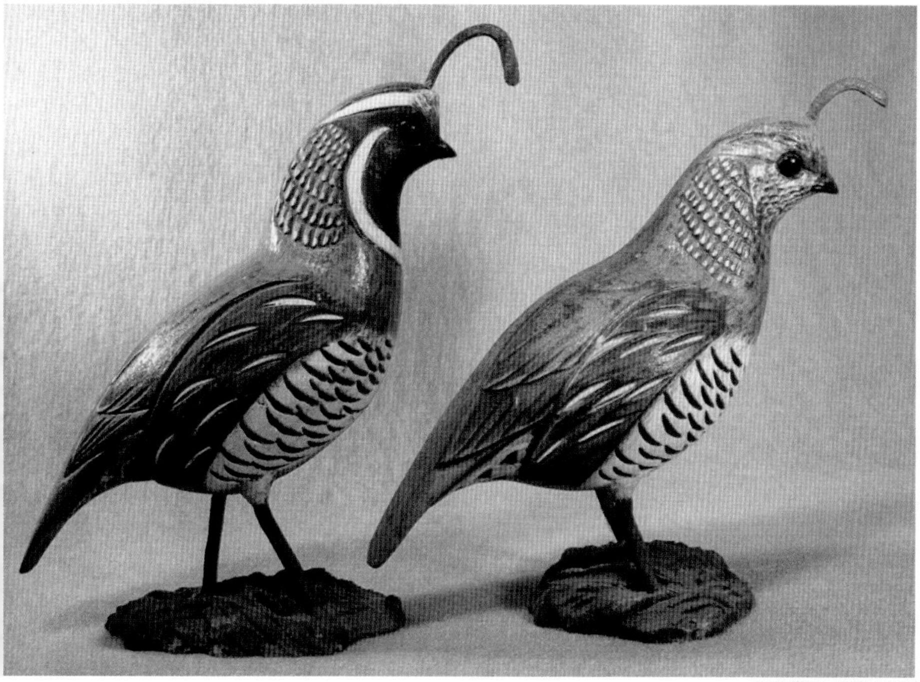

This male and female Quail pair were produced by Maureen during her Maureen Love Originals production period, so there are probably several of these in existence. They stand 7.5" and 6.5" tall and have an approximate value of $100-125 each.

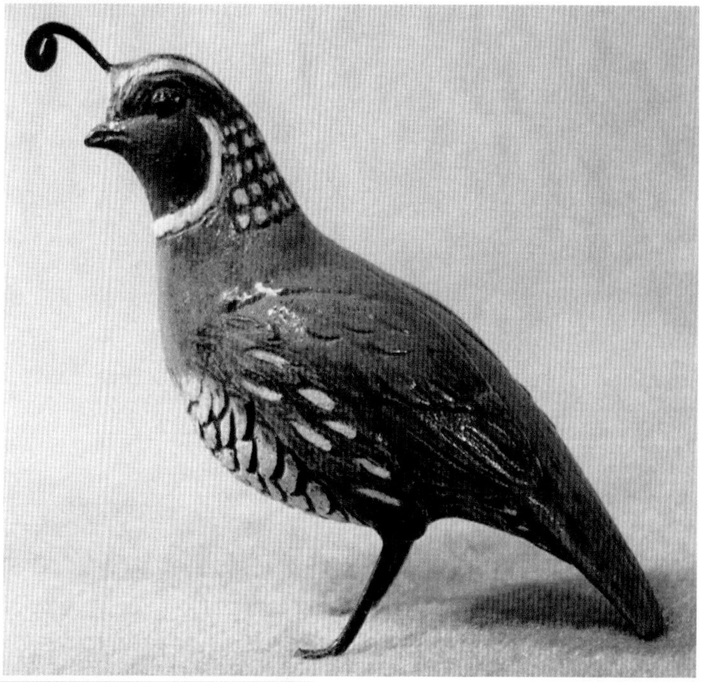

Standing only 2.5" tall, this small quail has an amazing amount of detail in the face, feathers, and even the topknot on his head. He has an approximate value of $35-50.

Known as a covey, this family group of Quail consists of the adult male (right), adult female (left), and the three chicks. All but the left check were eventually produced by Hagen-Renaker, but the production decoration cannot rival the wonderful hand-painted decoration seen on these pieces. These are also larger than the Hagen-Renaker models, with the adults standing 4.5" and 5" tall. Their approximate value is $90-110 for the adults and $35-50 for the young ones.

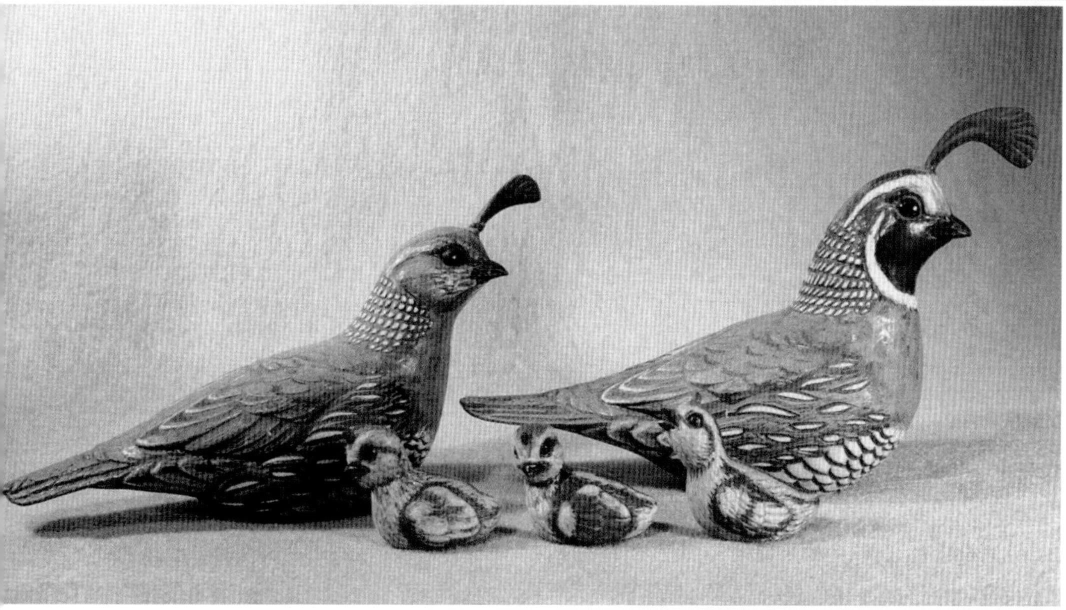

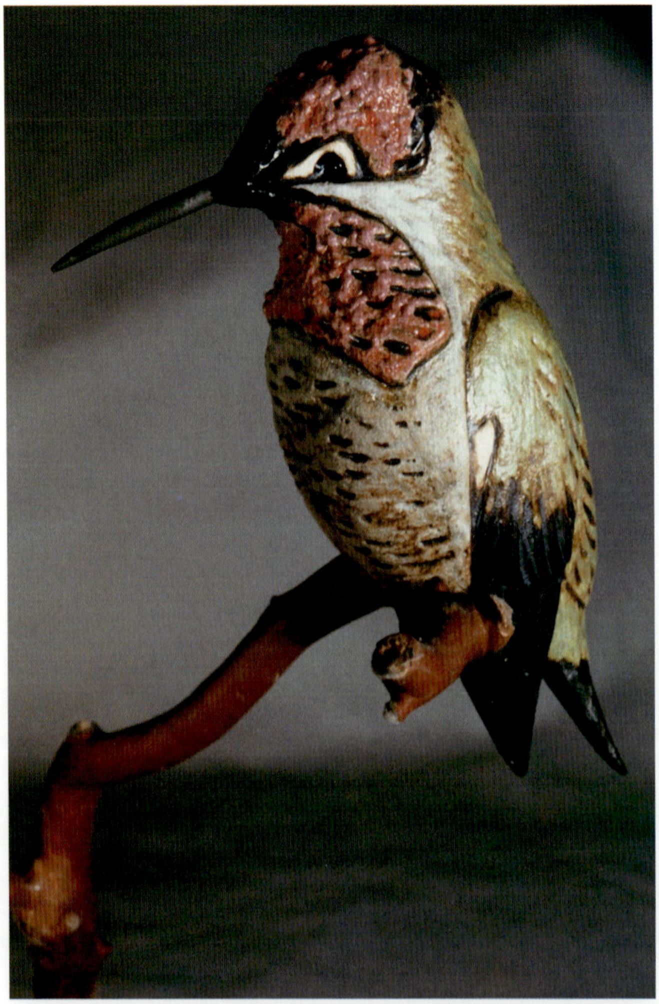

The Ruby-Throated Humming bird shown here is perched on a tree or bush. This piece was produced during the Maureen Love Originals years, so several of these may exist. The style of the branch varied, as did the number of leaves on it. The bird alone measures 3.5" tall, and the entire model is 7.75" tall. It has an approximate value of $110-125.

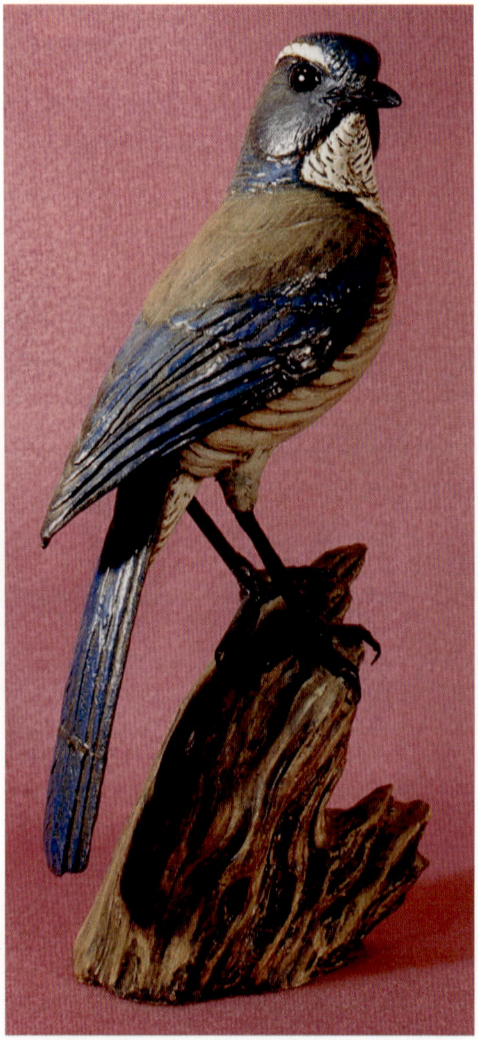

Looking quite saucy, this Western Scrub Jay stands 9.5" tall. Maureen has captured the personality of this active bird well. His approximate value is $100-125.

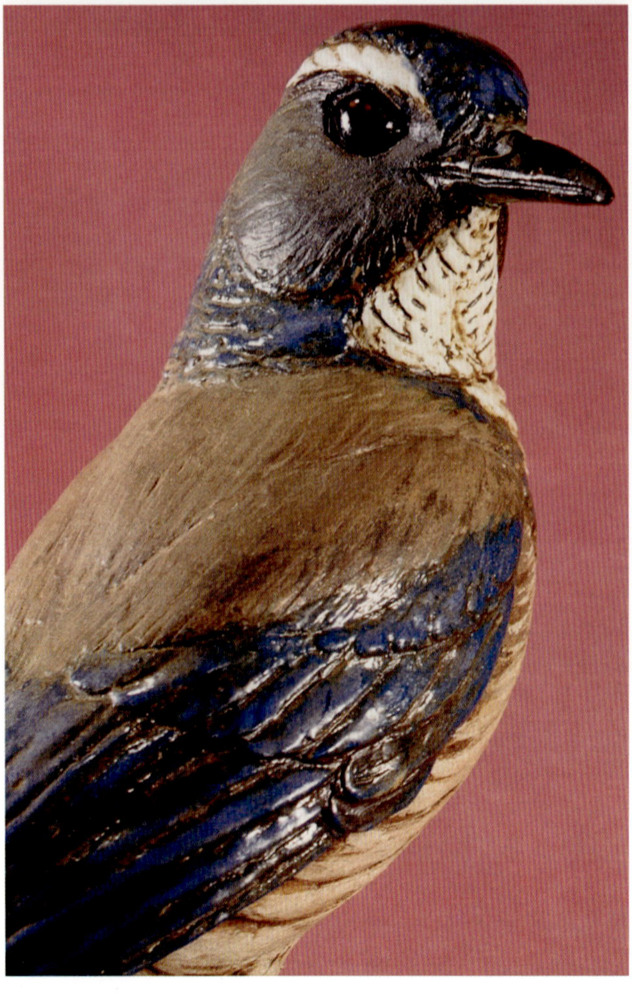

Looking in the brown over the shoulder area and the gray around the face, this close up of the Western Scrub Jay shows how Maureen achieves the appearance of feathers using texture as well as color.

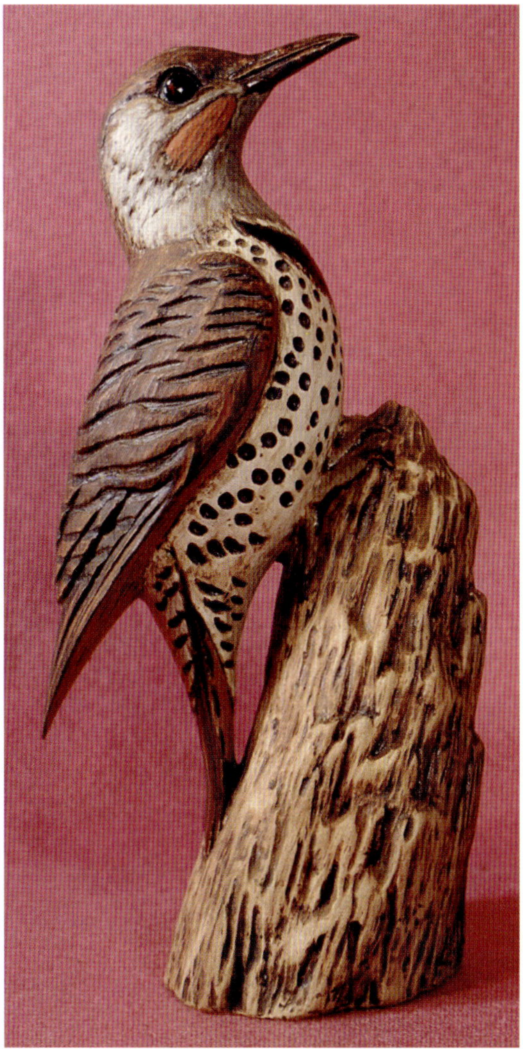

Looking like he was caught in the midst of pecking on a tree, the Flicker stands 7.25" tall mounted on this trunk. His approximate value is $110-130.

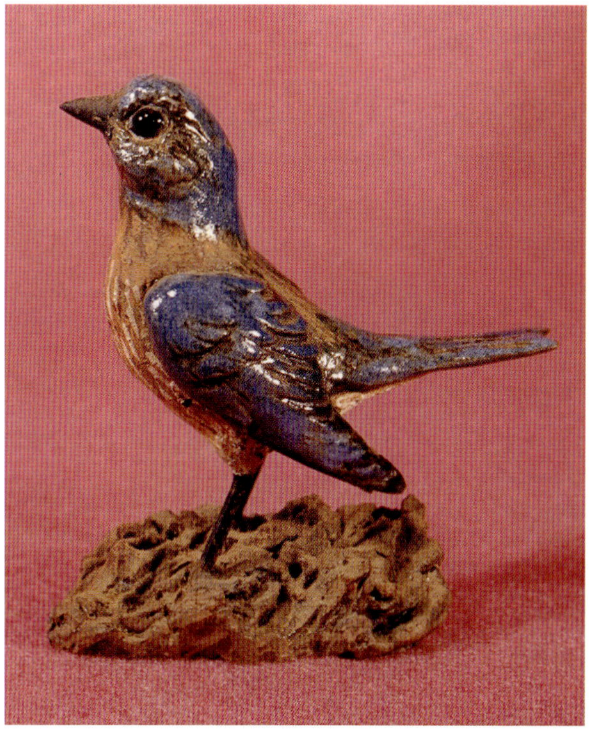

Ready to fly away, this Western Bluebird stands 2.75" tall. It has an approximate value of $40-55.

The Audubon's Warbler stands 5.5" tall mounted on this driftwood. The base is actually ceramic, but was cast from a piece of driftwood found on the beach. His approximate value is $60-75.

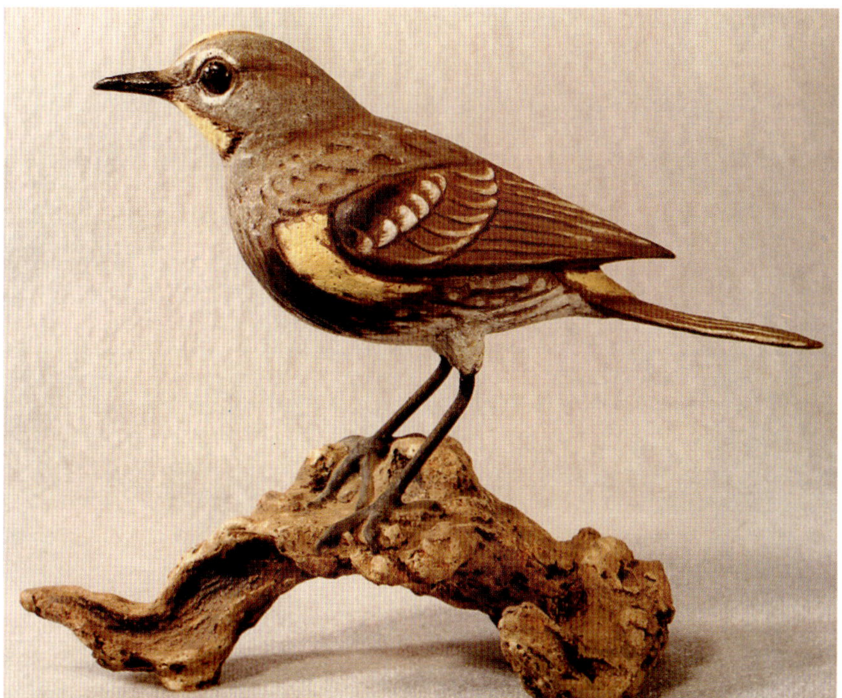

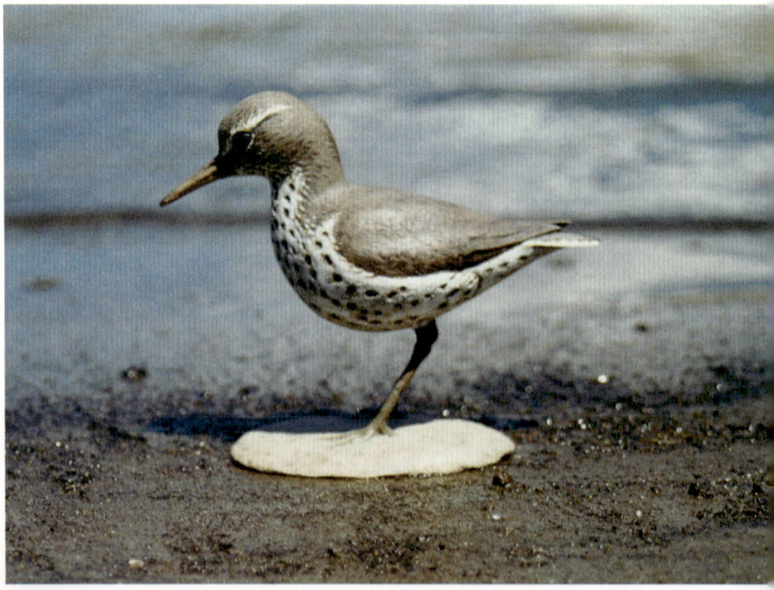

Posed in its natural habitat running along the beach searching for food, this model of the Spotted Sandpiper stands 4.4" tall and has an approximate value of $45-60.

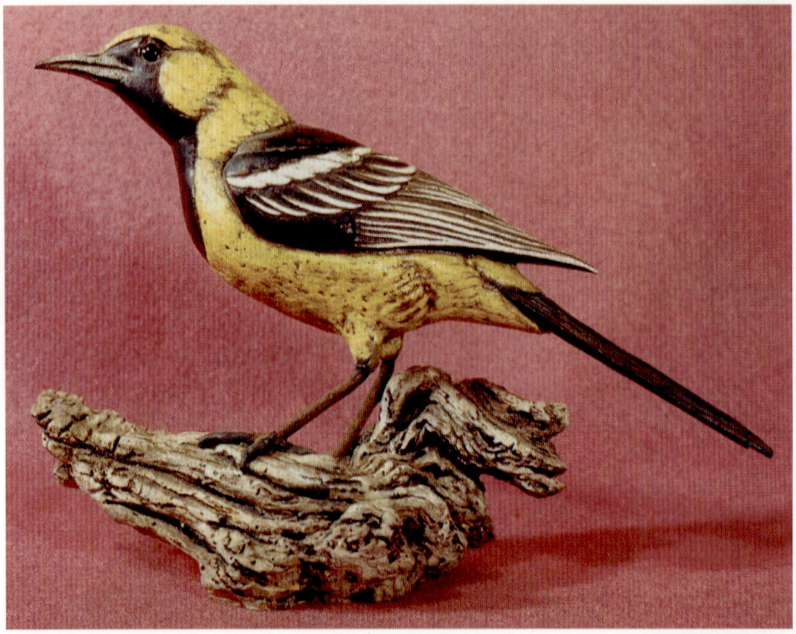

This male Hooded Oriole was modeled after a pair of birds that nest in Maureen's yard in the summer. She explains that the male of the songbird pairs usually has brighter plumage than the female. This model stands 5.75" tall on the base and has an approximate value of $60-75.

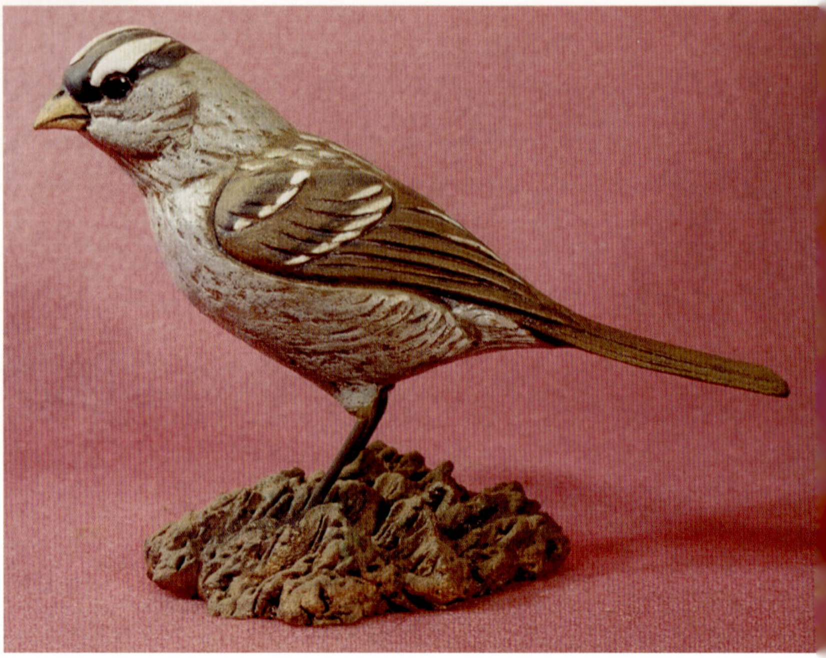

Most of the bird models produced by Maureen have metal legs, as shown on this White-Crowned Sparrow. He stands 4.5" tall on his base, and has an approximate value of $50-65.

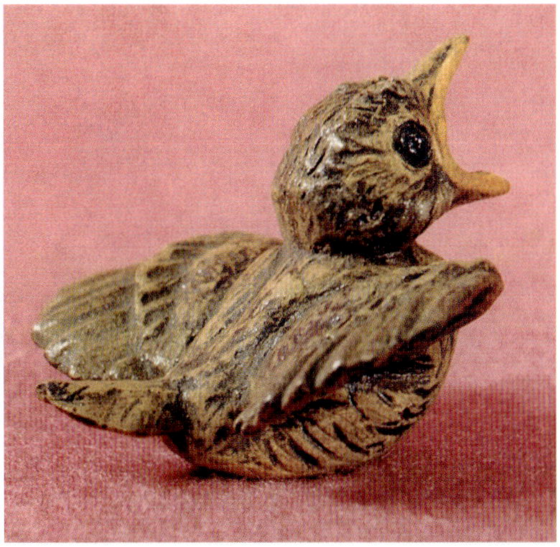

Being the nature lover that she is, Maureen has raised a few orphan birds over the years. This little baby represents one of those, although she doesn't claim it is any particular species of bird. The 1.5" fledgling has an approximate value of $25-40.

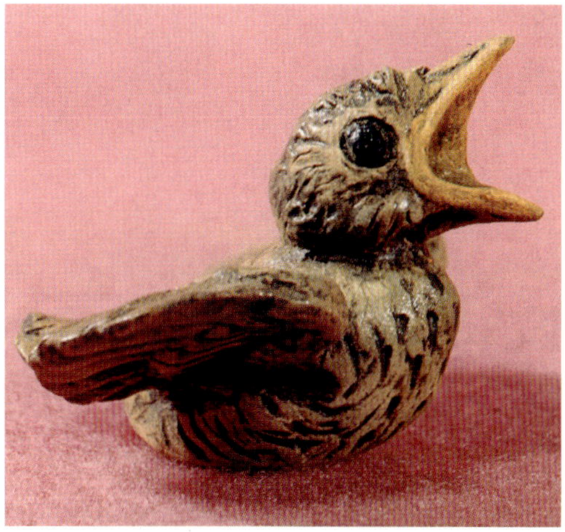

This front view of the fledgling bird exemplifies the relentless mouth and face demanding to be fed.

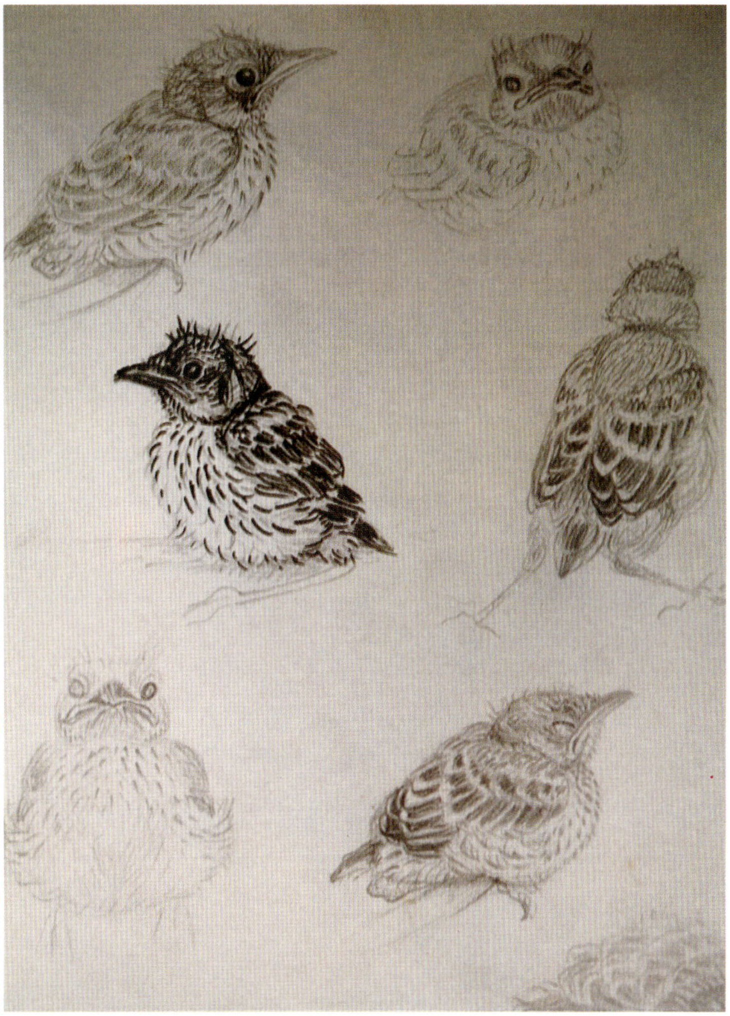

With a fledgling bird hopping about her house, Maureen was able to make several sketches of it before attempting the model.

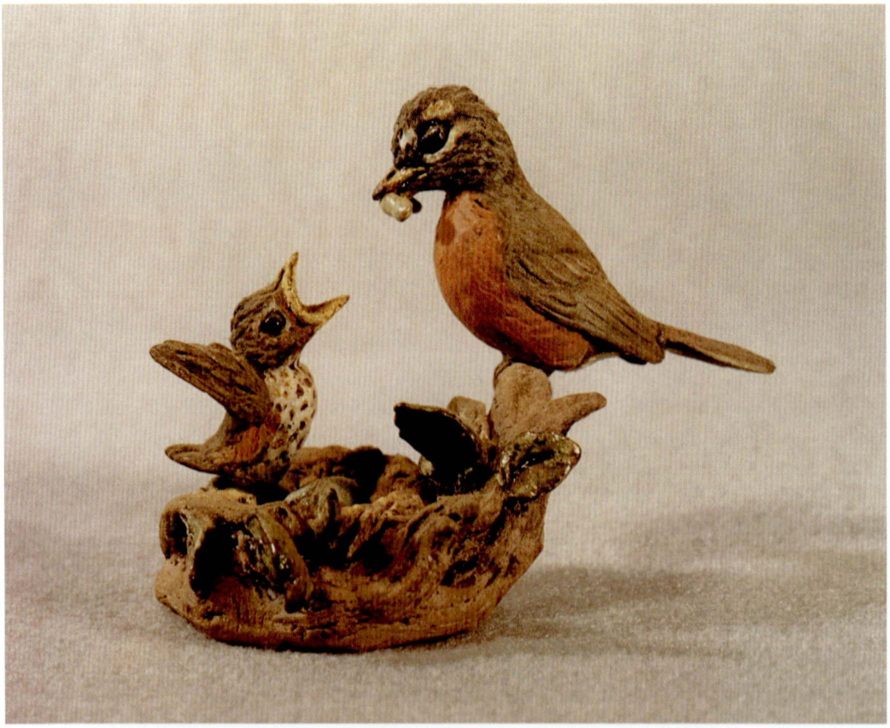

Baby Robin noisily requests his meal from his parent. At only 2.5" tall, this model contains a substantial amount of intricate detail. Its approximate value is $40-65.

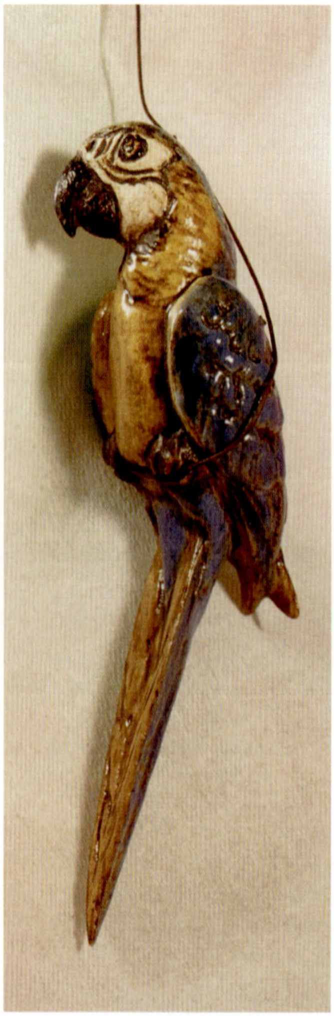

The Macaw Parrot has been separated from his base over time, but he still displays nicely on this wire hanger. Measuring 3.5" from head to tail tip, his approximate value is $35-50.

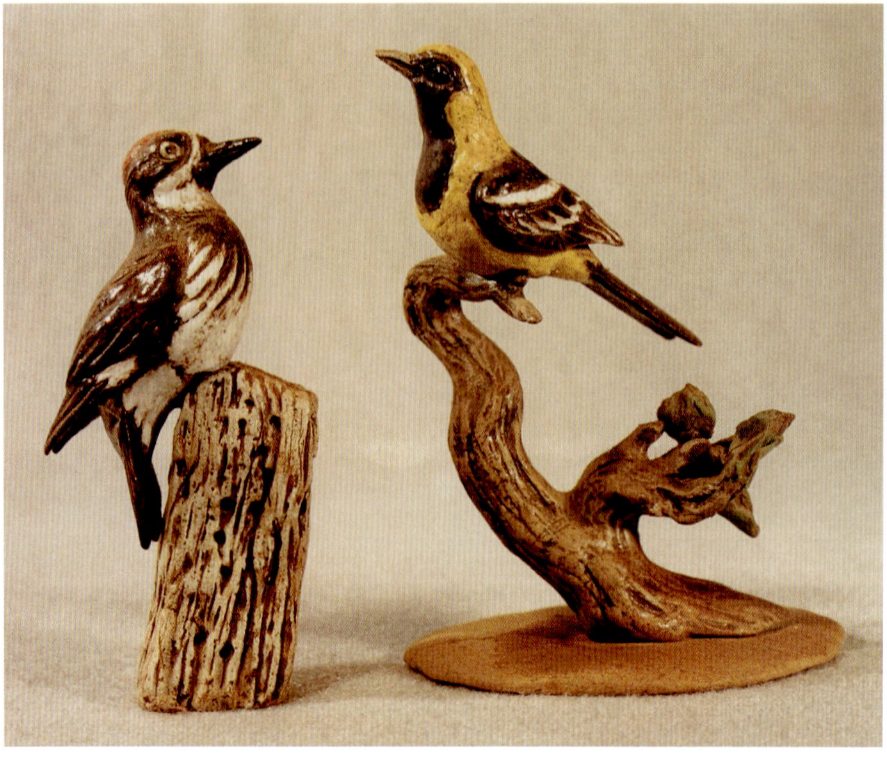

Maureen likes to experiment with different bases for her models. The Woodpecker on the left has holes pecked in his tree trunk. The Hooded Oriole is perched atop a tree branch complete with leaves. The Wood-pecker is 3.25" tall and the Hooded Oriole is 4" tall. Their approximate values are $50-65 each.

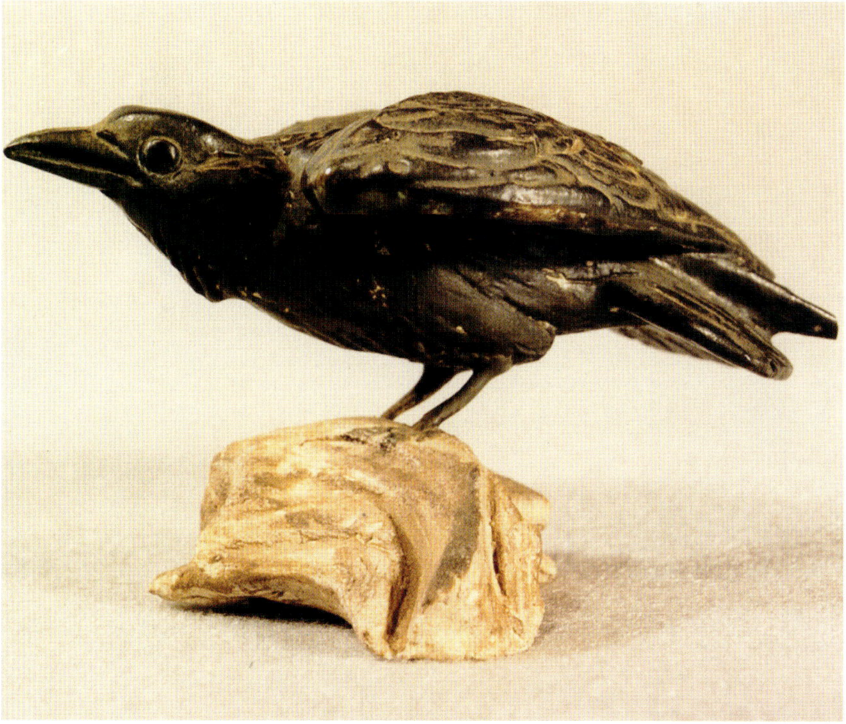

Looking positively ravenous, this crow perched on a rock measures a mere 2" tall. His approximate value is $35-50.

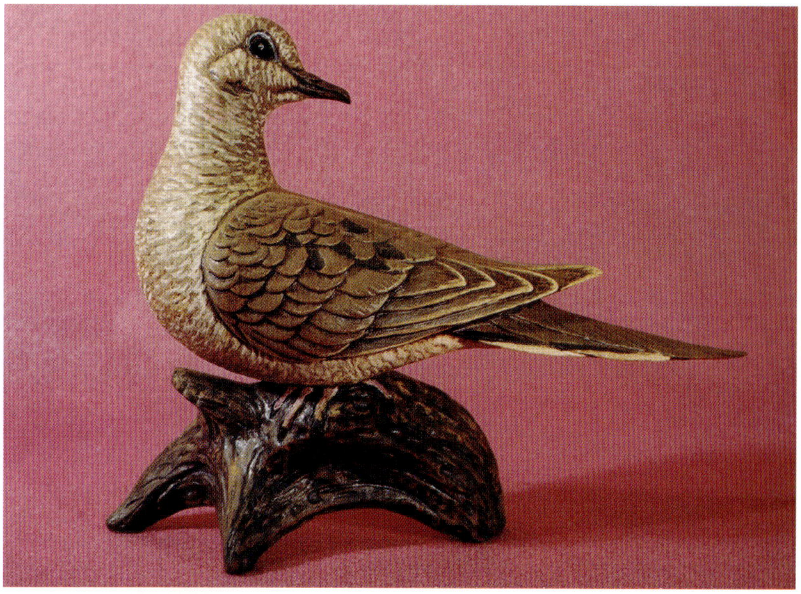

The peaceful mourning dove pauses here on her branch. She measures 6" tall, and was one of the birds produced by Maureen during her Maureen Love Originals period, so several of these might exist. The approximate value of this model is $100-125.

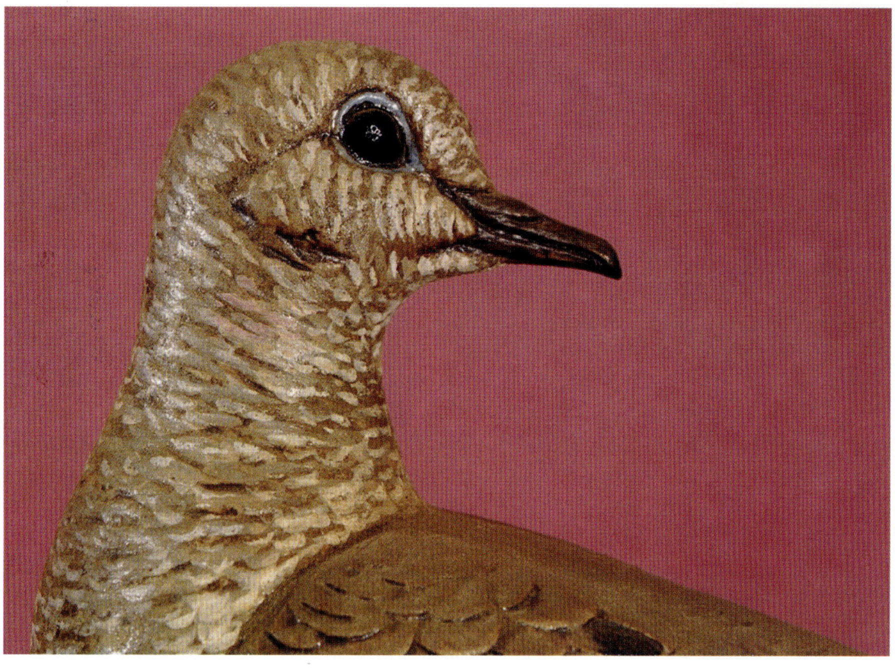

This close up of the Mourning Dove's head illustrates the intricate detail achieved through the texture of the clay and the shading of the painted patterns.

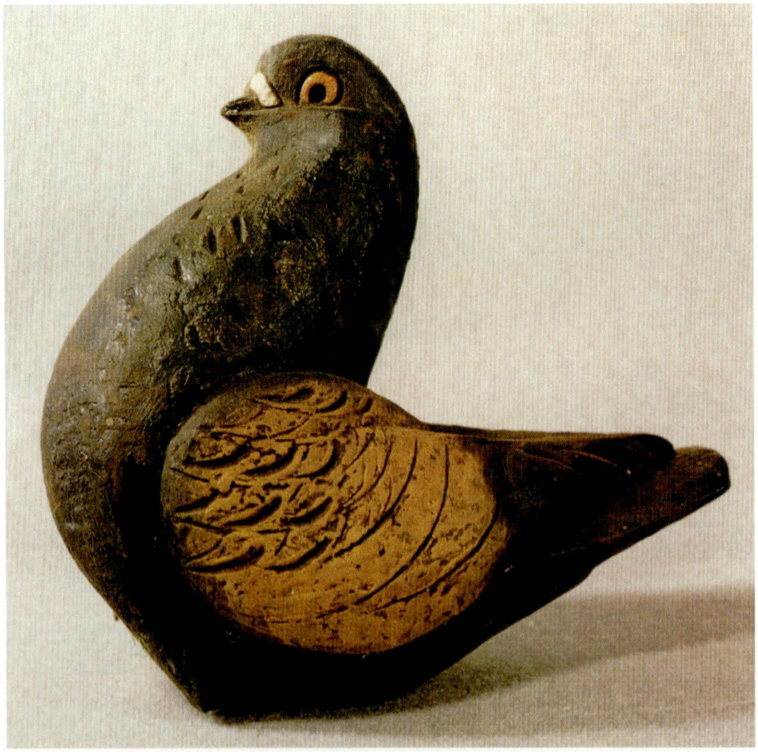

Known as the Modina Pigeon, this very unusual bird measures 5.75" tall. It has an approximate value of $50-65.

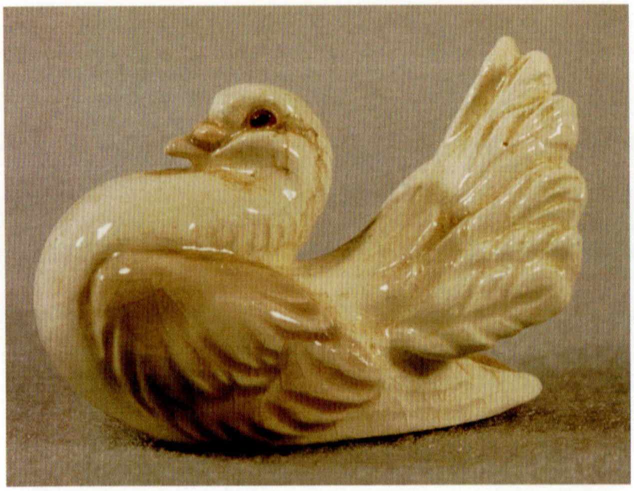

In a departure from her usual style, Maureen has created this Fantail Pigeon in a glossy finish. She usually prefers to work in matte, as she feels it is more realistic. This bird stands 1.2" tall, and has an approximate value of $25-40.

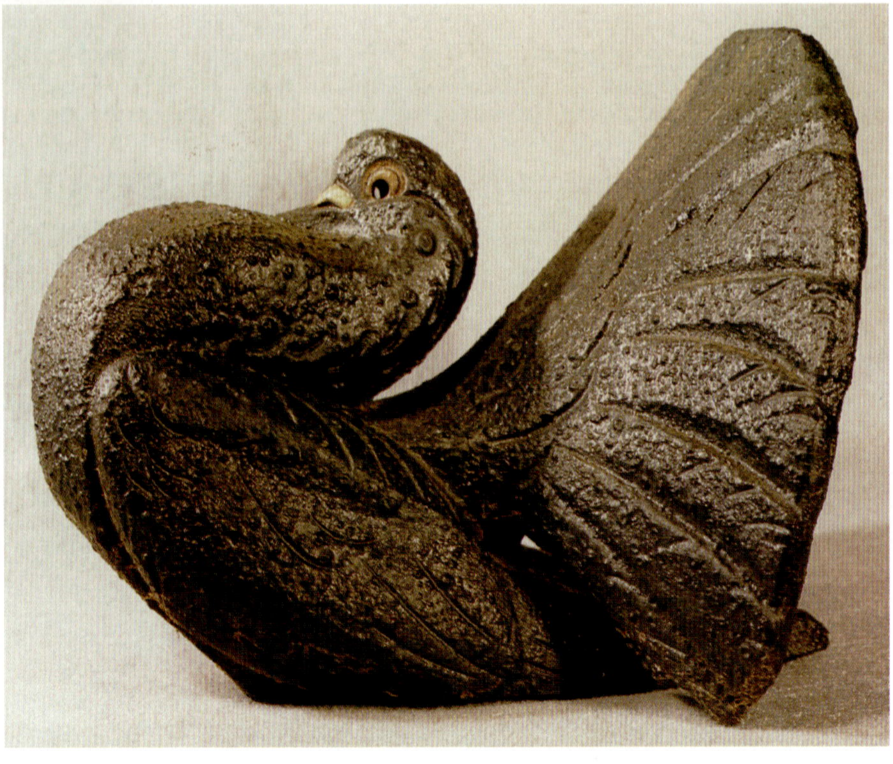

This puffed-up Fantail Pigeon measures 7" tall. Note the intricate design, with the wings passing under the large fantail. The approximate value of this bird is $70-85.

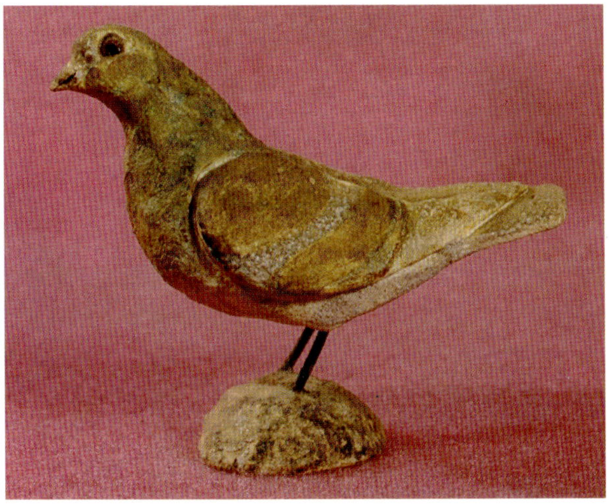

When asked about the species of this bird, Maureen called it "just a plain, old pigeon." It stands 2" tall and has an approximate value of $25-40.

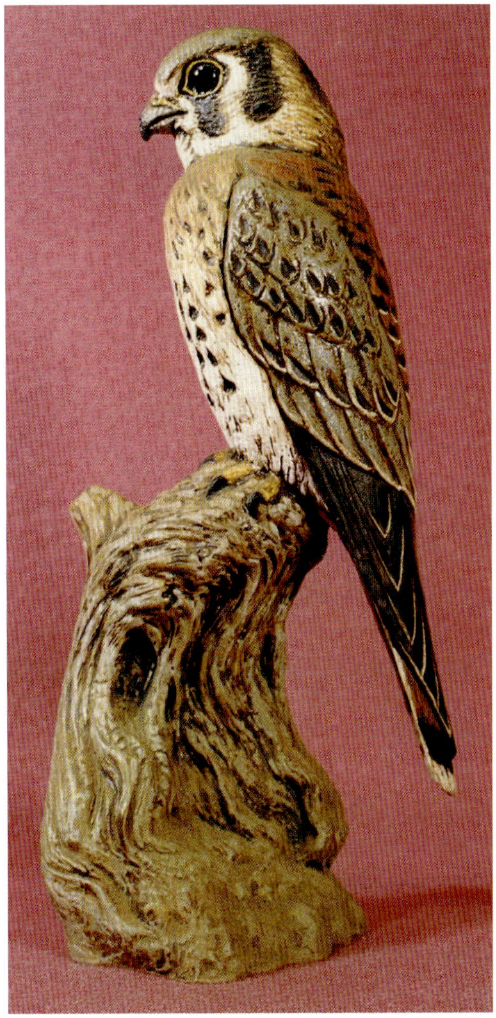

Measuring 8.25" atop the woody perch, this Kestrel is searching for prey. The approximate value of this model is $110-135.

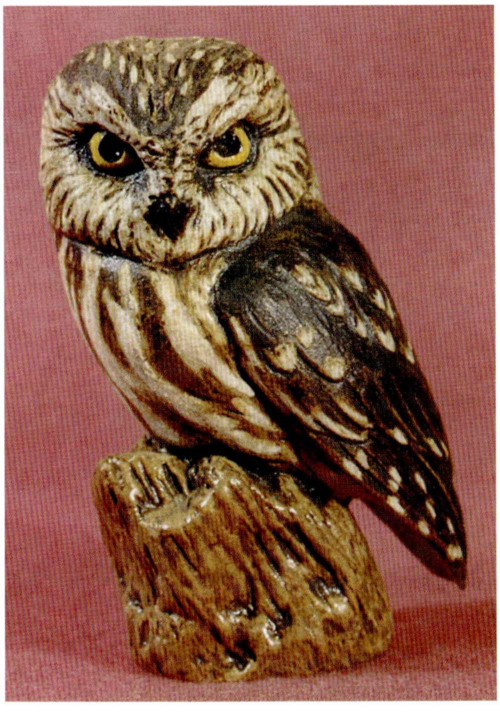

Known as the Saw-whet Owl, a smaller version of this model was later incorporated into the Hagen-Renaker Specialty line. Measuring only 3.75" tall, the detail in the texture and painting of the feathers adds so much to this hand-painted piece. The approximate value of this Owl is $45-60.

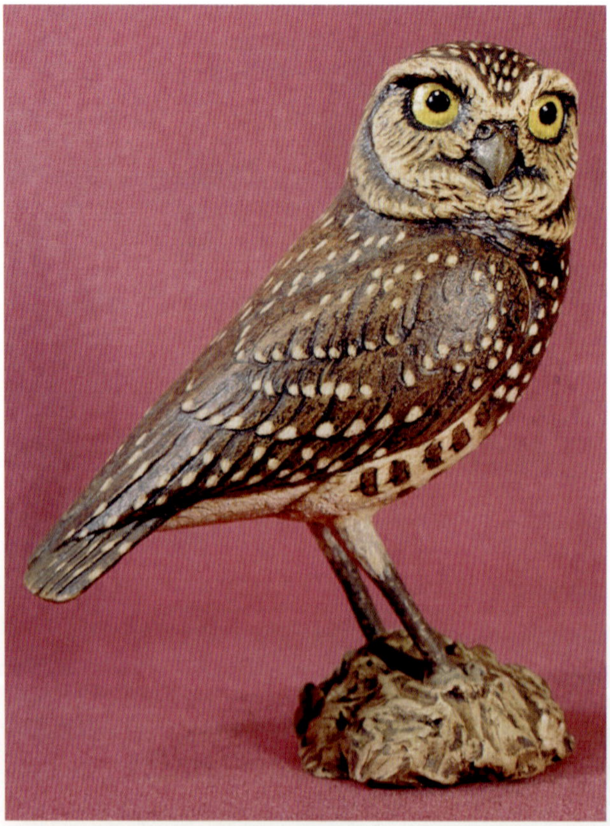

The alert, vigilant look of this Burrowing Owl has been beautifully captured in this model. It stands 5.25" tall by 4.25" long, and has an approximate value of $60-75.

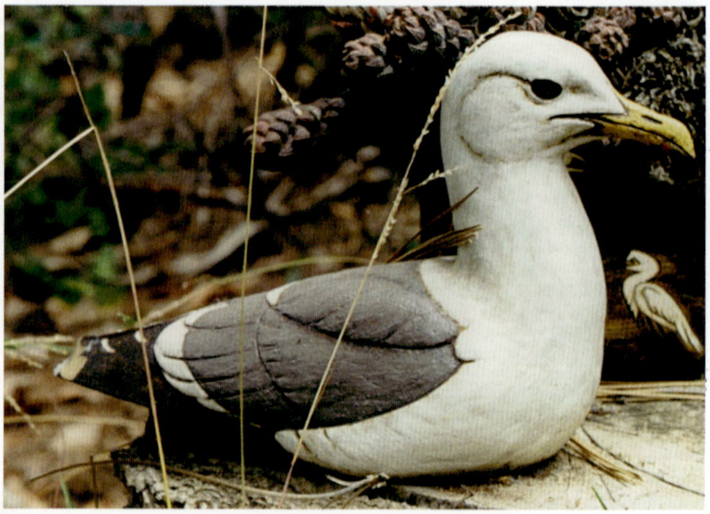

Maureen enjoys her artwork throughout her home and yard. This seagull appears right at home on this rock with the Egret planter in the background. He measures 7" tall and has an approximate value of $55-70.

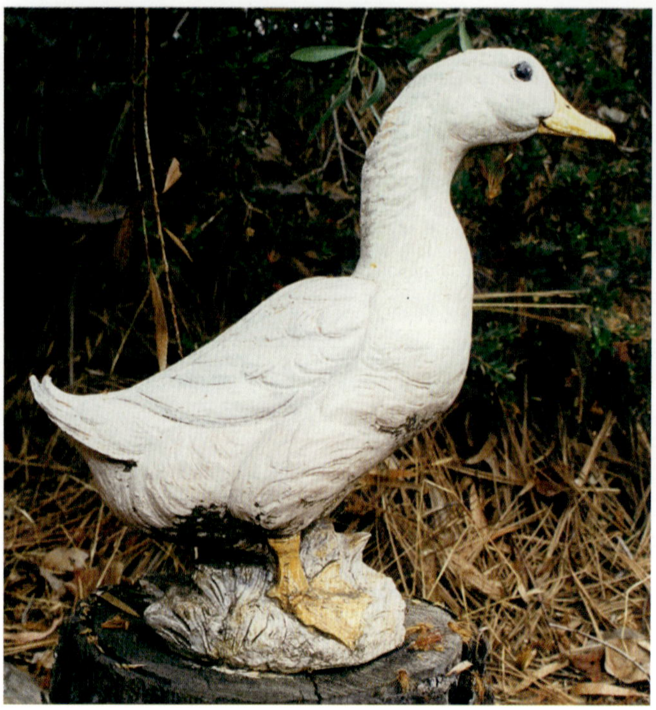

Perched out of harm's way on this tree stump, this Peking Duck measures 12" tall and has an approximate value of $100-125.

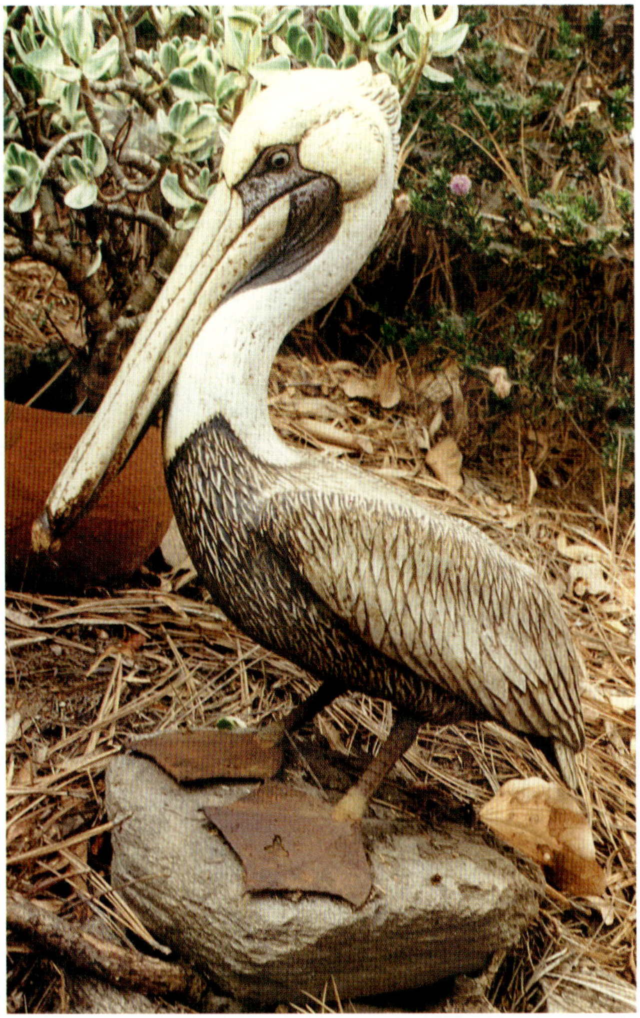

Standing at a near-life-sized 19", this pelican helps guard the garden outside. This view shows the copper sheet and metal bars used for the feet and legs to support such a large ceramic piece. His approximate value is $175-200.

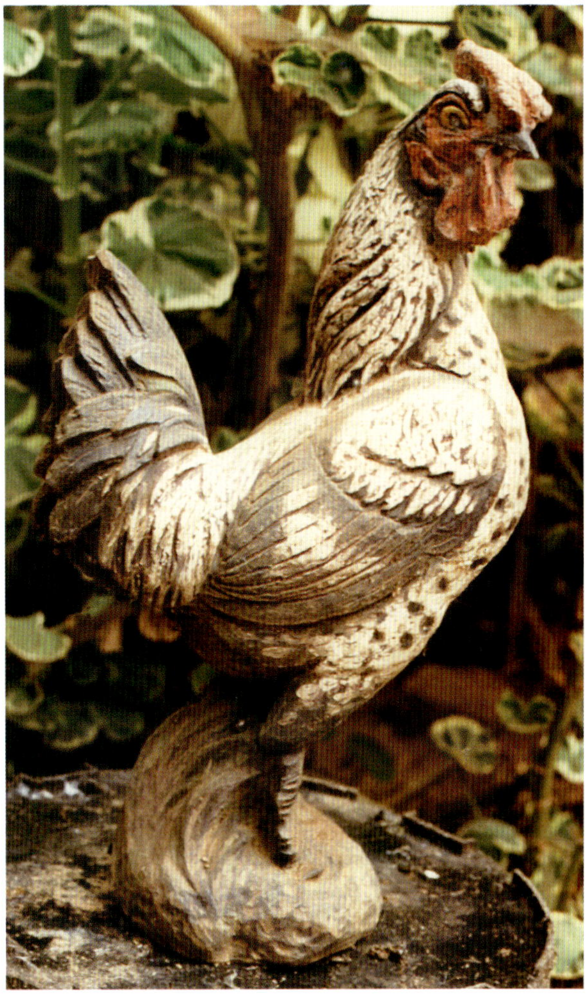

This model of a Bantam Rooster helps keep Maureen's pet chickens company in the yard. He measures 12.5" tall, and has an approximate value of $150-175.

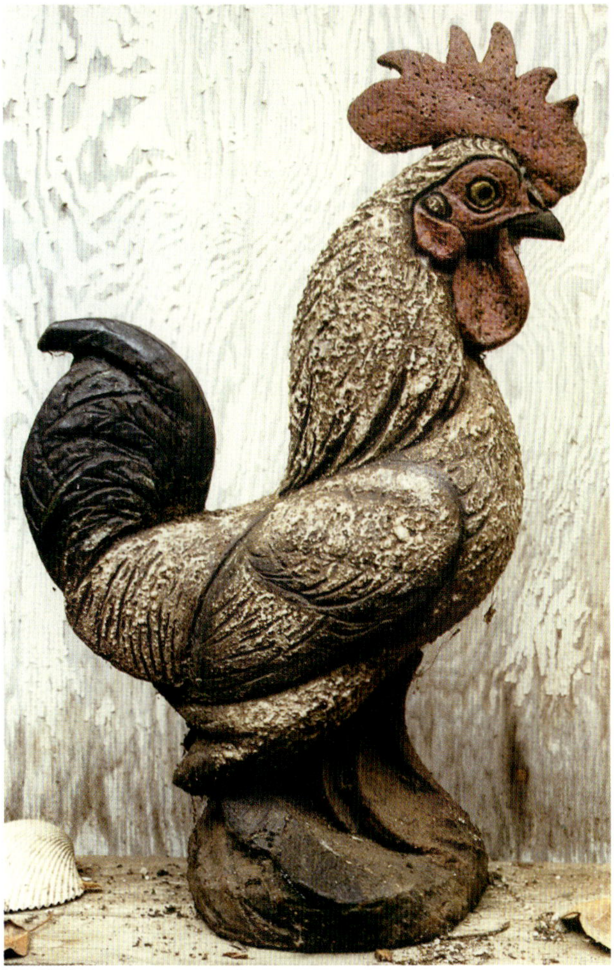

Looking a little more like stoneware than feathers, this Rooster stands guard outside the garden shed at a commanding 14.25" tall. His approximate value is $150-175.

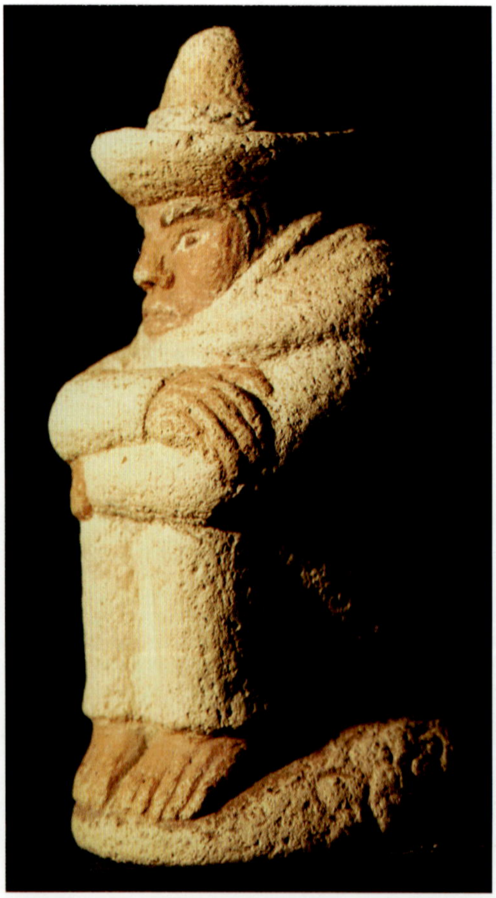

Since Maureen rarely produced human figures, this Mexican man sitting pensively is a very unusual piece. He measures 4.5" tall to the top of his sombrero and has an approximate value of $55-70.

This miniature rhino stands a petite .9" tall, but maintains a lot of muscular and facial detail like his larger comrades. Approximate value for this item is $25-40.

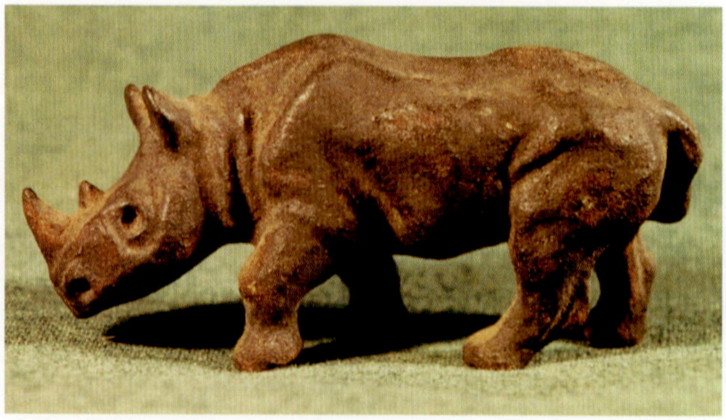

Standing an impressive 1.9" tall, this grasshopper rests on metal legs that have begun to rust from a life spent outdoors. The intricate overlapping V patterns in the rear legs and the facial details add charm to this piece. Approximate value for this creature is $20-35.

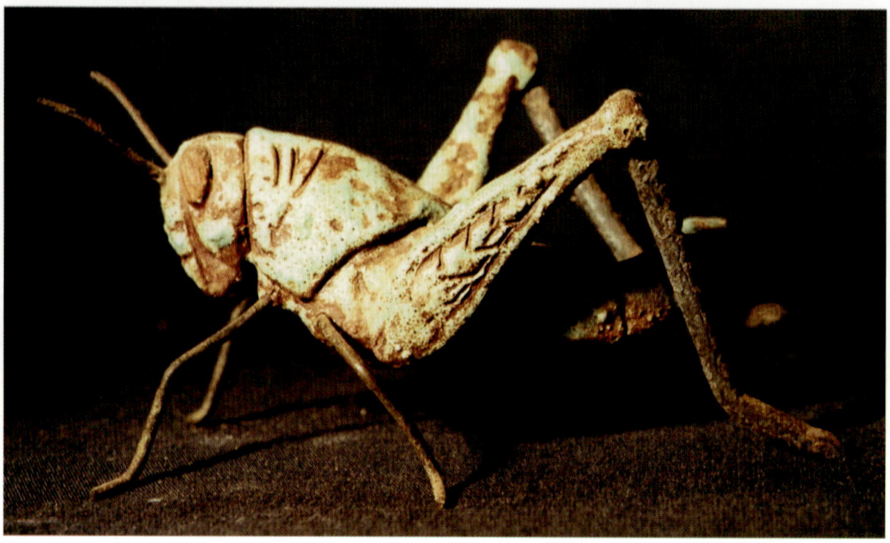

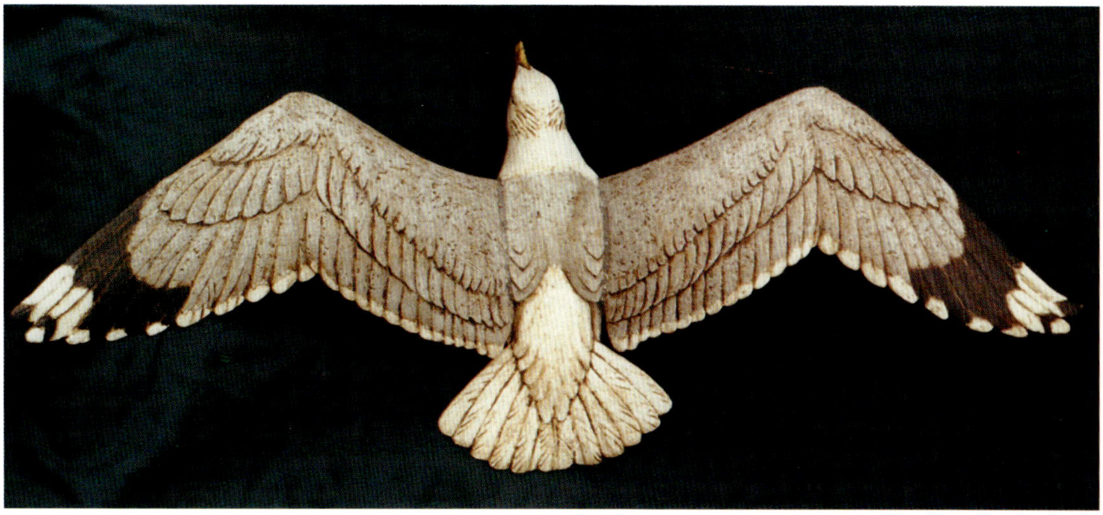

The feather patterns and textures on this gull are incredible. Even the tail feathers have realistic markings. His wingspan is 22" and the length of his body is 10.75" long. This poor fellow suffered a mishap during his lifetime and lost his legs.

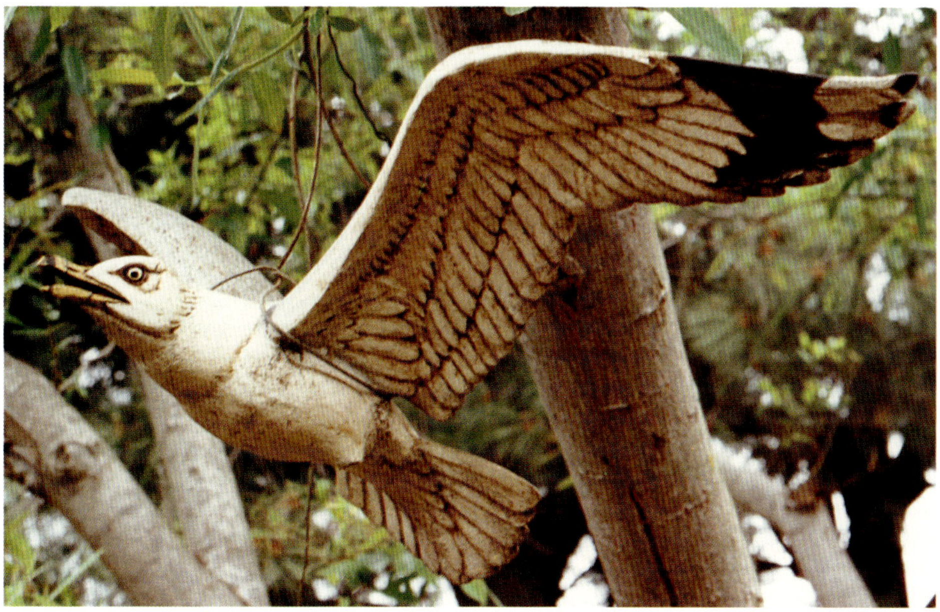

Using some ingenuity, Maureen took the broken seagull and gave him a new life. He now resides in a tree in her yard where he can appear to fly in a very life-like manner.

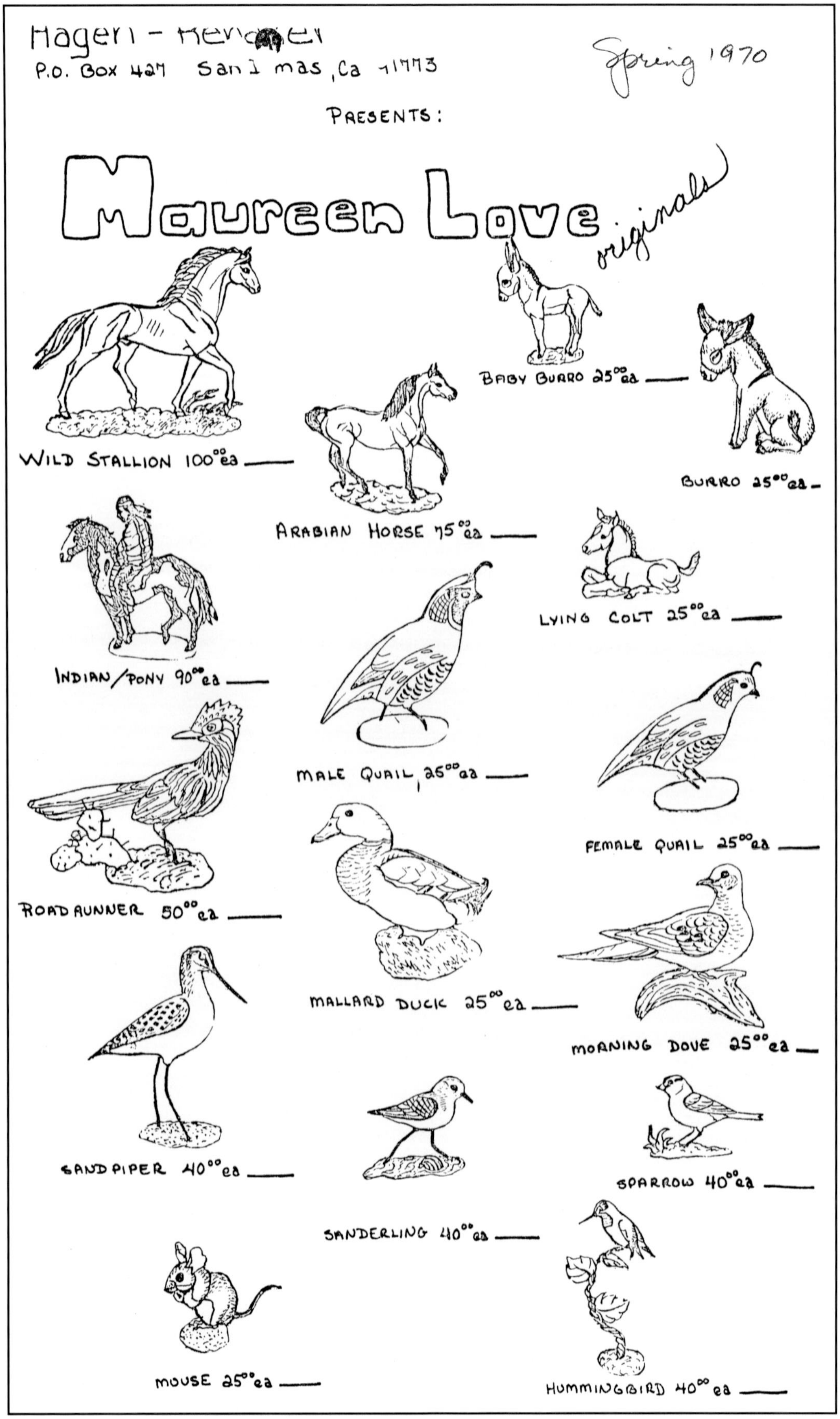

Hagen - Renaker
P.O. Box 427 San Dimas, Ca 91773

Spring 1970

PRESENTS:

Maureen Love originals

WILD STALLION 100^{00} ea ____

BABY BURRO 25^{00} ea ____

BURRO 25^{00} ea ____

ARABIAN HORSE 75^{00} ea ____

INDIAN/PONY 90^{00} ea ____

LYING COLT 25^{00} ea ____

MALE QUAIL 25^{00} ea ____

FEMALE QUAIL 25^{00} ea ____

ROADRUNNER 50^{00} ea ____

MALLARD DUCK 25^{00} ea ____

MORNING DOVE 25^{00} ea ____

SANDPIPER 40^{00} ea ____

SPARROW 40^{00} ea ____

SANDERLING 40^{00} ea ____

MOUSE 25^{00} ea ____

HUMMINGBIRD 40^{00} ea ____

Working independently of Hagen-Renaker, Maureen Love marketed her own ceramics for several years, mostly in the late 1960s and throughout the 1970s. She fired them in her kiln at home and decorated each one by hand. This line was called "Maureen Love Originals." This sales sheet is dated Spring, 1970.

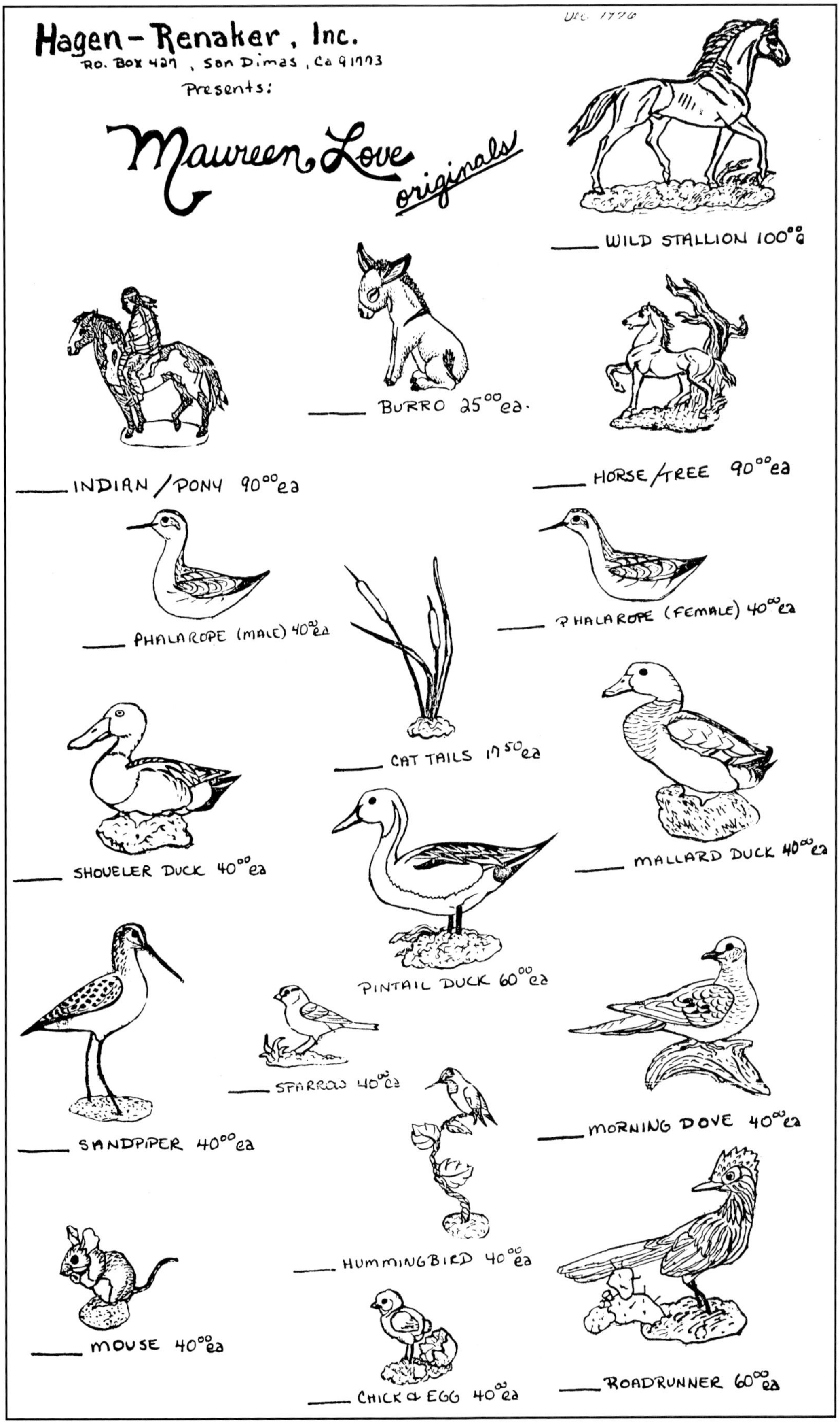

This sales sheet for Maureen Love Originals, dated December, 1976, shows some different birds than those seen on the first sheet. Note the cattails listed as a separate item.

Chapter Four

Close Association With Hagen-Renaker

While a very respectable artist in her own right, Maureen Love has become better known to collectors and art lovers through her association with Hagen-Renaker Pottery. Hired in 1951 by John and Maxine Renaker, she started working there as a decorator but quickly demonstrated her ability to design and sculpt. While working for Hagen-Renaker, Maureen continued to create models in her own kiln at home.

The first group of photos in this chapter shows Maureen's artistic decorating ability when she took home some blanks, or unfinished Hagen-Renaker models, that she then finished in her wonderful, realistic style. The few collectors who own these treasure them as unique creations.

The next several photos show some of the models that later gave rise to a Hagen-Renaker production model. These models enjoy the luxury of a hand-crafted design and a unique paint job that cannot be duplicated in the mass-production methods of the factory. Each one of these is an incredible work of original art.

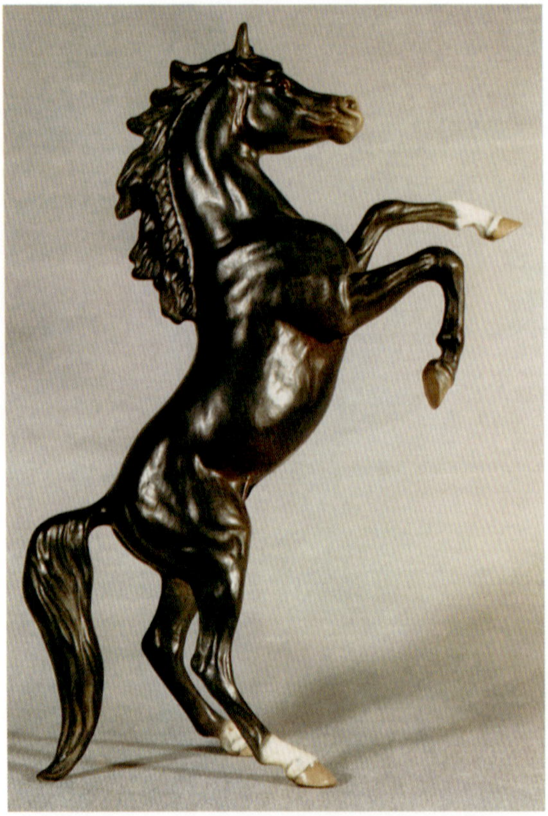

Maureen enjoys occasionally taking home unfinished Hagen-Renaker pieces and creating one-of-a-kind models on her own sculptures. The next several photos show examples of these. This 7.75" tall horse was sold as an Arabian stallion named "Fez" and designed by Maureen. However, it was never released in this black color. While the Hagen-Renaker version of this horse (in white or gray) is worth around $350, this piece is worth approximately $450-500.

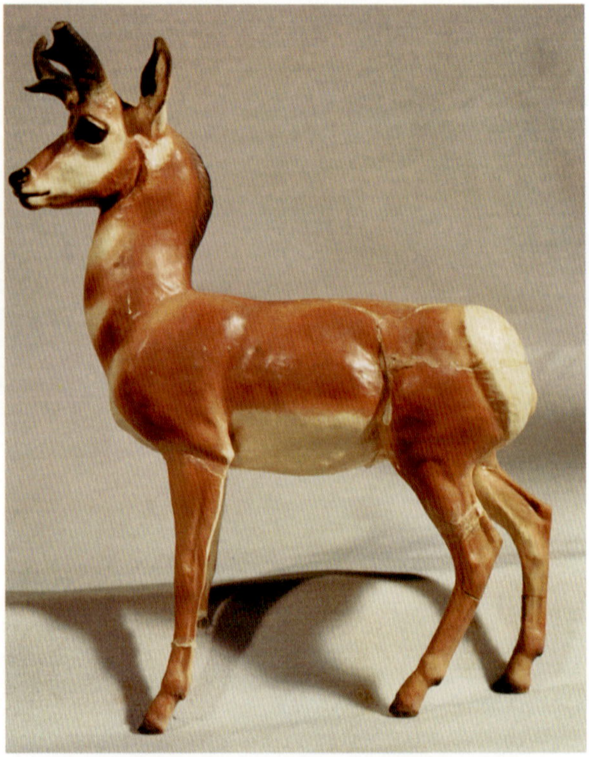

This Pronghorn Antelope was intended for Hagen-Renaker, but it may not have been produced. Maureen hand-decorated one herself, and even though the model has suffered numerous breaks through the years, it still stands proudly. It measures 6" tall, and in mint condition would have an approximate value of $275-300.

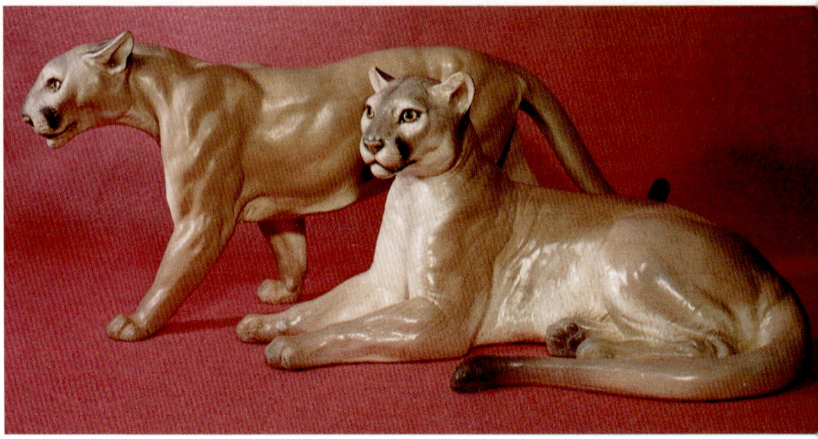

Designed for Hagen-Renaker, this walking mountain lion is 5.5" tall and 15" long. The lying mountain lion measures 5" tall. While the factory-produced pair is worth approximately $250 per lion, this pair was hand-decorated by Maureen and has incredible detail and shading. This pair is worth approximately $400-450 each.

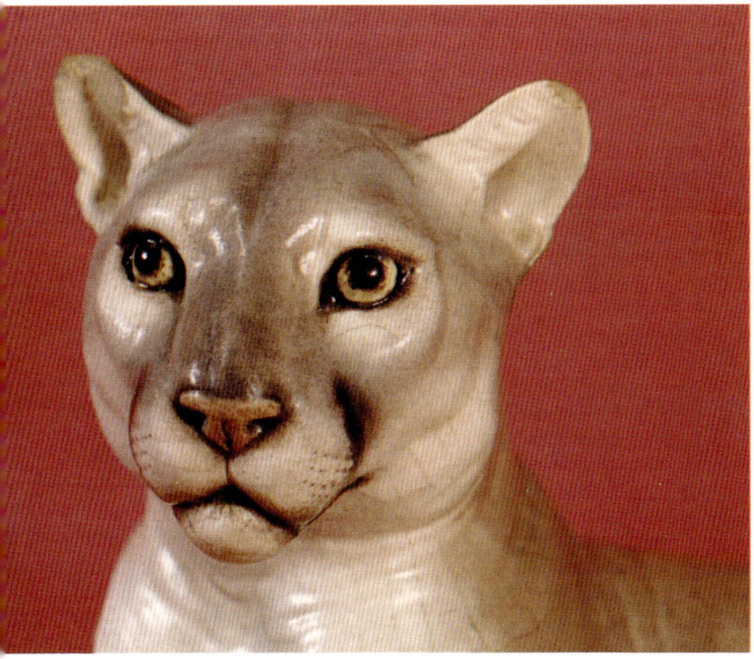

This close up of the face on the lying mountain lion illustrates the incredible detail Maureen puts into her work.

Once again, Maureen pulled an undecorated scrap horse from the Hagen-Renaker bin and created this magnificently shaded and detailed work of art. The model is "Crusader," a 6.25" tall Percheron designed for Hagen-Renaker by Maureen. The factory model is worth about $600, but this unique piece is valued at approximately $700-725.

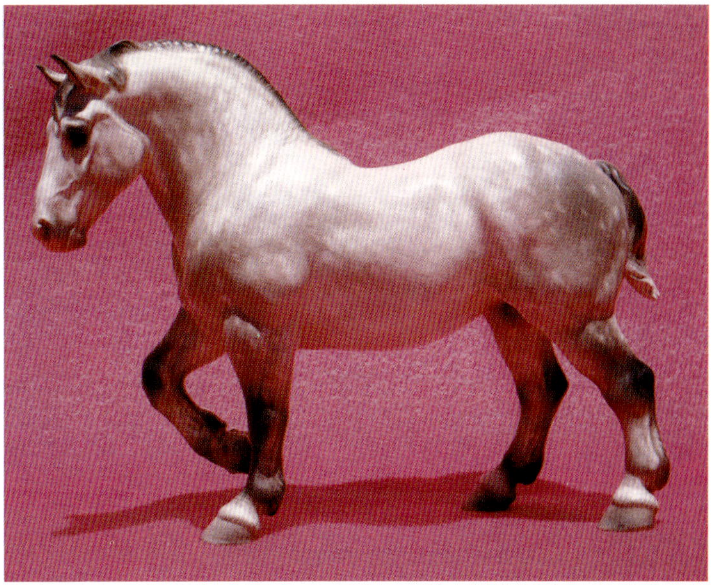

"Abdullah" the 6.25" Arabian stallion was produced for Hagen-Renaker in white. Maureen decorated this subtly gray shaded model for fun, resulting in this unique treasure. The Hagen-Renaker factory model is worth about $350, but this hand-painted work of art is worth approximately $500-550.

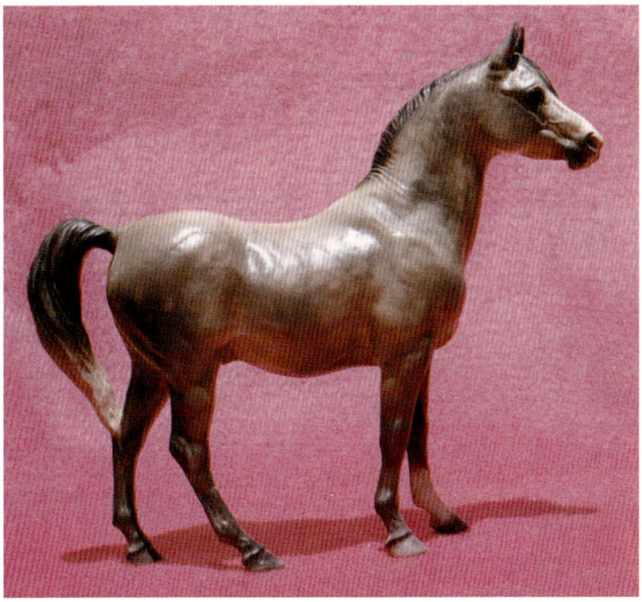

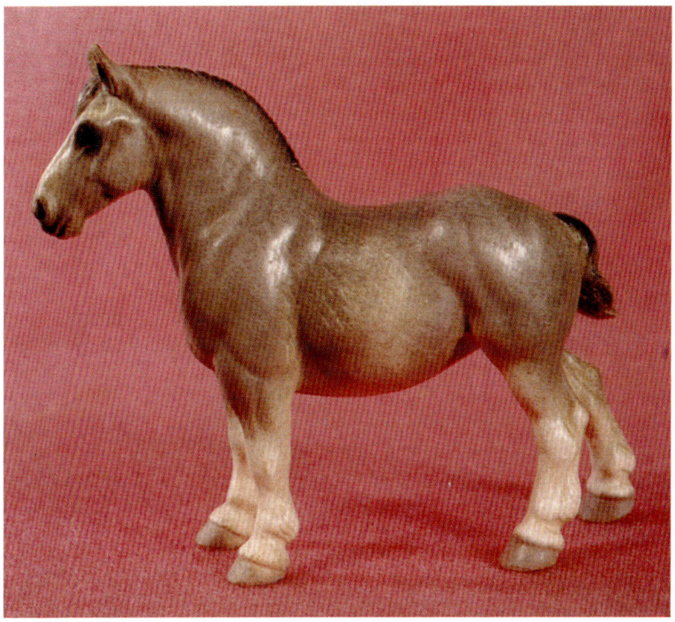

This Miniature draft horse was produced by Hagen-Renaker in white with gray shading, but never in this over-all gray coloring. Maureen decorated this 2.75" draft horse from one of the unfinished Hagen-Renaker models. The factory-produced piece is worth about $80, but this uniquely decorated horse is worth approximately $175-200.

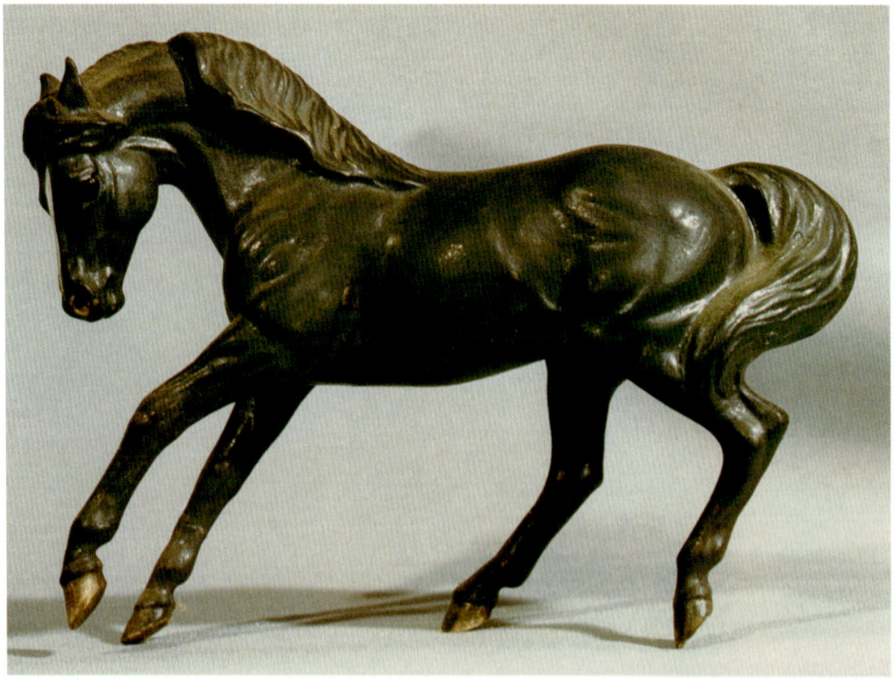

Later produced by Hagen-Renaker as the Morgan mare "Tria," this cantering horse measures 3.5" tall. The factory-produced piece can be seen on page 124. This unique model is worth approximately $250-300.

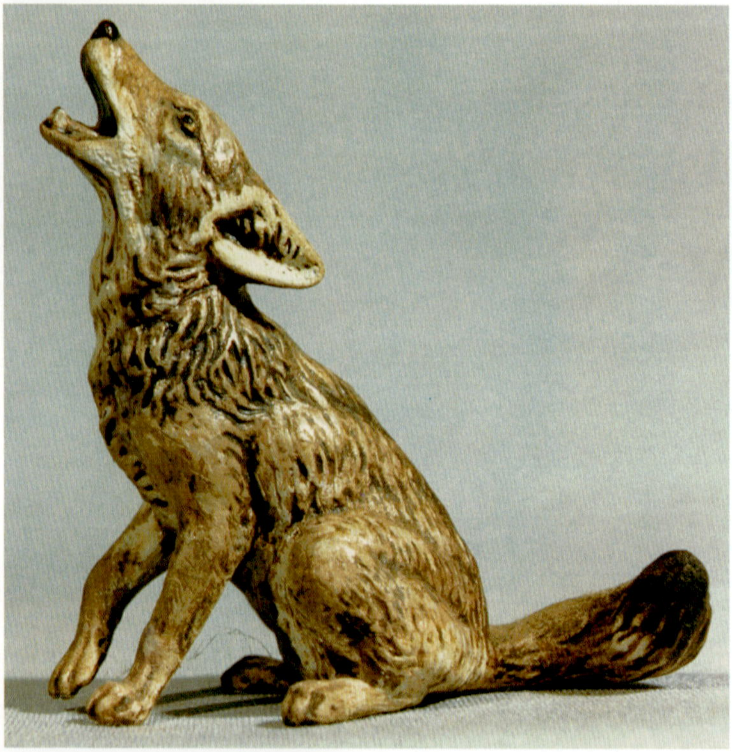

This original 2.5" stoneware ceramic howling coyote later appeared in the Hagen-Renaker Miniature line. The glossy tan factory model is worth about $8, while this matte handcrafted piece is valued at approximately $35-50.

The detail in the fur and face are very prominent in this original model. Even the pad under the raised front paw is visible. This 2" model later became a Hagen-Renaker Specialty line piece in gray gloss, with a value of about $12. This stalking wolf as pictured is worth approximately $35-50.

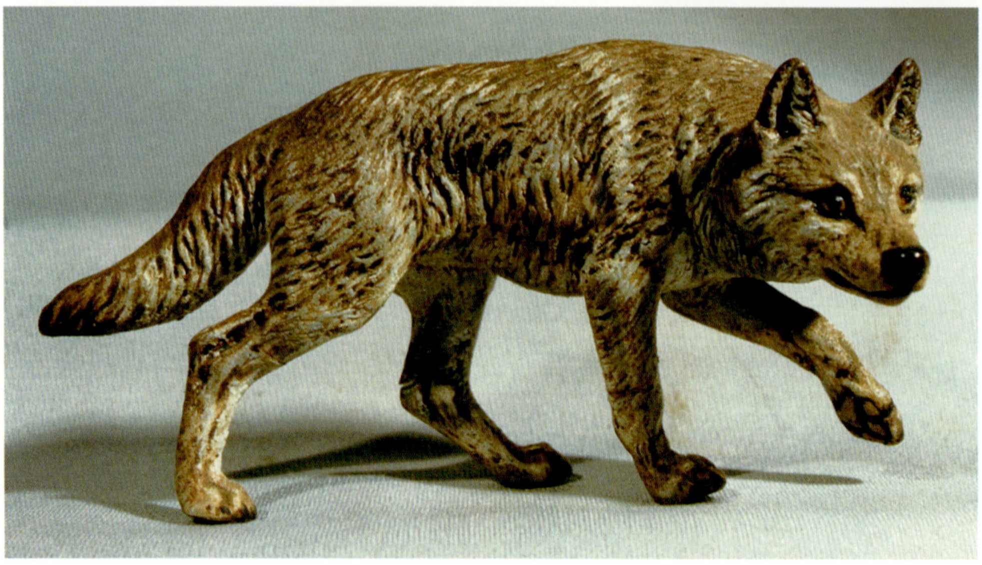

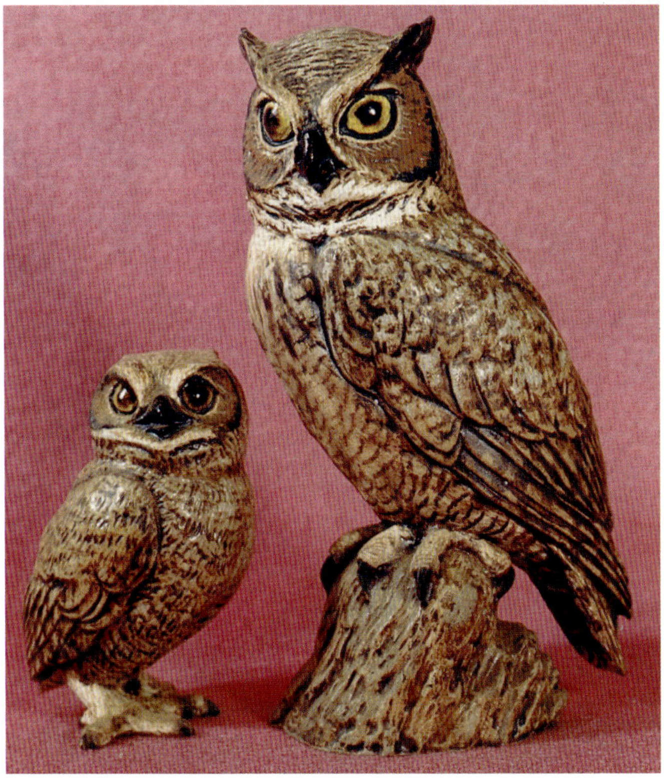

The tiny whirls and patterns in the feathers of this Horned Owl duo are realistically depicted in this stoneware ceramic medium. Measuring 5.25" and 2.8" tall, this owl and owlet were later produced by Hagen-Renaker in the Designers Workshop line. While the factory-produced pieces are currently valued at $50 and $35, these original creations are worth approximately $75-100 and $50-65 respectively.

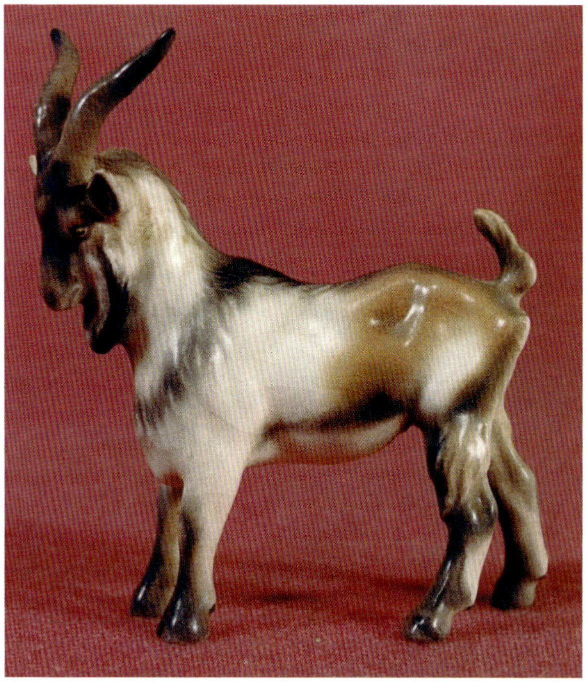

Measuring 2.5" tall, this adult male goat is attractively decorated in a calico pattern. The Hagen-Renaker factory piece has simpler decoration and striped horns. While the production piece is worth about $25, this handcrafted goat is worth approximately $45-60.

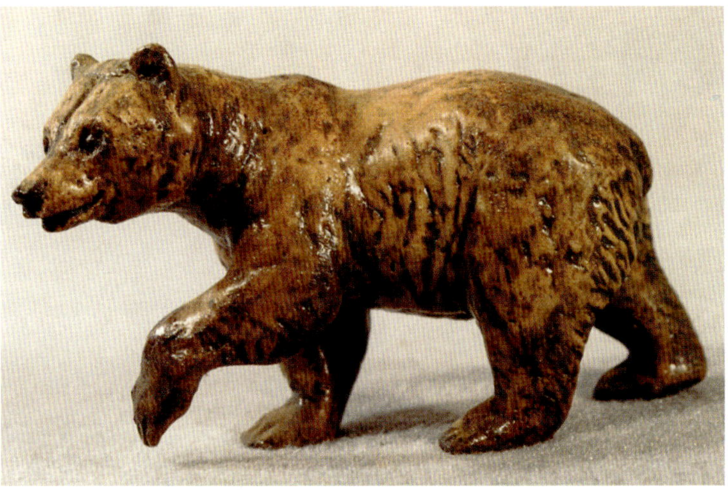

This bear model was produced briefly by Hagen-Renaker, in a smaller version, with a current value of approximately $8. This 2" original model captures much more of the bear's curious nature and furry detail. It has an approximate value of $35-50.

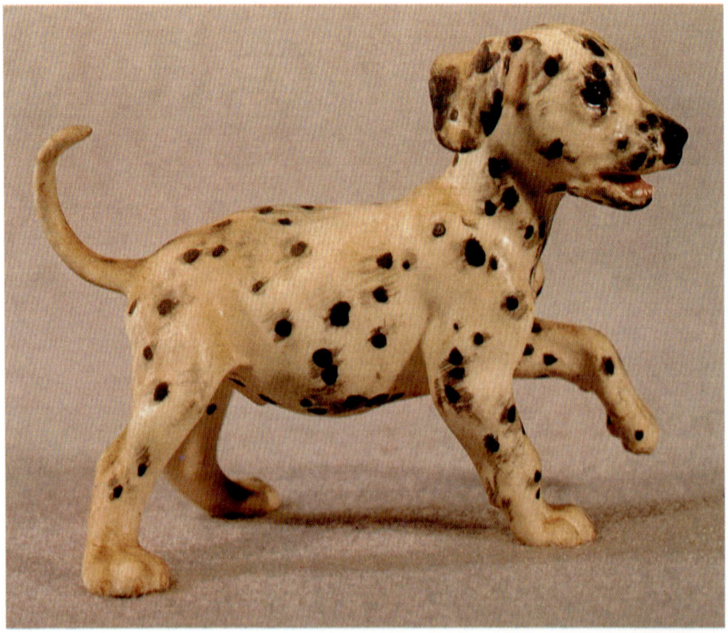

Delightfully hand-decorated and shaded, this original 2.5" sculpture later became the Hagen-Renaker Dalmatian puppy "Sparky." The less detailed factory piece is worth about $40, while this unique model is valued at approximately $65-80.

This Cockapoo-type dog was a portrait of Maureen's dog "Bear," who arrived at her home in a taxicab when the dog's original owner died. Hagen-Renaker later produced this dog in their Stoneware Specialty line. It looks amazingly similar to the original, but without the fine fur detail. The Hagen-Renaker piece is worth about $20, while this original piece, sitting 2.3" tall, is worth approximately $50-65.

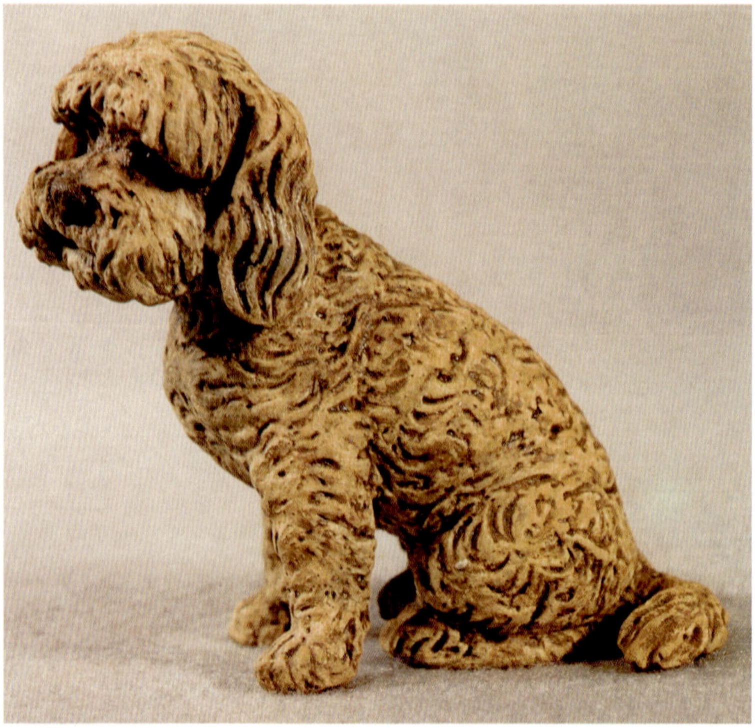

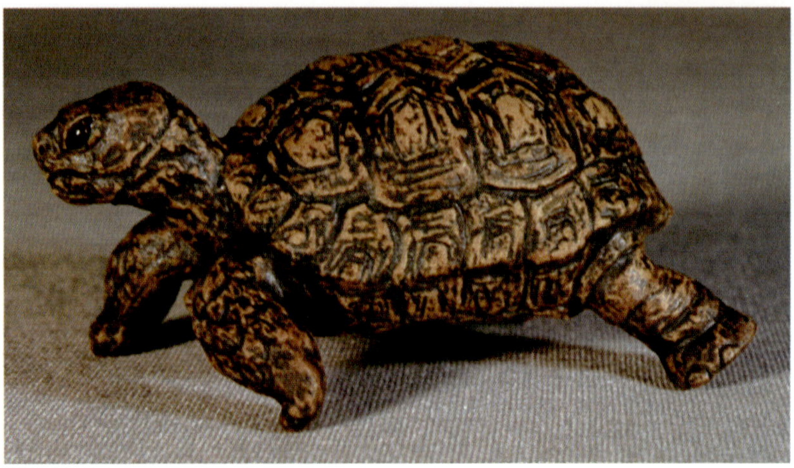

The desert tortoise shown here is 1.2" tall and was later produced by Hagen-Renaker. The incredible detail in the skin and shell were not duplicated in the factory piece, which is only light brown. While the Hagen-Renaker tortoise has a value of around $6, this unique piece has an approximate value of $35-50.

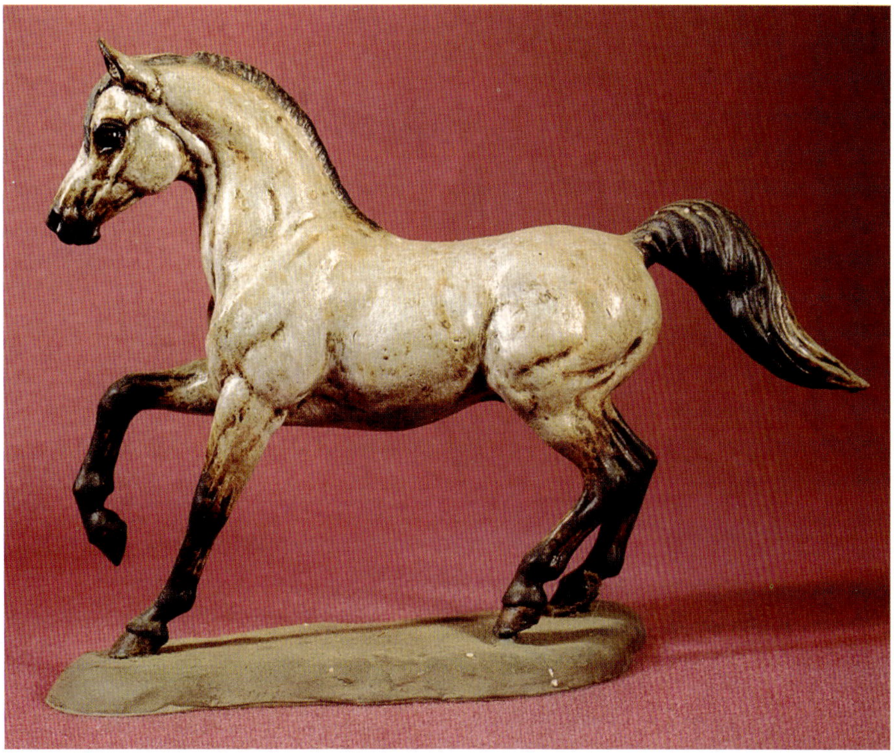

Named "Encore" the Arabian stallion by Hagen-Renaker, they produced this model in glossy bay, dapple-gray, white, and chestnut (see page 124). While the 5.5" factory piece is valued at around $165, this unique artwork has an approximate value of $250-275. Note the appealing, rough texture of the body and the delicate details of the face and legs.

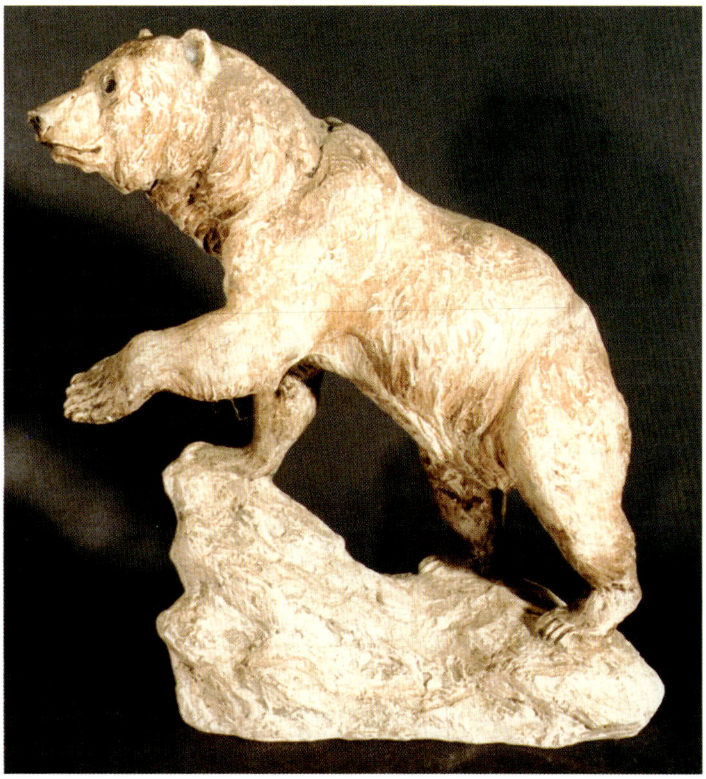

This Grizzly Bear atop his rock ledge was later produced by Hagen-Renaker (see page 114). Standing 7.75" tall, this original sculpture is worth approximately $250-275.

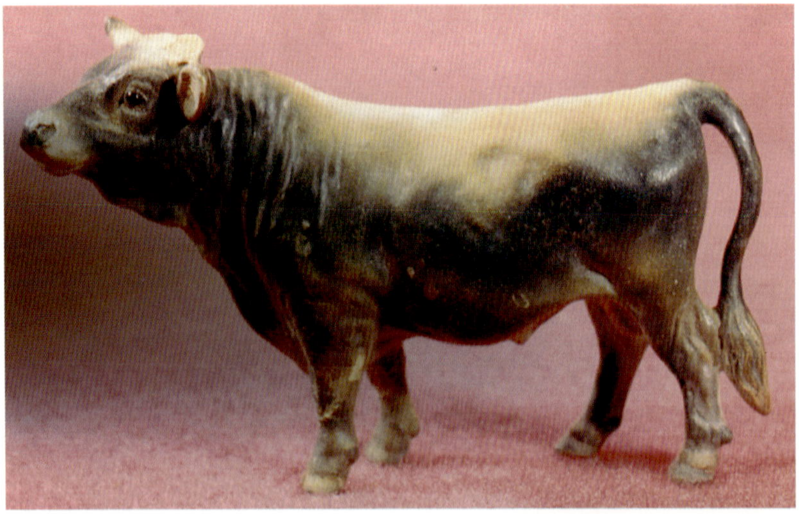

Later produced by Hagen-Renaker in black, light brown, or black spotted, this Jersey bull shows much more detail and delicacy than the factory models. Standing 1.75" tall, the Hagen-Renaker models are worth about $15-25 while this unique bull is worth approximately $40-55.

Accurate models result from detailed sketches. It is interesting to see how closely the finished model of the Jersey bull resembles this sketch. All that appears to be missing is the nose ring.

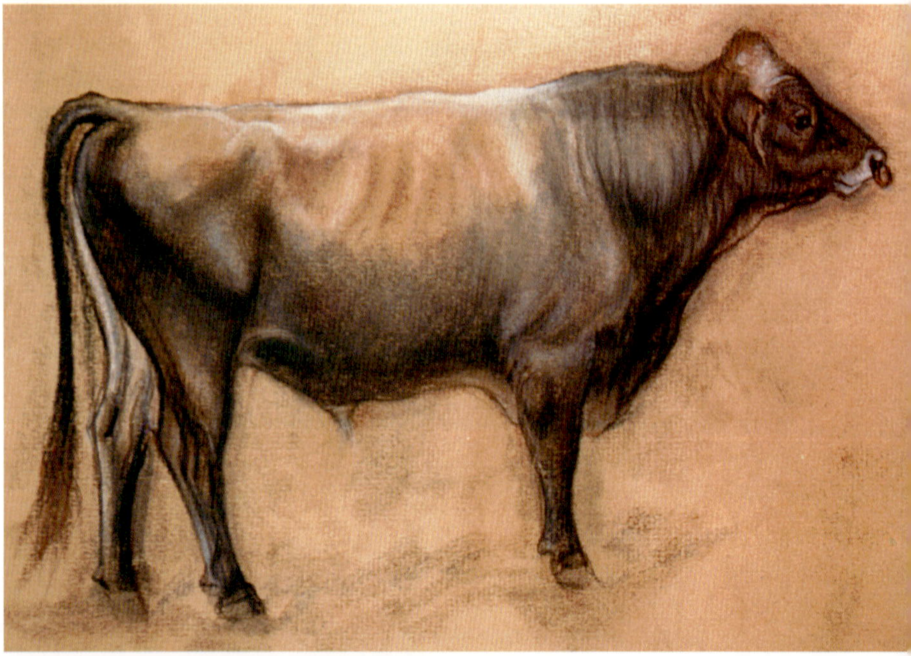

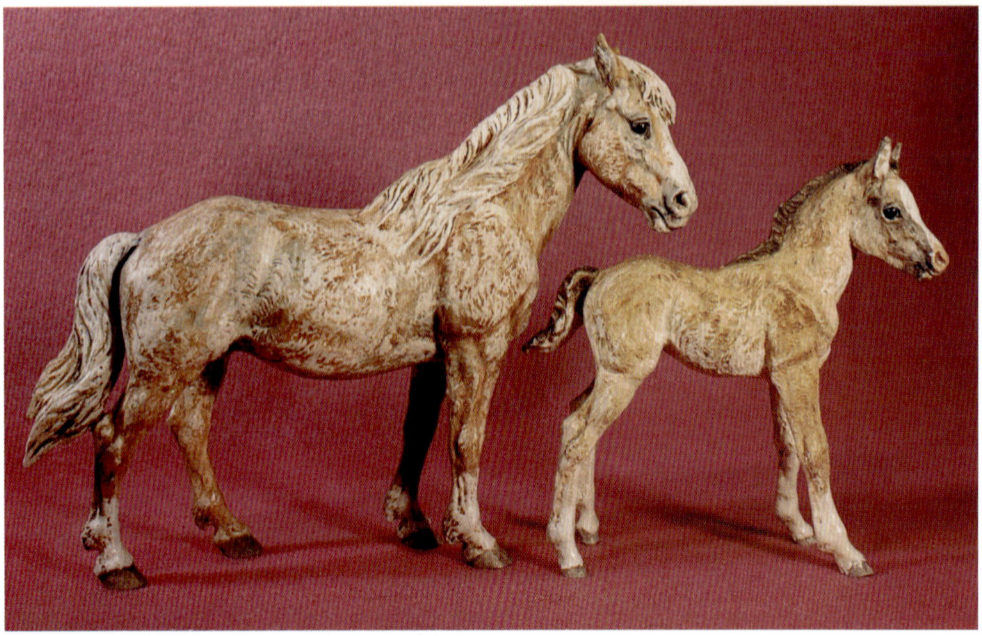

Produced as a Mustang mare and foal named "Daisy" and "Butch" by Hagen-Renaker, this appealing duo measures 6" and 4.6" tall. The texture of their wild coats cannot be duplicated in the factory-produced pieces as it appears here in the original sculptures. The Hagen-Renaker pieces are valued at about $250 and $175, while these original models are worth approximately $325-350 and $225-250 respectively.

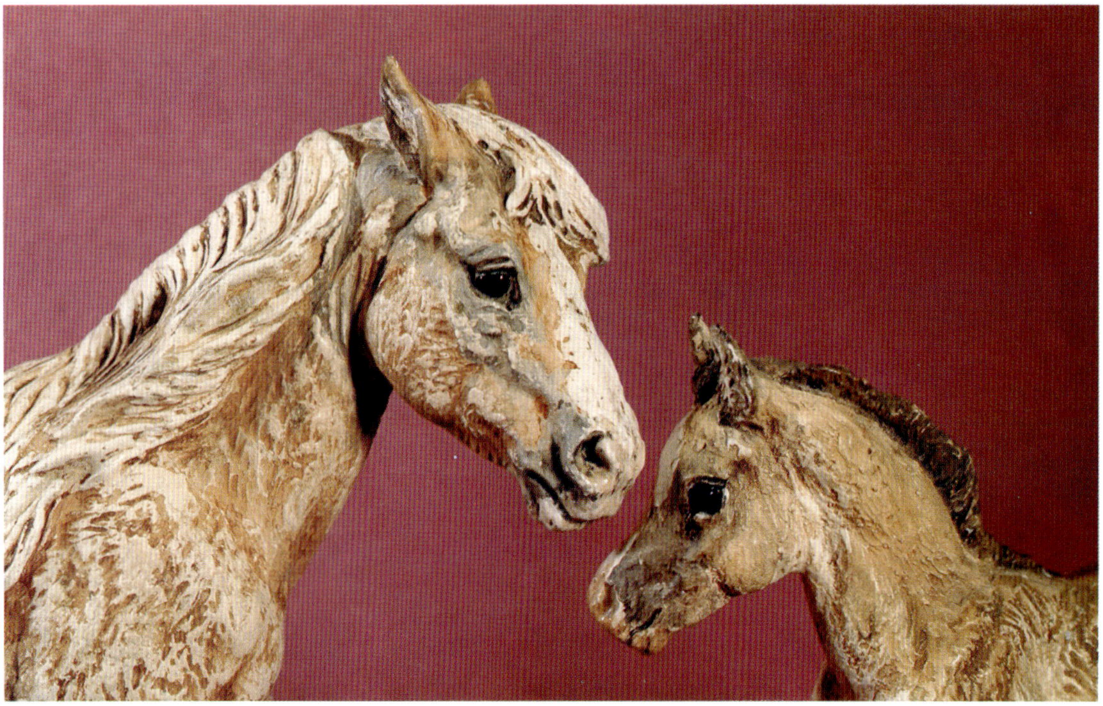

The facial detail and finely defined textures of these original models cannot be reproduced in the factory process. Maureen has instilled unique personalities into every one of her animals, gleaned from watching them interact in their natural environments.

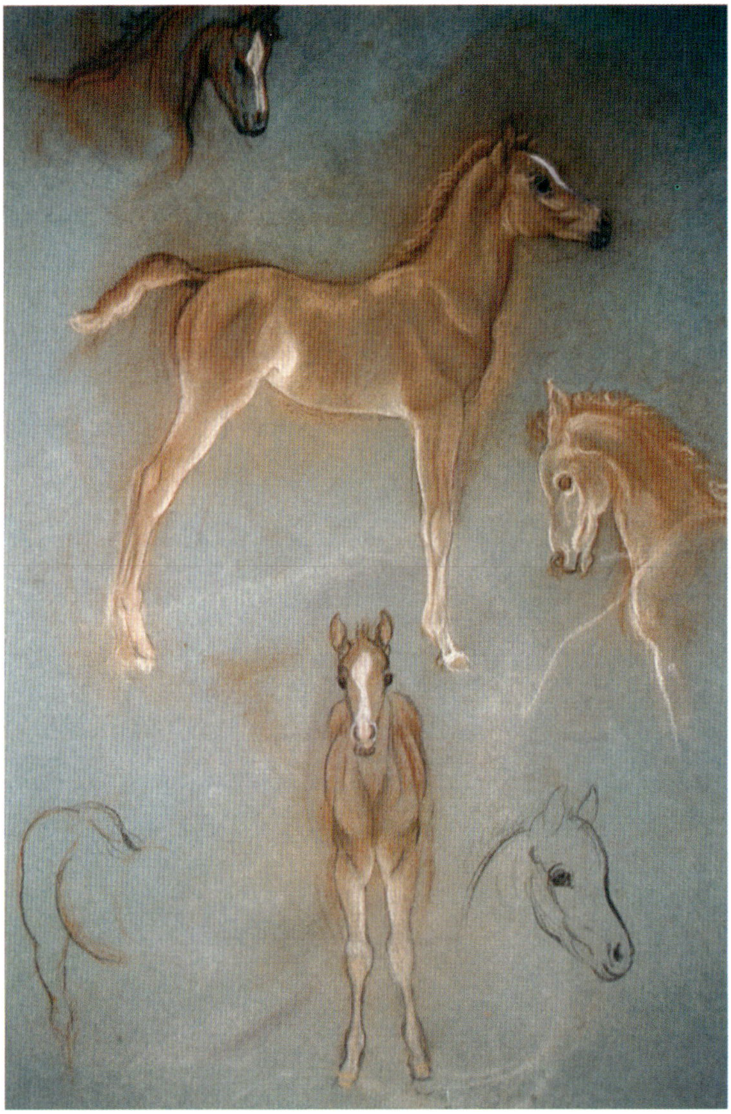

These adorable, playful baby sketches resulted in the adorable Mustang foal.

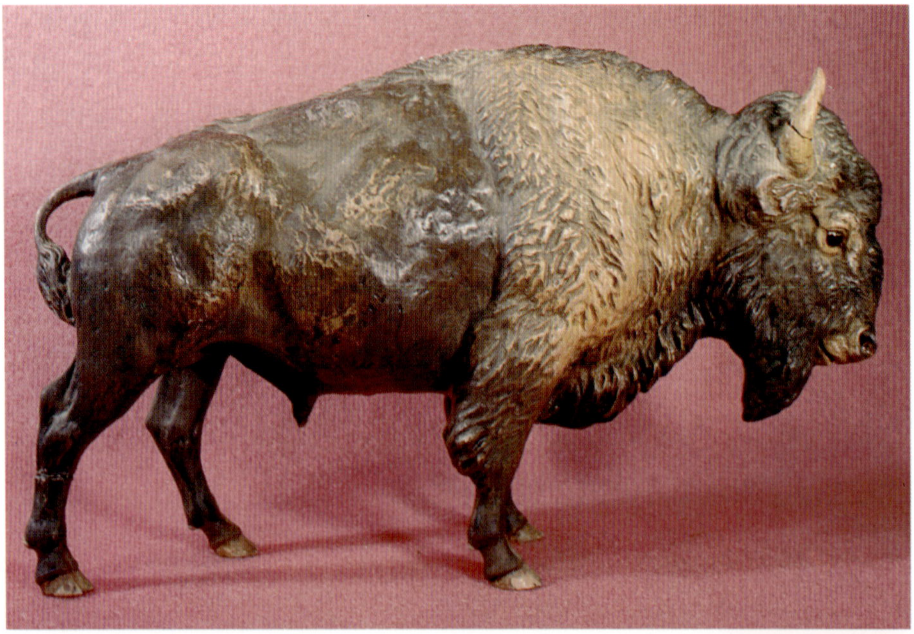

This majestic Bison stands 5.75" tall and has the appearance of a bronze statue rather than ceramic. Hagen-Renaker later produced it in the Designers Workshop line in tan and dark brown, but some of the fur and facial details were lost. The Hagen-Renaker pieces are valued at about $150, while this unique Bison is worth approximately $250-275.

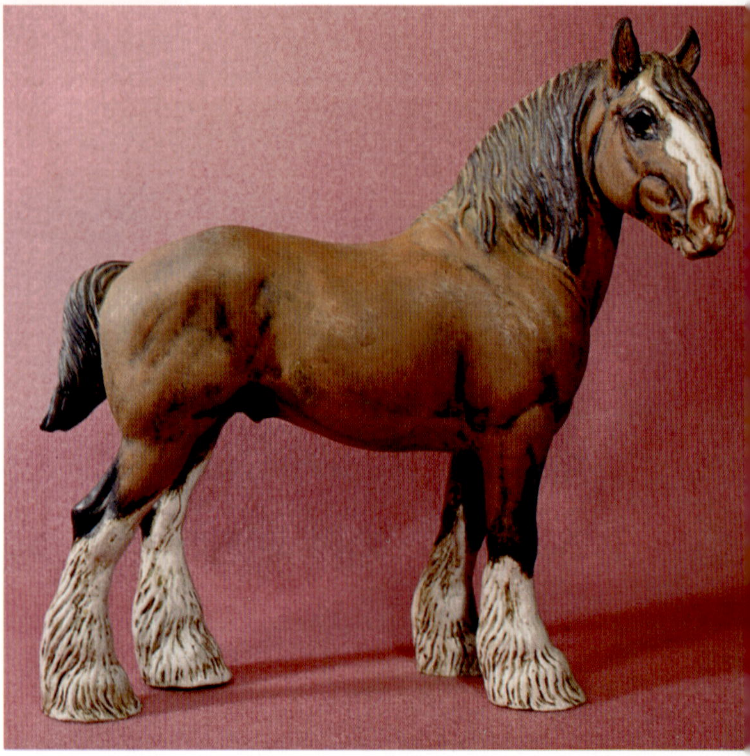

Based on a California Clydesdale named "Benny," this original model stands 7.75" tall. Hagen-Renaker later issued this horse in the 1980s, slightly smaller and with less detail in the legs and face. The Hagen-Renaker version is worth about $225, while this stunning original sculpture is worth approximately $325-350.

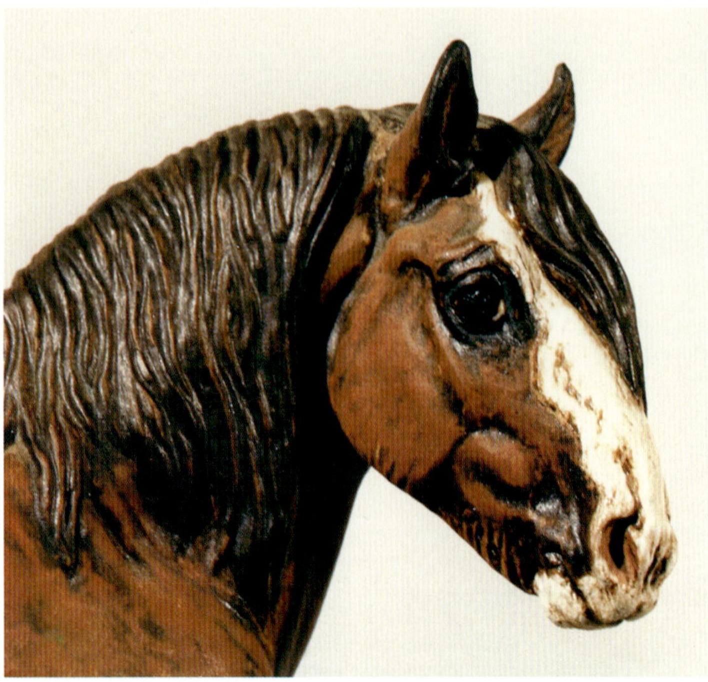

This close up photograph of the face of the Clydesdale highlights the lifelike details of this horse, including the wrinkles in the lips and the long fur under the chin.

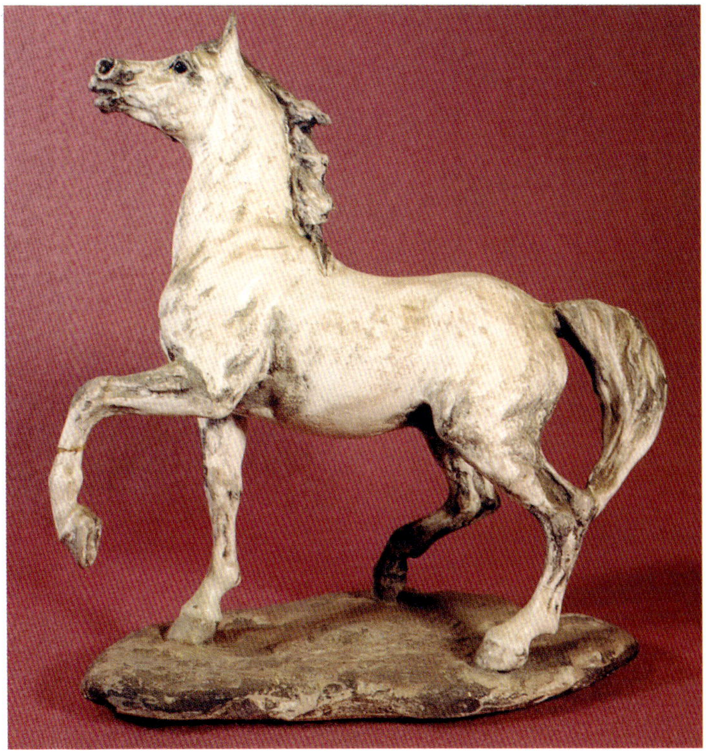

A 6.5" spirited, prancing Arabian stallion with head held high makes a lively sculpture. Hagen-Renaker later adapted this model, calling it the "Turning Arabian." It was produced in white and chestnut at the factory, but the detail of this original piece is unmistakable. The Hagen-Renaker horse is valued at $300, while this unique model is worth approximately $400-425.

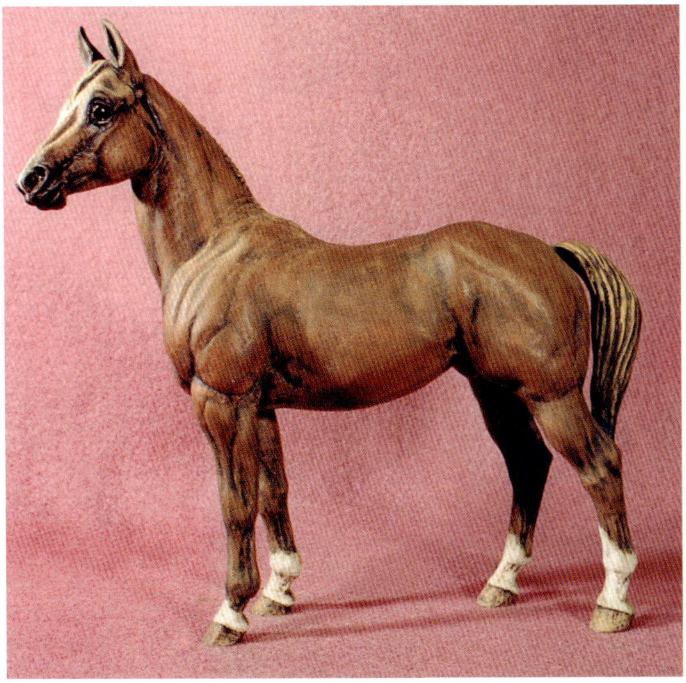

A Quarter Horse mare named "Cocoa Silk" was the subject for this equine model. Standing 7.5" tall, the rough appearance of the stoneware ceramic provides a suitable texture for her fur. Hagen-Renaker later produced this model as the Quarter Horse mare, unnamed, in bay, gray, chestnut, and Appaloosa. The value of the Hagen-Renaker model is about $175, while this original figure is worth approximately $300-325.

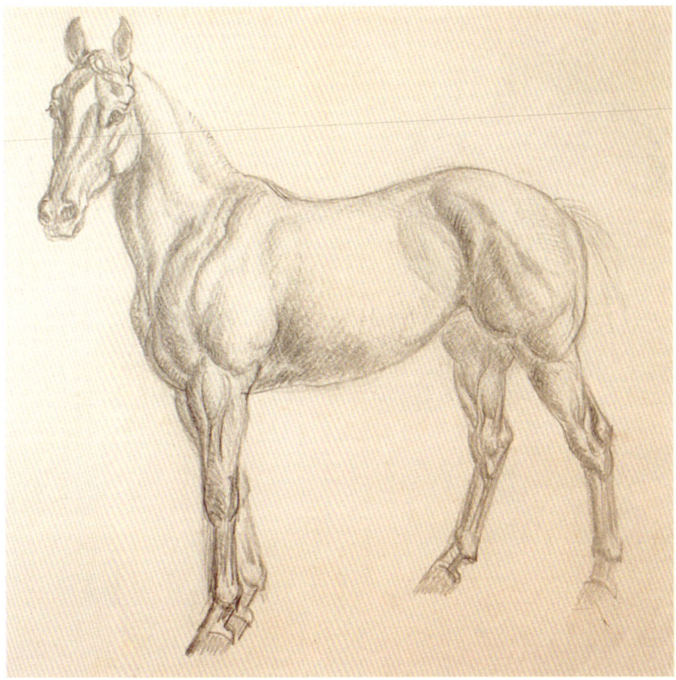

This sketch helped in the creation of the model of the Quarter Horse mare "Cocoa Silk."

The stoneware ceramic material simulates the skin of an iguana very accurately. Complete with desert flowers, this iguana measures 2.5" tall. Hagen-Renaker later produced this model in a glossy glaze. That factory-produced piece has a value of $25. This original artwork is worth approximately $60-75.

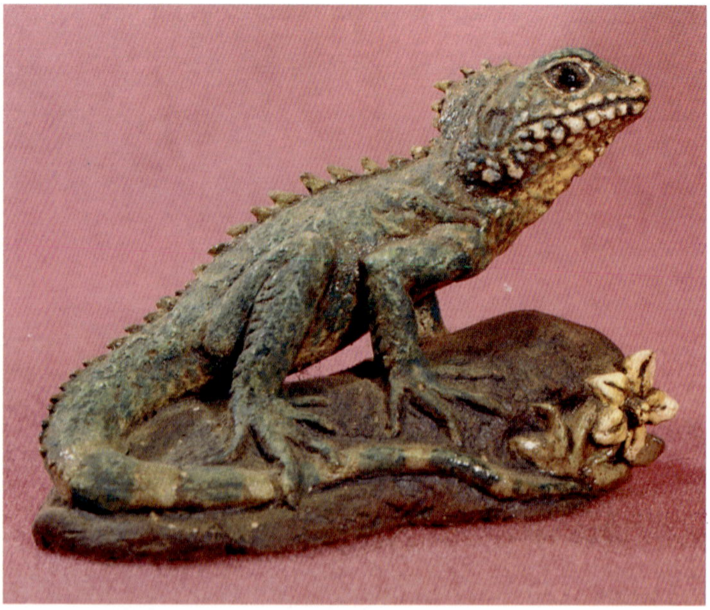

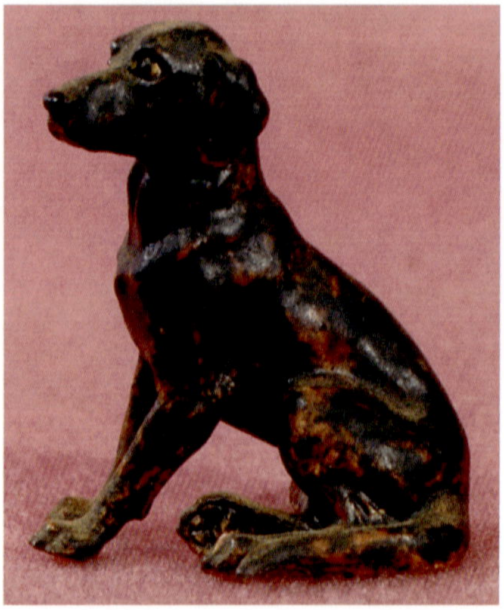

This black Labrador Retriever is a portrait of "Mia," a dog Maureen used to own. Maureen remembers her as the best-behaved dog she ever had, and she would walk her without a leash everywhere they went. She refers to her as a "volunteer dog," as the dog voluntarily came home with Maureen one day and just stayed. Hagen-Renaker produced this model in their Miniatures line in both black and golden tan, and it can be seen on page 109. This original sculpture, sitting 1.75" tall, has an approximate value of $35-50.

The rough texture of these figures seems to appropriately portray the spirit of the west. The cutting horse is missing the tips of his ears and the steer his left horn tip, but otherwise everything is in place and very detailed. The horse and rider are 8.5" tall, and the steer is 3.5" tall. The Hagen-Renaker version of these models can be seen on page 96. This original horse and rider is worth approximately $400-450 and the steer approximately $110-130.

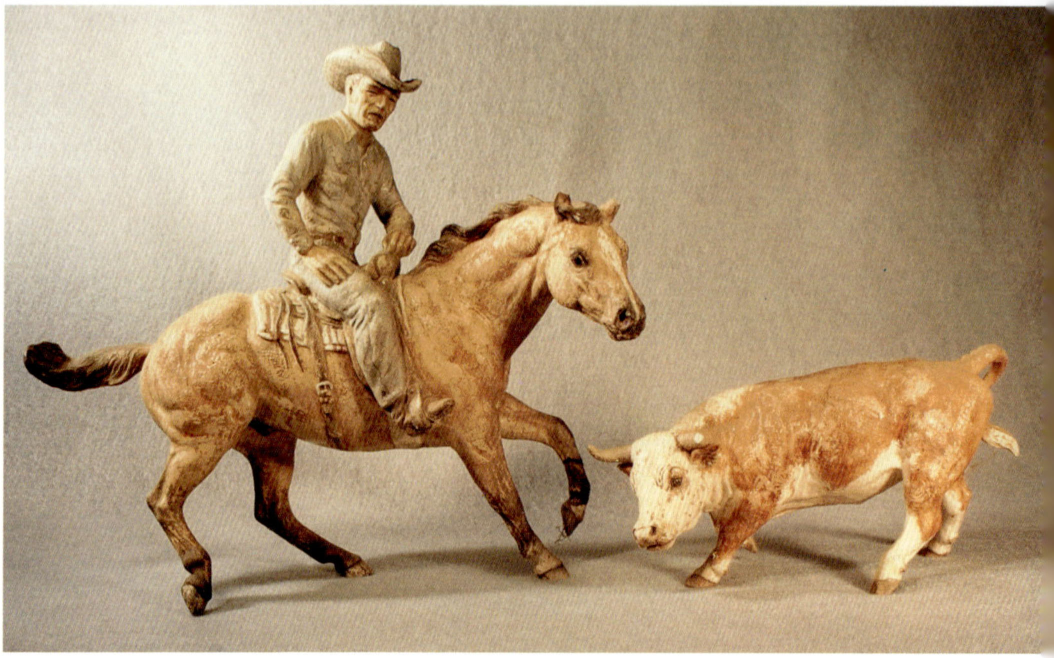

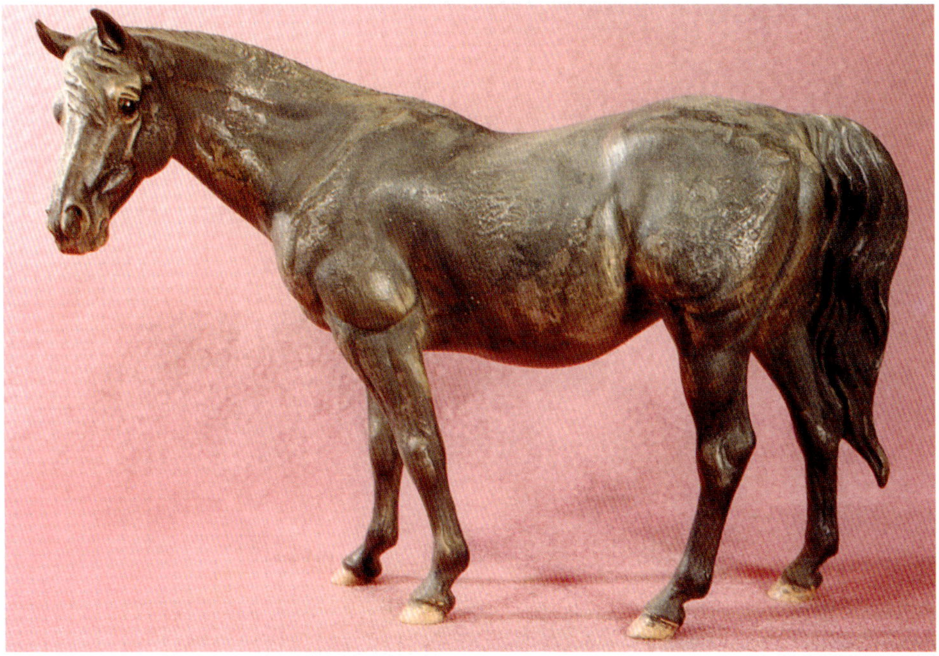

This gentle-looking horse is a sweet Morgan mare. She stands 5" tall, and was later produced as "Forever Amber" by Hagen-Renaker. That model can be seen on page 106. This original sculpture is worth approximately $200-225.

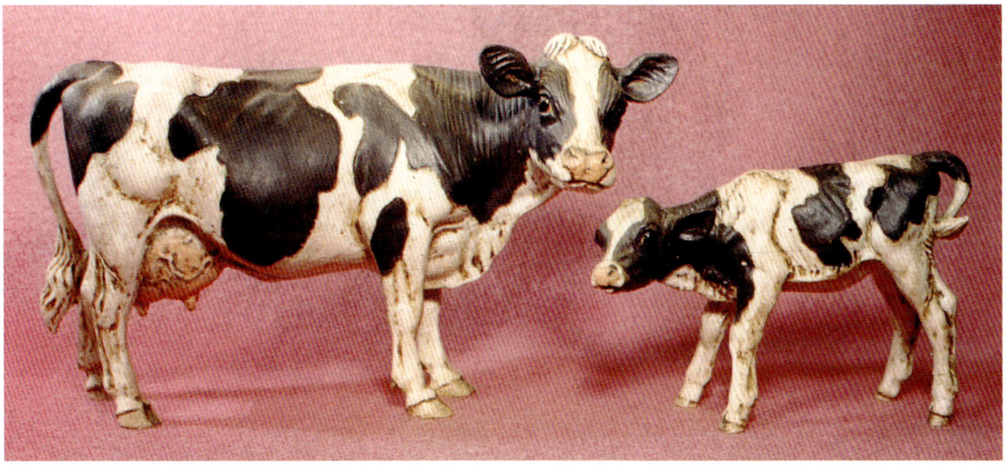

The Holstein cow and calf were designed using the 4-H judging standards manual, according to Jim Renaker. The cow stands 5" tall and the calf is 3.25" tall. Hagen-Renaker later produced them in the Designers Workshop line, but without the intricate detail in the tail hair, utter, and faces. The Hagen-Renaker pieces are valued at about $75 and $40, while these original models are worth approximately $200-225 and $75-100 respectively.

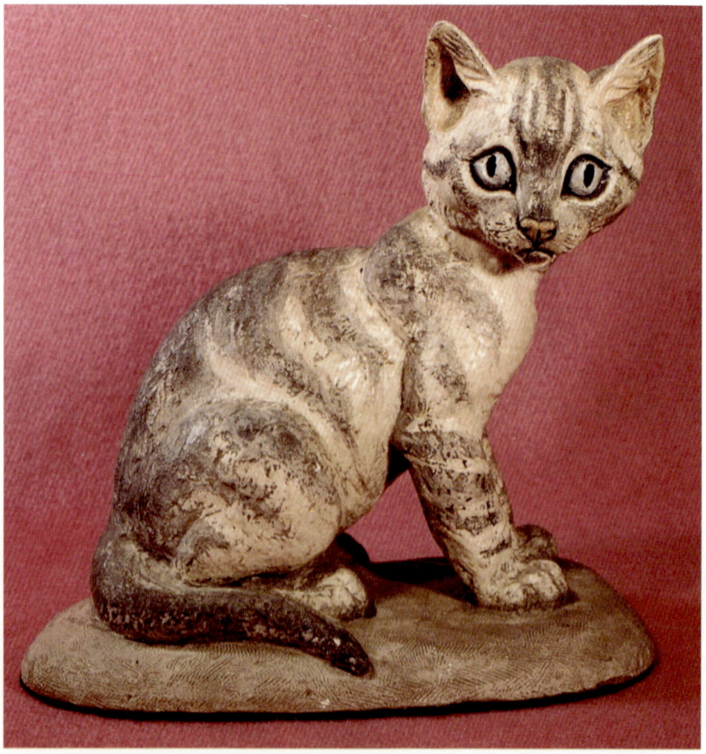

Maureen produced this cat in a few variations, both on and off the base. This one is 6" tall.

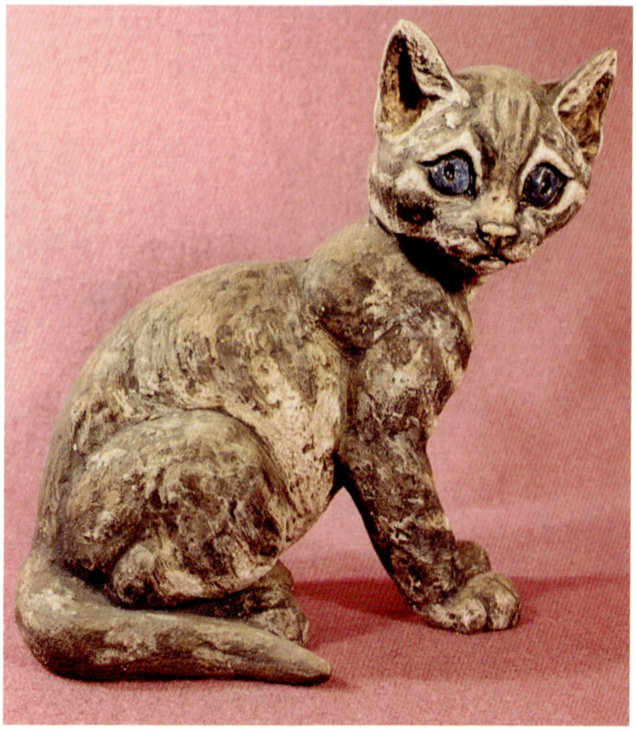

This version has slightly different coloring, and is not mounted on a base. It was later produced by Hagen-Renaker. The factory piece has a value of about $50, while this original artwork has an approximate value of $100-125.

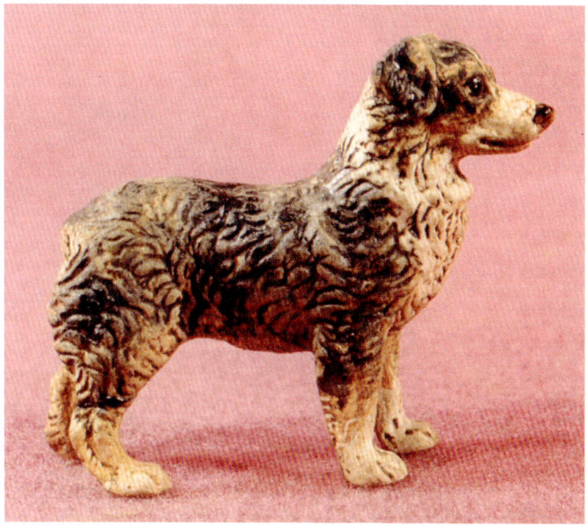

With lots of fuzzy fur, this Australian Shepherd stands 1.75" tall. Hagen-Renaker later had to tame his fur in order to produce him, as seen on page 108. Maureen's original model is worth approximately $30-45.

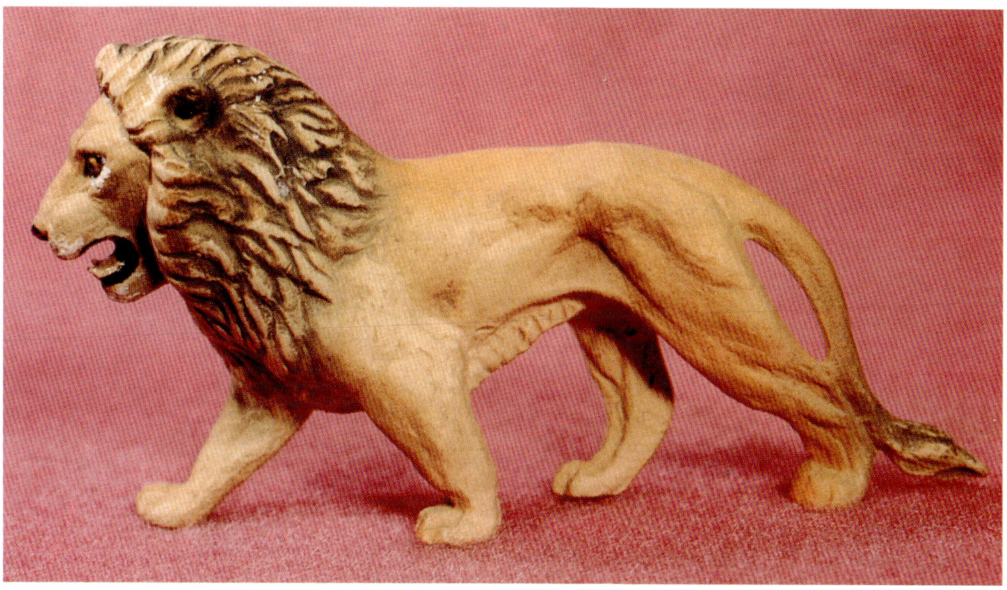

Maureen has captured interesting texture and detail in the mane, tail, and face of this walking lion. Standing 1.8" tall, he was later produced in the Hagen-Renaker Specialty line. The factory piece is worth about $20, while this life-like artwork is worth approximately $35-50.

The mule "Big Red Loretta" served as the subject for this model. Hagen-Renaker later produced this mule in the 1980s, and it has an approximate value of $200. Standing 7" tall, this incredible original piece has an approximate value of $325-350.

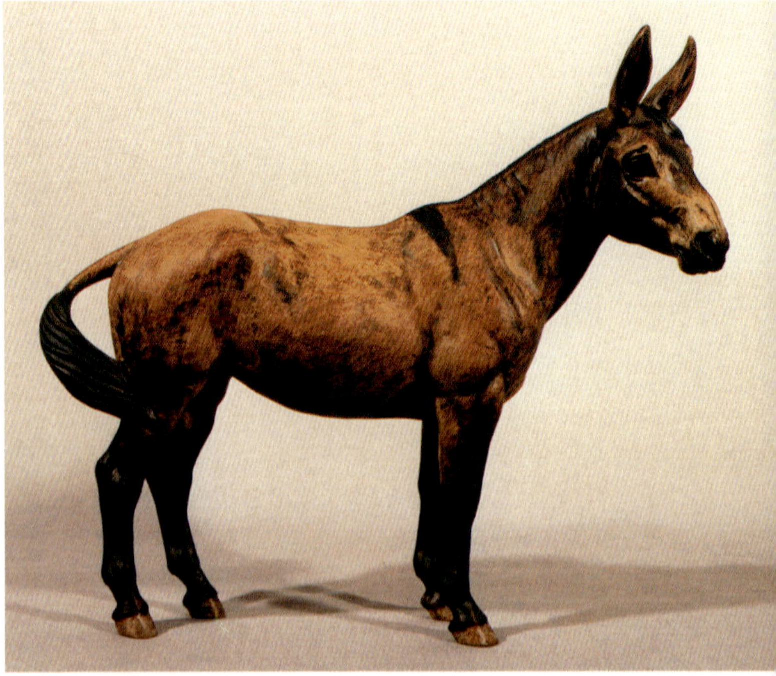

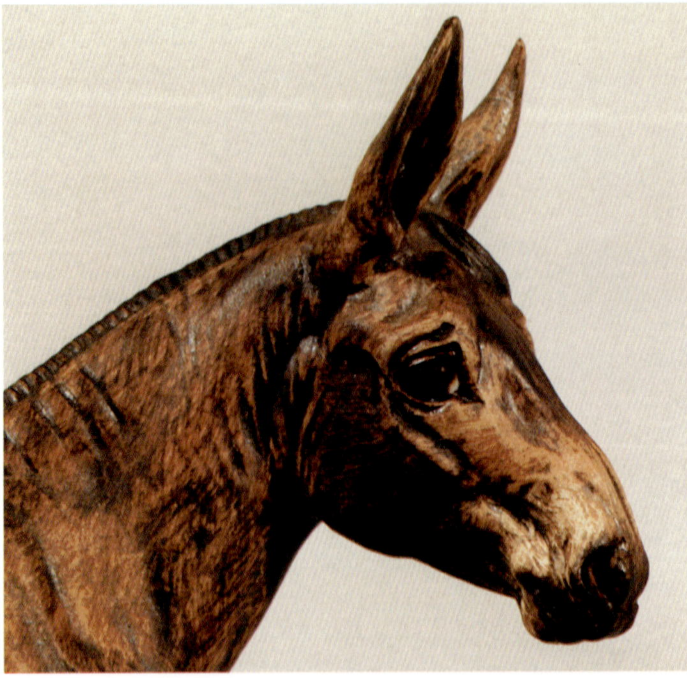

This close up view of the head of the mule shows the personality, texture, and detail of this amazing model.

In this sketch of the mule, the name "Loretta" appears in the lower left corner. The model turned out very close to the appearance of the sketch.

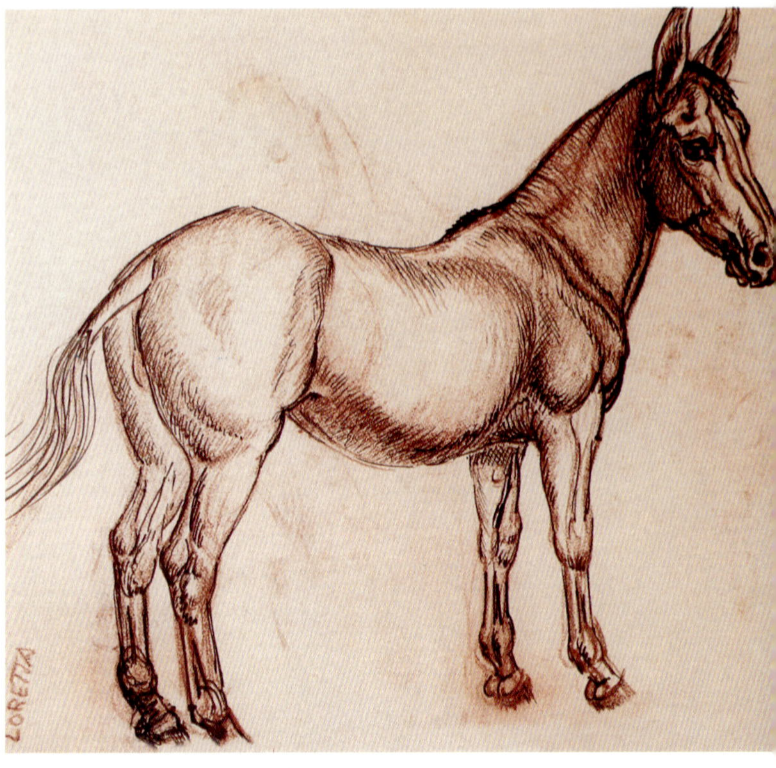

The final grouping in this chapter shows some sketches from Maureen's many sketchbooks along with the resulting animals that were produced by Hagen-Renaker. Comparing the original sketch to the final model gives one a sense of appreciation for Maureen's ability as an artist both on the drawing board and in the final, three-dimensional model.

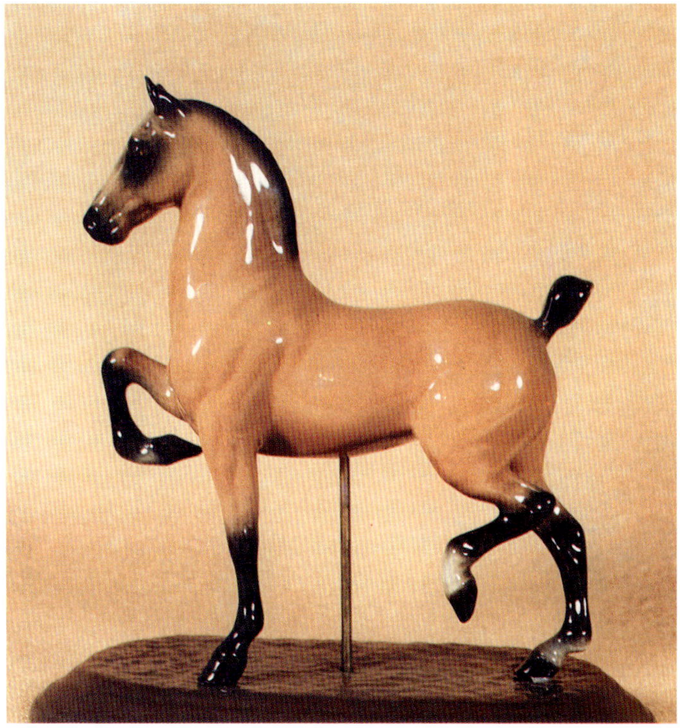

This Hackney horse was modeled after the mare "Brookside Stella." This Hagen-Renaker model stands 5.5" tall and has an approximate value of $225-250.

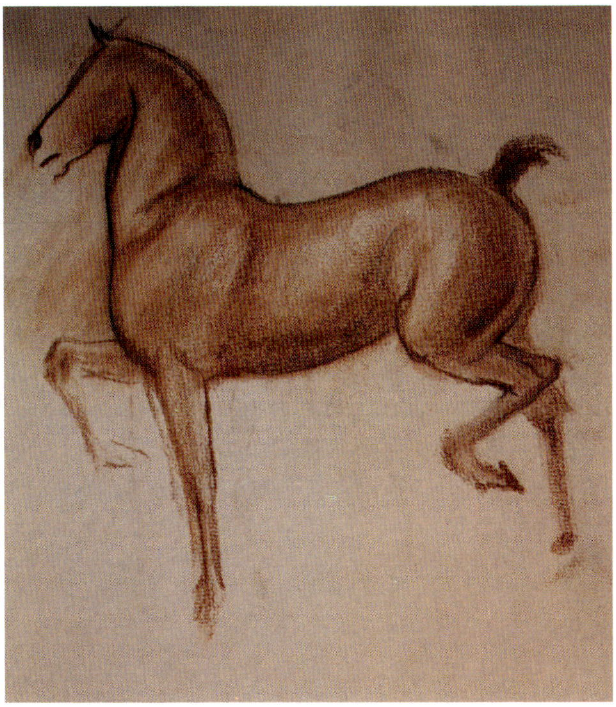

This initial sketch helped develop the model that became the Hackney mare "Brookside Stella."

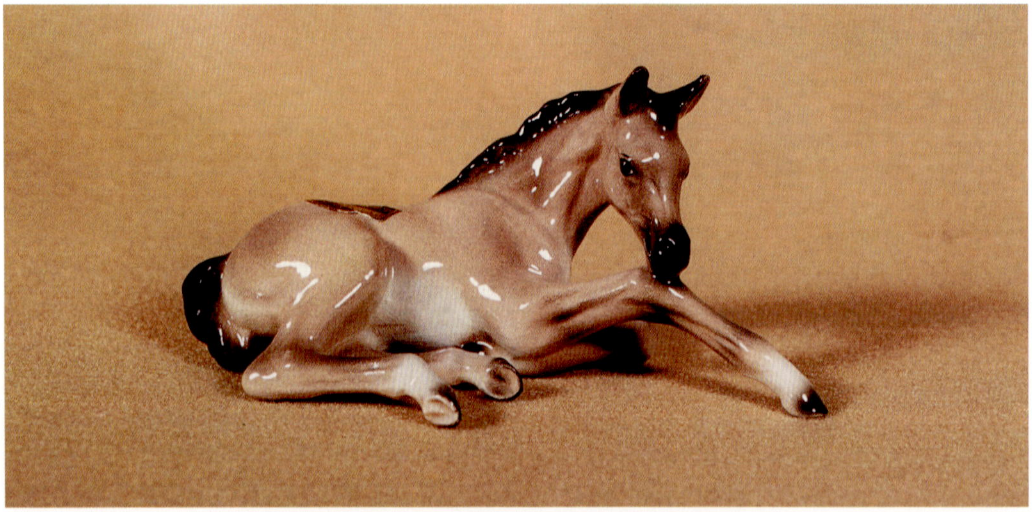

Maureen designed this pretty Morgan foal that Hagen-Renaker produced and called "Clover." There is nice detail around the eyes, and even on the underside of the hooves. It is 2.5" tall, was made in brown, palomino, and white, and has an approximate value of $125-150.

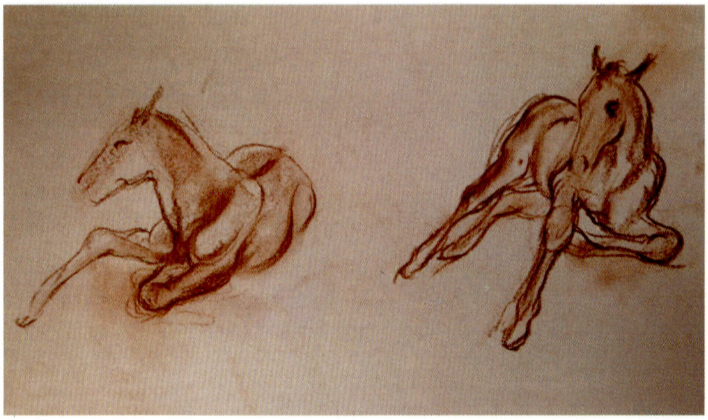

Maureen would sketch her subjects from many views before attempting to create a three-dimensional model. Here are sketches that served as the inspiration for the Morgan foal "Clover."

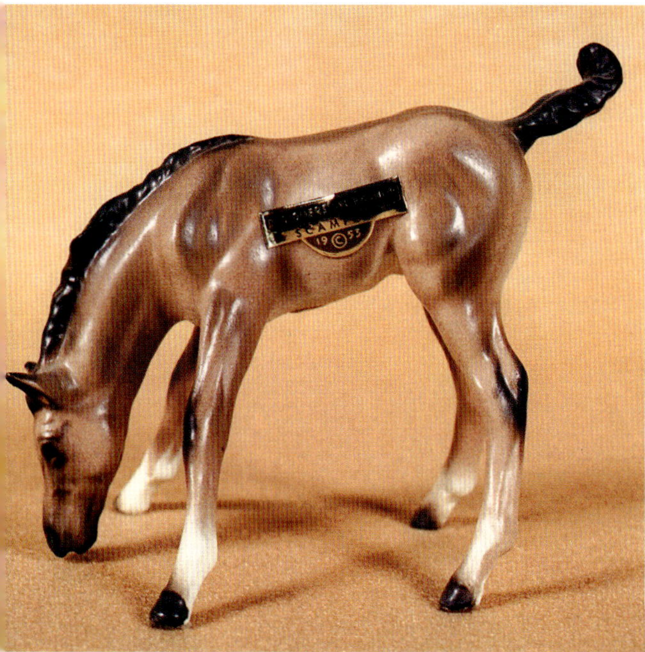

This Hagen-Renaker Morgan foal named "Scamper" wears its identifying foil sticker. Standing 3" tall, this foal was produced by the factory in brown, palomino, and white. It has an approximate value of $125-150.

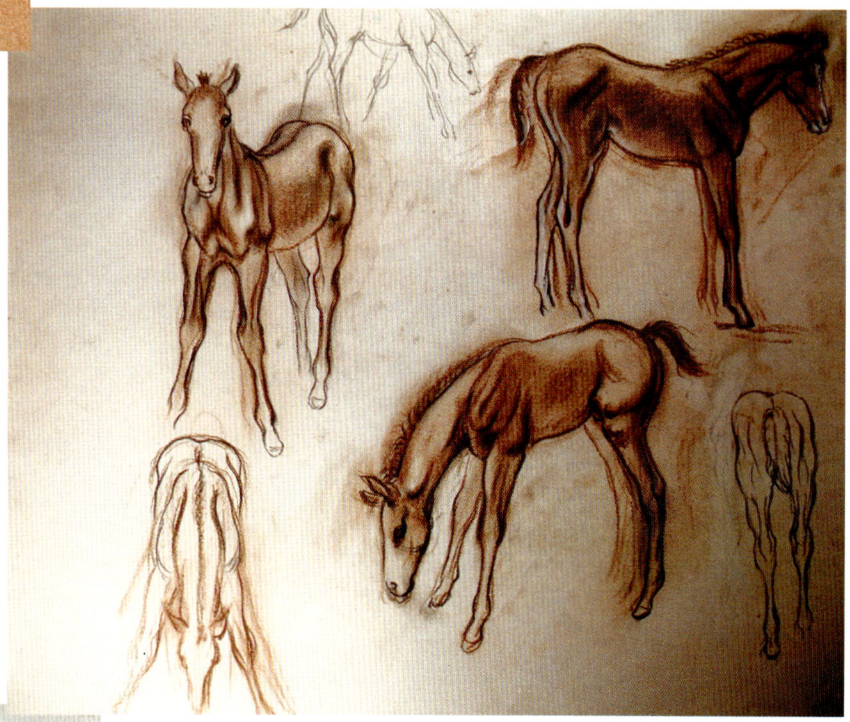

Maureen stood in the fields and pastures for hours, sketching the horses and foals while they moved through several potential poses.

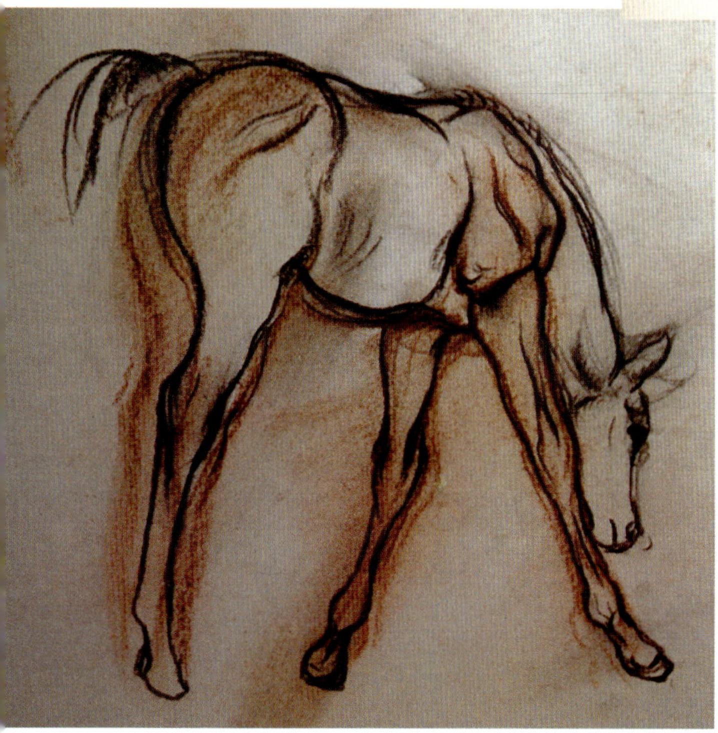

The more positions she was able to sketch, the better the model. Even this unusual view is helpful.

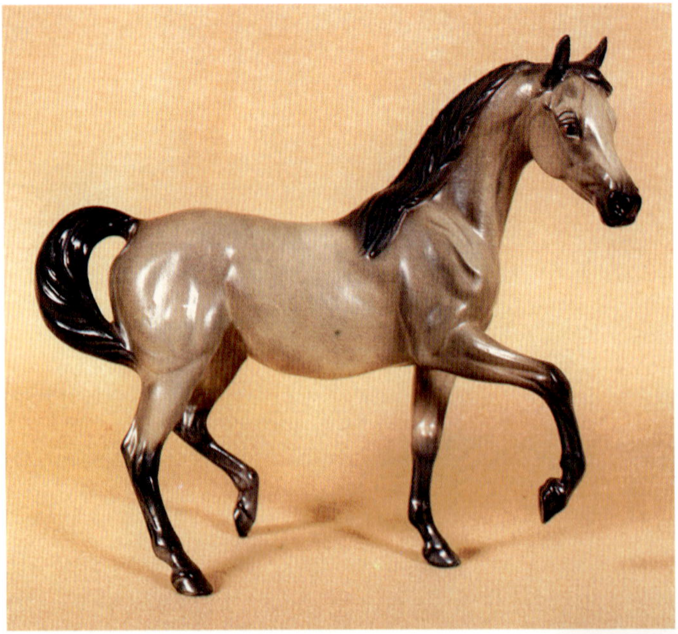

Hagen-Renaker named this Arabian mare "Sheba" and produced her in gray and in white. She stands 7" tall and has an approximate value of $250-300.

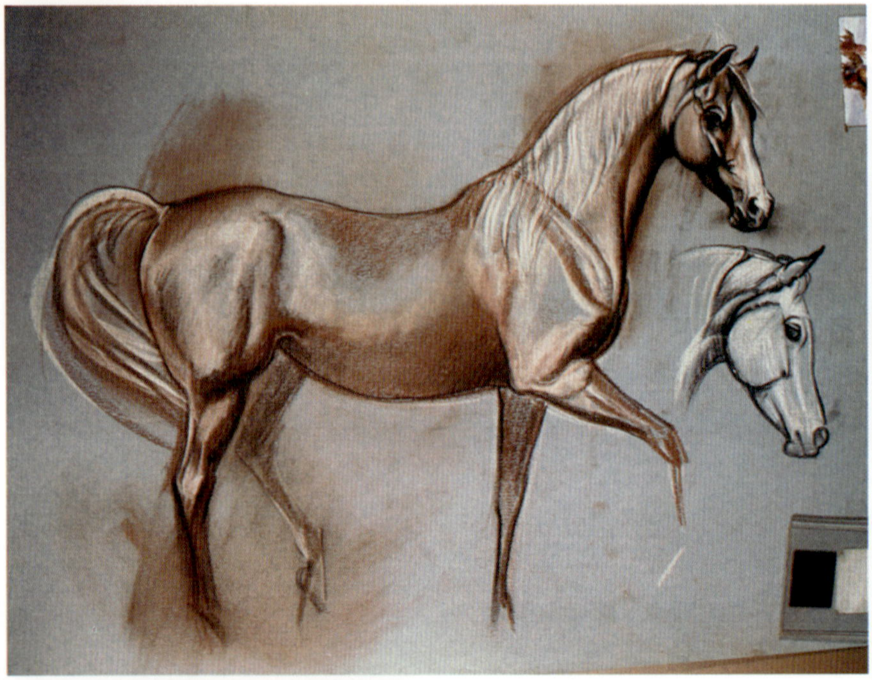

This sketch of the Arabian mare named "Sheba" is a good study in forward motion and flow.

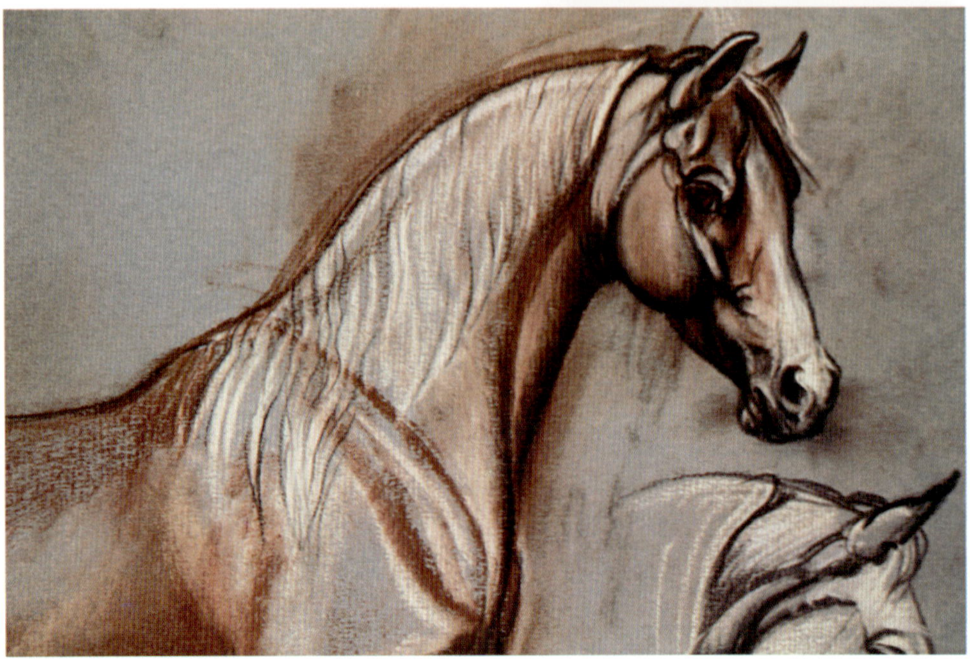

Maureen has a special touch for capturing the kind, gentle nature of horses on paper and in ceramic.

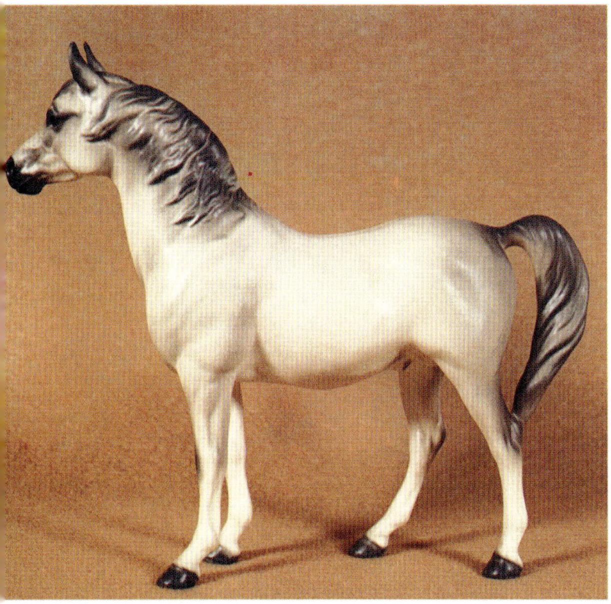

Standing 6" tall, this Arabian stallion was designed by Maureen. He was produced by Hagen-Renaker and named "Abdullah." He has an approximate value of $250-300

This gorgeous sketch of the white Arabian stallion translated well into the Hagen-Renaker model "Abdullah."

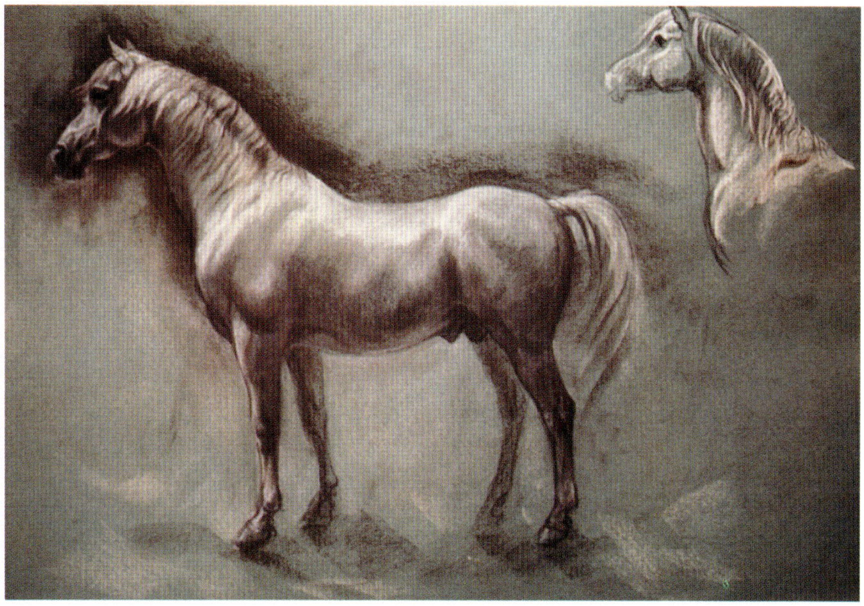

Hagen-Renaker also produced the Arabian stallion "Abdullah" in this attractive chestnut color.

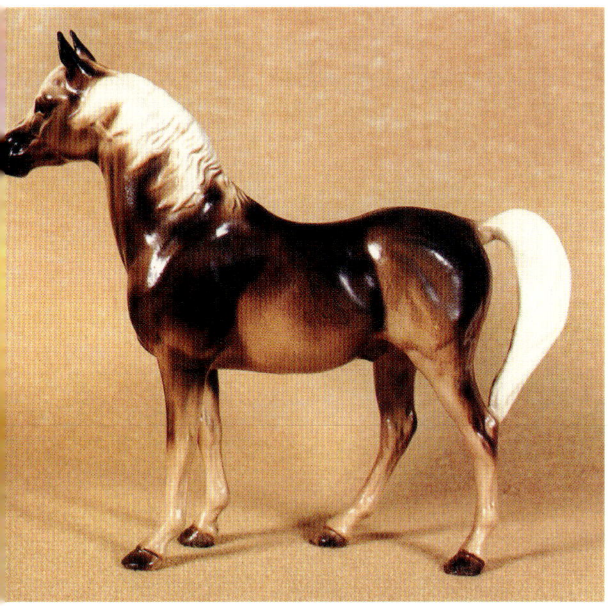

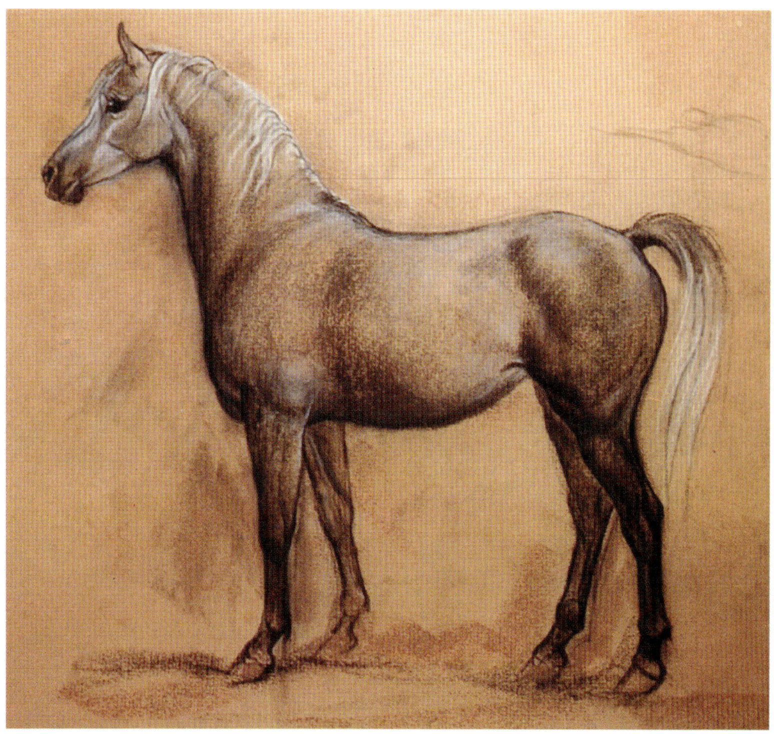

The designer usually does not have input into the production color of a piece, but since Maureen sketched this Arabian stallion as a rich chestnut, it may have had some influence on the factory decisions.

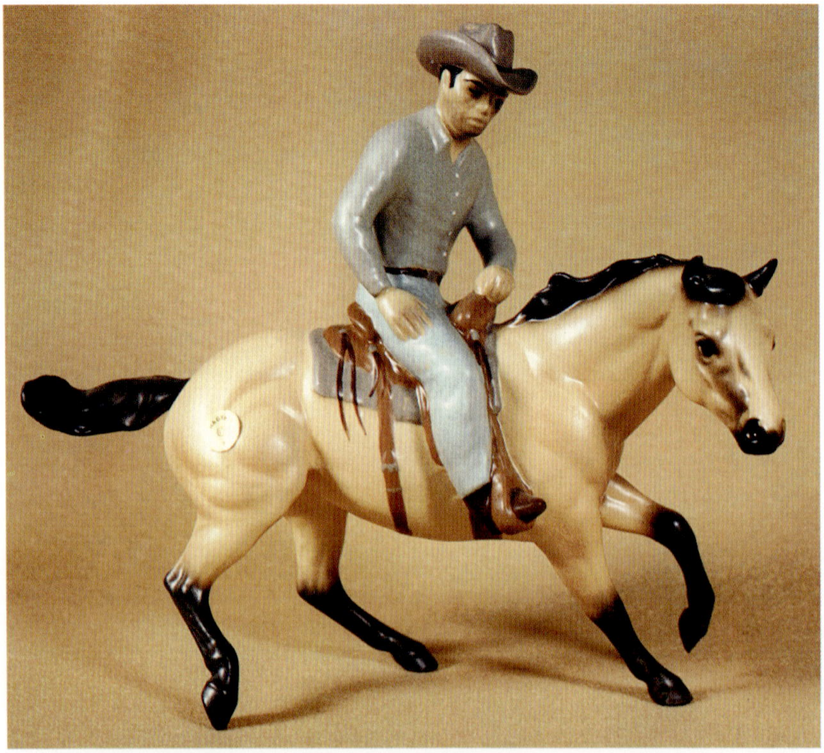

This beautifully detailed cutting horse and rider are 8.5" tall and were produced in buckskin, chestnut, and black by Hagen-Renaker. The approximate value for this piece is $250-275.

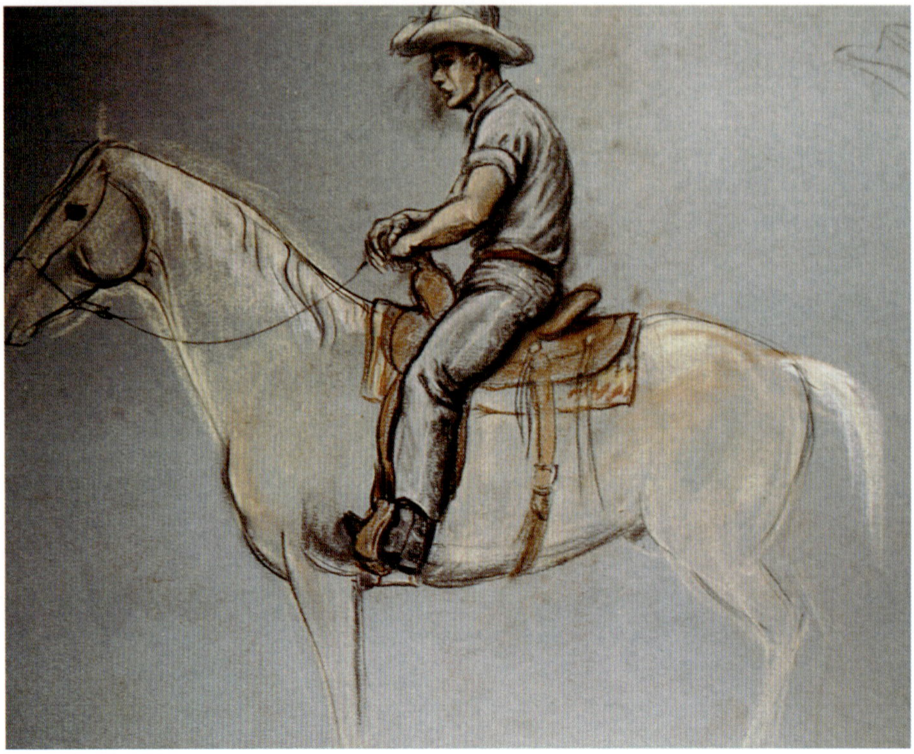

While working on the cutting horse and rider model, Maureen had to study the rider's clothing and the saddle equipment to make an accurate piece.

Hagen-Renaker produced this American Saddlebred horse in brown, palomino (shown) and white. It stands 6.75" tall and has an approximate value of $135-150.

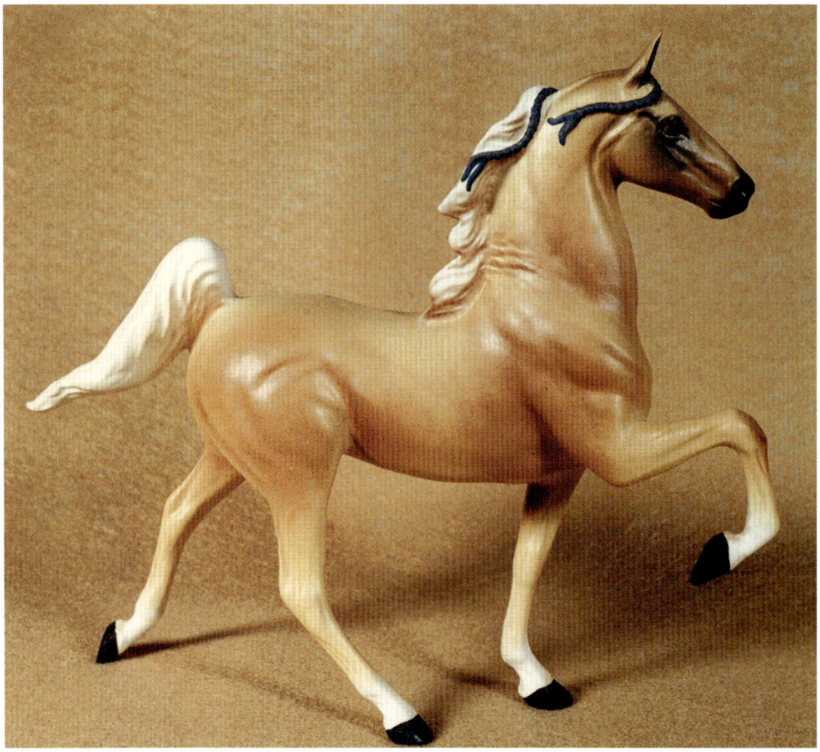

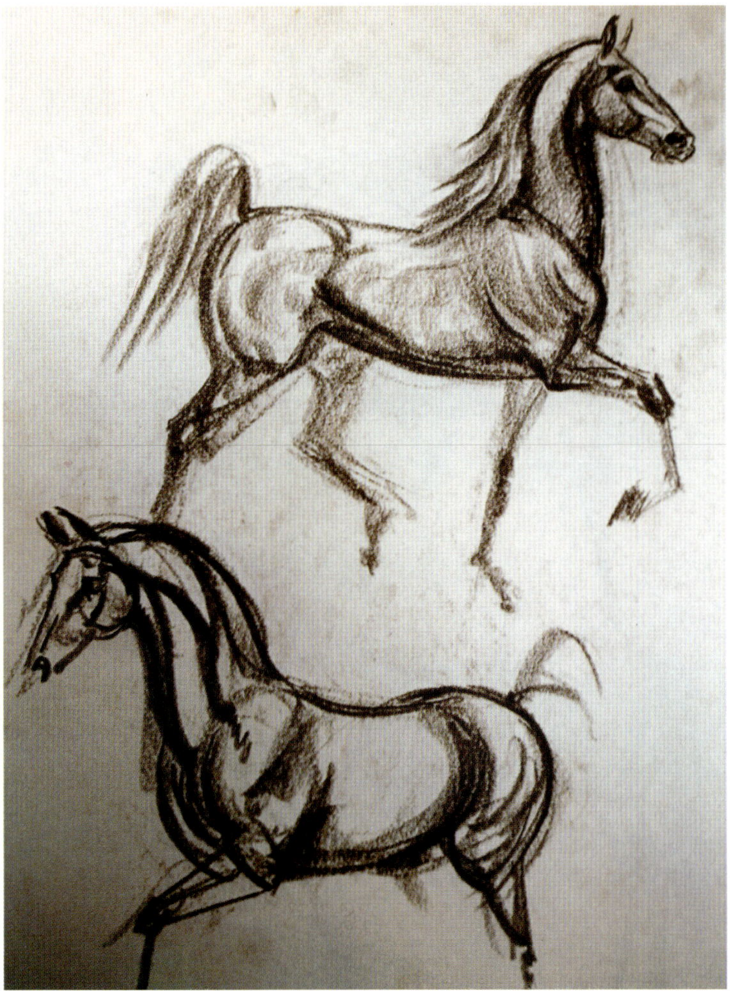

Sometimes the reality of making models has to overcome the beauty of real life. These sketches show the American Saddlebred standing on two hooves, with two in the air. To make a model that would stand without a base required putting at least three of the horse's hooves down.

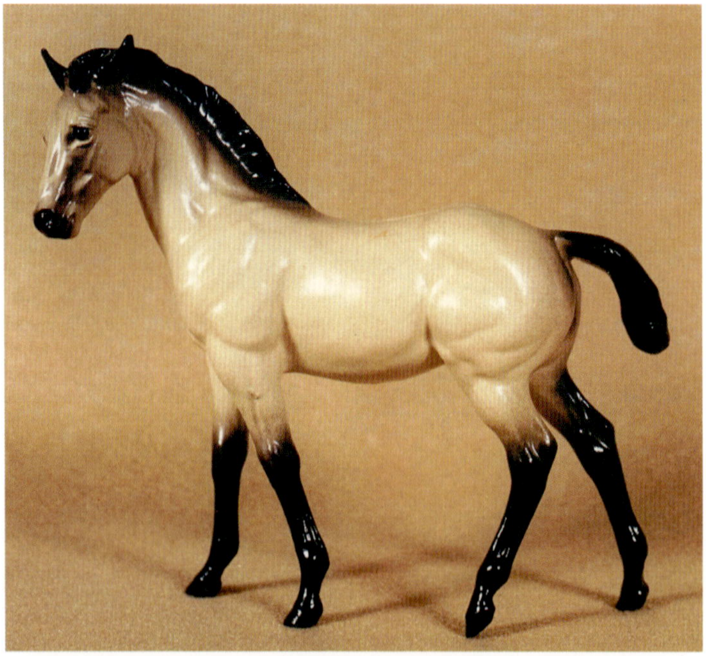

Named "Shamrock" by Hagen-Renaker, this Quarter Horse foal stands 5" tall, was produced in buckskin (shown), bay and palomino, and has an approximate value of $75-100.

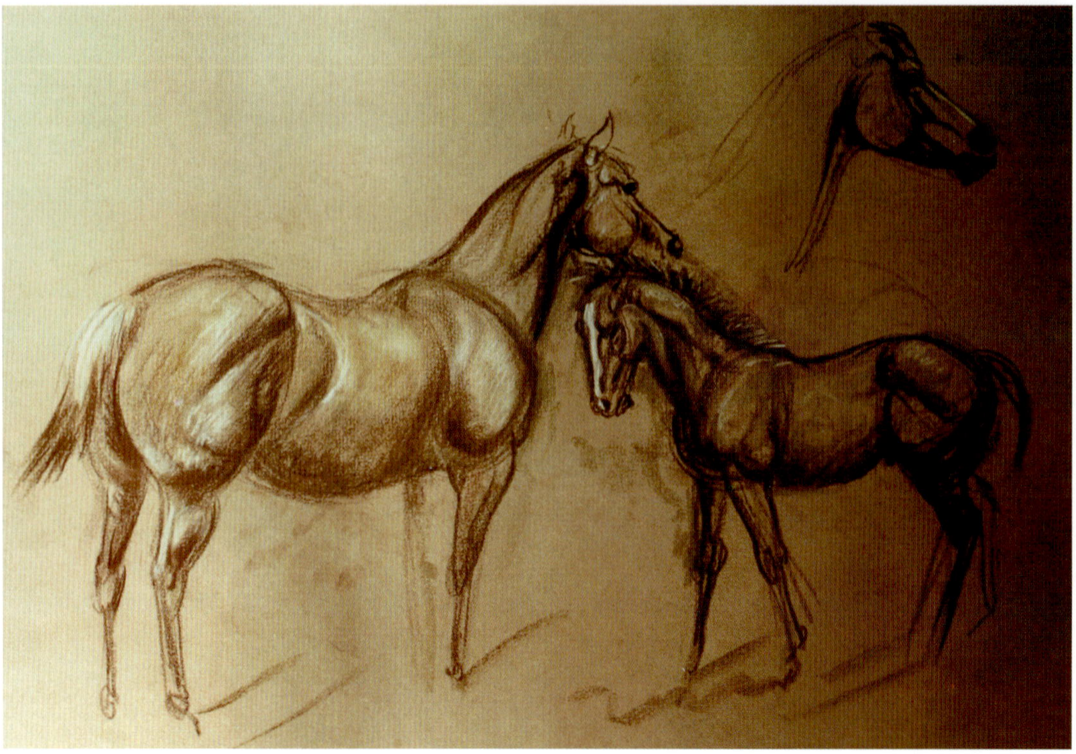

This sketch gave rise to the Quarter Horse foal "Shamrock," and also one of the adult Quarter Horses produced by Hagen-Renaker.

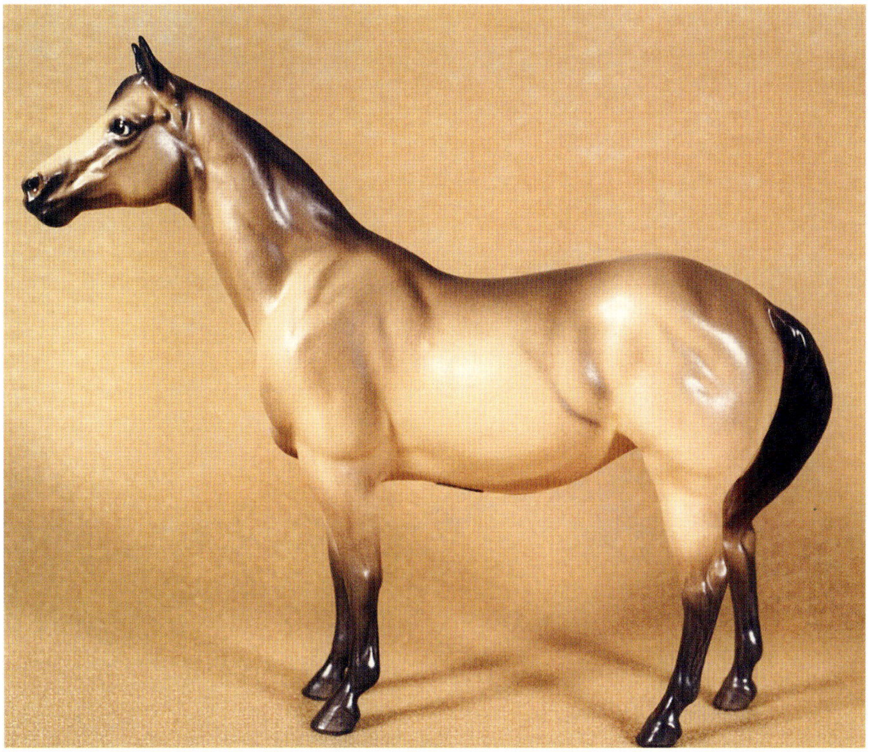

The adult female Quarter Horse produced by Hagen-Renaker was named "Erin." She stands 6" tall, was produced in buckskin (shown), bay, and palomino, and has an approximate value of $125-150.

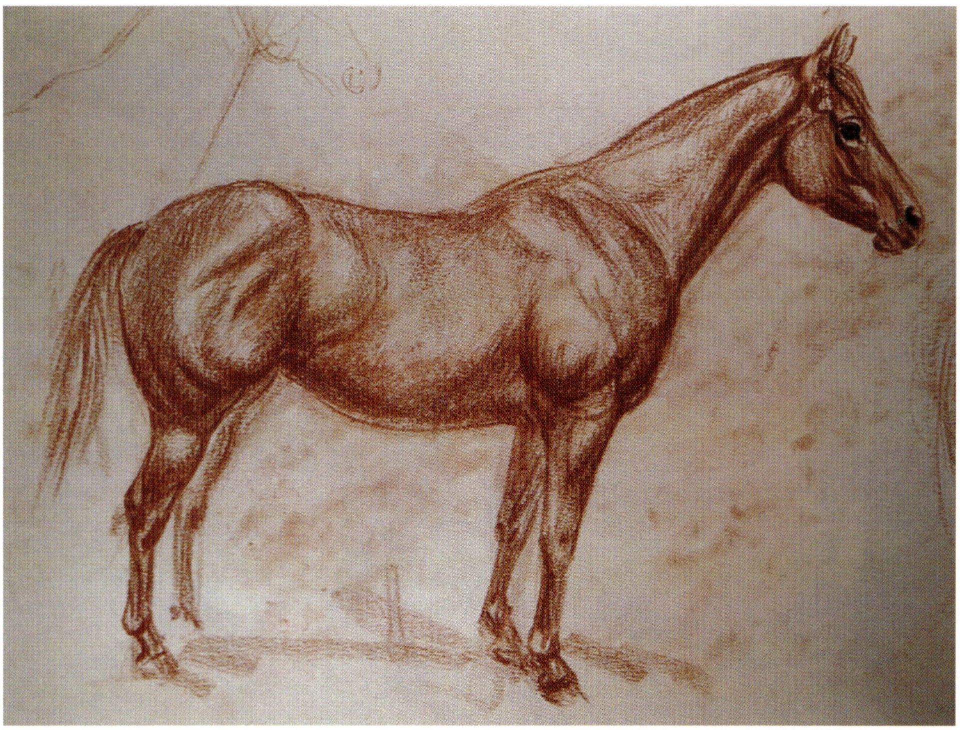

Here is another sketch of an adult Quarter Horse to represent the side view of the muscles, face, and legs.

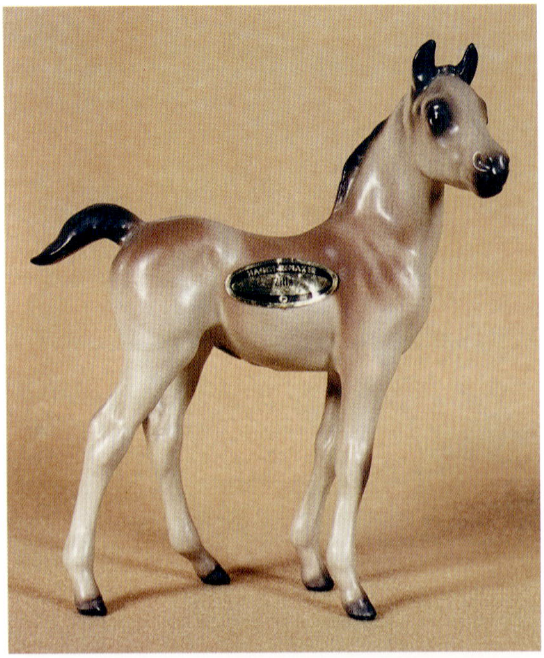

This petite Arabian foal was produced by Hagen-Renaker in this unusual color of rose gray, white, and gray. Note the oval Hagen-Renaker foil sticker. Named "Zilla," she stands 5" tall and has an approximate value of $80-100.

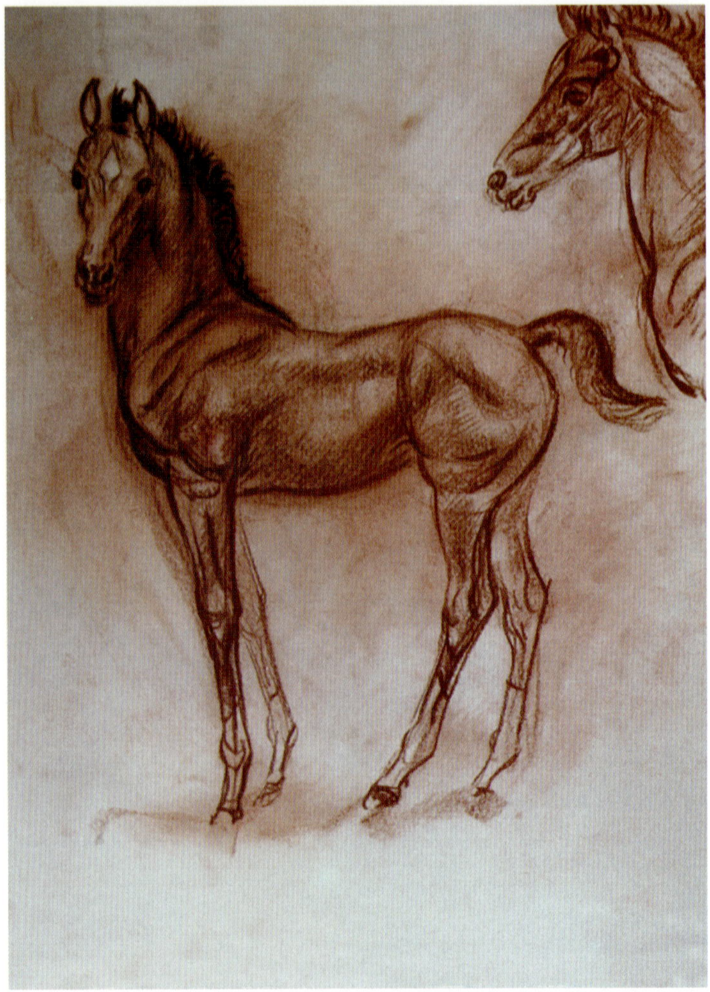

The perky likeness of this sketch translated well into ceramic for the creation of the Arabian foal "Zilla."

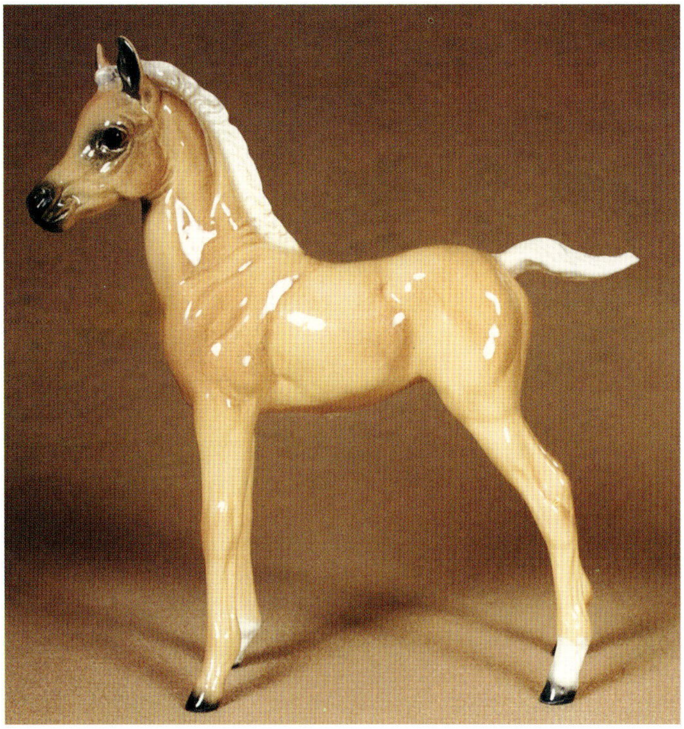

On a larger scale, this 7" Arabian foal was also named "Zilla." Hagen-Renaker released her in palomino (shown), white, and gray. Her approximate value is $125-150.

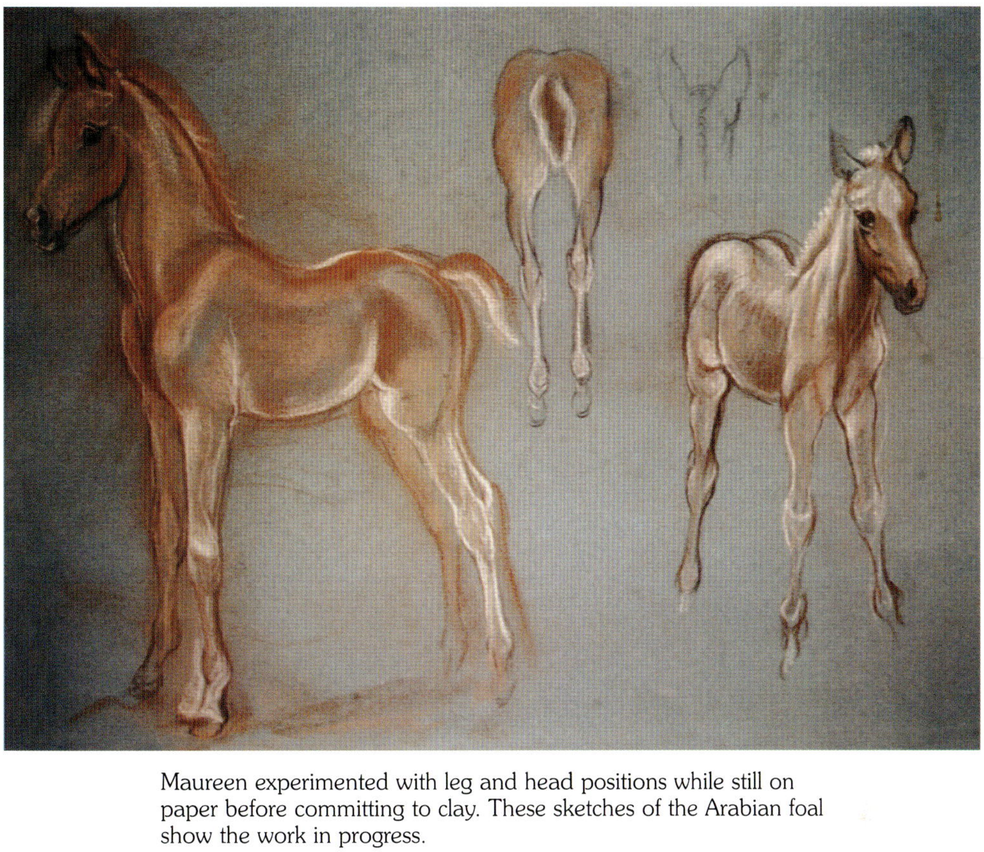

Maureen experimented with leg and head positions while still on paper before committing to clay. These sketches of the Arabian foal show the work in progress.

This female donkey shows a lot of fur detail around the face, neck and shoulders. Produced by Hagen-Renaker with the name "Adelaide," she stands 5.25" tall and has an approximate value of $80-100.

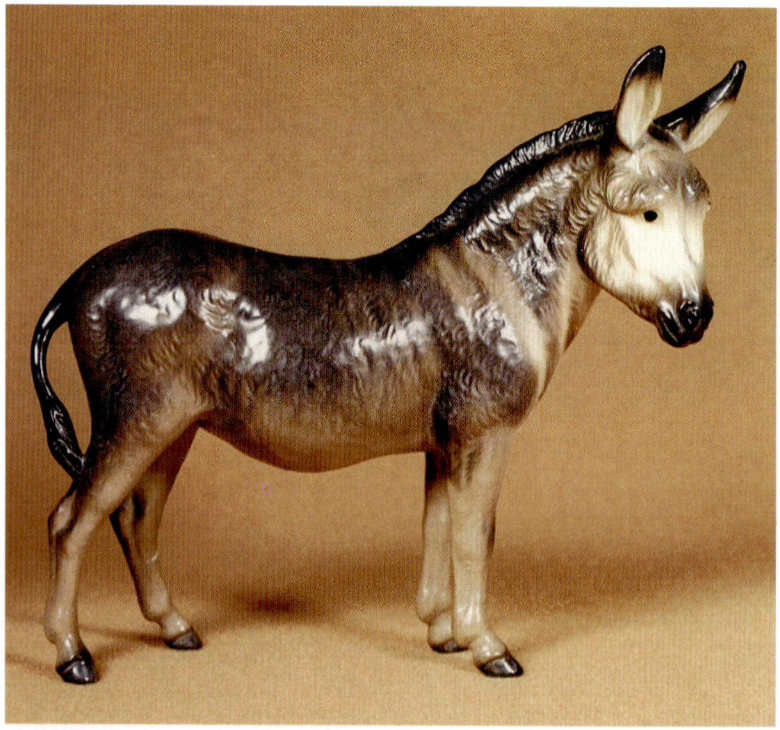

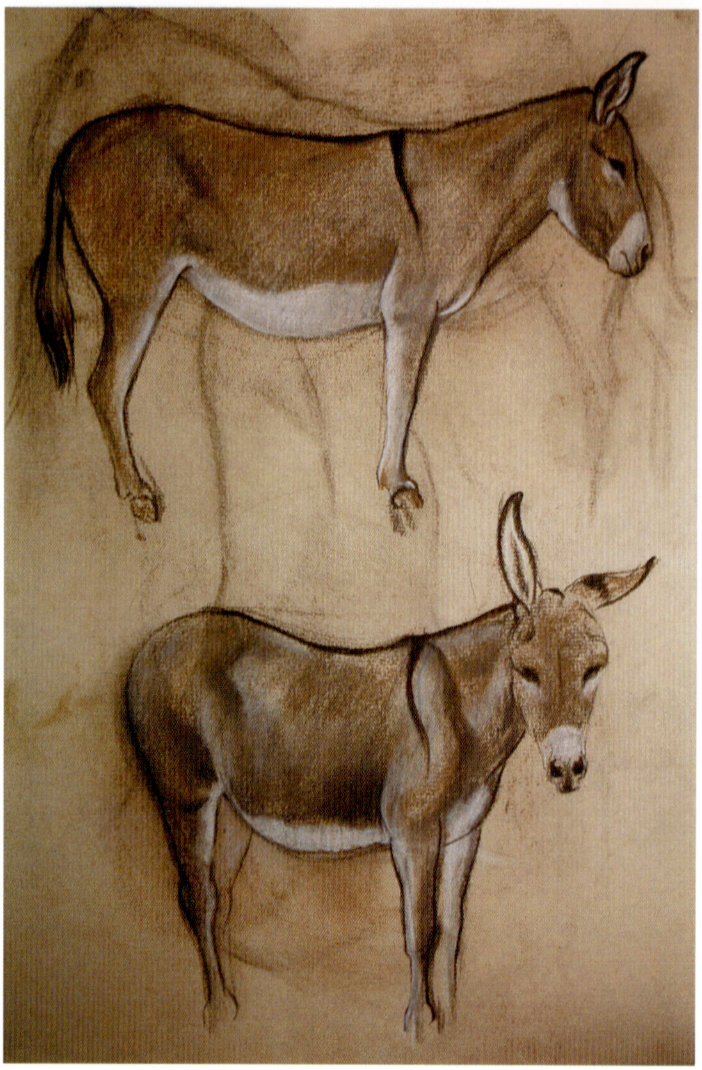

The texture of the smooth, short coat on these donkey sketches looks soft enough to feel.

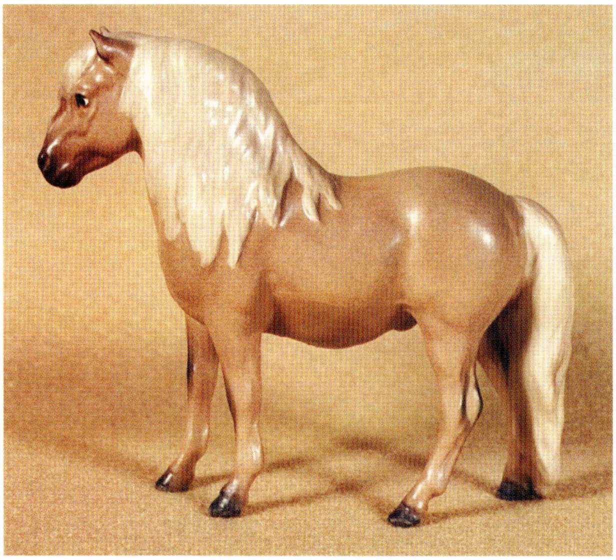

"Wrangler" the Shetland Pony produced by Hagen-Renaker was made in chestnut (shown), brown pinto, and gray pinto. Standing 4" tall, he has an approximate value of $225-250.

The Shetland Pony stallion model "Wrangler" very closely resembles this work sketch created by Maureen.

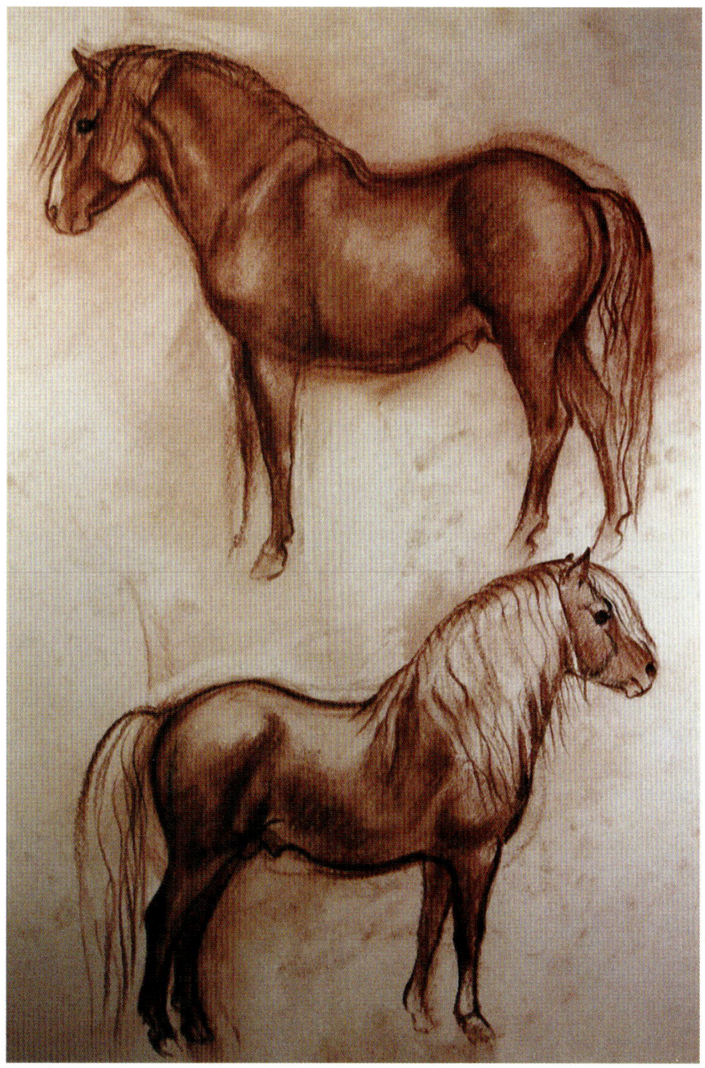

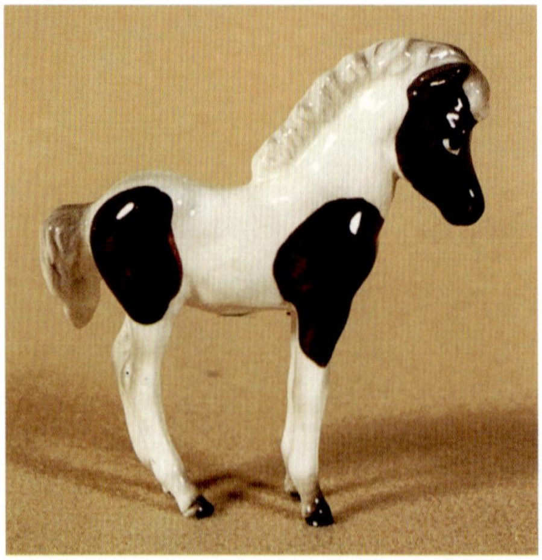

Hagen-Renaker produced Maureen's adorable Shetland Pony foal and called it "Rascal." He stands 2.75" tall, and was made in brown pinto (shown), chestnut, and gray pinto. His approximate value is $175-200.

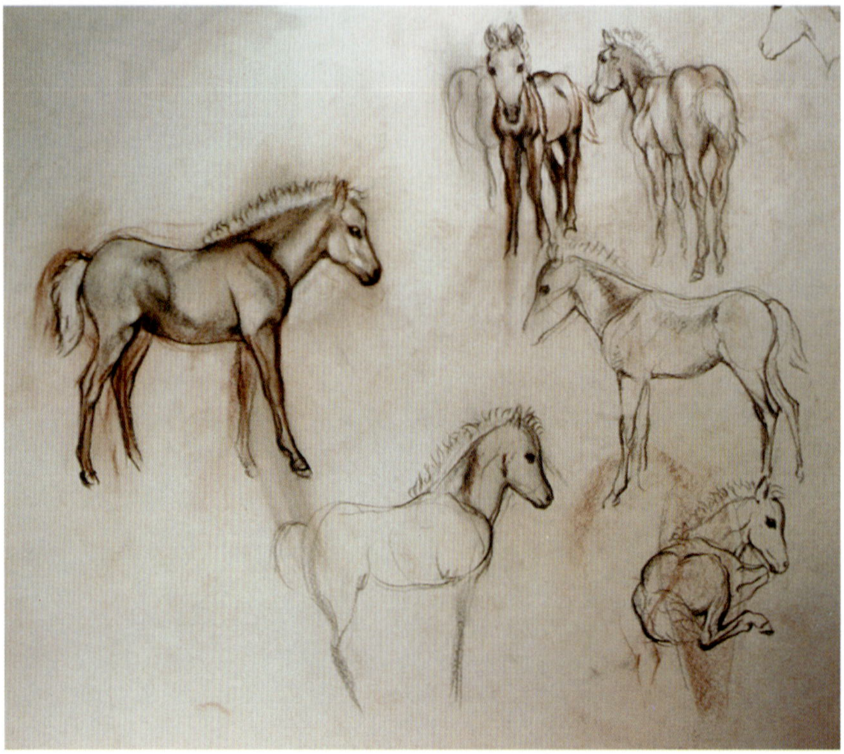

Maureen tried several poses for the Shetland Pony foal before deciding how to sculpt the model.

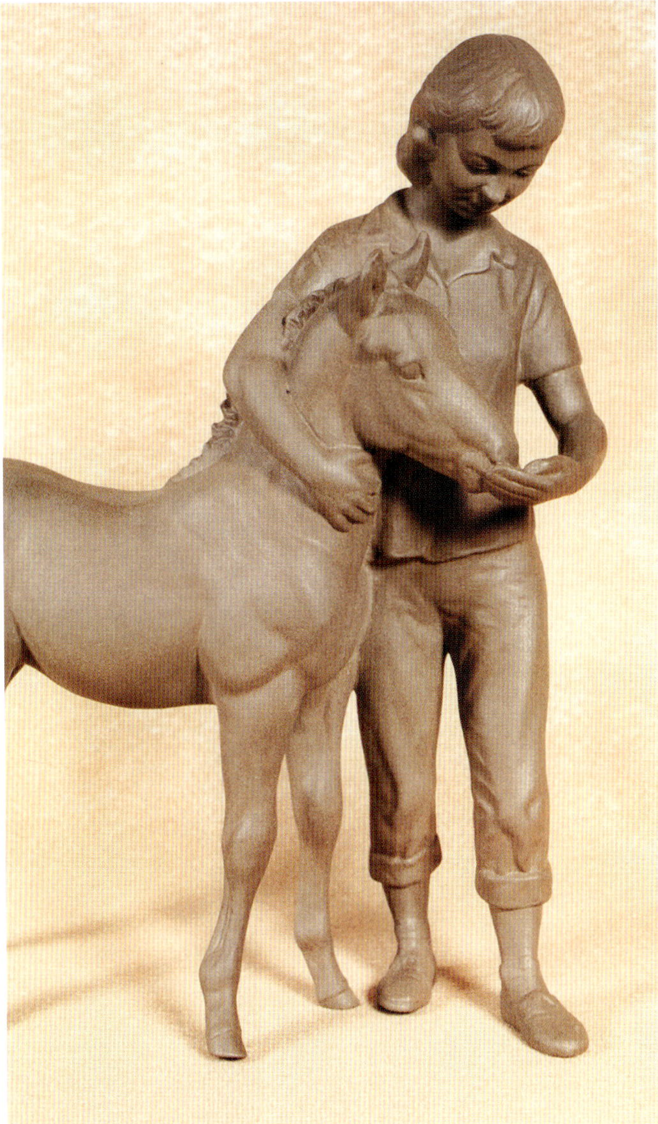

The girl and foal figure was tried by Hagen-Renaker in their Stoneware line, but never put into regular production. The piece stands 10.8" tall, and is considered rare.

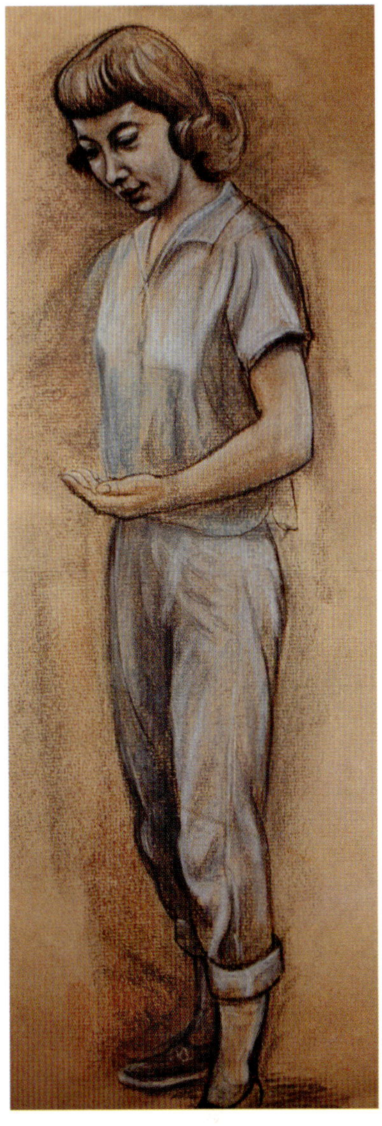

Maureen used the daughter of a Hagen-Renaker employee as a model for this sketch.

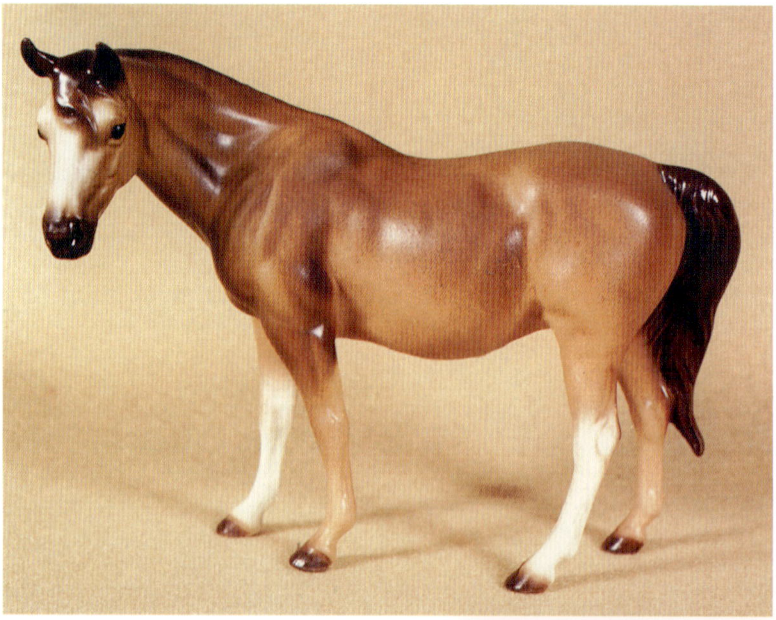

Hagen-Renaker produced this Morgan mare and named her "Forever Amber." Offered in chestnut (shown) and palomino, she stands 5" tall and has an approximate value of $90-110.

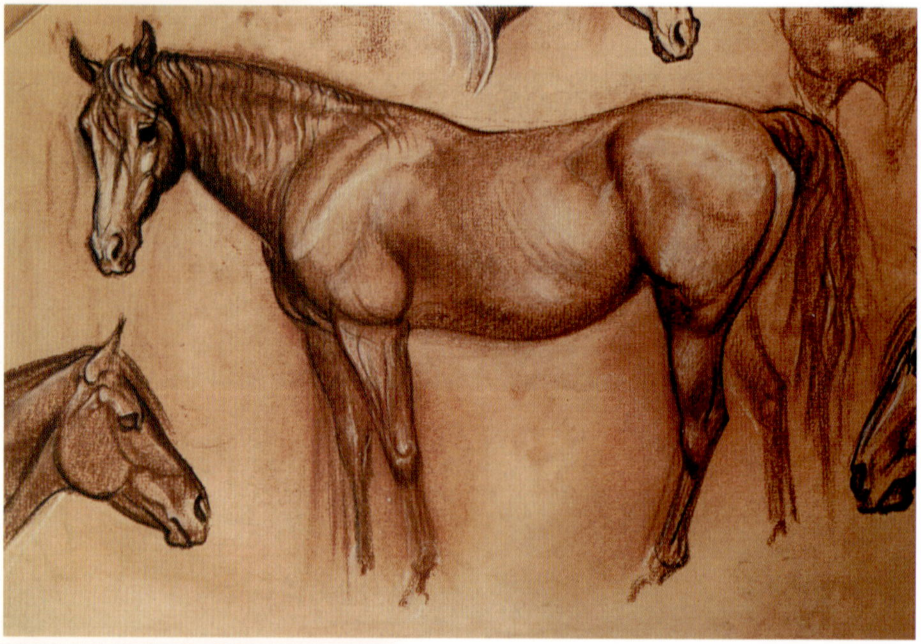

This sketch of a Morgan mare helped define the model that later became "Forever Amber."

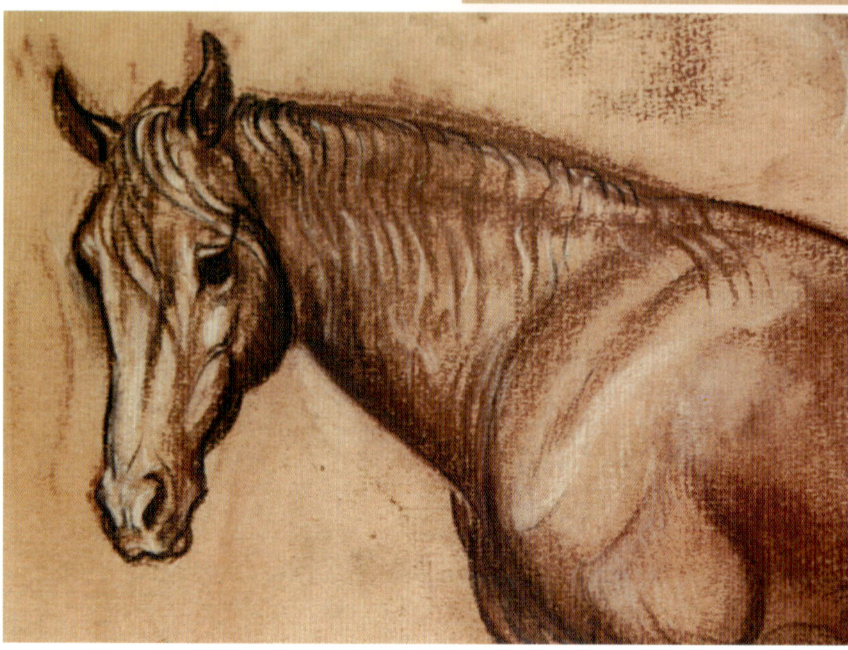

Compare this head study to the original sculpture shown on page 87 to see how well the facial details transferred to the clay model.

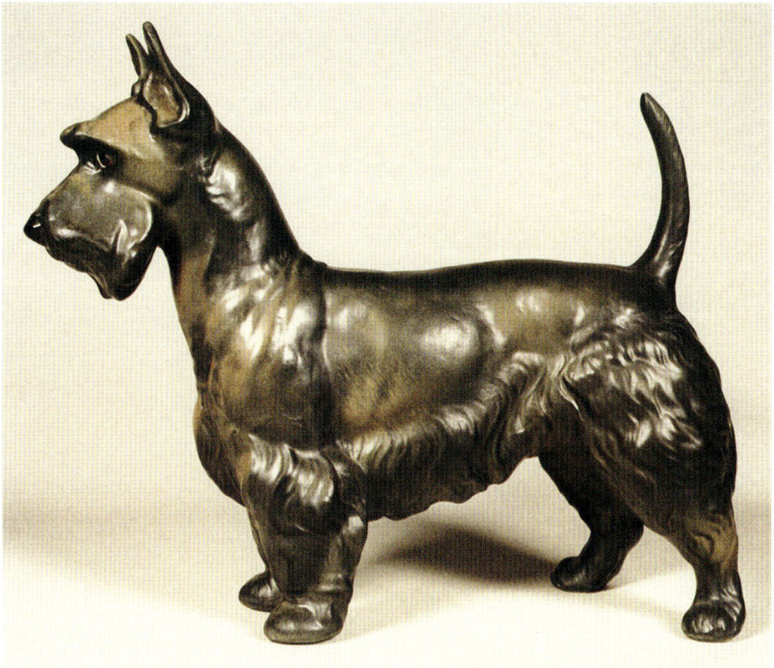

Given the good Scottish name "Mac" by Hagen-Renaker, this Scottish Terrier stands 5.5" tall and has an approximate value of $50-65.

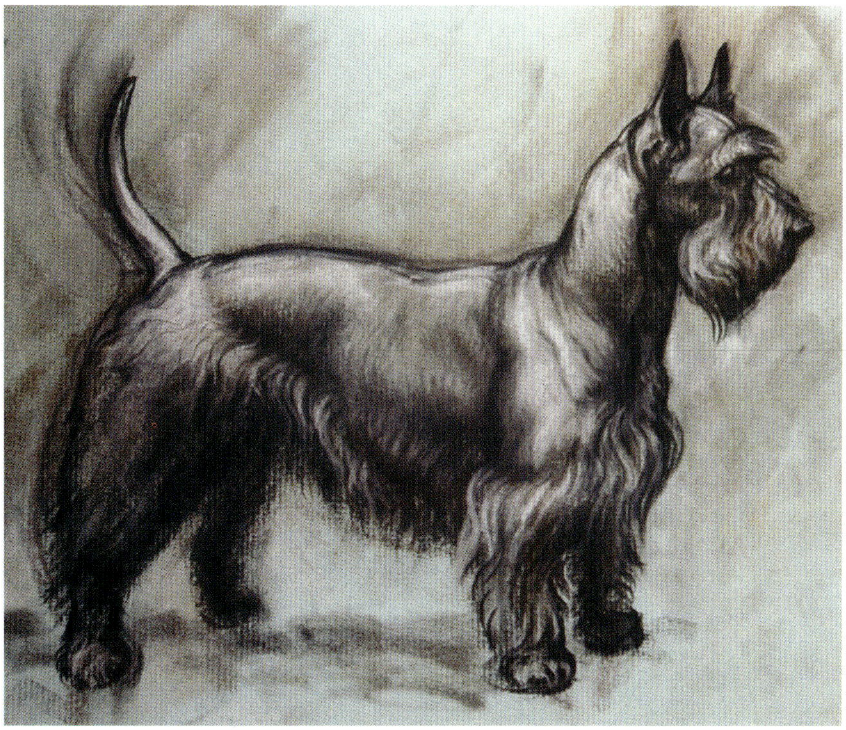

The inspiration for this Scottish Terrier sketch was a dog that Maureen owned.

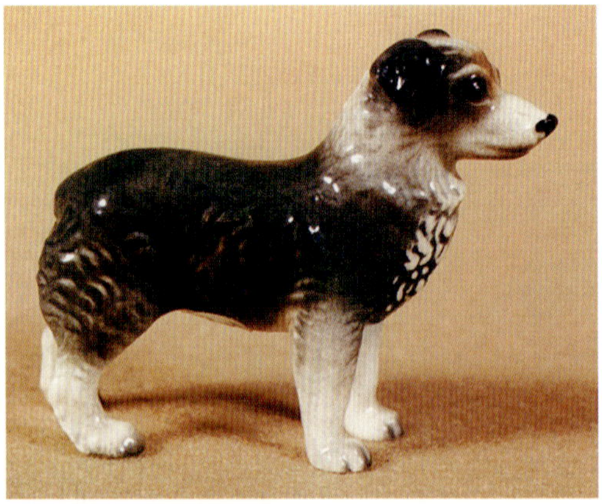

Hagen-Renaker recently added this Australian Shepherd to their Miniature line. Standing 1.75" tall, it has an approximate value of $6-8.

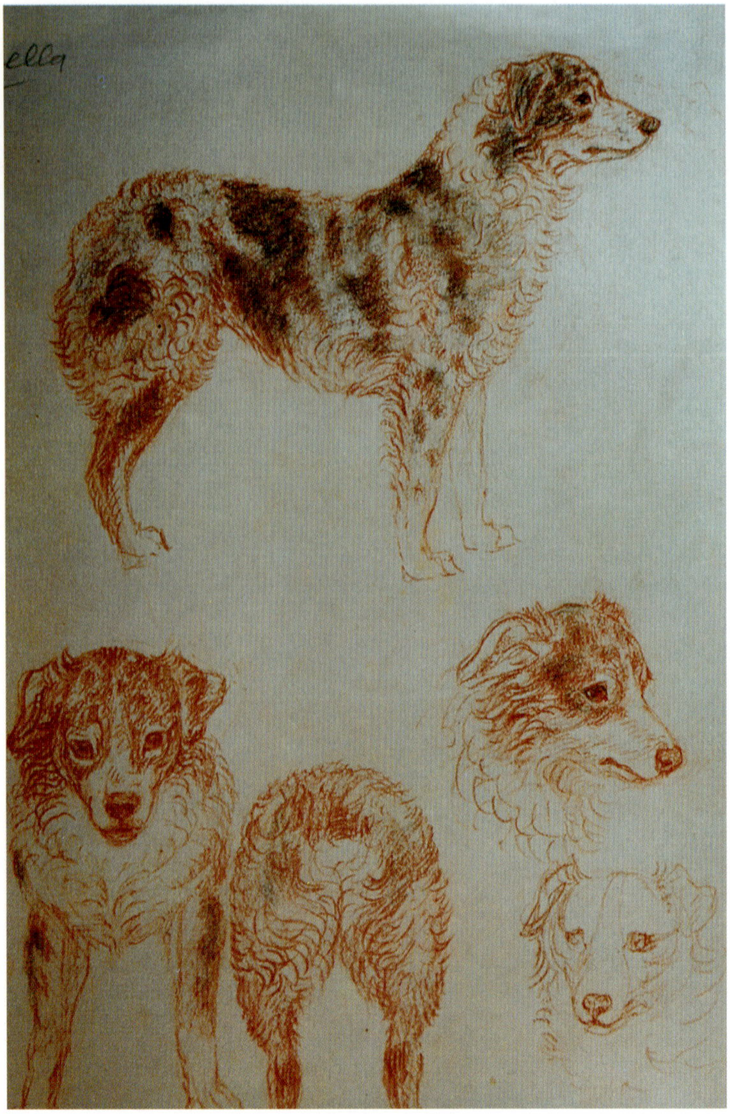

The curly, rough appearance of the fur of this Australian Shepherd shows up well in this sketch, and in the original model on page 89, but is not easy to duplicate in the factory produced piece.

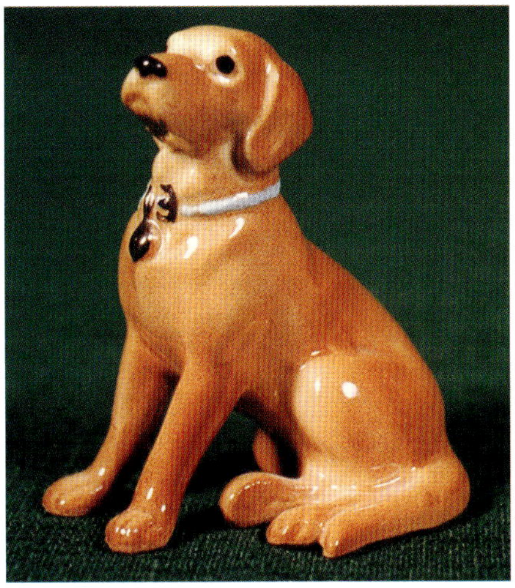

The Labrador Retriever was produced by Hagen-Renaker in this golden brown color and in black. It measures 2" tall and has an approximate value of $4-6.

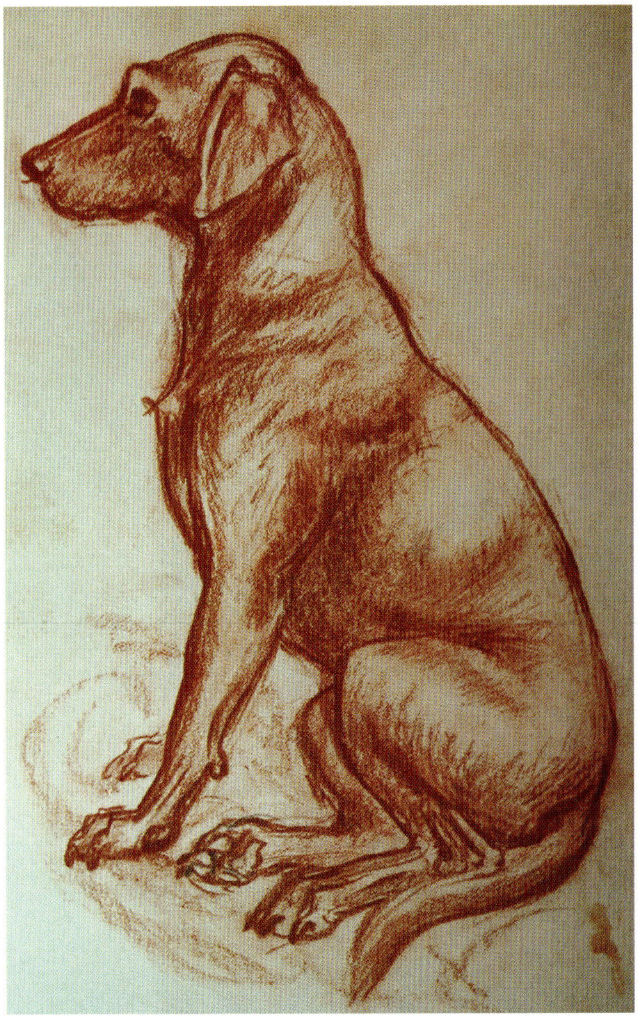

Maureen's Labrador Retriever "Mia" served as the subject for this sketch and the resulting model.

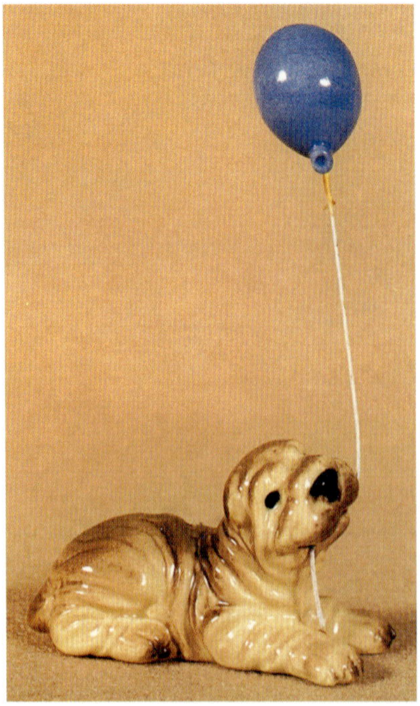

This Shar Pei adult dog holding the balloon was recently produced by Hagen-Renaker in their Miniature line. The dog measures 1.3" tall and has an approximate value of $4-6.

There was an incredible amount of detail put into this sketch, including trying to capture all of the dog's wrinkles.

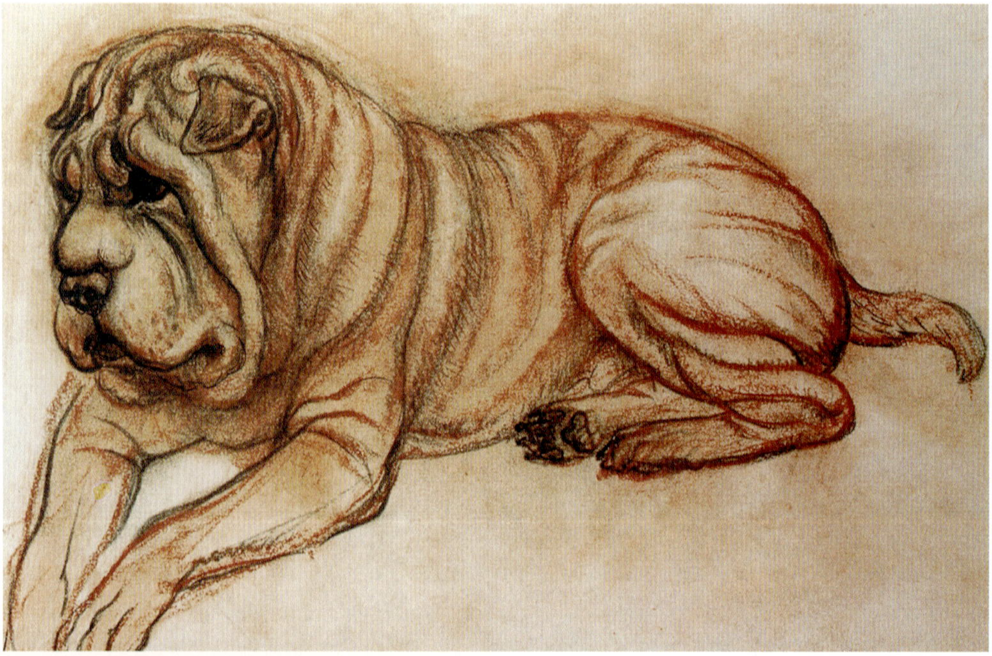

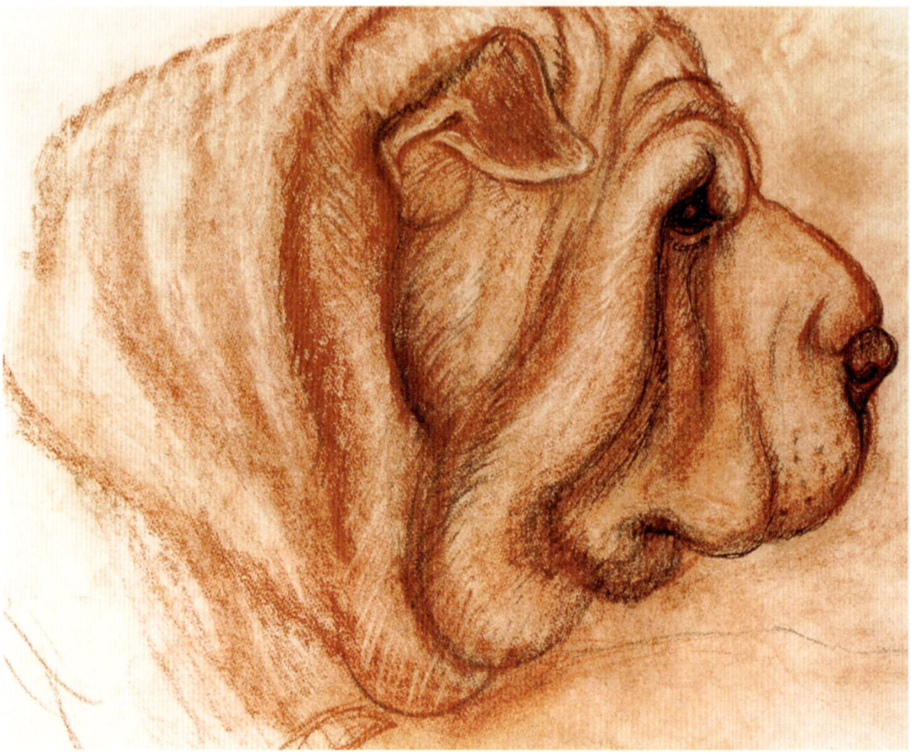

Here is another view of the amazing detail, including fur texture, found in this dog's sketches.

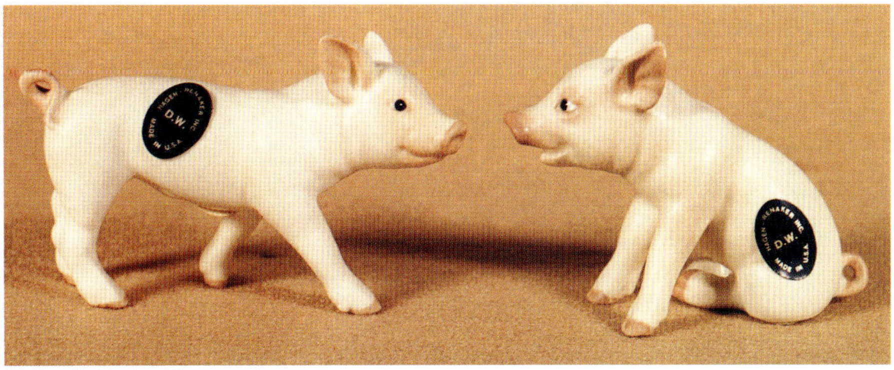

These two piglets were produced for the Hagen-Renaker Designers Workshop series. Note the "DW" sticker on each piglet. They are both 1.75" tall and have an approximate value of $18-22 each.

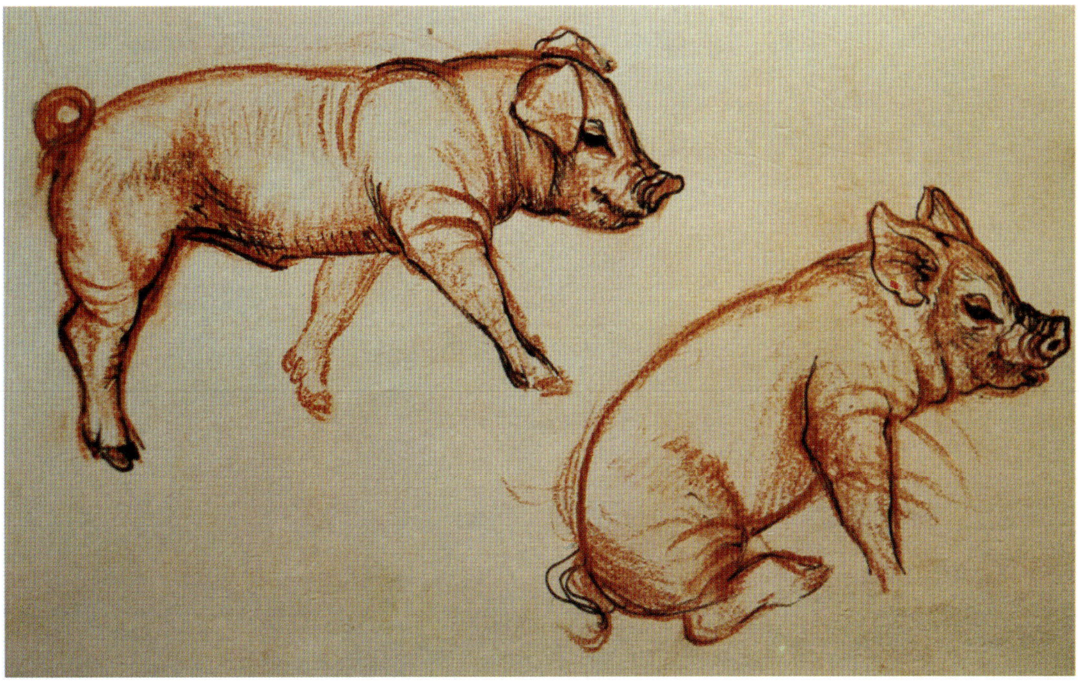

All of the important details, from wrinkled snouts to curly tails, were captured in these working sketches.

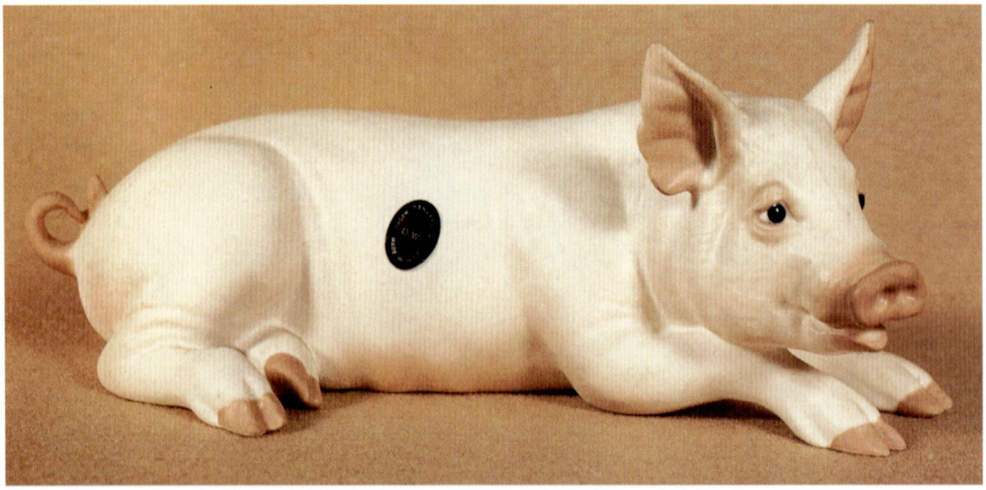

Produced by Hagen-Renaker in their Designers Workshop (DW) line in the 1980s, this adult pig measures 3" tall by 7" long. Her approximate value is $40-50.

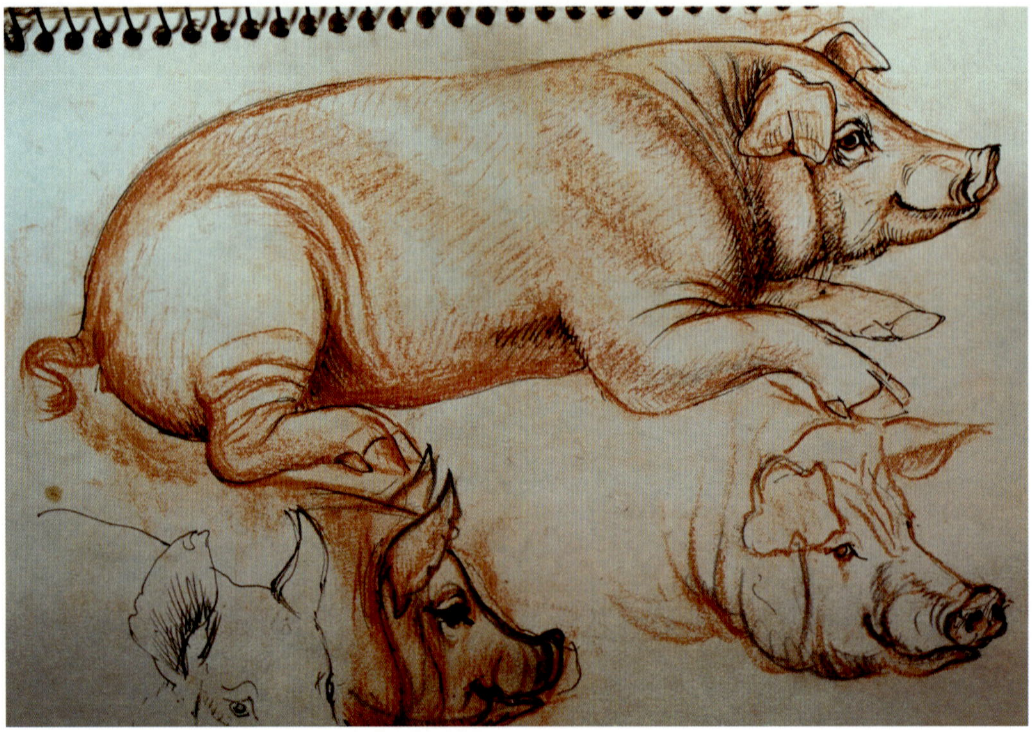

Several views of this sow's head helped develop the shape of her massive features.

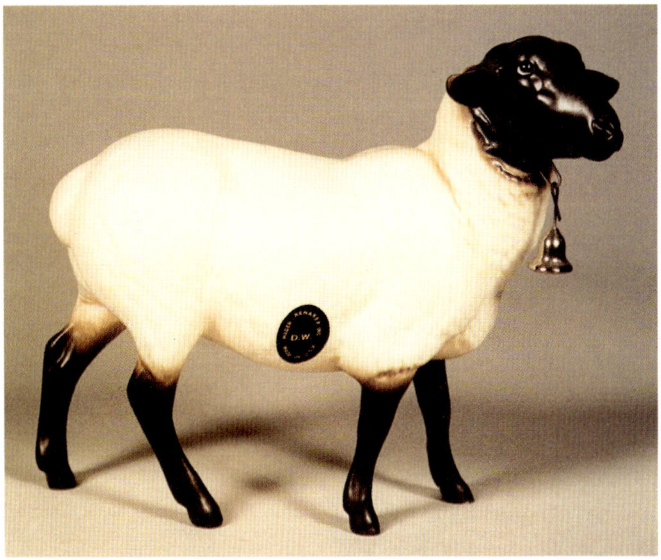

This ewe named "Lady Jane" stands 4" tall and was produced by Hagen-Renaker as part of the Designers Workshop line (note sticker). Her approximate value is $50-75.

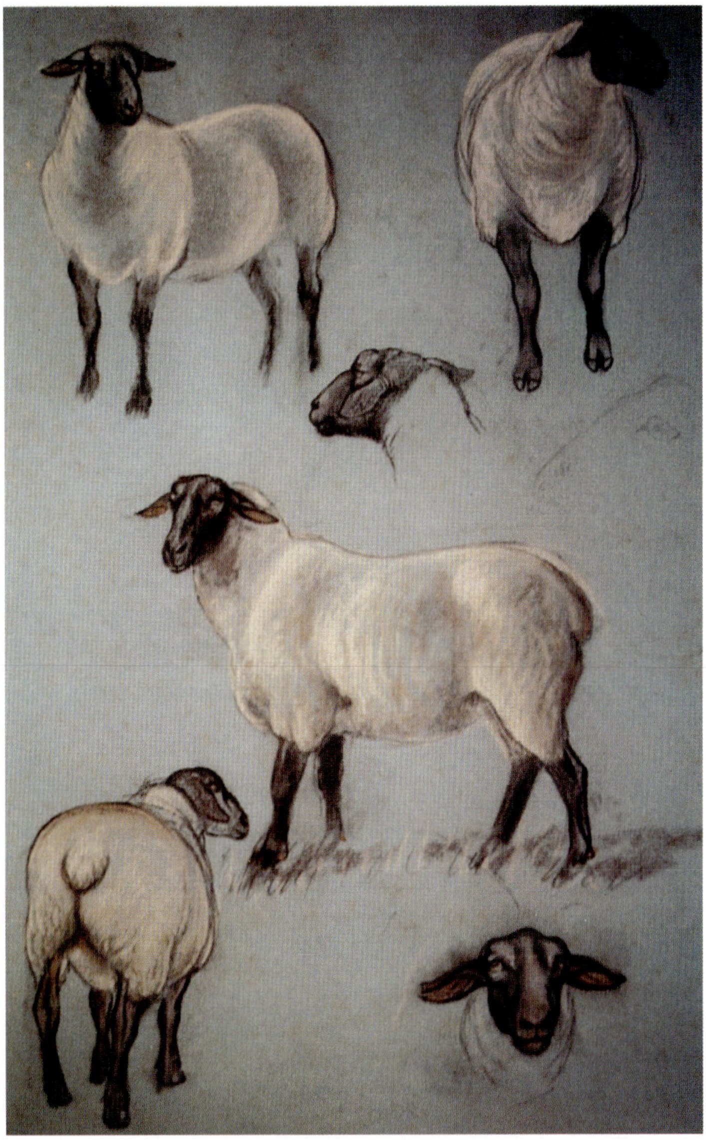

Here are several sketches of the peaceful ewe, at rest in her pasture where Maureen sketched her.

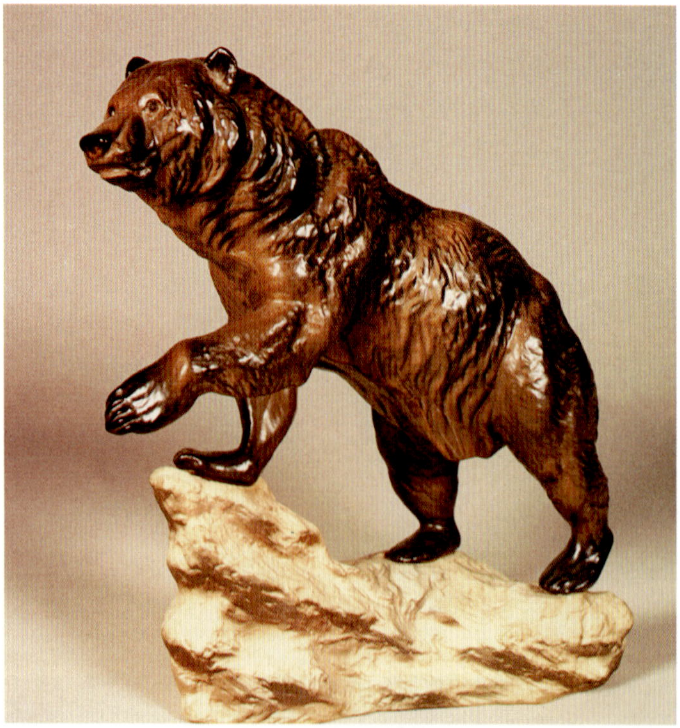

The fierce Grizzly Bear was produced by Hagen-Renaker in varying shades of brown, as well as gold and white for a short time. It stands 7.75" tall and has an approximate value of $125-150.

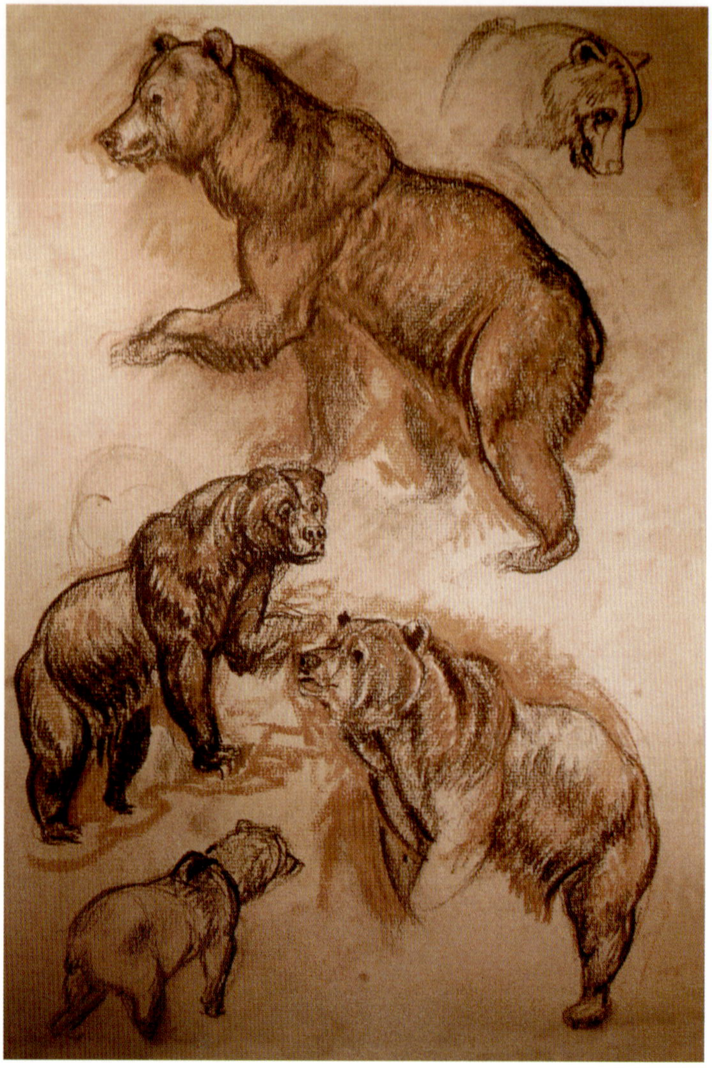

These sketches were drawn during one of Maureen's visits to the San Diego. She recalls, "It's not really fun sketching at the zoo because you attract an audience."

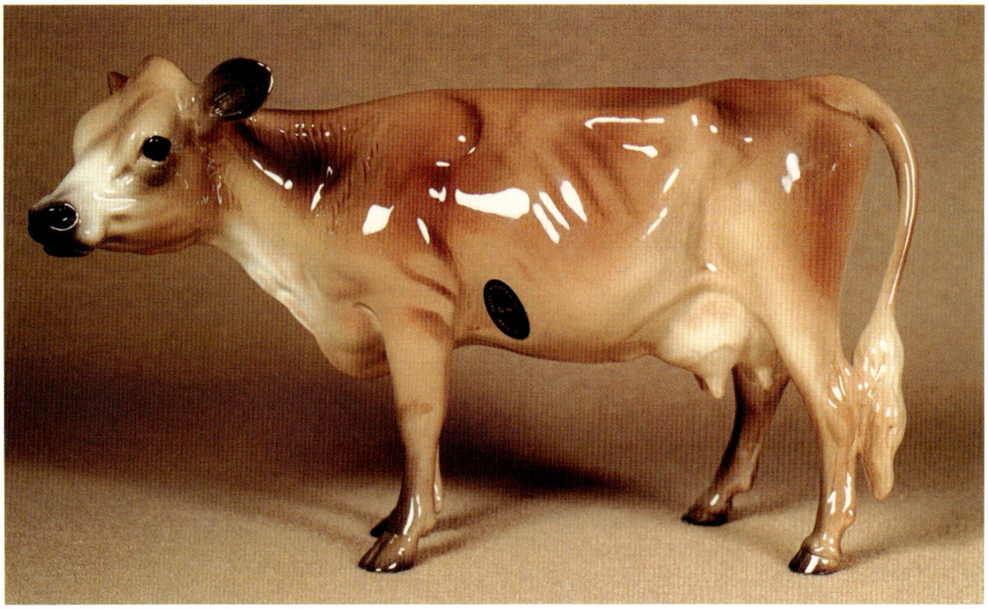

Hagen-Renaker produced this peaceful Jersey cow for a short time in the mid-1980s. She stands 5" tall and has a value of approximately $75-100.

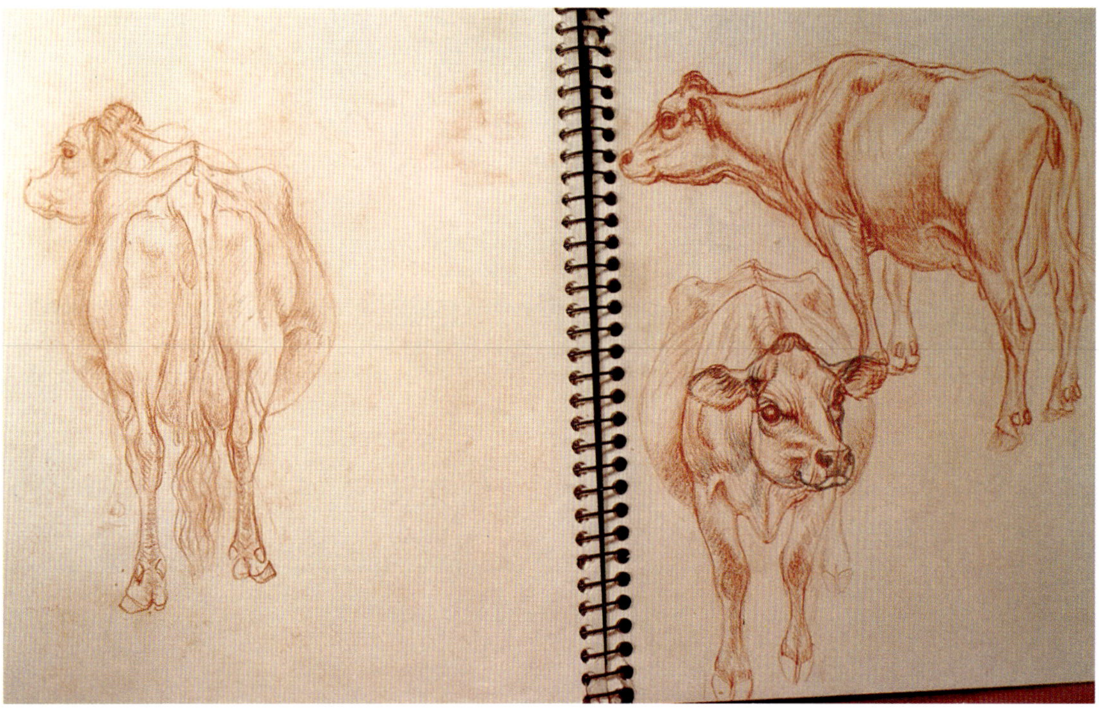

From the bony hips to the gentle brown eyes, Maureen has captured the personality of this Jersey cow in her sketches.

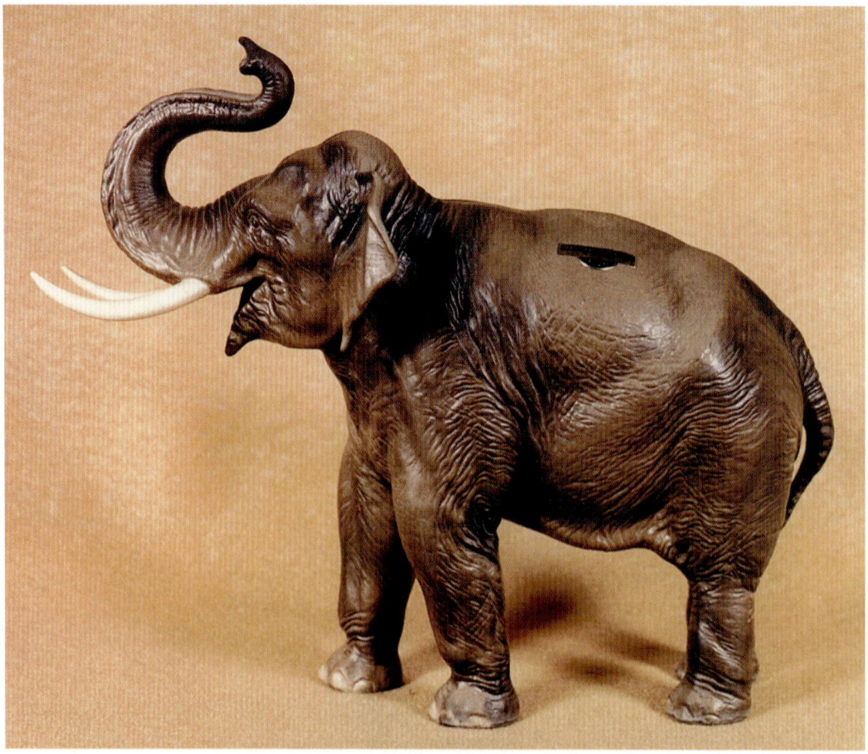

Named "Rajah" by Hagen-Renaker, this Designers Workshop series elephant stands 8.75" tall and shows an incredible amount of detail in the skin wrinkles throughout the body and head. Note the gold foil Hagen-Renaker sticker on his side. His approximate value is $100-125.

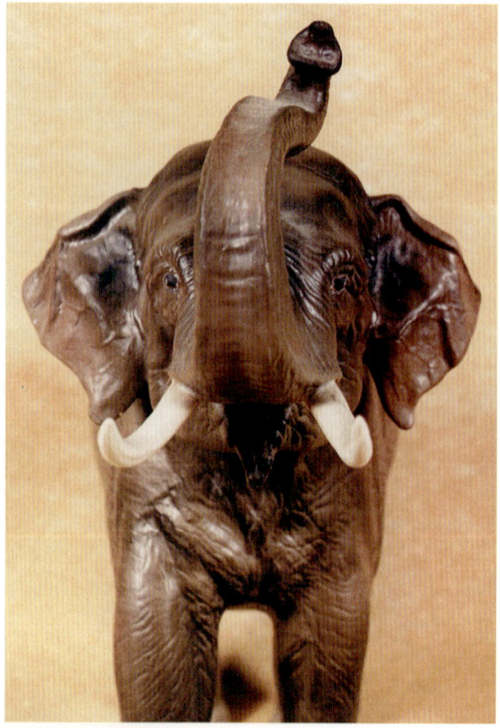

This front view of "Rajah" shows off more of the intricate detail in this model.

These sketches provided the basis for the "Rajah" model, but Maureen embellished the model quite a bit while sculpting it.

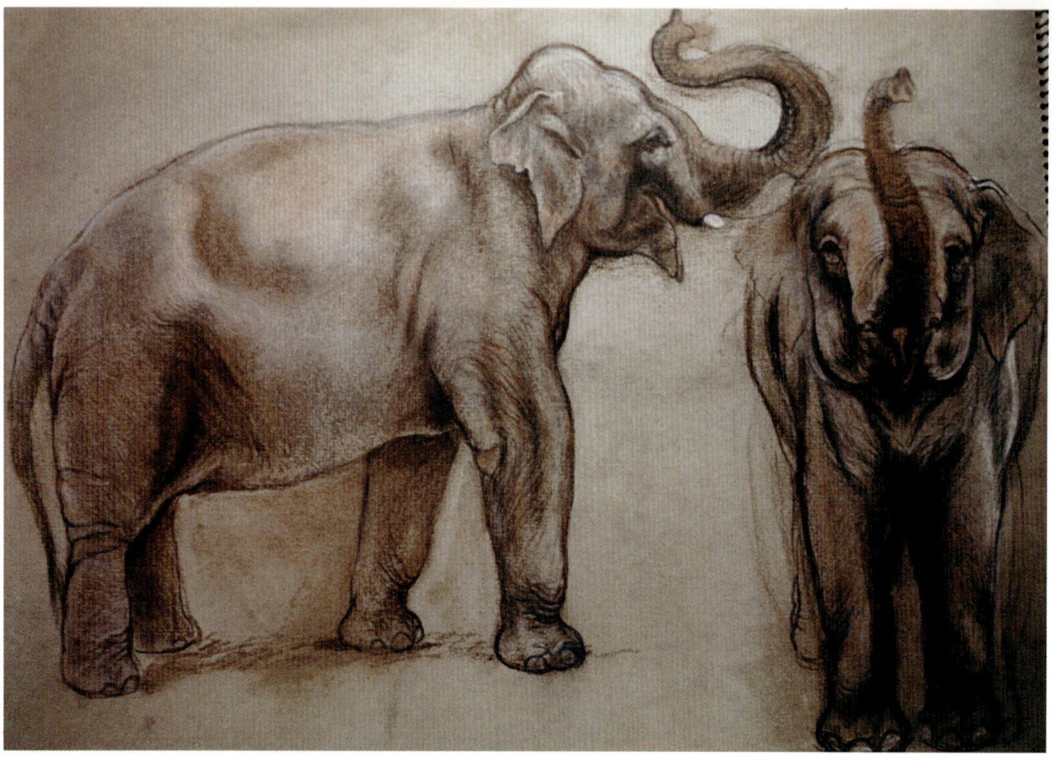

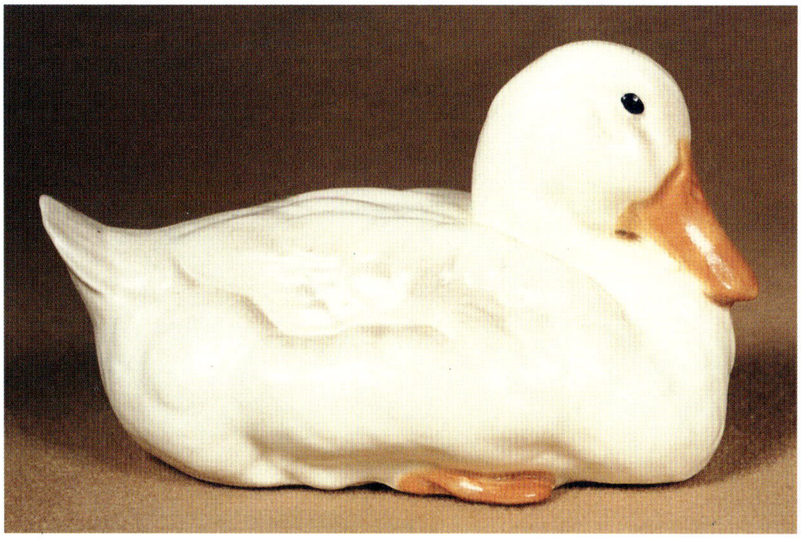

Known as "Jill," this female duck was produced by Hagen-Renaker along with her drake "Jack." She measures 2.75" tall and has an approximate value of $25-40.

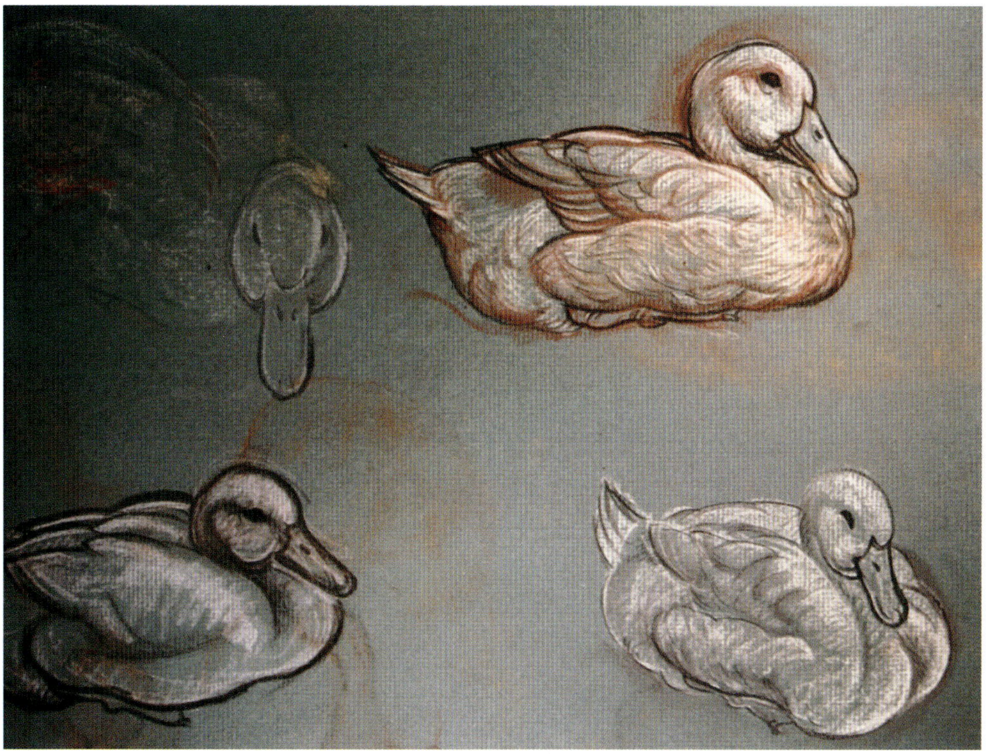

Through this series of sketches, Maureen explored different head positions for the duck. There were actually two versions of "Jill" produced by Hagen-Renaker, one with her bill on her chest and one with her bill slightly elevated.

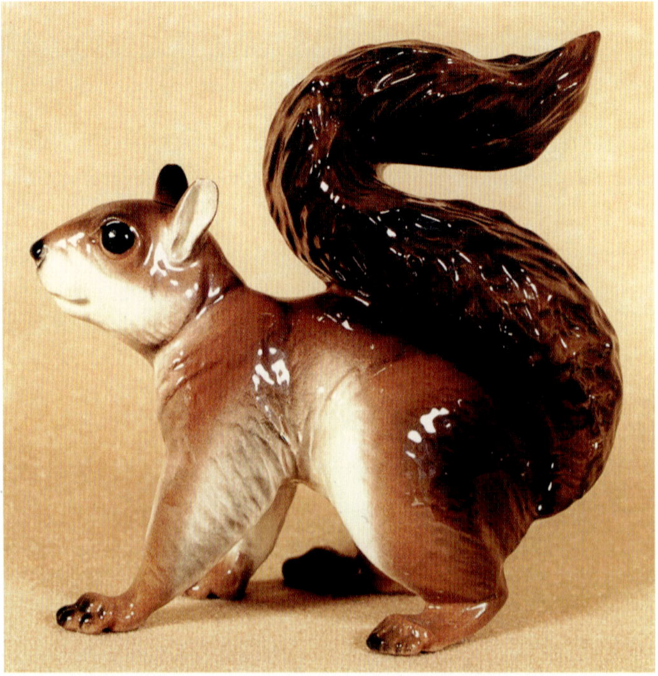

The squirrel "Jane" is quite large, standing 5.25" tall at tail tip. She was made by Hagen-Renaker in both gray bisque and brown (shown) and has an approximate value of $50-75.

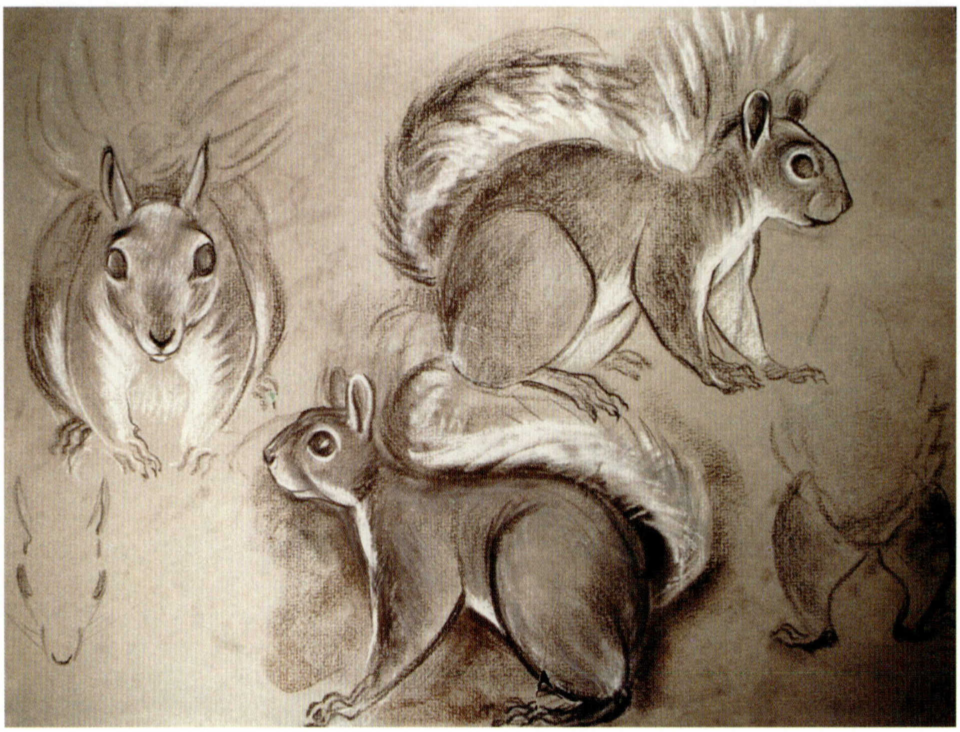

Maureen had plenty of opportunities to observe and sketch the big gray squirrels that lived in a walnut tree grove near her home.

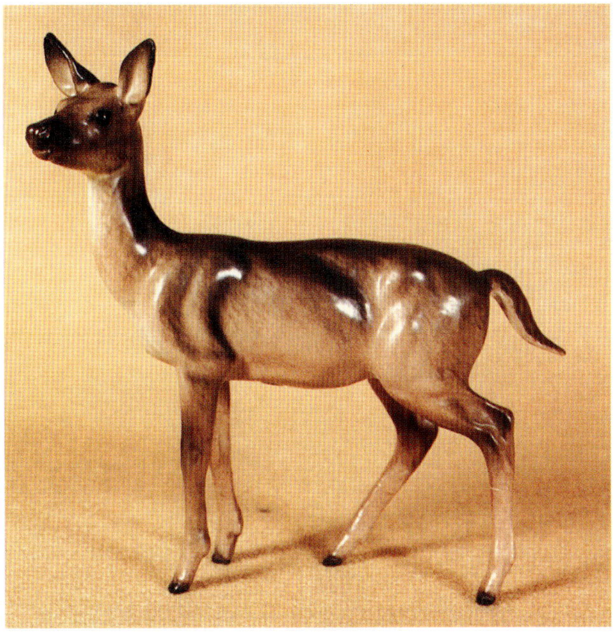

This delicate dark brown doe was produced by Hagen-Renaker for a short time in the early 1960s. She stands 4.2" tall and has an approximate value of $125-150.

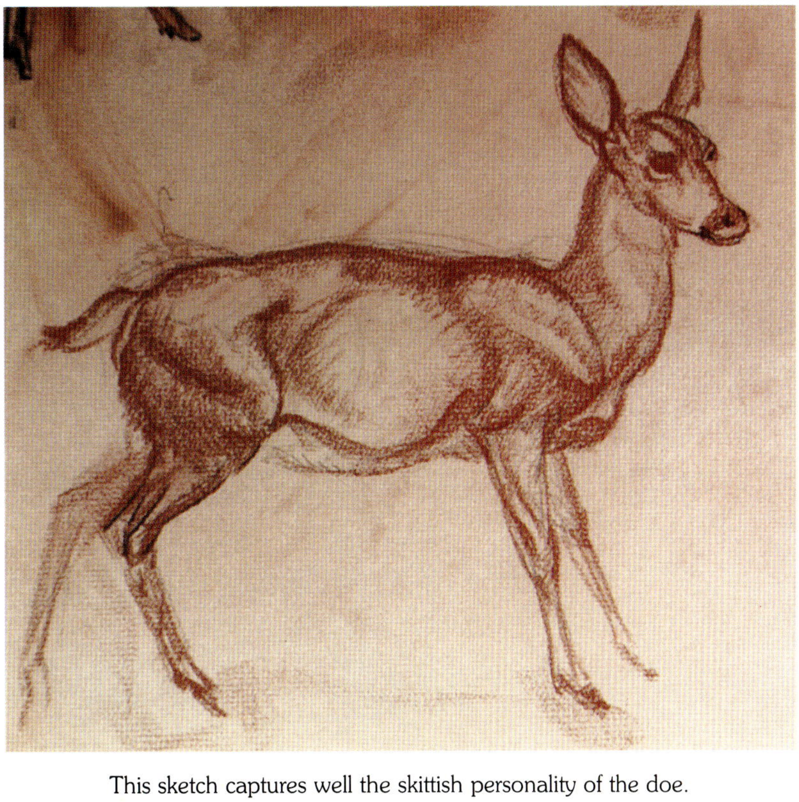

This sketch captures well the skittish personality of the doe.

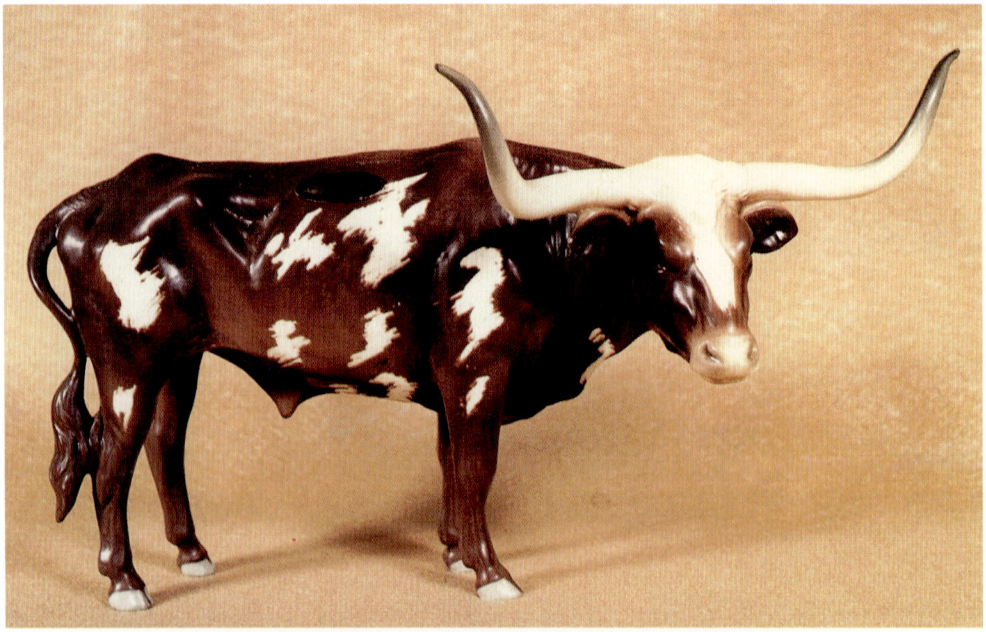

Hagen-Renaker produced this Longhorn bull in a variety of shades of brown, as well as this brown and white coloring. Standing 5.75" tall, he has an approximate value of $125-150.

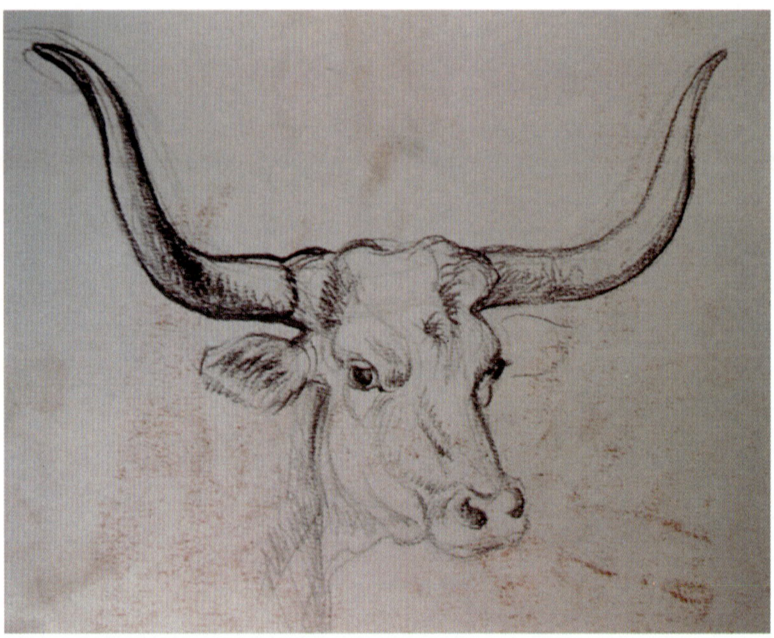

This impressive face represents a creature not to be meddled with.

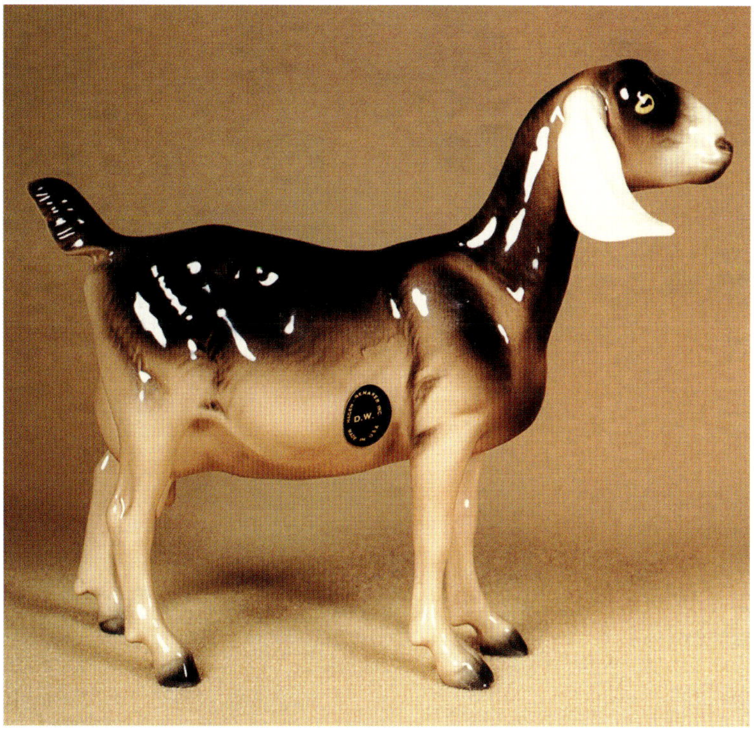

This Nubian Goat doe was produced by Hagen-Renaker in the 1980s. She stands 5" tall and has an approximate value of $50-75.

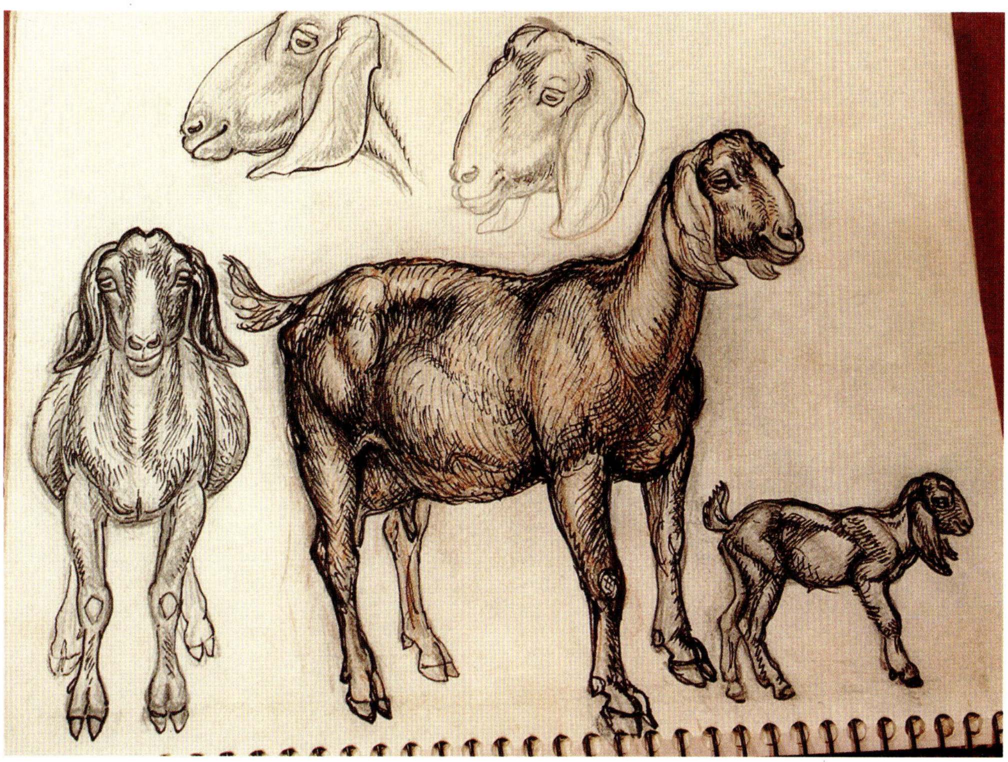

The unique facial features of the Nubian Goat are captured well in these sketches.

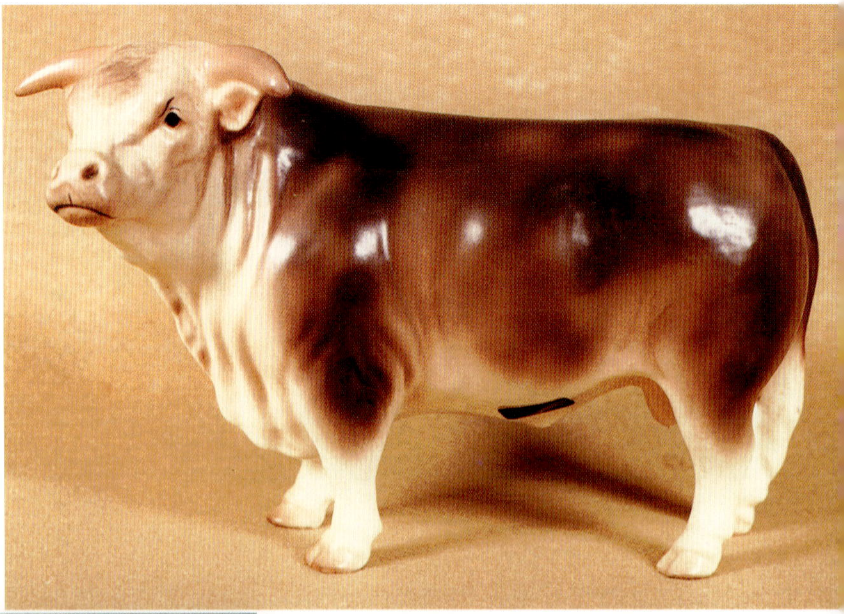

Named "Domino" by Hagen-Renaker, this Hereford Bull has a blue rectangular Hagen-Renaker foil sticker (shown) on his belly. Standing 5.25" tall, he has an approximate value of $80-100.

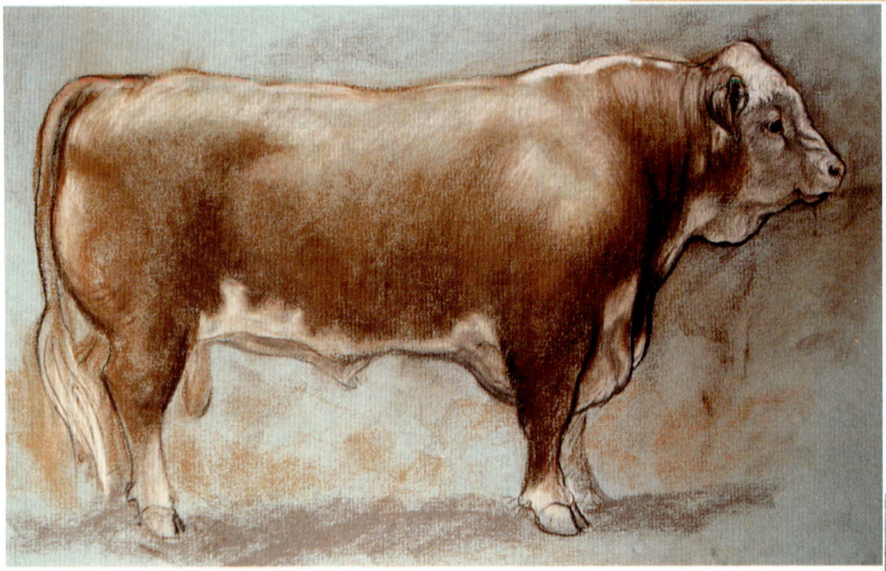

The sketch of this massive Hereford Bull translated well into the model "Domino."

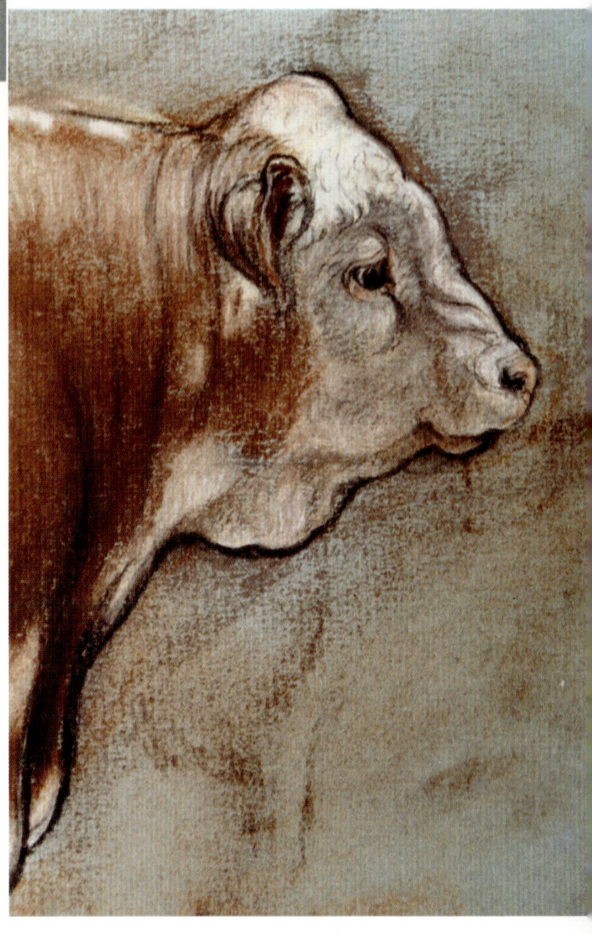

Wonderful facial details, including the pink nose, are captured in this sketch of the Hereford Bull.

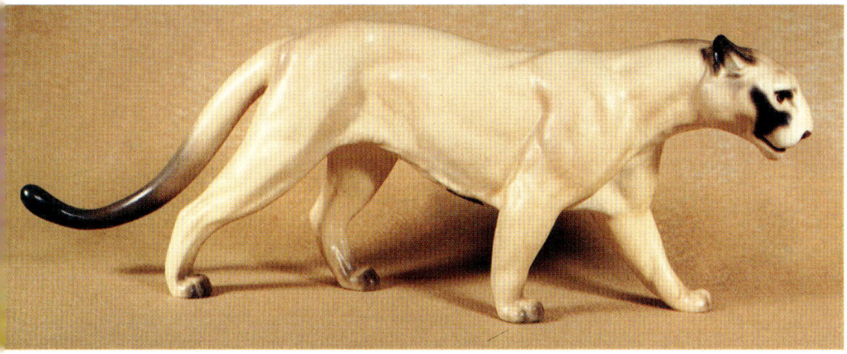

This walking Mountain Lion was produced by Hagen-Renaker as a set with a lying lion. This one stands 5.25" tall and has an approximate value of $225-250.

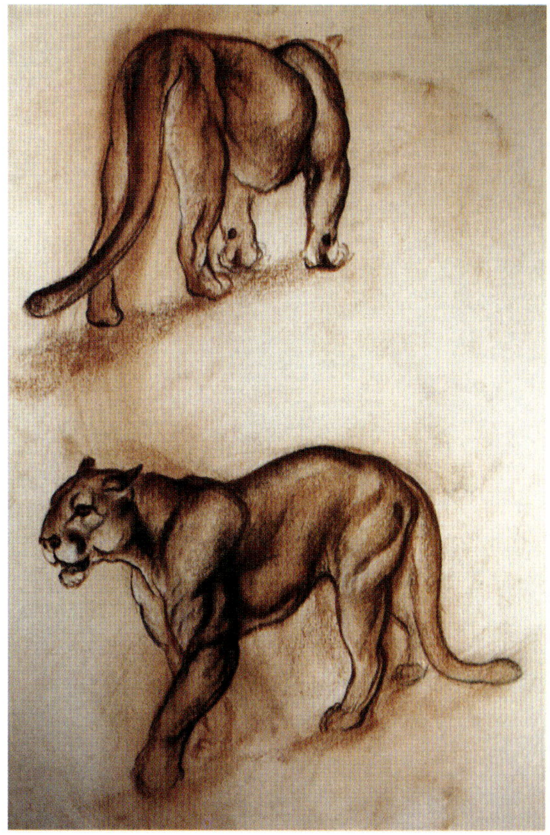

The incredible grace of the Mountain Lion is expressed well in these sketches.

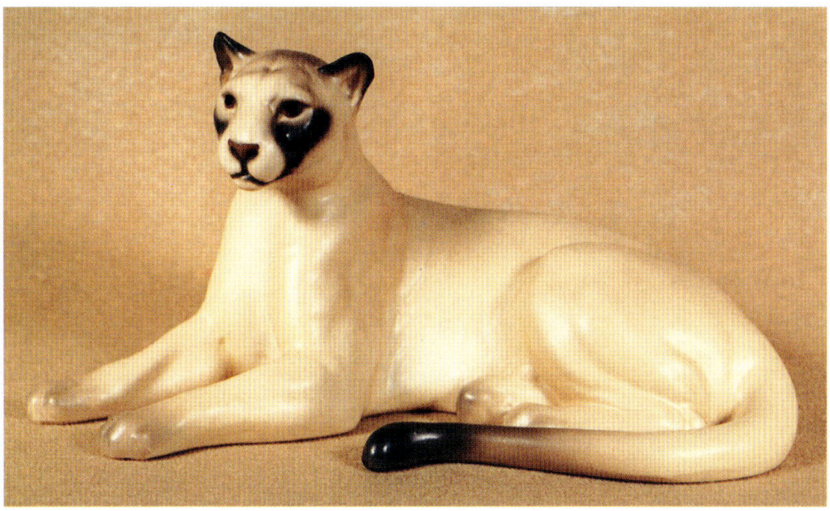

Produced by Hagen-Renaker along with the walking Mountain Lion, this lying Mountain Lion model measures 5" tall, and has an approximate value of $200-225.

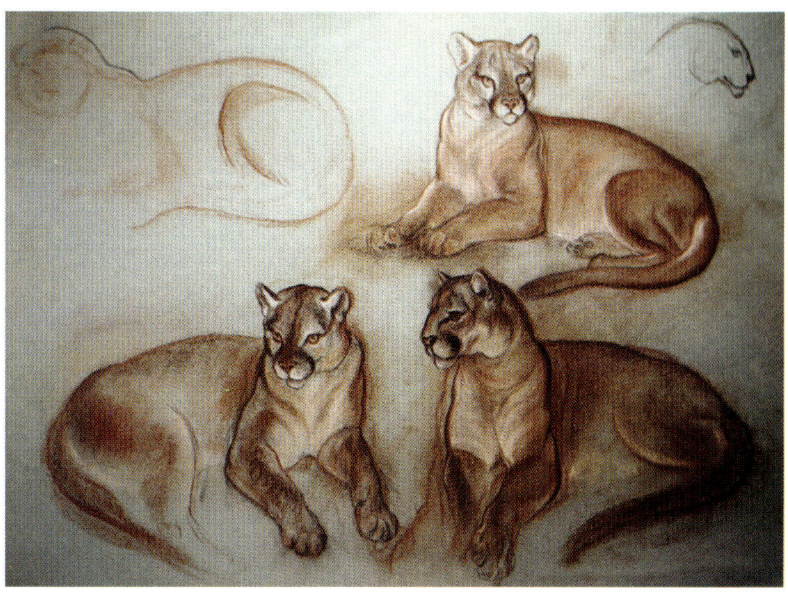

These sketches of the lying Mountain Lion show an animal that is alert and ready for action.

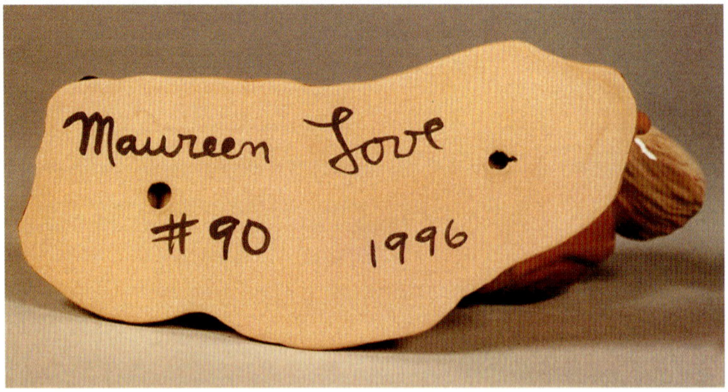

Hagen-Renaker developed a special line of horses for collectors beginning in the 1990s. These horses are in the 4-6" scale, and each one is signed on the base by Maureen and has the run number. (Ninetieth horse produced on this one.). However, they are factory-produced and should not be confused with her original artwork.

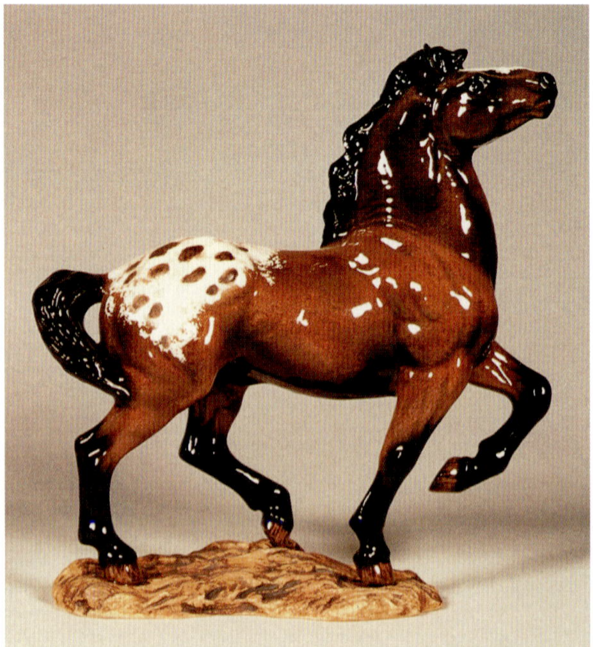

"Jamboree" the Appaloosa was the first in the Collectors Series. Standing 5" tall, he came in tan, gray, and bay (shown). Laurilyn Burson applied the white blanket at the factory. Maureen Love's signature plus the number in the run is on the underside of the base. The approximate value of this horse is $120-135.

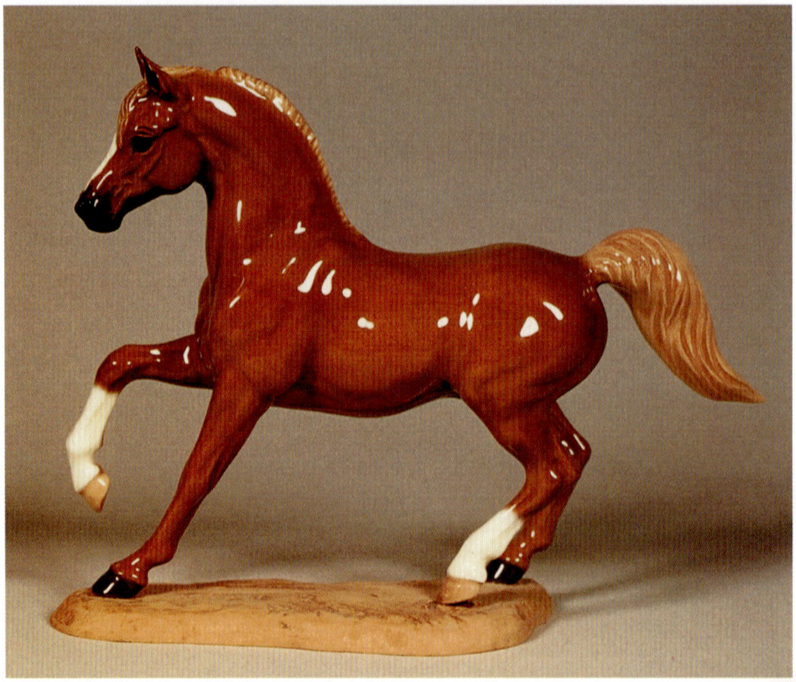

Second in the Collectors Series by Hagen-Renaker was "Encore," the Arabian stallion. Offered in white, dapple-gray, bay, and chestnut (shown), he has Maureen Love's signature and a run number on the underside of his base. Standing 5.5" tall, he has an approximate value of $165-180.

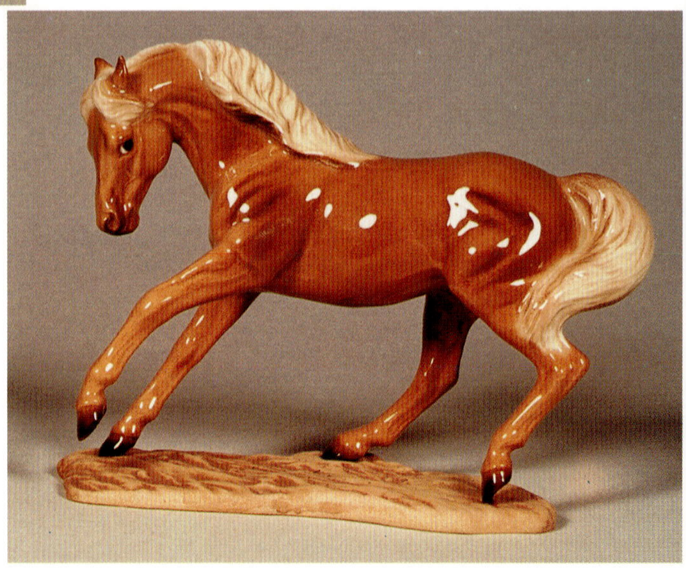

The cantering mare "Tria" is the third in the series for collectors by Hagen-Renaker. She was produced in palomino (shown) and in bay. She stands 4" high, has Maureen's signature and a run number under her base, and has an approximate value of $120-130.

"Quartet" the Quarter Horse came next in the Collectors Series by Hagen-Renaker. "Quartet" was produced in gray (shown) white, bay, and chestnut, with and without white facial and leg markings. Signed by Maureen Love and numbered under the base, this horse stands 4.75" tall and has an approximate value of $90-110.

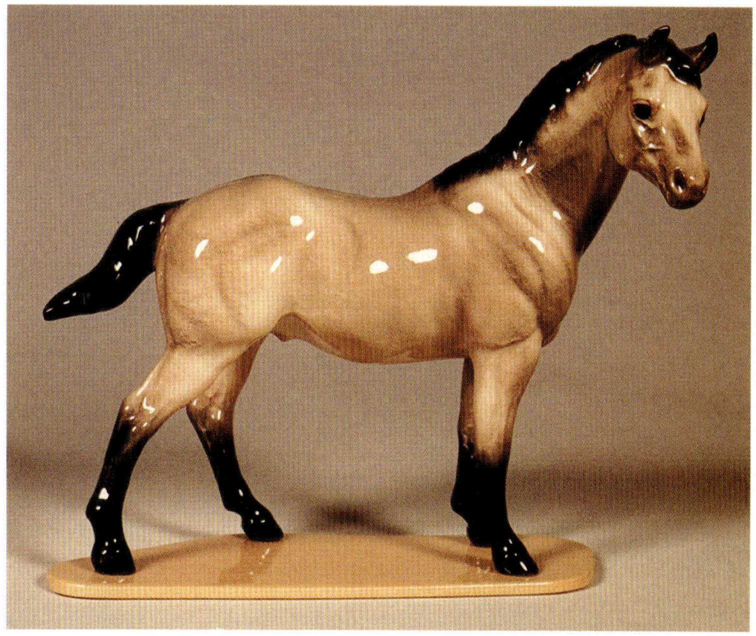

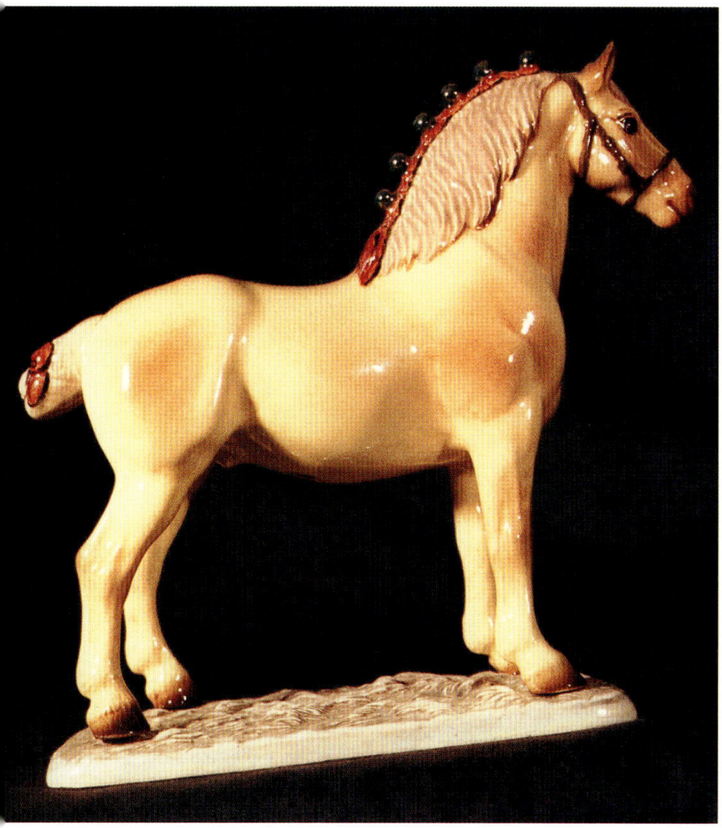

The fifth horse in this special series is a draft horse named "Cinco." This is a prototype of the model, showing the intricate hand-painted detail in the mane, tail, and face. The retail price for this horse is $140.

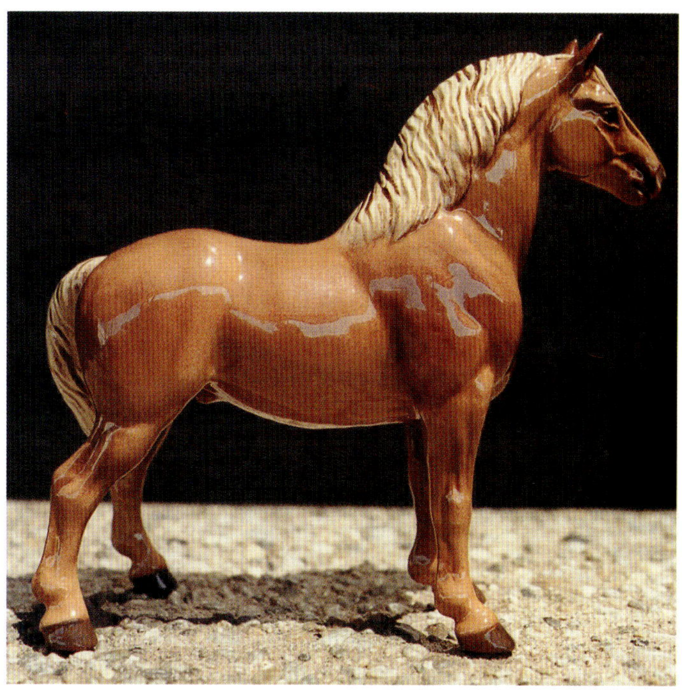

The first attempt at the draft horse model was this handsome horse with a full mane and tail. It was later decided to retool the mold and give "Cinco" a bobbed mane and tail, for a special, dressy effect. This full-tail version is considered rare, with only two or three models like this in existence.

Chapter Five

Made With Love

In 1997 Maureen Love and former Hagen-Renaker coworker Laurilyn Burson teamed up to form a new company. They felt that there was interest in medium scale (5-6") horses from the collecting community and "Made With Love" was formed. Maureen sculpts the horses, then Laurilyn produces them. Many of the Made With Love pieces have been offered in both standard and custom colors. Laurilyn enjoys working with the collectors and sharing their excitement when their new horse arrives.

As this collaboration flourished, Laurilyn discovered that Maureen still had molds for many of her Maureen Love Originals pieces. They were stored in the garage, pretty much out of the way and forgotten. This sparked yet another endeavor, with Laurilyn revitalizing these molds and producing new versions of the 1970s favorites. This venture has been dubbed "Molds From Maureen's Garage." The majority of the garage mold horses shown in this chapter were produced in 2001 and 2002.

The inevitable question arises as to whether or not these reissued models will lessen the value of the primary Maureen Love Originals of the 1970s. Because the new pieces are not decorated by Maureen, they have a very different appearance. While they are beautiful models, the style is quite unlike Maureen's and therefore they exist as pieces from a different era. Because Maureen will probably never again produce and decorate models as she did in the 1960s, 70s, and 80s, those original pieces will exist as unique and valuable collectibles.

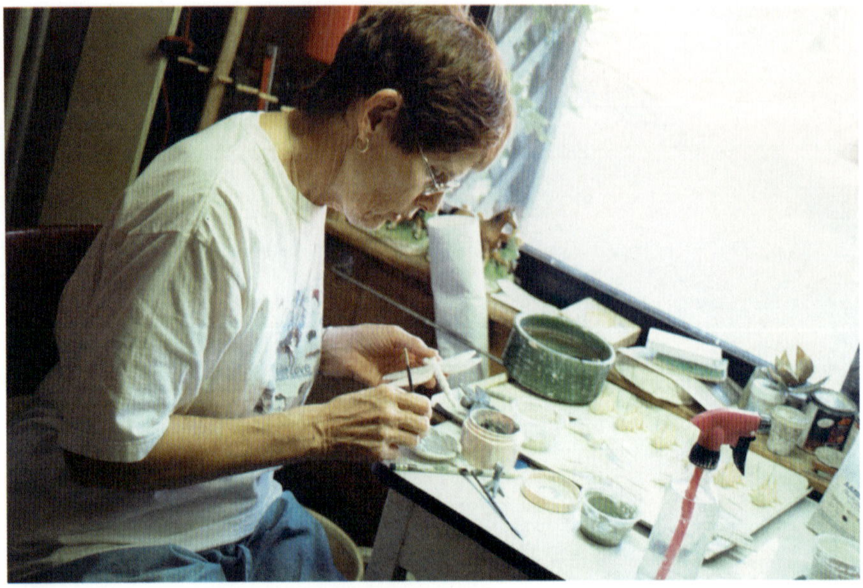

Laurilyn Burson, former Hagen-Renaker mold-maker, is also a very talented artist. Besides her collaborative projects with Maureen, she also creates her own work. Here she is decorating a dragonfly she produced.

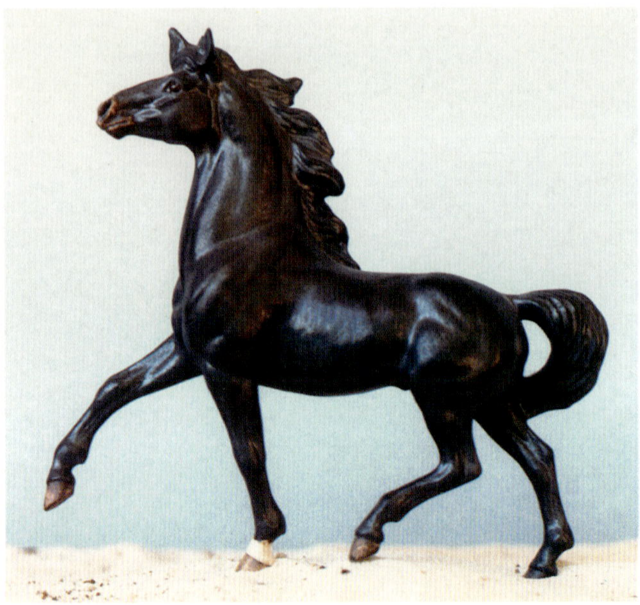

This Wild Horse was the first model sculpted by Maureen to be produced by Made With Love. It stands 6.5" tall at the ear tips and is usually mounted on a base. This particular model was photographed with the base under sand to better show off the horse. Black (shown) was the original color, then some custom variations were produced. The value of this model is $110-135.

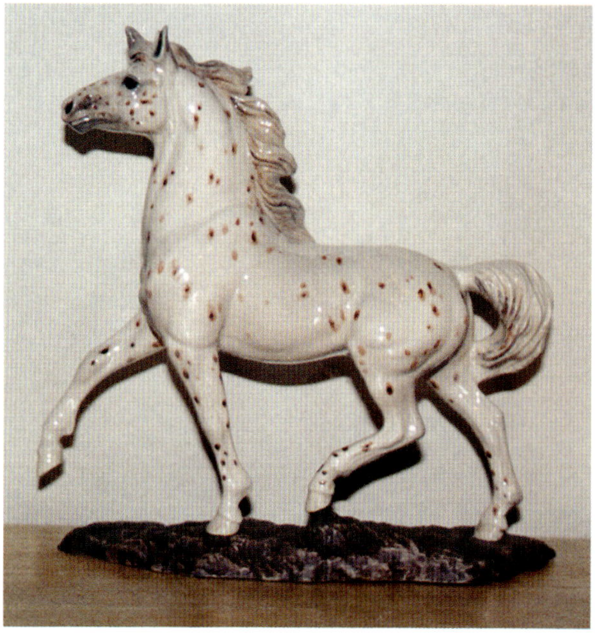

Here the Wild Horse model is custom-finished as an eye-catching Leopard Appaloosa.

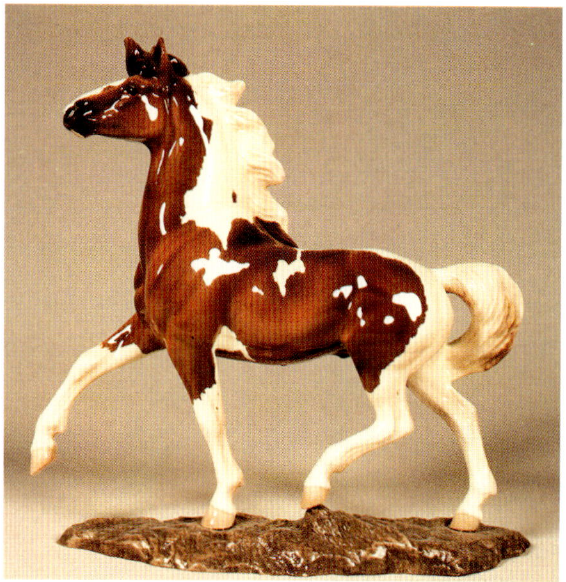

This wonderful brown and white pinto coloring was copied from a horse that lives near Laurilyn's home. Note how the bump in the base raises up to support the left rear hoof of this model.

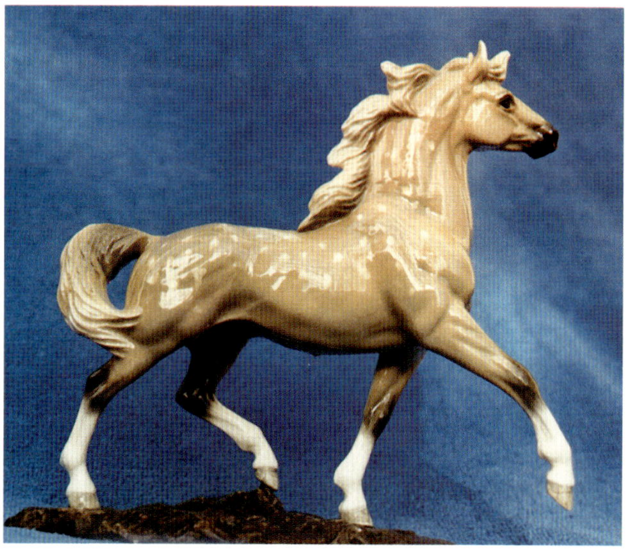

Each color of this model gives it a totally different appearance. Here the Wild Horse is featured in a custom dapple gray.

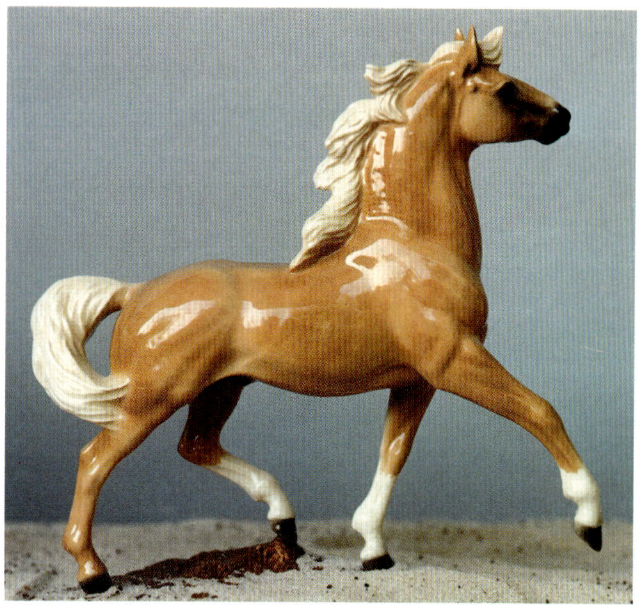

This palomino Wild Horse with a creamy mane and tail was photographed in sand to try to disguise the base.

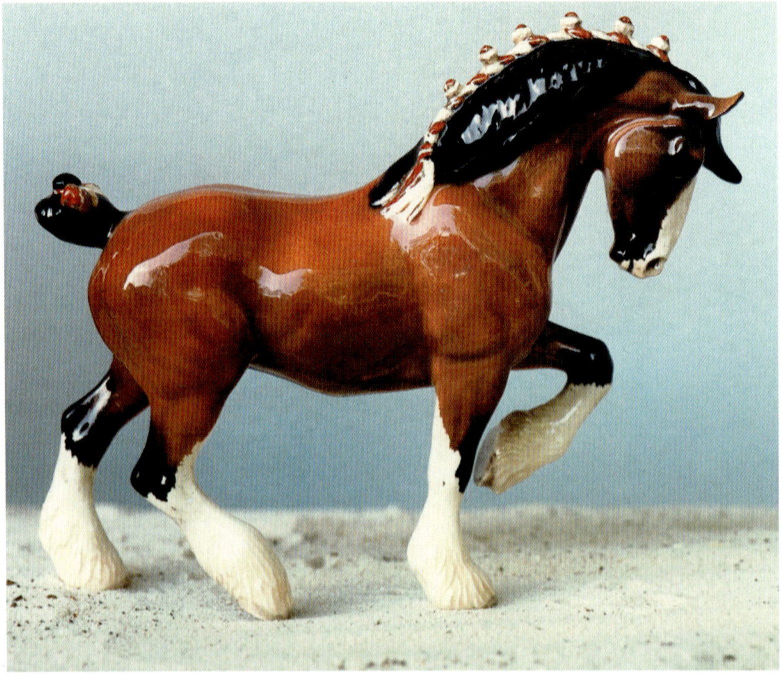

The second horse offered by Maureen and Laurilyn through Made With Love was this adult walking Clydesdale. He was sold freestanding, without a base. The mane bobs were painted in a variety of color combinations. Standing 5.25" tall, his approximate value is $110-135.

The walking Clydesdale was offered in both a glossy finish, and in matte (shown). This rough, stoneware finish is very reminiscent of the older Maureen Love horses. Matte finish horses were done in both this bay color, and in black with white stockings.

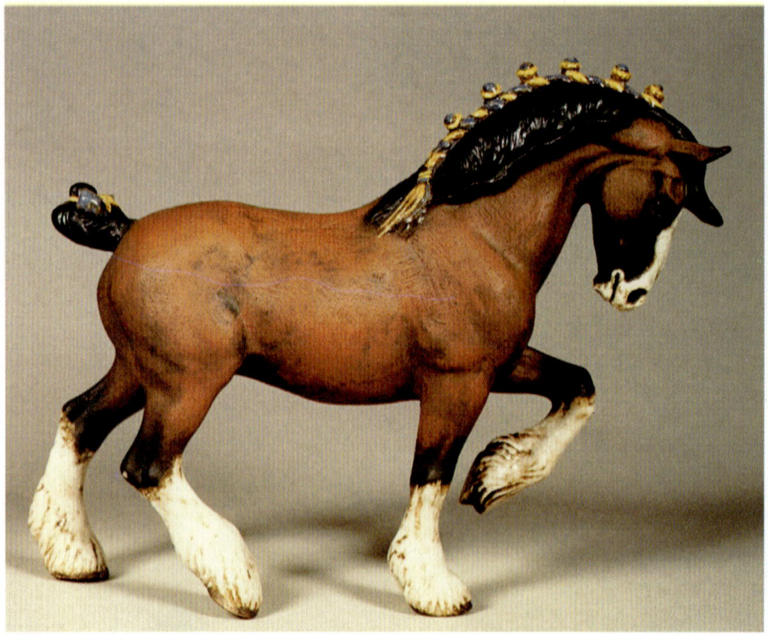

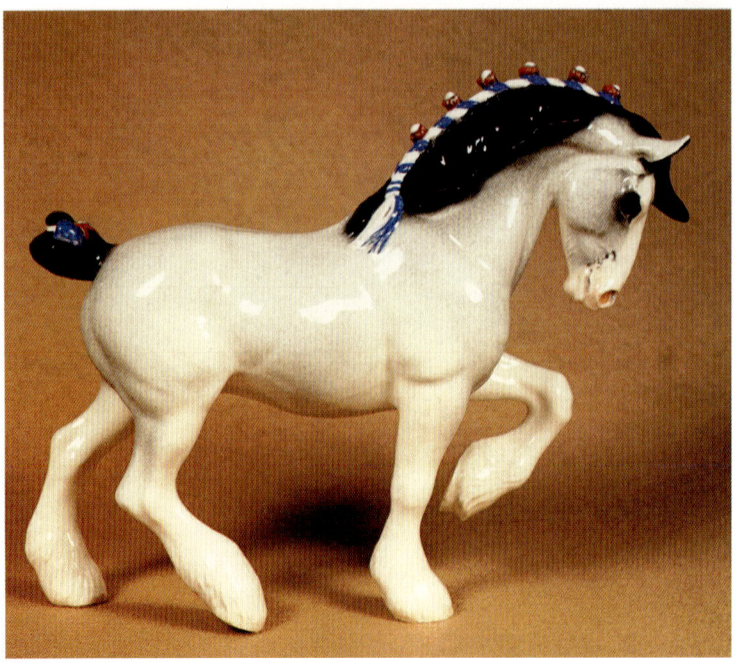

This light gray Clydesdale with his black mane and tail and red, white, and blue mane bobs was a custom finish model. Most of the custom Made With Love pieces are one-of-a-kind items.

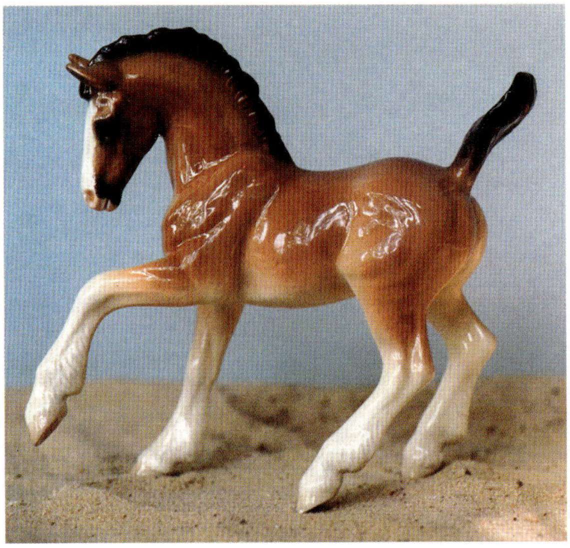

To accompany the Clydesdale adult, Maureen next designed this Clydesdale foal. Roughly in scale to the adult, it measures 4.5" tall. Out of a final count of ninety-four models, only twenty-five were made in this regular run bay color. The rest were stoneware (nine), bisque (seven), or custom (forty-seven), with six seconds. This model has an approximate value of $85-100.

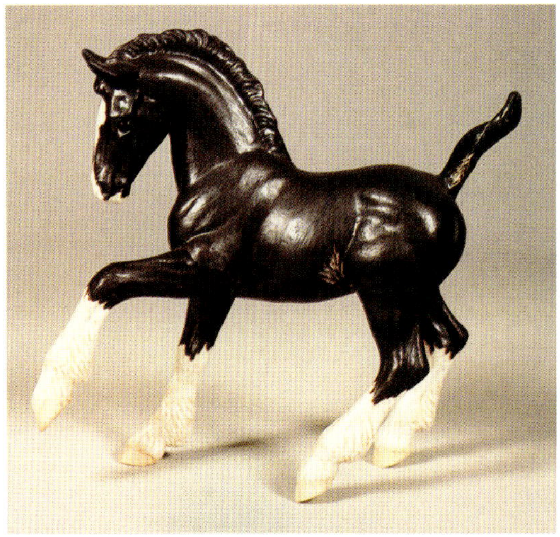

This matte finish black Clydesdale foal was decorated to match the adult. Note the hair detail on the belly. There is similar detail on the inside of the ears, and on the side of the tail.

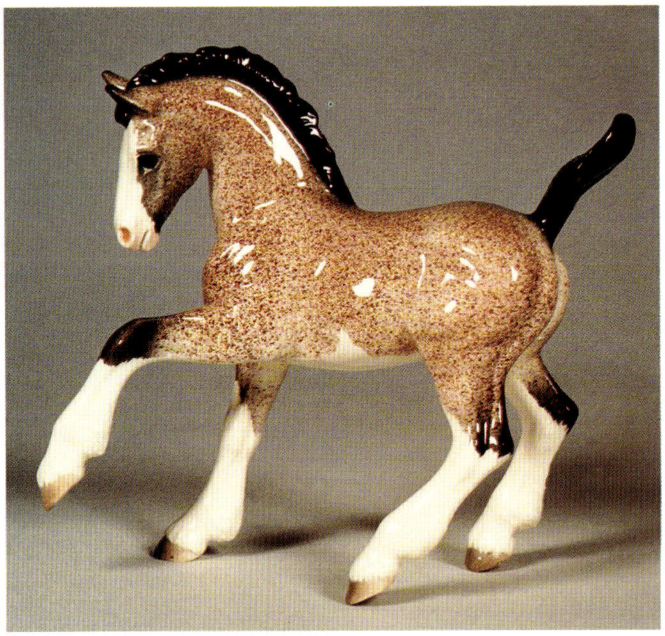

Laurilyn admits she had a lot of fun with the spray gun the day she decorated this red roan Clydesdale foal. This piece was done as a special request.

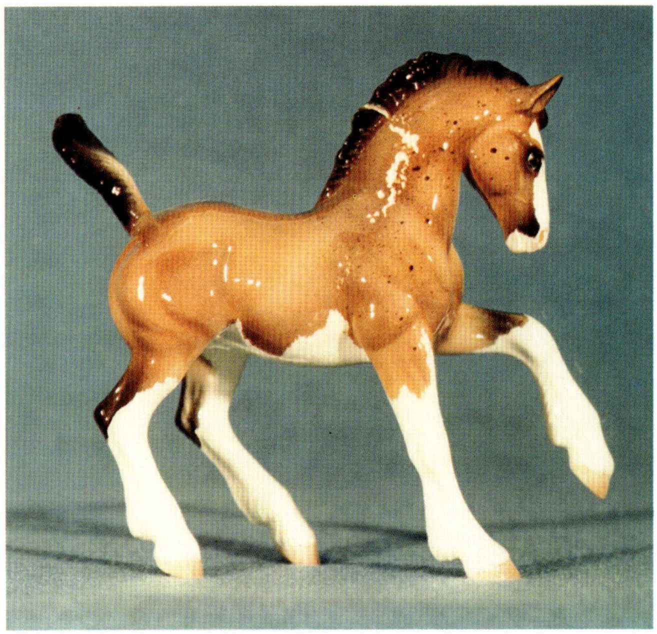

This coloring might not be found in real life, but it is certainly showy with the high white on the legs and the speckles in the chestnut body color.

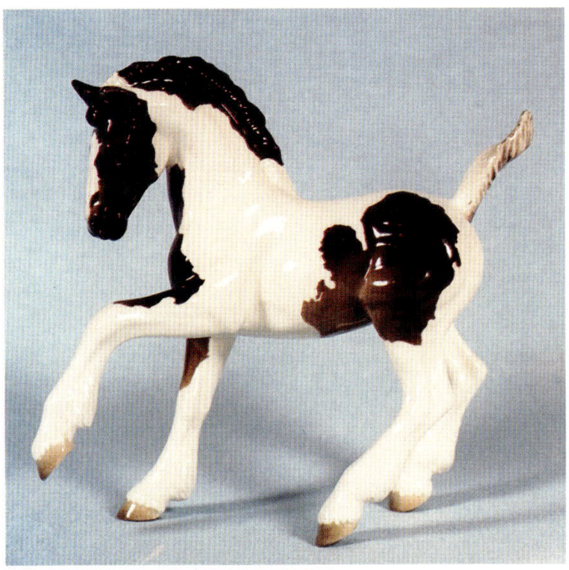

To be technically correct, the Clydesdale does not come in this attractive pinto pattern, but there are other draft horse breeds that do.

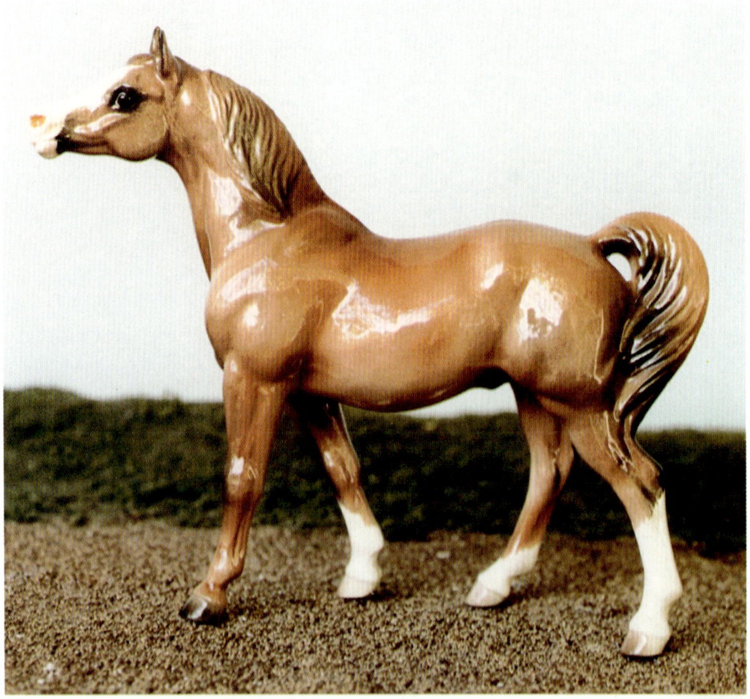

Made With Love produced a very small run (thirty-three pieces) of this Arabian stallion. Each of the horses had a unique coloring, with no two being alike. Needless to say, this limited edition sold out quickly in 2001. This stallion measures 5" tall and has an approximate value of $110-135

Here is the Arabian stallion in a subtle dapple-gray. He was also produced in dapple brown, with brown legs, mane, and tail.

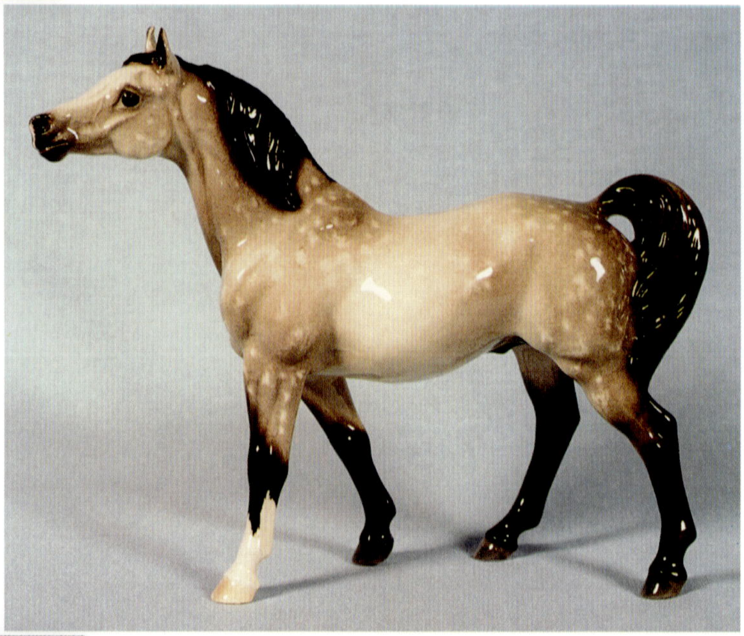

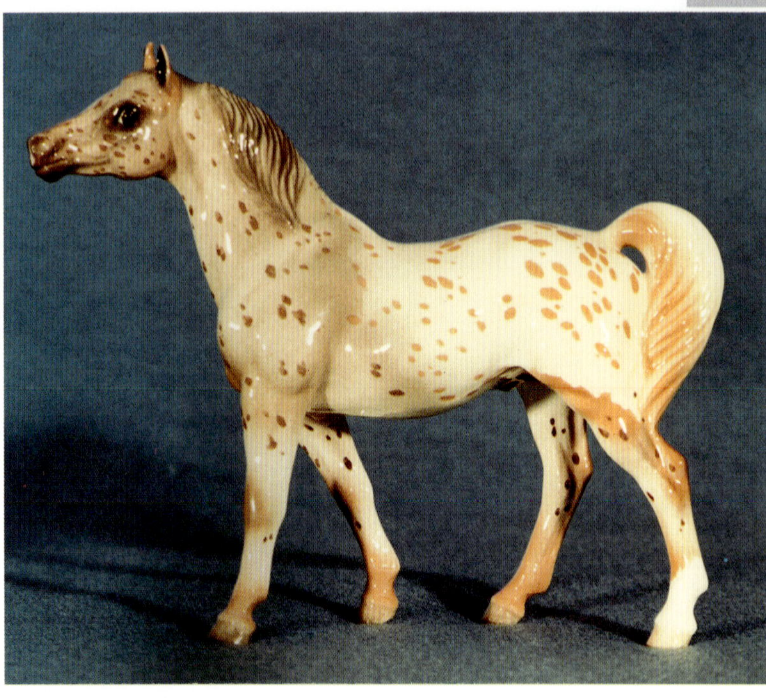

Technically, Arabians are not found in this Leopard Appaloosa coloring, but perhaps this model represents a crossbreed. There is a lot of hand-painted detail in this flashy horse.

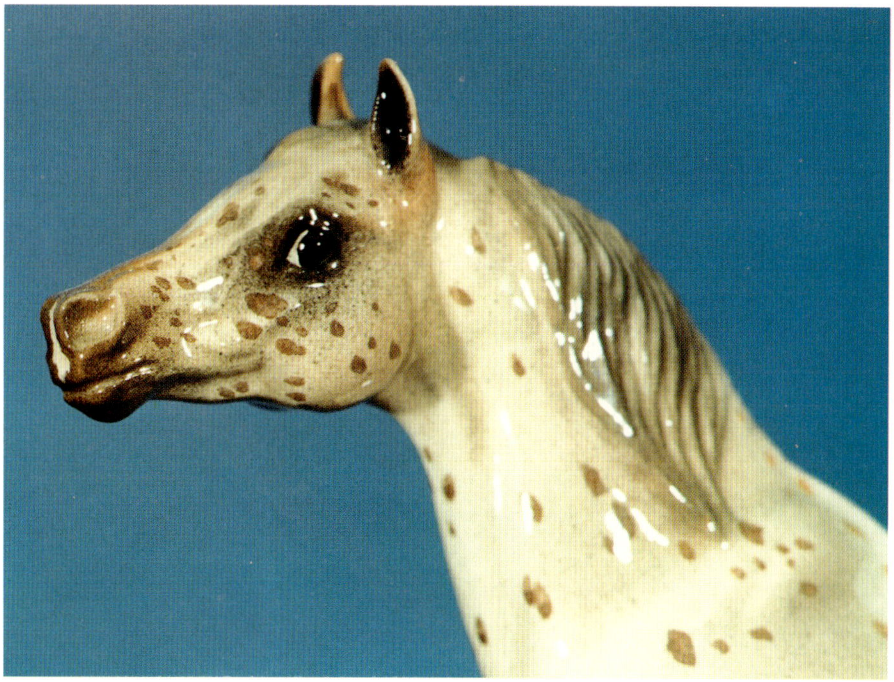

This head study close up gives an excellent view of the incredible detail in this Leopard Appaloosa. Note in particular the white snip at the end of the nose, and the eye whites.

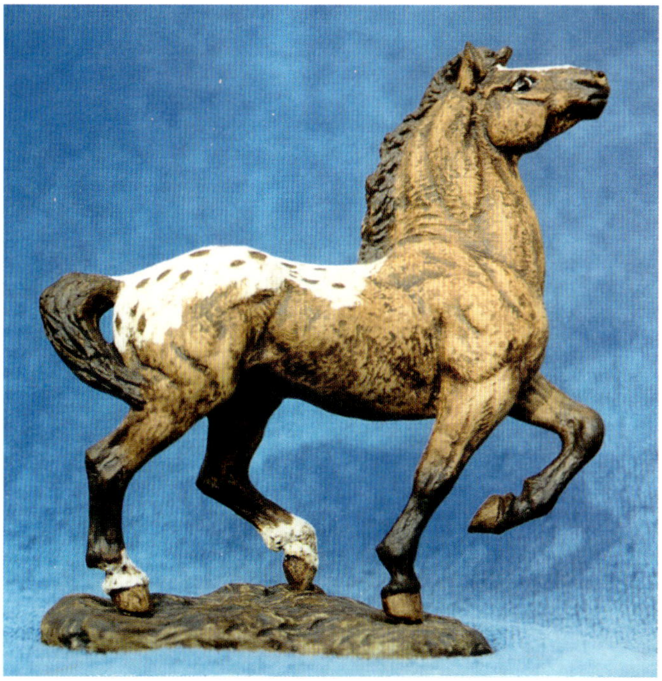

Designed by Maureen, this spunky Appaloosa is a little more "artsy" than her usual, realistic horses. This model is signed by her, and is dated 1993. He stands 5.5" tall and has an approximate value of $150-175.

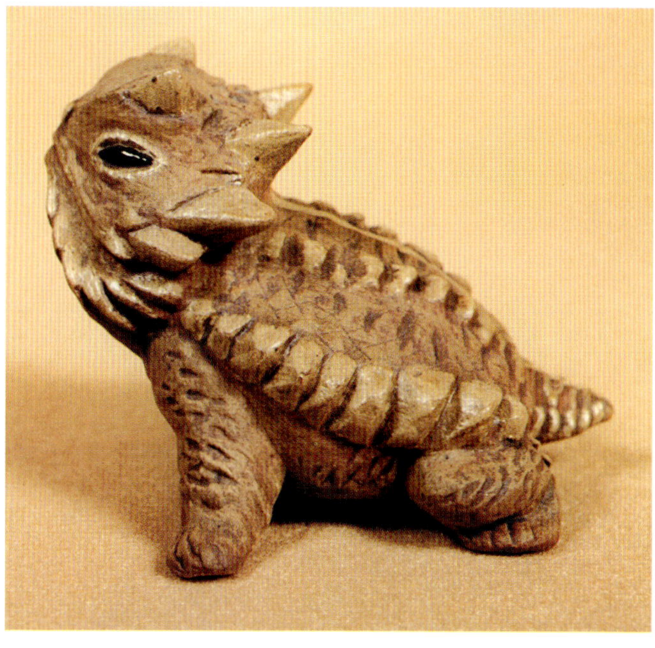

When Laurilyn excavated the molds from Maureen's garage, she found more than just horses. This adorable horned toad was quickly cast, decorated, and sold by Laurilyn to a few lucky collectors. It stands 1.5" tall and has an approximate value of $40-55. The original piece designed and decorated by Maureen can be seen on page 38.

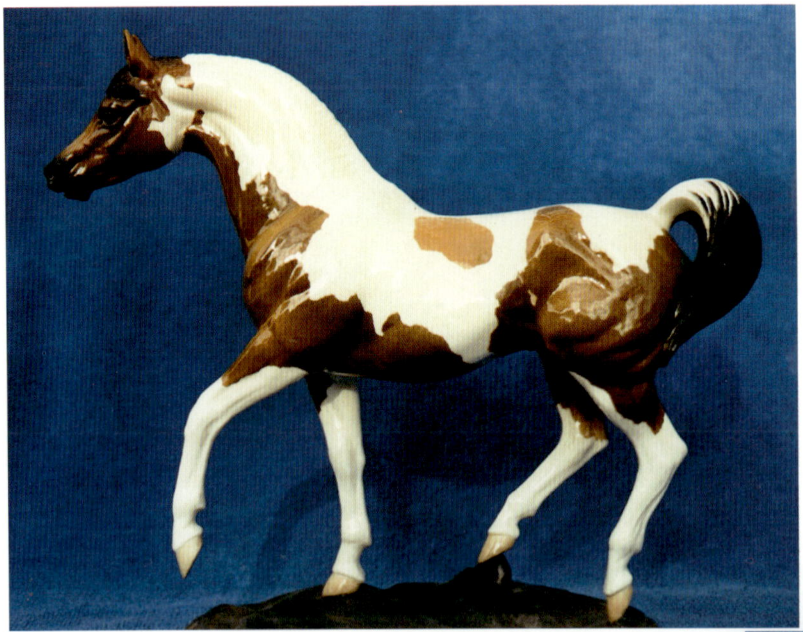

This next horse was another mold reclaimed from Maureen's garage. The original horse produced by Maureen can be seen on page 35. This flashy Pintabian is #17 in the Molds from Maureen's Garage series. It stands 8" tall, was produced in 2000, and has an approximate value of $250-275.

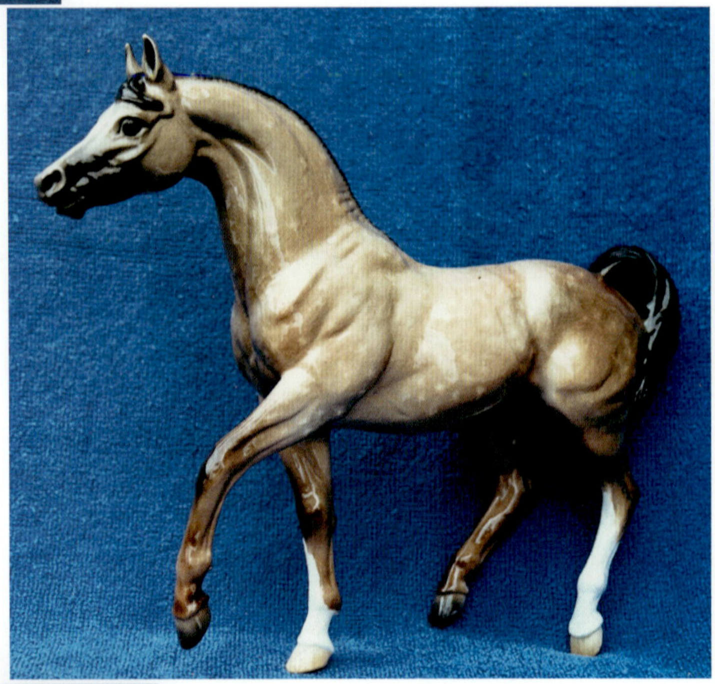

Decorated in a subtle glossy dapple-brown, this walking Arabian stallion was decorated by Laurilyn Burson. It stands 7.5" tall because it was removed from its base. It has an approximate value of $250-275.

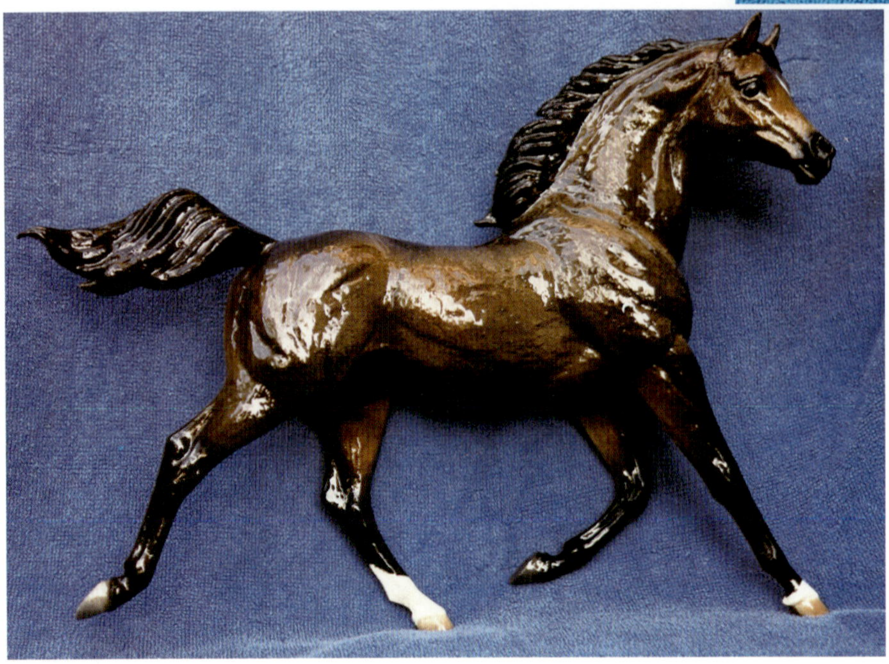

This stunning chocolate bay model of the Arabian horse "Marranas" was first produced by Maureen Love in the 1970s, and can be seen on page 30. Laurilyn decorated this reissued model. It stands 9" tall without its base, and has an approximate value of $375-400. Laurilyn also produced this model in other colors, including dapple-gray, chestnut, and buttermilk buckskin.

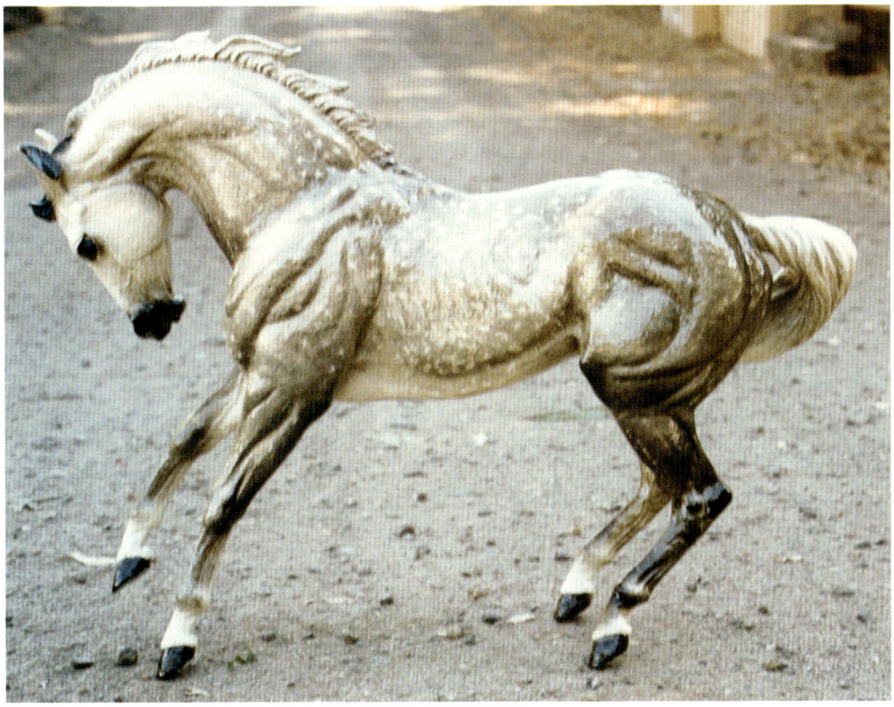

So large he had to be photographed outside, Laurilyn dubbed this Thoroughbred horse "Gig," short for gigantic. Originally produced by Maureen and mounted on a wooden base, the early piece can be seen on page 26. Laurilyn has cast and decorated this model, producing them in bay, dun, and dapple-gray (shown) so far. Standing 17" tall, this reissued model has an approximate value of $600-700.

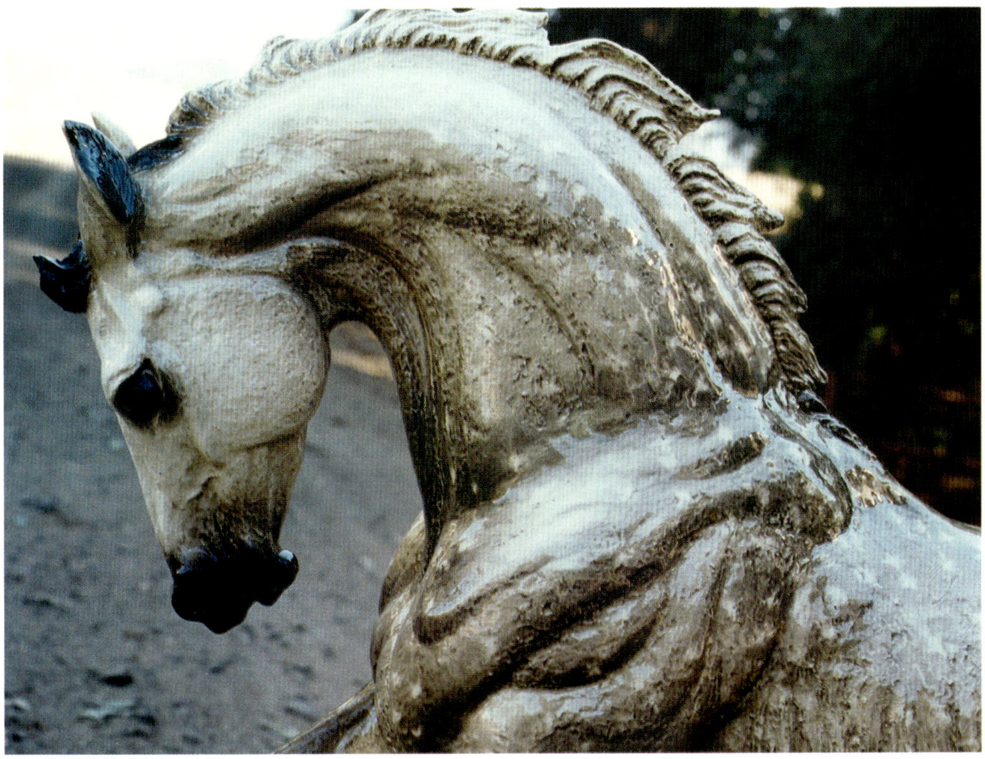

This close up head study of the gigantic Thoroughbred really captures the energy and motion of this incredible model.

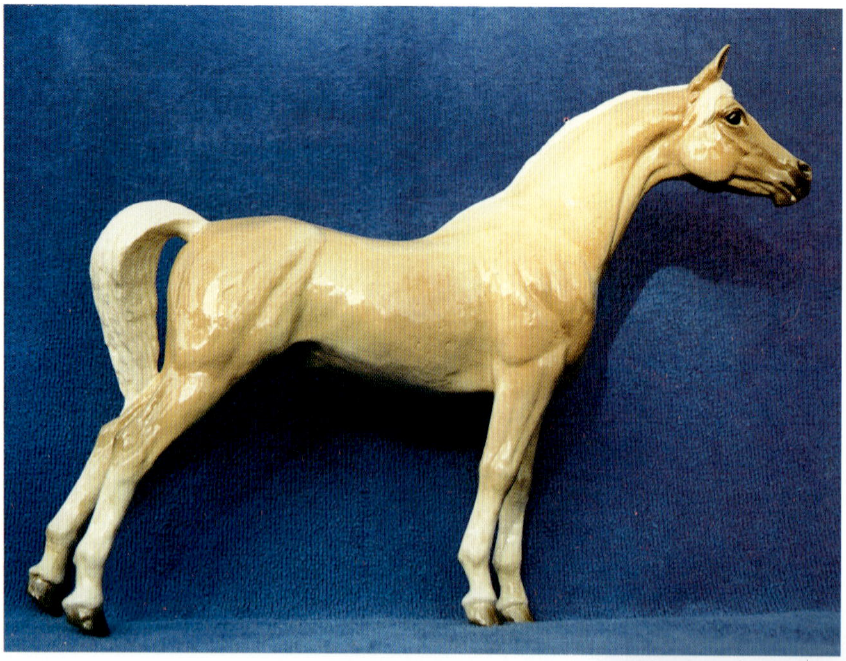

While sculpting horses in the 1960s, Maureen Love made models of several of the horses at the Wagon Wheel Ranch, owned by friends Jimmie and Edna Nelson. "Skowranas" was one of the horses she produced, as seen on page 31. Laurilyn rescued the old mold and produced a few models from it, including this palomino colored horse. He stands 8" tall and has an approximate value of $275-300.

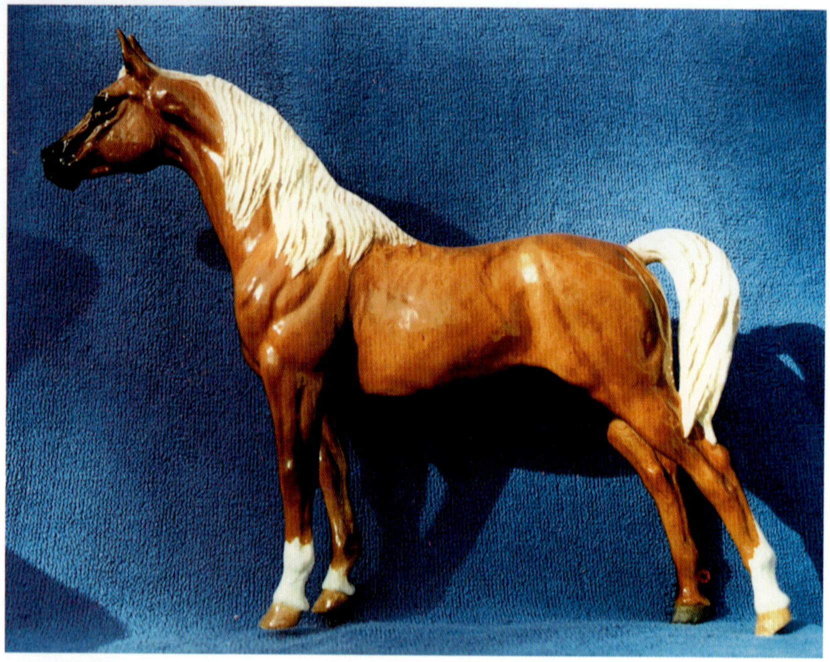

This reissued version of the Arabian horse "Skowranas" was also produced by Laurilyn Burson is this flashy chestnut color.

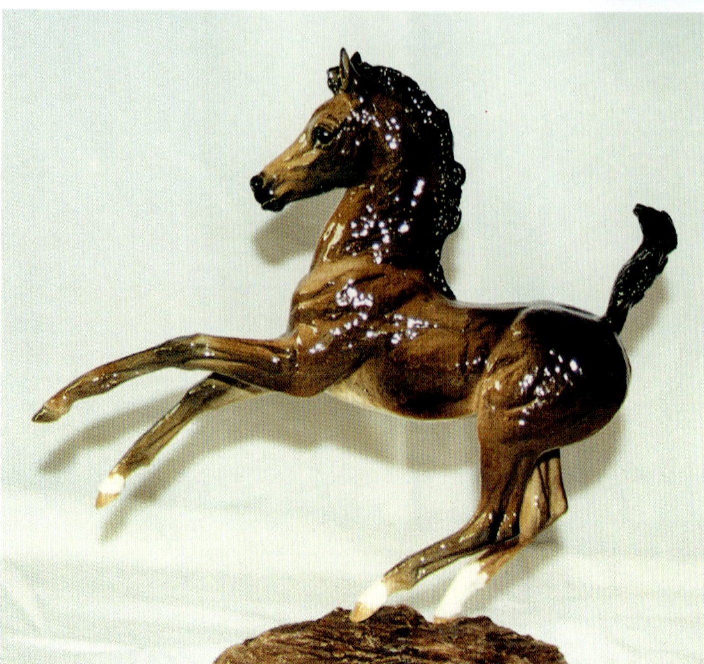

The Arabian foal "Ibn Nataf" was originally produced by Maureen in the 1970s, and can be see on page 37. Reissued and decorated by Laurilyn, this spunky model measures 8.5" tall and is #13 in the Molds from Maureen's Garage series. Produced in 2001, it has an approximate value of $275-300.

This Maureen Love model was produced in the 1970s and the original can be seen on page 34. Laurilyn has enjoyed experimenting with this foal, as it is very compact and easy to handle. The black matte foal shown here was finished using the Raku process. This piece was actually created by a collector, under Laurilyn's guidance.

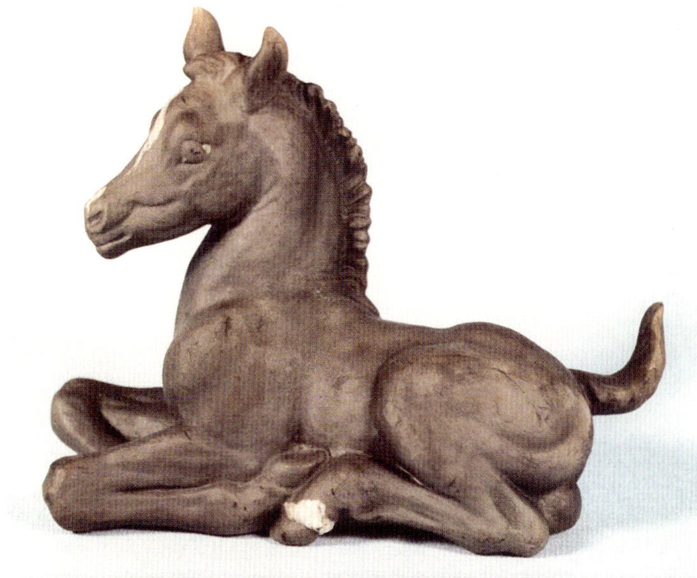

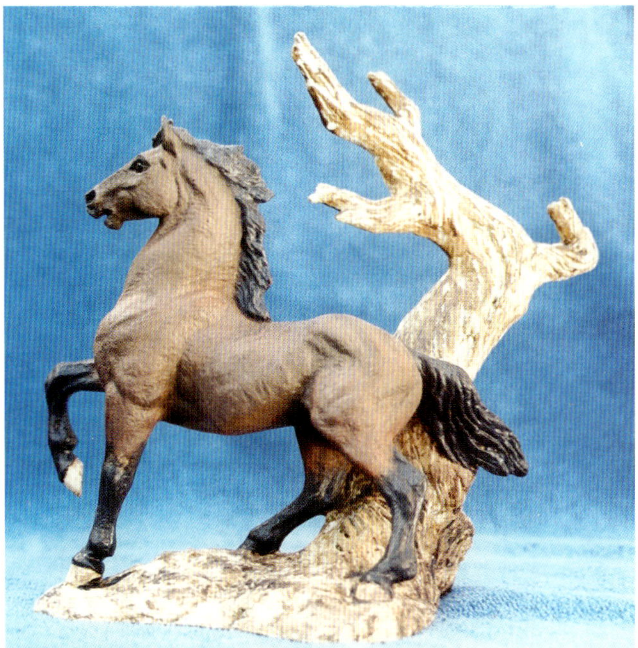

Another mold rescued from Maureen's garage was this unique "Tree Horse." Maureen first offered it in the 1970s as horse/tree, as seen on page 28. This bay horse and tree stands 7" tall, was decorated by Laurilyn Burson, and has an approximate value of $150-175.

With this flashy dapple-gray coloring, the horse with the tree takes on an entirely different appearance from the bay model. The shading on this model really accents the muscles in the horse's neck, shoulders, and rump.

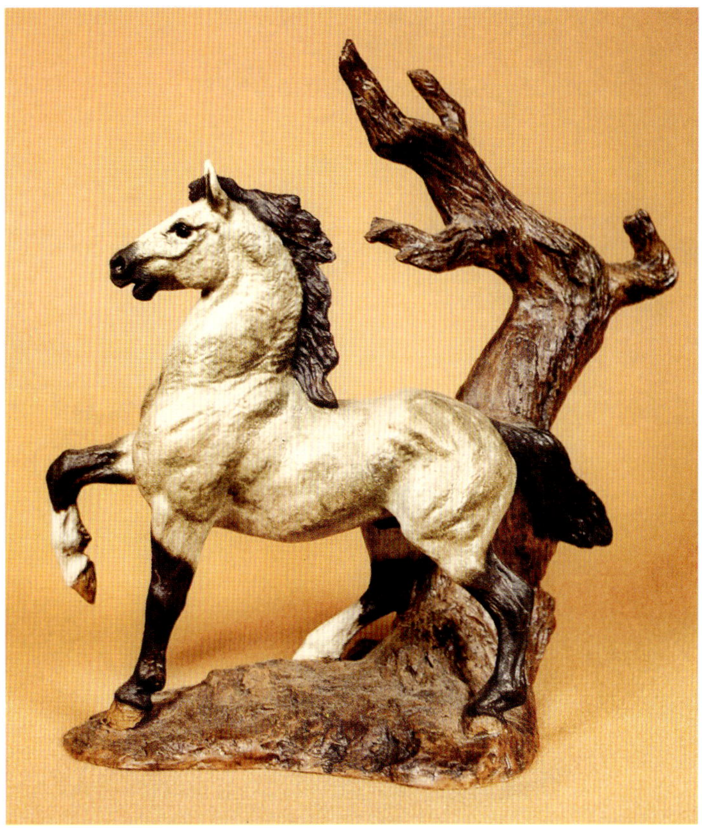

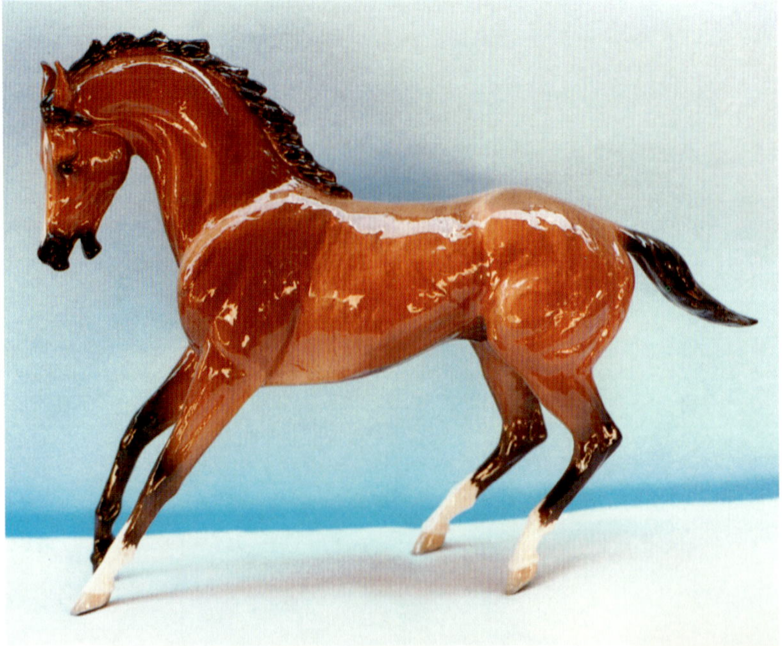

This energetic racehorse was reissued by Laurilyn in 2001. His spirited pose and brilliant color make him quite the eye-catching model. Standing 8" tall by 10.5" long, his approximate value is $250-275.

This unusual Overo Pinto pattern was copied from a real horse. This special set with the racehorse and the jockey was offered to collectors as a one-of-a-kind model. Measuring 9" tall, this horse and rider has an approximate value of $300-350.

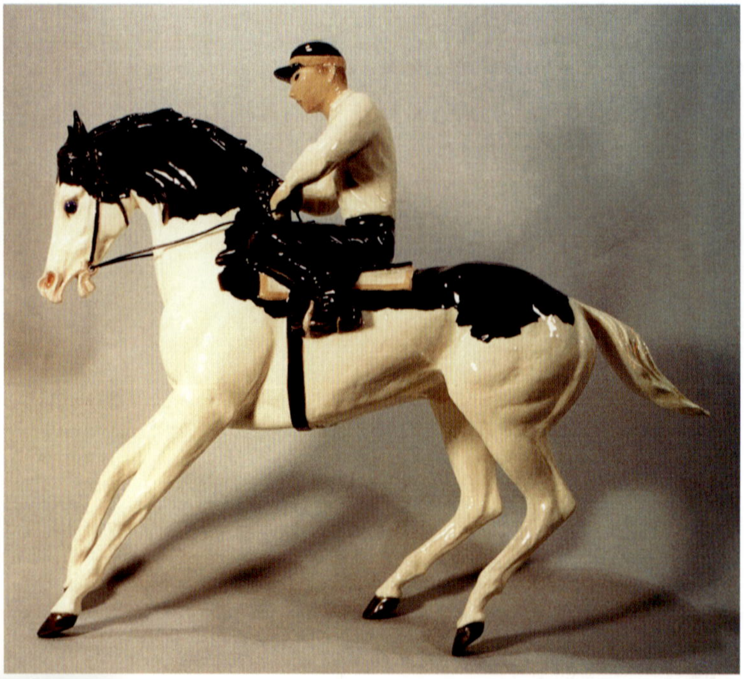

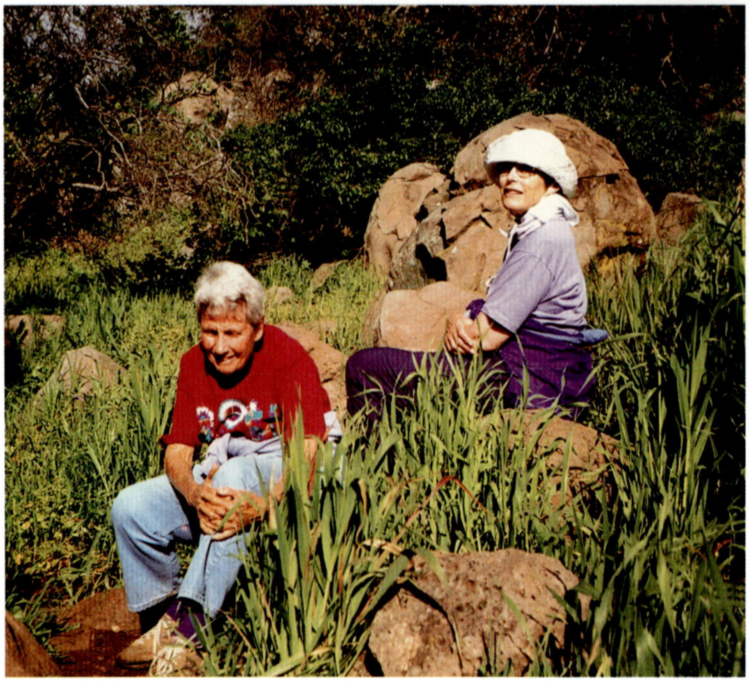

Maureen Love (left) and Laurilyn Burson on the Santa Rosa Plateau. They both enjoy hiking, and looking at the wild flowers.

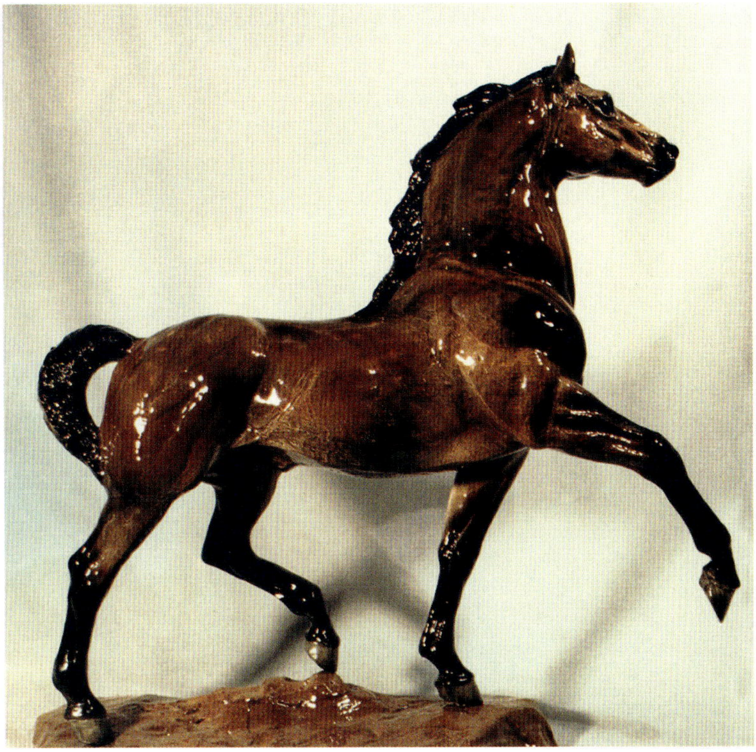

In a wonderfully-shaded bay color, this 11" tall horse comes from one of the garage molds that reportedly is in bad condition and will not be used to produce many models. Only the second one taken from this mold, his approximate value is $325-360.

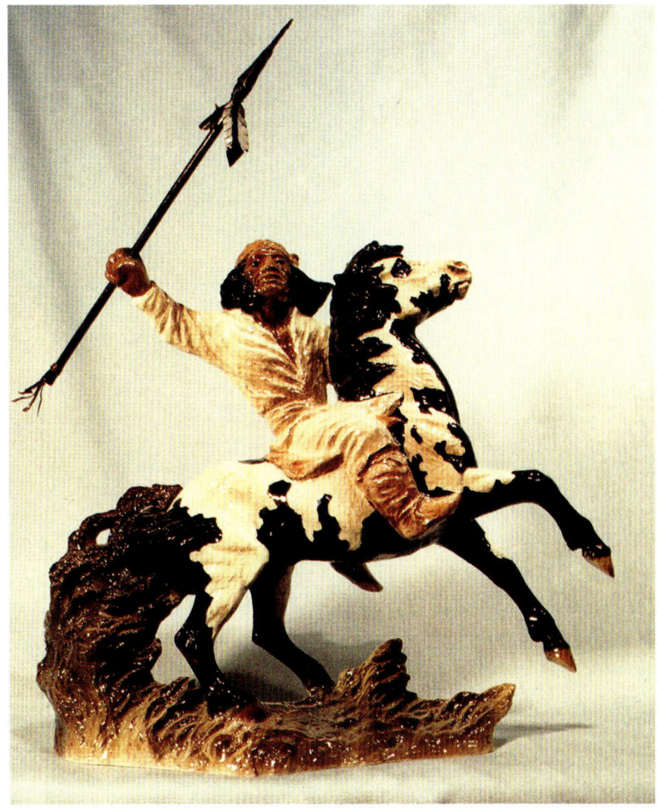

Portraying a fierce Apache warrior and his horse, this model measures 10" high to the tip of the spear. The horse and rider are ceramic, but the spear is metal. This is the second model made from this garage mold and has an approximate value of $275-325.

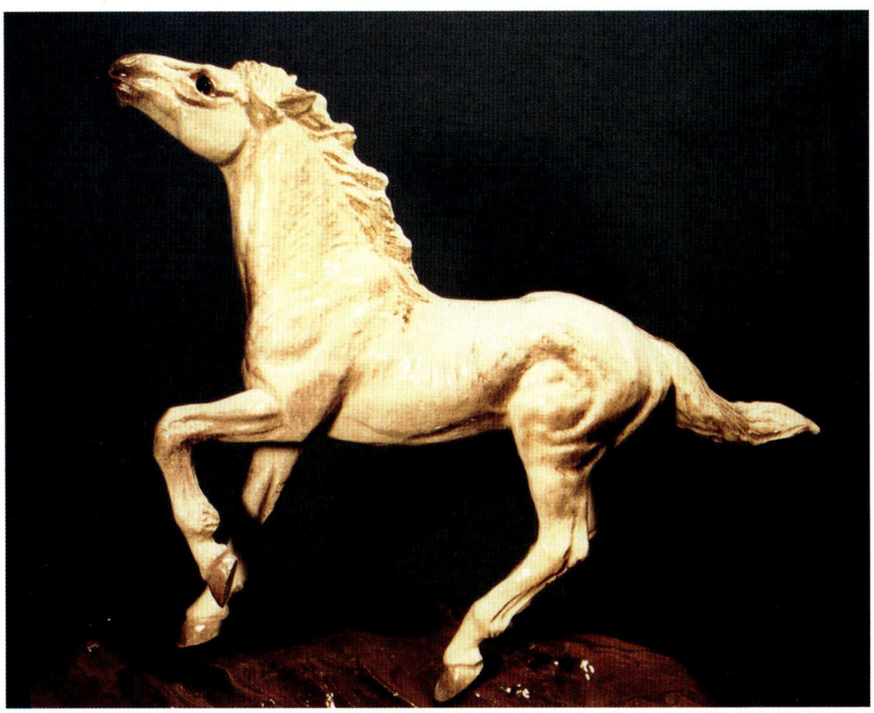

This dun-colored wild horse stallion stands 6.5" tall. He is the second one made from this garage mold, and has an approximate value of $200-225.

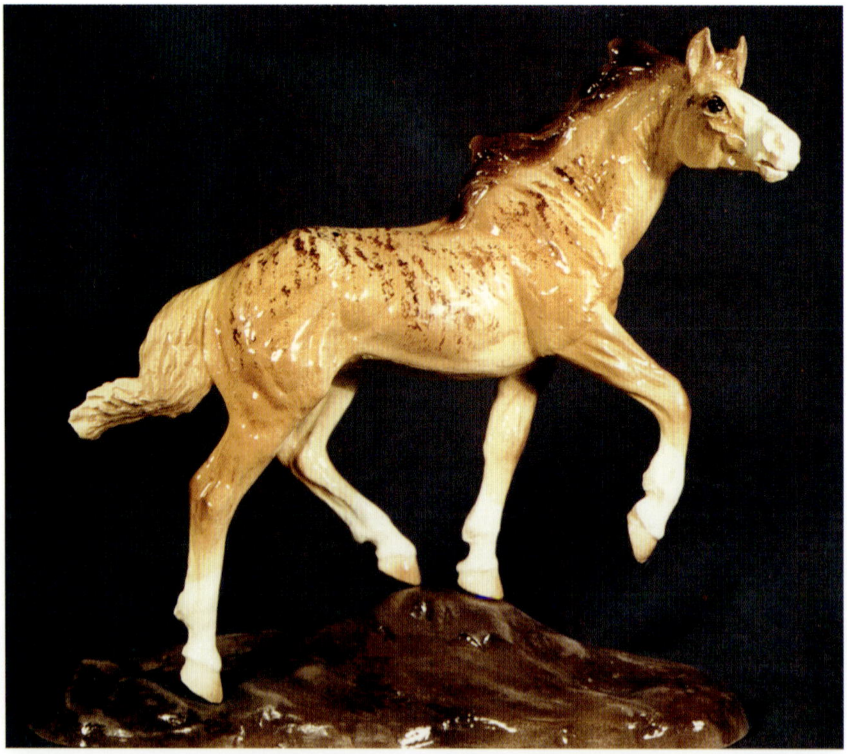

Laurilyn researched all of the horse colors on these garage mold horses before producing them, including this unusual brindle coloring. This model measures 6.25" tall and has an approximate value of $200-225.

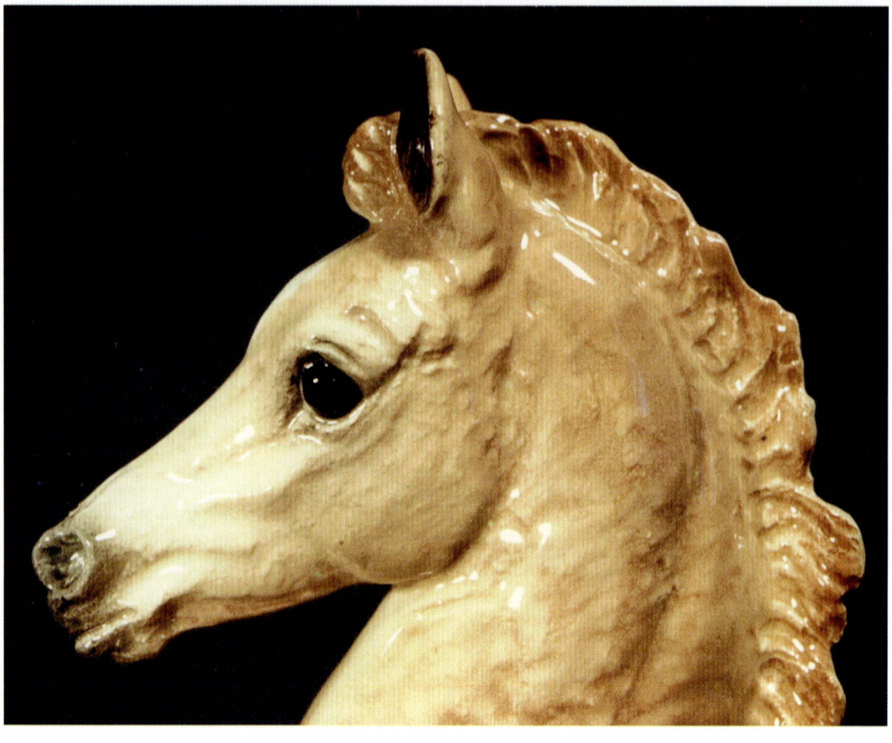

The head can be called the most important part of the model. These models, originally designed by Maureen in the 1960s and 1970s, have stood the test of time well. Here the foal "Ibn Nataf" is shown in a close-up head study, as reproduced by Laurilyn in 2002.

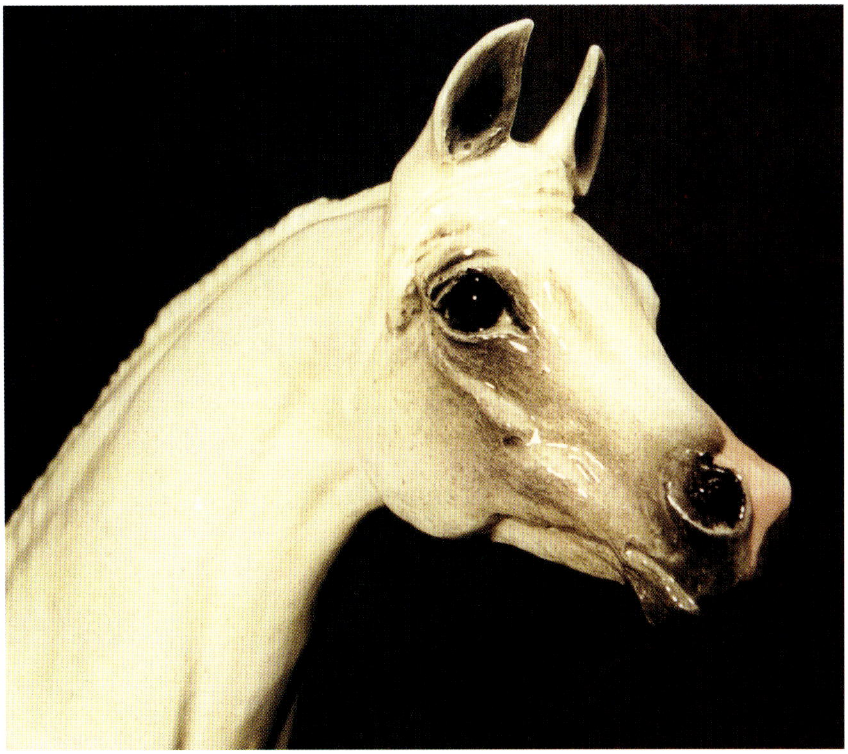

This close-up head study of "Skowranas" certainly conveys the majesty of this Arabian Stallion model.

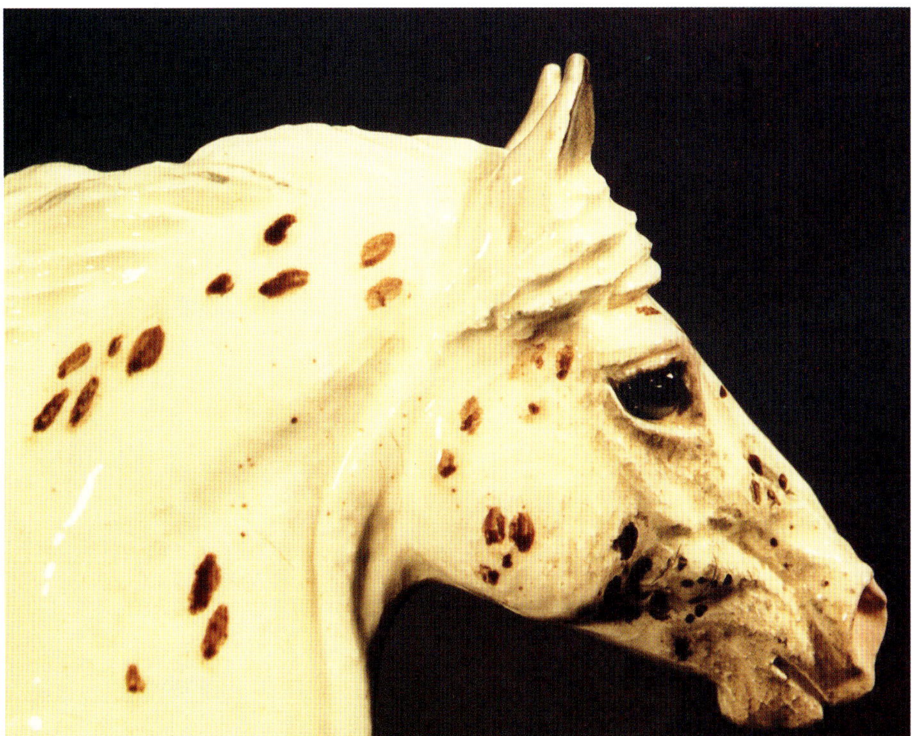

There is deep fire and emotion captured in the face of this leopard Appaloosa stallion, another garage mold horse.

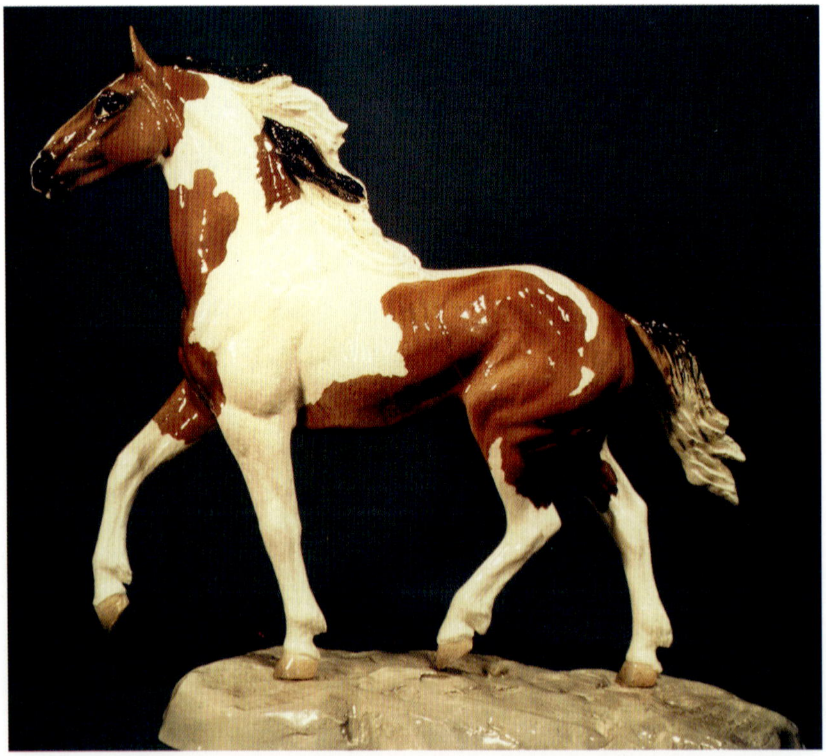

This beautifully-finished pinto stallion was created as a special order by Laurilyn from one of Maureen's old molds. It stands 9" tall and has an approximate value of $325-375.

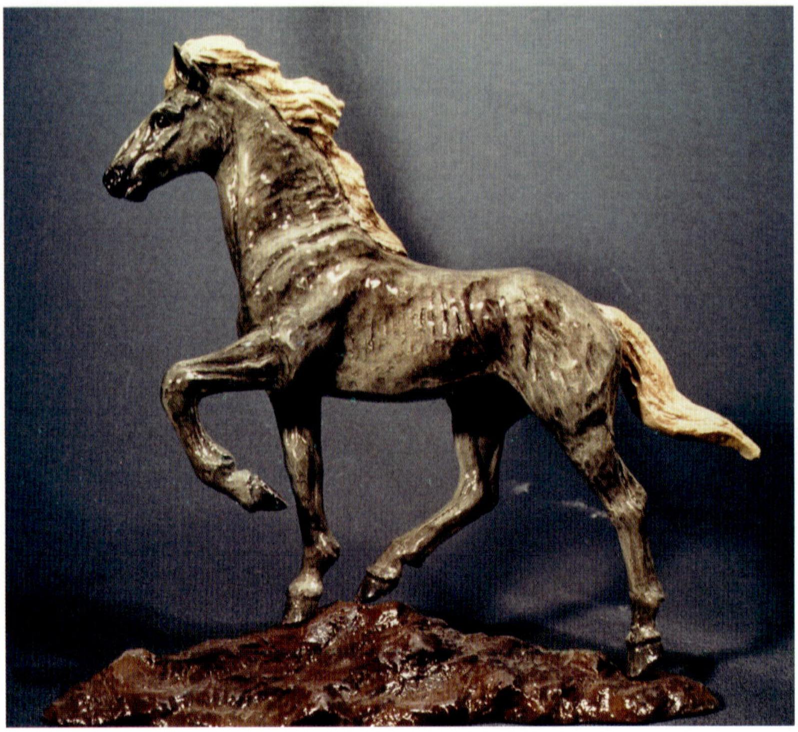

The unusual smoky coloring on this model shows off the detail well. He stands 6.5" tall and has an approximate value of $175-225.

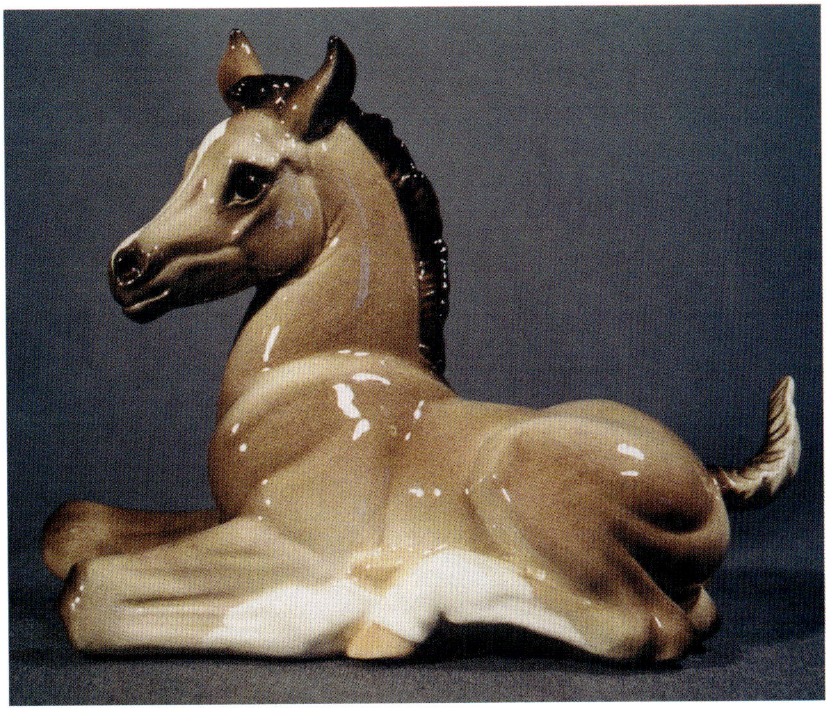

Originally produced as a Maureen Love Originals piece, this 3.5" lying Arabian foal looks adorable in this delicate bay color. During 2002 Laurilyn offered this foal in various colors for $75 retail.

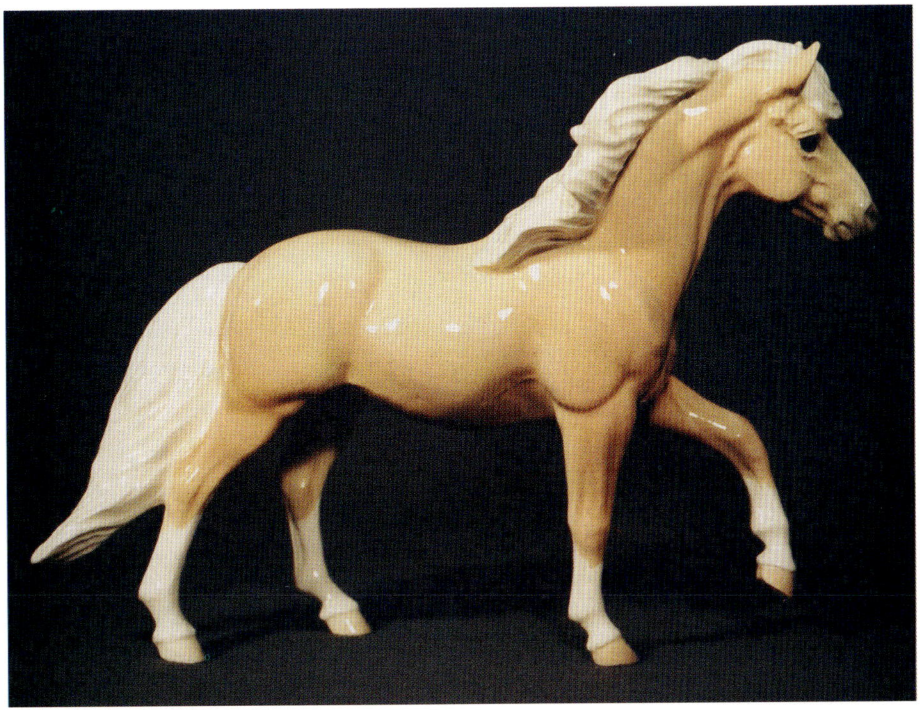

"My Pal" was a new model offered by Made With Love, beginning in 2002. He was available with various markings in this palomino color or in custom colors. This model stands 5.25" tall and the retail price was $200 palomino or $230 in a custom color.

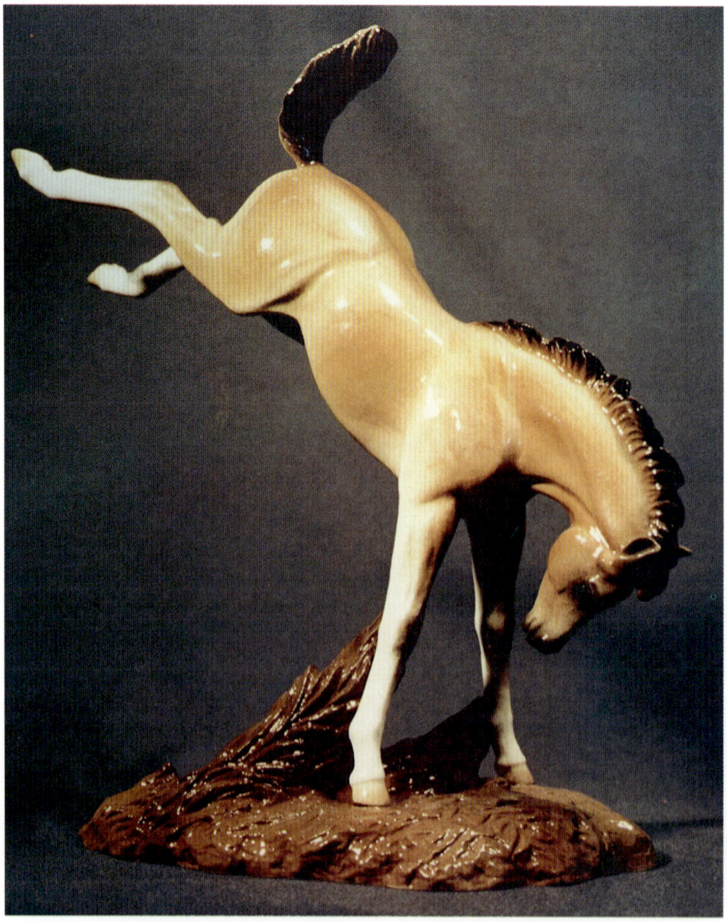

"Froli," the bucking filly, was sculpted by Maureen and produced by Laurilyn in response to collectors who wanted another large, active foal. She measures 8" tall and was available in this light bay or in custom colors for $300 and $330 retail.

Maureen's closest friends were treated to this beautiful Wood Duck as a Christmas gift in 2001.

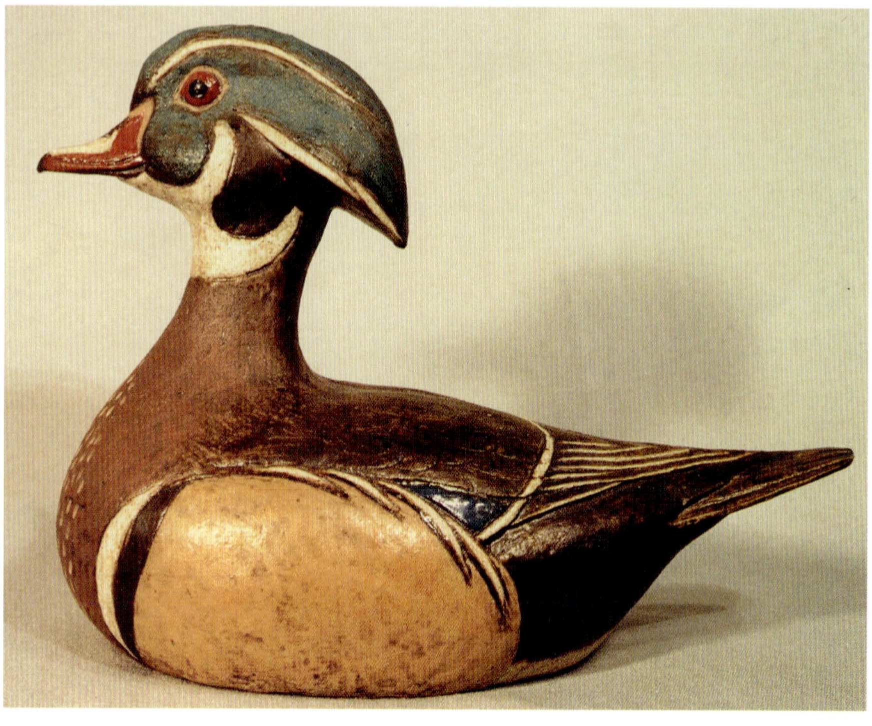

Bibliography

Kelly, Nancy. *Hagen-Renaker Pottery: Horses and Other Figurines.* Atglen, Pennsylvania: Schiffer Publishing Ltd., 2000.

Roller, Gayle *The Charlton Standard Catalogue of Hagen-Renaker, 2nd Edition.* Toronto, Canada: The Charlton Press, 1999.

Index